A
HISTORY
OF
PHILOSOPHY

VOLUME I

Greek, Roman, and Medieval

harper ✦ corchbooks

*A reference-list of Harper Torchbooks, classified
by subjects, is printed at the end of this volume.*

A
HISTORY
OF
PHILOSOPHY

VOLUME I

Greek, Roman, and Medieval

WILHELM
WINDELBAND

HARPER TORCHBOOKS ❧ The Cloister Library

Harper & Row · Publishers · New York

A HISTORY OF PHILOSOPHY: I—Greek, Roman, and Medieval

Printed in the United States of America

Reprinted by arrangement with The Macmillan Company, New York, from
the revised edition of 1901, translated by James H. Tufts.

First HARPER TORCHBOOK edition published 1958

Library of Congress catalog card number: LC-58-7114—Vol. I

TRANSLATOR'S PREFACE.

REGARDED simply as a historical discipline, the history of thought might fairly claim a prominent place in education, and an equal share of the attention now given to comparative and historical studies. The evolution of an idea is in itself as interesting and valuable an object of study as the evolution of a word, of an institution, of a state, or of a vegetable or animal form.

But aside from this interest which it has in common with other historical sciences, the history of philosophy has a peculiar value of its own. For the moment we attempt any serious thinking in any field, — natural science, history, literature, ethics, theology, or any other, — we find ourselves at the outset quite at the mercy of the words and ideas which form at once our intellectual atmosphere and the instruments with which we must work. We cannot speak, for example, of mind or matter, of cause or force, of species or individual, of universe or God, of freedom or necessity, of substance or evolution, of science or law, of good or true or real, without involving a host of assumptions. And the assumptions are there, even though we may be unconscious of them, or ignore them in an effort to dispense with metaphysics. To dispense with these conceptions is impossible. Our only recourse, if we would not beg our questions in advance, or remain in unconscious bondage to the instruments of our thought, or be slaves to the thinking of the past generations that have forged out our ideas for us, is to "criticise our categories." And one of the most important, if not the only successful, means to this end is a study of the origin and development of these categories. We can free ourselves from the past only by mastering it. We may not hope to see beyond Aristotle or Kant until we have stood on their shoulders. We study the history of philosophy, not so much to learn what other men have thought, as to learn to think.

For an adequate study of the history of thought, the main requisites are a careful study of the works of the great thinkers — a requisite that need not be enlarged on here, although such study is a comparatively recent matter in both Britain and America, with a few notable exceptions — and a text-book to aid us in singling out the important problems, tracing their development, disentangling their complications, and sifting out what is of permanent value. To meet this second need is the especial aim of the present work, and, with all the excellencies of the three chief manuals already in use, it can scarcely be questioned that the need is a real one. Those acquainted with the work here translated (W. Windelband's *Geschichte der Philosophie*, Freiburg i. B., 1892) have no hesitation in thinking that it is an extremely valuable contribution toward just this end. The originality of its conception and treatment awaken an interest that is greater in proportion to the reader's acquaintance with other works on the subject. The author shows not only historical learning and vision, but philosophical insight; and in his hands the comparative treatment of the history of thought proves as suggestive and fruitful as the same method applied to other subjects in recent times. A work like the present could only have been written with some such preparation as has come in this case from the previous treatment of Greek and Modern Philosophy at greater length, and in presenting it to English readers I am confident that it will meet the wants, not only of special students of philosophy, but also of all who wish to understand the development of thought. Teachers will, I think, find it very valuable in connection with lecture courses.

As regards the work of the Translator, little need be said. He has tried — like many others — to make a faithful translation into intelligible English, and is fully conscious that it has been with varying success. Of course translation in the strict sense is often impossible, and I cannot hope to have adopted the happiest compromise or found the most felicitous rendering in all cases. "Being" (spelled with a capital) is used for "*Sein.*" Where the German "*Form*" seemed to differ enough from the ordinary English sense of the word to make "form" misleading, I have spelled it "Form," and the same course has been taken with "*Real*," "*Realität*," where the German seemed to desire to distinguish them from "*wirklich*," which has been translated sometimes by "real," sometimes by "actual." "*Vorstellung*" is usually rendered by "idea," following Locke's usage, except in connection with the system of Leibniz, where "representation" is necessary to bring out his thought. "*Idee*," in the Platonic and Kantian use, is rendered "Idea" (spelled with a capital). The convenient word "*Geschehen*" has no exact counterpart, and has been variously rendered, most frequently perhaps by "cosmic processes." In the additions made to the bibliography, no attempt has been made to be exhaustive; I have simply tried to indicate some works that might aid the student. It is scarcely necessary to say that any corrections or suggestions will be gratefully received and utilised if possible. Material in square brackets is added by the translator.

In conclusion, I desire to express my indebtedness to my colleagues, Professors Shorey, Strong, and Cutting, and Dr. Schwill for helpful suggestions. My chief indebtedness, however, is to the critical taste and unwearied assistance of my wife. If I have in any degree succeeded in avoiding German idioms, it is largely due to her.

JAMES H. TUFTS.

UNIVERSITY OF CHICAGO,
July, 1893.

———◦◦×◦◦———

TRANSLATOR'S NOTE TO THE SECOND EDITION.

IN preparing this second edition all changes made by the author in the second German edition have been incorporated either in the text or in the appendix at the close. In addition, I have included a brief notice (pp. 663–670) of certain aspects of recent English thought, which naturally have more interest for the readers of this translation than for those of the original.

JAMES H. TUFTS.

UNIVERSITY OF CHICAGO,
May, 1901.

AUTHOR'S PREFACE.

———∘o;•;oo———

AFTER many painful delays and interruptions I now present at last the conclusion of the work whose first sheets appeared two years ago.

The reader will not confuse this with the compendiums which have very likely sometimes been prepared by dressing out lecture notes on the general history of philosophy. What I offer is a serious *text-book*, which is intended to portray in comprehensive and compressed exposition the evolution of the ideas of European philosophy, with the aim of showing through what motives the principles, by which we to-day scientifically conceive and judge the universe and human life, have been brought to consciousness and developed in the course of the movements of history.

This end has determined the whole form of the book. The literary-historical basis of research, the biographical and biblio-graphical material, were on this account necessarily restricted to the smallest space and limited to a selection that should open the way to the best sources for the reader desiring to work farther. The philosophers' own expositions, too, have been referred to in the main, only where they afford a permanently valuable formulation or rationale of thoughts. Aside from this there is only an occasional citation of passages on which the author supports an interpretation differing from that ordinarily adopted. The choice of material has fallen everywhere on what individual thinkers have produced that was new and fruitful, while purely individual turns of thought, which may indeed be a welcome object for learned research, but afford no philosophical interest, have found at most a brief mention.

As is shown even by the external form of the exposition, chief emphasis has been laid upon the development of what is weightiest from a philosophical standpoint: *the history of problems and conceptions.* To understand this as a connected and interrelated whole has been my chief purpose. The historical interweaving of the various lines of thought, out of which our theory of the world and life has grown, forms the especial object of my work, and I am convinced that this problem is to be solved, not by any *a priori* logical construction, but only by an all-sided, unprejudiced investigation of the facts. If in this exposition a relatively large part of the whole seems to be devoted to antiquity, this rests upon the conviction that for a historical understanding of our intellectual existence, the forging out of the conceptions which the Greek mind wrested from the concrete reality found in Nature and human life, is more important than all that has since been thought — the Kantian philosophy excepted.

The task thus set required, however, a renunciation which no one can regret more than myself. The purely topical treatment of the historical movement of philosophy did not permit of giving to the personality of the philosophers an impressiveness corresponding to their true worth. This could only be touched upon where it becomes efficient as a causal factor in the combination and transformation of ideas. The æsthetic fascination which dwells in the individual nature of the great agents of the movement, and which lends its especial charm to the academic lecture, as well as to the more extended exposition of the history of philosophy, had to be given up here in favour of a better insight into the pragmatic necessity of the mental process.

Finally, I desire to express at this place also my lively gratitude to my colleague, Dr. Hensel, who has not only aided me with a part of the proofs, but has also essentially increased the usefulness of the book by a subject index.

WILHELM WINDELBAND.

STRASSBURG, November, 1891.

AUTHOR'S PREFACE TO THE SECOND EDITION

———◦◦⦂⦂◦◦———

A LARGE edition of my *History of Philosophy* had been exhausted more than two years ago, and in the meantime its use had been further extended by English and Russian translations. This permits me to assume that the new treatment which I gave to the subject has filled an existing gap, and that the synoptical and critical method which I introduced has gained approval so far as the principle is concerned. While therefore I could leave the book unchanged in its main outlines when preparing this new edition, I could be all the more careful in making evidently needed improvements and in fulfilling certain specific requests.

Under the head of improvements I have undertaken such corrections, condensations, and expansions upon particular points as are requisite for a text-book which seeks to represent the present condition of investigation, and in this work the literature which has appeared since the first edition has been utilised. In consequence of the great condensation of material the exposition had become sometimes difficult to follow, and 1 have aimed in many cases to give more fluent form to the expression by breaking up some of the longer sentences, and occasionally omitting what was of merely secondary importance.

A desire has been expressed by readers of the book for a more extended notice of the personalities and personal relations of the philosophers. In the preface to my first edition I had myself recognised the justice of this demand, but had disclaimed the intention of satisfying it because the special plan of my work and the necessary limitations of space prevented. Now I have sought to fulfil this demand so far as it has seemed possible within the limit of my work, by giving brief and precise characterisations of the most important thinkers.

A desire for a more extended treatment of the philosophers of the nineteenth century has also been reckoned with. The few pages originally accorded to the subject have been expanded to three times the former compass, and I hope that although one will miss one topic and another another, it will nevertheless be possible to gain a fairly complete general view of the movements of philosophy down to the more immediate present, in so far as this is to be expected from a history of principles.

Finally, I have remade the subject index, and so expanded it that in connection with the text it may, as I hope, have the value of a dictionary of the history of philosophy. This gives to my work a second distinctive feature; namely, that of a work of reference of a systematic and critical sort.

By all these expansions the size of the book has been considerably increased, and I express here to my esteemed publisher, Dr. Siebeck, my heartiest gratitude for the cordial response with which he has made possible these essential improvements.

WILHELM WINDELBAND.

STRASSBURG, September, 1900.

CONTENTS.

INTRODUCTION.

PART I.

THE PHILOSOPHY OF THE GREEKS.

PART II.

THE HELLENISTIC–ROMAN PHILOSOPHY.

PART III.

THE PHILOSOPHY OF THE MIDDLE AGES.

HISTORY OF PHILOSOPHY.

INTRODUCTION.

---

§ 1. The Name and Conception of Philosophy.

R. Haym, Art. *Philosophie* in Ersch und Grüber's *Encyclopädie*, **III. Abth.**, Bd. 24.

W. Windelband, *Praeludien* (Freiburg i. B., 1884), 1 ff.

[A. Seth, Art. *Philosophy* in *Enc. Brit.*]

[G. T. Ladd, *Introduction to Philosophy*. N.Y. 1891.]

By philosophy present usage understands the scientific treatment of the general questions relating to the universe and human life. Individual philosophers, according to the presuppositions with which they have entered upon their work, and the results which they have reached in it, have sought to change this indefinite idea common to all, into more precise definitions,[1] which in part diverge so widely that the common element in the conception of the science may seem lost. But even the more general meaning given above is itself a limitation and transformation of the original significance which the Greeks connected with the name philosophy, — a limitation and transformation brought about by the whole course of the intellectual and spiritual life of the West, and following along with the same.

1. While in the first appearance in literature[2] of the words φιλοσοφεῖν and φιλοσοφία the simple and at the same time indefinite meaning, "striving after wisdom," may still be recognised, the word "philosophy" in the literature after Socrates, particularly in the school of Plato and Aristotle, acquired the fixed significance accord-

---

[1] Cited in detail in Ueberweg-Heinze, *Grundriss der Geschichte der Philosophie*, I. § 1. [Eng. trans. Ueberweg's *History of Philosophy*, trans. by G. S. Morris. N.Y. 1871.]

[2] Herodotus, I. 30 and 50; Thucydides, II. 40; and frequently also even in Plato, *e.g. Apol.* 29; *Lysis*, 218 A; *Symp.* 202 E ff.

ing to which it denotes exactly the same as the German word
"*Wissenschaft.*"[1] According to this meaning philosophy in general[2]
is the methodical work of thought, through which we are to know
that which "is"; individual "philosophies" are the particular sci.
ences in which individual realms of the existent are to be investi.
gated and known.[3]

With this first *theoretical meaning* of the word "philosophy" a
second was very early associated. The development of Greek
philosophy came at the time when the naïve religious and ethical
consciousness was in process of disintegration. This not only
made the questions as to man's vocation and tasks more and more
important for scientific investigation (cf. below, Part I. ch. 2), but
also made instruction in the right conduct of life appear as an
essential aim, and finally as the main content of philosophy or
science. Thus philosophy in the Hellenistic period received the
practical meaning of an *art of life, based upon scientific principles,*[4] —
a meaning for which the way had already been prepared by the
Sophists and Socrates.

In consequence of this change, purely theoretical interest passed
over to the particular "philosophies," which now in part assumed
the names of their special subjects of research, historical or belonging to natural science, while mathematics and medicine kept all the
more rigorously that independence which they had possessed from
the beginning with relation to science in general.[5] The name of
philosophy, however, remained attached to those scientific efforts
which hoped to win from the most general results of human knowledge a conviction for the direction of life, and which finally culminated in the attempt (made by Neo-Platonism) to create from such
a philosophy a new religion to replace the old that had been lost.[6]

---

[1] A conception which it is well known is of much greater compass than the
English and French "science." [In this translation the words "science" and
"scientific" are used in this larger sense. The term "natural science" will be
used for the narrower meaning which "science" alone often has. If it should
serve to remind the beginner that philosophy and scientific thought should be
one, and that natural science is not all of science, it may be of value.]

[2] Plato, *Rep.* 480 B; Aristotle, *Met.* VI. 1, 1026 a 18.

[3] Plato, *Theæt.* 143 D. Aristotle sets the doctrine "of Being as such" (the
later so-called Metaphysics) as "First Philosophy" over against the other
"philosophies," and distinguishes further theoretical and practical "philosophy." In one passage (*Met.* I. 6, 987 a 29) he applies the plural φιλοσοφίαι also
to the different systems of science which have followed in historical succession,
as we should speak of the philosophies of Kant, Fichte, Hegel, etc.

[4] Cf. the definition of Epicurus in Sext. Emp. *Adv. Math.* XI. 169, and on
the other hand that of Seneca, *Epist.* 89.

[5] Cf. below, Part I.

[6] Hence Proclus, for example, would prefer to have philosophy called
theology.

There was at first little change in these relations, when the remains of ancient science passed over into the culture of the present peoples of Europe as the determining forces of their intellectual life. Content and task of that which the Middle Ages called philosophy coincided with the conception held by later antiquity.[1] And yet the meaning of philosophy underwent an essential change by finding philosophy's task already performed, in a certain sense, by religion. For religion, too, afforded not only a sure conviction as a rule for the guidance of personal life, but also in connection with this, a general theoretical view of all reality, which was the more philosophical in its character, as the dogmas of Christianity had been formulated entirely under the influence of ancient philosophy. Under these circumstances, during the unbroken dominance of Church doctrine, there remained for philosophy, for the most part, only the position of a handmaid *to ground, develop, and defend dogma scientifically.* But just by this means philosophy came into a certain opposition to theology as regards method; for what the latter taught on the ground of divine revelation, the former was to win and set forth by means of human knowledge.[2]

But the infallible consequence of this relation was, that the freer individual thinking became in its relation to the Church, the more independently philosophy began the solution of the problem which she had in common with religion; from presentation and defence of doctrine she passed to its criticism, and finally, in complete independence of religious interests, sought to derive her teaching from the sources which she thought she possessed in the "natural light" of human reason and experience.[3] The opposition to theology, as regards methods, grew in this way to an opposition in the subject matter, and modern philosophy as "world-wisdom" set itself over against Church dogma.[4] However manifold the aspects which this relation took on, shading from a clinging attachment to a passionate conflict, the office of "philosophy" remained always that which

---

[1] Cf., for example, Augustine, *Solil.* I. 7 ; *Conf.* V. 7; Scotus Erigena, *De Div. Prædest.* I. 1 (Migne, 358) ; Anselm *Proslog.*, ch. 1. (Migne, I. 227) ; Abelard, *Introd. in Theol.* II. 3 ; Raymundus Lullus, *De Quinque Sap.* 8.

[2] Thomas Aquinas, *Summa Theol.* I. 32, 1 ; *Contr. Gent.* I. 8 f., II. 1 ff. ; Duns Scotus, *Op. Ox.* I. 3, qu. 4 ; Durand de Pourçain, *In Sent. Prol.*, qu. 8 ; Raymundus of Sabunde, *Theol. Natur. Prooem.*

[3] Laur. Valla, *Dialect. Disp.* III. 9 ; B. Telesio, *De Nat. Rer. Prooem.;* Fr. Bacon, *De Augm.* III. 1 (Works, Spedding, I. 539 = III. 336) ; Taurellus, *Philos. Triumph.* I. 1 ; Paracelsus, *Paragr.* (ed. Huser) II. 23 f. ; G. Bruno, *Della Causa*, etc., IV. 107 (Lagarde, I. 272) ; Hobbes, *De Corpor.* I. (Works, Molesworth, I. 2 and 6 f.).

[4] Characteristic definitions, on the one hand, in Gottsched, *Erste Gründe der gesammten Weltweisheit* (Leips. 1756), pp. 97 ff. ; on the other hand, in the article *Philosophie*, in the *Encyclopédie* (Vol. XXV. pp. 632 ff.).

antiquity had assigned to it, to supply from scientific insight a foundation for a theory of the world and of human life, where religion was no longer able to meet this need, or at least to meet it alone. In the conviction that it was equal to this task, the philosophy of the eighteenth century, like that of the Greeks, considered it its right and duty to enlighten men with regard to the nature of things, and from this position of insight to rule the life of the individual and of society.

In this position of self-security philosophy was shaken by *Kant*, who demonstrated the impossibility of a philosophical (*i.e.* metaphysical) knowledge of the world beside of or above the individual sciences, and thereby restricted once more the conception and the task of philosophy; for after this quitclaim the realm of *philosophy, as a particular science*, was narrowed to just that *critical consideration by Reason of itself,* from which *Kant* had won his decisive insight, and which needed only to be extended systematically to activities other than that of knowing. With this function could be united what *Kant*[1] called the universal or cosmical conception of philosophy, — its vocation in the practical direction of life.

It is, to be sure, far from true that this new and apparently final conception of philosophy gained universal acceptance at once. It is rather the case that the great variety of philosophical movements of the nineteenth century has left no earlier form of philosophy unrepeated, and that a luxuriant development of the "metaphysical need"[2] even brought back, for a time, the inclination to swallow up all human knowledge in philosophy, and complete this again as an all-embracing science.

2. In view of these mutations through which the meaning of the word "philosophy" has passed in the course of time, it seems impracticable *to pretend to gain a general conception of philosophy from historical comparison.* None of those brought forward for this purpose[3] apply to all those structures of mental activity which lay claim to the name. Even the subordination of philosophy under the more general conception "science" is questionable in the case of those types of teaching which place a one-sided emphasis on the

---

[1] *Critique of Pure Reason*, A. 839; B. 866.
[2] Schopenhauer, *World as Will and Idea*, Vol. II. ch. 17.
[3] Instead of criticising particular conceptions it is sufficient here to point to the widely diverging formulas in which the attempt has been made to perform this impossible task: cf., for example, only the introductions to works such as those of Erdmann, Ueberweg, Kuno Fischer, Zeller, etc. All these conceptions thus determined apply only in so far as the history of philosophy has yielded the *result* which they express, but they do not apply with reference to the *intentions* expressed by the philosophers themselves.

practical significance of their doctrine :[1] still less can we define the subject-matter and form of philosophy considered as a special science, in a way that shall hold good for all cases. For even aside from the primitive or the revived standpoint for which philosophy is a universal science,[2] the attempts to limit it are extremely various. The problems of natural science form at first almost the sole objects of interest for philosophy, then for a long period are included in its scope, and do not separate from it until modern times. History, on the other hand, has remained an object of indifference to most philosophical systems, and has emerged as an object of philosophical investigation relatively late and in isolated cases. Metaphysical doctrines, again, in which the centre of philosophy is usually sought, we see either pushed one side at important turning-points in history or declared to be entirely impossible [3]; and if at times the ability of philosophy to determine the life of the individual or of society is emphasised, a proud standpoint of pure theory has renounced such a menial occupation.[4]

From still another side it has been claimed that philosophy treats the same subjects as the other sciences, but in another sense and by another method; but neither has this specific characteristic of form historical universality. That there is no such acknowledged historical method would of course be no objection if only the endeavour after such a method were a constant characteristic of all philosophies. This is, however, so far from being the case that in fact many philosophers imprint on their science the method of other disciplines, *e.g.* of mathematics or of investigation of nature,[5] while others will have nothing at all to do with a methodical treatment of their problems, and regard the philosophic activity as analogous to the creations of genius in art.

3. From these circumstances is explained also the fact that there is no fixed *relation of philosophy to the other sciences,* which is capable of a definition valid for all history. Where philosophy presents itself as the universal science, the other sciences appear only as its more or less distinctly separated parts.[6] Where, on the contrary, philosophy is assigned the task of grasping the results of the par-

---

[1] So in the case of the majority of the philosophers of later antiquity.

[2] As for Chr. Wolf; cf. his *Logica,* §§ 29 ff.

[3] This is especially the case where philosophy is regarded solely as "science of cognition." Cf., *e.g.,* W. Hamilton in his notes to Reid's works, II. 808. Among the French at the close of the eighteenth and the beginning of this century, philosophy = *analyse de l'entendement humain.*

[4] *E.g.* with Plotinus.

[5] So Descartes and Bacon.

[6] So, for example, in the Hegelian system.

ticular sciences in their general significance, and harmonising them
into a comprehensive knowledge of the world, we have as the result
peculiarly complex relations: in the first place, a dependence of
philosophy upon the existing condition of insight reached in the particular disciplines — a dependence which expresses itself principally
in the furtherance of philosophy by the prominent advances made
by individual sciences; [1] in the next place, an influence in the
opposite direction, when philosophy takes part in the work of the
particular sciences. This action is felt as help or as hindrance,
according as the philosophical treatment of the questions embraced
under the particular disciplines sometimes contributes valuable
factors for their solution, by means of its wider range of vision and
its tendency toward unity,[2] but at other times presents itself only
as a duplication which, if it leads to like results, appears useless, or
if it wishes to furnish other results, dangerous.[3]

From what has been said it is evident farther, that the *relations
of philosophy to the other activities of civilisation* are no less close than
its relation to the individual sciences. For the conceptions arising
from the religious and ethical and artistic life, from the life of the
state and of society, force their way everywhere, side by side with
the results won from scientific investigation, into the idea of the
universe which the philosophy of metaphysical tendencies aims to
frame; and the reason's valuations (*Werthbestimmungen*) and standards of judgment demand their place in that idea the more vigorously, just in proportion as it is to become the basis for the practical
significance of philosophy. In this way humanity's convictions and
ideals find their expression in philosophy side by side with its
intellectual insights; and if these convictions and ideals are regarded,
erroneously often, as gaining thereby the form of scientific intelligence, they may receive under certain circumstances valuable clarification and modification by this means. Thus this relation also of
philosophy to general culture is not only that of receiving, but also
that of giving.

It is not without interest to consider also the mutations in *external position*
and *social relations* which philosophy has experienced. It may be assumed that
science was from the first, with perhaps a few exceptions (Socrates), pursued in
Greece in closed schools.[4] The fact that these, even at a later time, had the form

---

[1] As the influence of astronomy upon the beginnings of Greek, or that of
mechanics upon those of modern, philosophy.

[2] The Protestant theology of the nineteenth century stands in this relation
to German philosophy.

[3] Cf. the opposition of natural science to Schelling's philosophy of nature.

[4] H. Diels, *Ueber die ältesten Philosophenschulen der Griechen* in Philos.
Aufsätze zum Jubiläum E. Zeller's, Leips. 1887, pp. 241 ff.

of societies with religious laws [1] would not in itself alone, in view of the religious character of all Greek judicial institutions, prove a religious origin of these schools, but the circumstance that Greek science worked out its contents directly from religious ideas, and that certain connections with religious cults present themselves unmistakably in a number of directions,[2] makes it not improbable that the scientific societies sprang originally from religious unions (the Mysteries) and continued in a certain connection with them. But when the scientific life had developed to complete independence, these connections fell away and purely scientific schools were founded as free unions of men who, under the guidance of persons of importance, shared with each other the work of research, exposition, defence, and polemic,[3] and at the same time had an ethical bond in a common ideal of the conduct of life.

With the advent of the larger relations of life in the Hellenistic and Roman period, these unions naturally became loosened, and we frequently meet writers, especially among the Romans, who are active in the field of philosophy in a purely individual way, neither members of a school nor professional teachers. Such were Cicero, Seneca, and Marcus Aurelius. Not until the latest period of antiquity were the ties of the schools drawn more closely again, as in Neo-Pythagoreanism and Neo-Platonism.

Among the Romanic and Germanic peoples the course of events has been not unlike that in the ancient world. The science of the Middle Ages also appears in the train of the Church civilisation ; it has its seats in the cloister-schools, and is stimulated toward independent development primarily by questions of religious interest. In it, too, the oppositions of various religious orders, such as the Dominicans and Franciscans, assert themselves for a time, and even the freer scientific associations out of which the universities gradually developed, had originally a religious background and an ecclesiastical stamp.[4] Hence there was always but a slight degree of independence with reference to Church doctrine in this corporate philosophy of the universities, and this held true on into the eighteenth century for the Protestant universities also, in the foundation and development of which ecclesiastical and religious interests had a foremost place.

On the other hand, it is characteristic of the " world-wisdom " or secular philosophy which was gaining its independence at the beginning of the modern period, that those who bring and support it are not at all men of the schools, but men of the world and of life. An escaped monk, a state-chancellor, a cobbler, a nobleman, a proscribed Jew, a learned diplomat, independent men of letters and journalists, — these are the founders of modern philosophy, and in accord with this, their work takes for its outer form not the text-book or the deposit of academical disputations, but the free literary production, the essay.

Not until the second half of the eighteenth century did philosophy again become corporate, and domesticated in the universities. This took place first in Germany, where the most favourable conditions were afforded by the rising independence of the universities, and where a fruitful interchange between teachers and students of the university was beneficial to philosophy also.[5]

---

[1] v. Wilamowitz-Möllendorf, *Antigonos von Karystos* (Philol. Stud. IV. Berlin, 1881, pp. 263 ff.).

[2] The Pythagoreans, as is well known, offer a pre-eminent example of this ; but sympathies with the Apollo cultus are plain enough in the Platonic Academy also. Pfleiderer has lately sought to bring the apparently isolated Heraclitus into connection with the Mysteries (E. Pfleiderer, *Heraklit von Ephesus.* Berlin, 1886).

[3] Cf. H. Usener, *Ueber die Organisation der wissenschaftlichen Arbeit im Alterthum* (Preuss. Jahrb., Jahrg. LIII., 1884, pp. 1 ff.), and E. Heitz, *Die Philosophenschulen Athens* (Deutsche Revue, 1884, pp. 326 ff.).

[4] Cf. G. Kaufmann, *Geschichte der deutschen Universitäten* I. pp. 98 ff. (Stuttg. 1888).

[5] *Schelling* has erected the finest monument to the ideal conception of science in the activity of German universities, in his *Vorlesungen über die Methode des akademischen Studiums* (2. and 3. Vorlesung. Ges. Werke, I. Abth., Vol. 5. pp. 223 ff.).

From Germany this spread to Scotland, England, France, and Italy, and in general it may be said that in the nineteenth century the seat of philosophy is essentially to be sought in the universities.[1]

In conclusion, the *share of the various peoples* in the development of philosophy deserves a brief mention. As with all developments of European culture, so with philosophy, — the Greeks created it, and the primitive structure of philosophy due to their creative activity is still to-day an essential basis of the science. What was added in antiquity by the mixed peoples of Hellenism and by the Romans does not, in general, amount to more than a special form and practical adaptation of the Greek philosophy. Only in the religious turn which this last movement took (cf. below, Part II. ch. 2) do we find something essentially new which sprang from the harmonising of national differences in the Roman Empire. The scientific culture of the Middle Ages was also international, as is implied in the universal employment of the Latin language. It is with modern philosophy that the special characters of particular nations first present themselves as of decisive influence. While the traditions of mediæval scholasticism maintain themselves most vigorously and independently in Spain and Portugal, the Italians, Germans, English, and French supply the first movements of the new science which reached its highest point in the classical period of German philosophy. Compared with these four nations, the rest stand almost entirely in a receptive attitude ; a certain independence is noticeable, if anywhere, in more recent time among the Swedes.

§ 2. The History of Philosophy.

The more varied the character assumed by the problems and content of philosophy in the course of time, the more the question rises, what meaning there can be in uniting in historical investigation and exposition products of thought which are not only so manifold, but also so different in kind, and between which there seems to be ultimately nothing in common but the name.

For the anecdotal interest in this checkered diversity of various opinions on various things, which was perhaps formerly the chief motive of a "History of Philosophy," stimulated too by the remarkable and strange nature of many of these views, cannot possibly serve as the permanent centre of a genuine scientific discipline.

1. At all events, however, it is clear that the case stands otherwise with the history of philosophy than with that of any other science. For with all these the field of research remains fixed, on the whole at least, however many the variations to which its extent, its separation from a still more general field, and its limitation with reference to neighbouring fields, may be subject in the course of history. In such a case there is no difficulty in tracing the development of knowledge over a field which can be determined in this way, and in eventually making just those variations intelligible as the natural consequences of this development of insight.

---

[1] The best evidence for this statement is afforded by just the passionate attacks which Schopenhauer directed against the relation between philosophy and the universities.

Quite otherwise, however, in the case of philosophy, which has no such subject-matter common to all its periods, and whose "history," therefore, sets forth no constant advance or gradual approximation to a knowledge of the subject in question. Rather, it has always been emphasised that while in other sciences, a quiet building up of knowledge is the rule, as soon as they have once gained a sure methodical footing after their rhapsodical beginnings, — a rule which is interrupted only from time to time by a sudden new beginning, — in philosophy the reverse is true. There it is the exception that successors gratefully develop what has been already achieved, and each of the great systems of philosophy begins to solve its newly formulated problem *ab ovo*, as if the other systems had scarcely existed.

2. If in spite of all of this we are still to be able to speak of a "history of philosophy," the unity of connection, which we find neither in the objects with which philosophers busy themselves, nor in the problems they have set themselves, can be found only in the *common work which they have accomplished* in spite of all the variety in their subject-matter and in the purposes with which they have worked.

But this common product, which constitutes the meaning of the history of philosophy, rests on just the changing relations which the work of philosophers has sustained in the course of history, not only to the maturest results of science in general and of the special sciences in particular, but also to the other activities of European civilisation. For was it that philosophy had in view the project of a general scientific knowledge of the universe, which she would win either in the role of universal science, or as a generalising comprehension of the results of the special sciences, or was it that she sought a view of life which should give a complete expression to the highest values of will and feeling, or was it finally that with a clearly defined limitation of her field she made reason's self-knowledge her goal, — the result always was that she was labouring to bring to conscious expression the necessary forms and principles in which the human reason manifests its activity, and to transfer these from their original form of perceptions, feelings, and impulses, into that of *conceptions*. In some direction and in some fashion every philosophy has striven to reach, over a more or less extensive field, a formulation in conception of the material immediately given in the world and in life; and so, as these efforts have passed into history, the constitution of the mental and spiritual life has been step by step disclosed. *The History of Philosophy is the process in which European humanity has embodied in scientific conceptions its views of the world and its judgments of life.*

It is this common fruit of all the intellectual creations which present themselves as "philosophies," which alone gives to the history of philosophy as a genuine science its content, its problem, and its justification. This, too, is the reason why a knowledge of the history of philosophy is a necessary requirement, not only for all scholarly education, but for all culture whatever; for it teaches how the conceptions and forms have been coined, in which we all, in every-day life as well as in the particular sciences, think and judge the world of our experience.

The beginnings of the history of philosophy are to be sought in the historical compositions (for the most part lost) of the great schools of antiquity, especially the Peripatetic School. As we may see in the examples given by Aristotle,[1] these works had the critical purpose of preparing for the development of their own views by a dialectical examination of views previously brought forward. Such collections of historical material were planned for the various fields of science, and doxographies[2] in philosophy arose in this way side by side with histories of particular disciplines, such as mathematics, astronomy, physics, etc. As inclination and power for independent philosophic thought later declined, this literature degenerated into a learned scrap-book work, in which were mingled anecdotes from the lives of the philosophers, individual epigrammatic sayings, and sketches of their doctrines.

Those expositions belonging to the modern period which were based upon the remains of ancient tradition had this same character of collections of curiosities. Such were *Stanley's*[3] reproduction of Diogenes Laertius, and *Brucker's* works.[4] Only with time do we find critical discernment in use of the sources (*Buhle,*[5] *Fülleborn*[6]), a more unprejudiced apprehension of the historical significance of individual doctrines (*Tiedemann,*[7] *Degérando*[8]), and systematic criticism of these upon the basis of the new standpoint (*Tennemann,*[9] *Fries,*[10] and *Schleiermacher*[11]).

It was, however, through *Hegel*[12] that the history of philosophy was first made an independent science, for he discovered the essential point that the

---

[1] *E.g.* in the beginning of the *Metaphysics.*

[2] More in detail on these below.

[3] Th. Stanley, *The History of Philosophy.* Lond. 1685.

[4] J. J. Brucker, *Historia Critica Philosophiæ.* 5 vols. Leips. 1742 ff. *Institutiones Historiæ Philosophiæ.* Leips. 1747.

[5] J. G. Buhle, *Lehrbuch der Geschichte der Philosophie.* 8 vols. Göttingen, 1796 ff.

[6] G. G. Fülleborn, *Beiträge zur Geschichte der Philosophie.* 12 Studien. Züllichau, 1791 ff.

[7] D. Tiedemann, *Geist der Speculativen Philosophie.* 7 vols. Marburg, 1791 ff.

[8] De Gérando, *Histoire Comparée des Systèmes de Philosophie.* 2d ed. in 4 vols. Paris, 1822 f.

[9] W. G. Tennemann, *Geschichte der Philosophie.* 11 vols. Leips. 1798 ff. *Grundriss der Geschichte der Philosophie für den akademischen Unterricht.* Leips. 1812. [Eng. trans. 1833 and 1852.]

[10] J. Fr. Fries, *Geschichte der Philosophie.* 2 vols. Halle, 1837 ff.

[11] Fr. Schleiermacher, *Geschichte der Philosophie,* from his literary remains in the Coll. Works. III. Abth., 4 Bd., 1 Th. Berlin, 1839.

[12] Cf. the introductions of the *Phänomenologie des Geistes,* of the lectures on the *Philosophy of History,* and those on the *History of Philosophy.* Ges. Werke, Bd. II. pp. 62 ff.; IX. pp. 11 ff.; XIII. pp. 11–134. In Hegel's works the *Geschichte der Philosophie,* edited from his lectures by Michelet, occupies Vols. XIII.–XV. Berlin, 1833–36. [*Lectures on the History of Philosophy,* by G. W. Hegel. Trans. by E. S. Haldane in 3 vols. Vol. I. Lond. 1892.] On his standpoint

history of philosophy can set forth neither a motley collection of opinions of various learned gentleman "*de omnibus rebus et de quibusdam aliis,*" nor a constantly widening and perfecting elaboration of the same subject-matter, but rather only the limited process in which the "categories" of reason have successively attained distinct consciousness and reached the form of conceptions.

This valuable insight was, however, obscured and injured in the case of Hegel by an additional asumption, since he was convinced that the chronological order in which the above "categories" have presented themselves in the historical systems of philosophy must necessarily correspond with the logical and systematic order in which these same categories should appear as "elements of truth" in the logical construction of the final system of philosophy (*i.e.* in Hegel's view, his own). The fundamental thought, right in itself, thus led to the mistake of a construction of the history of philosophy under the control of a philosophical system, and so to a frequent violation of historical fact. This error, which the development of a scientific history of philosophy in the nineteenth century has set aside in favour of historical accuracy and exactness, arose from the wrong idea (though an idea in logical consistence with the principles of Hegel's philosophy) that the historical progress of philosophical thought is due solely, or at least essentially, to an ideal necessity with which one "category" pushes forward another in the dialectical movement. In truth, the picture of the historical movement of philosophy is quite a different one. It depends not solely upon the thinking of "humanity" or even of the "*Weltgeist,*" but just as truly upon the reflections, the needs of mind and heart, the presaging thought and sudden flashes of insight, of philosophising individuals.

3. The history of philosophy, considered as such a sum-total, in which the fundamental conceptions of man's views of the world and judgments of life have been embodied, is the product of a great variety of single movements of thought. And as the actual motives of these movements, various factors are to be distinguished, both in the setting of the problems and in the attempts at their logical solution.

The logical, *pragmatic factor* is no doubt sufficiently important. For the problems of philosophy are in the main given, and this is shown by the fact that they are constantly recurring in the historical movement of thought as the "primeval enigma of existence," and are ever anew demanding imperiously the solution which has never completely succeeded. They are given, however, by the inadequacy and internal contradictions of the material which consciousness presents for philosophical consideration.[1] But just for

---

stand G. O. Marbach, *Lehrbuch der Geschichte Philosophie* (2. Abth. Leips. 1838 ff.), C. Hermann, *Geschichte der Philosophie in pragmatischer Behandlung* (Leips. 1867), and in part also the survey of the entire history of philosophy which J. Braniss has published as the first (only) volume of a *Geschichte der Philosophie seit Kant* (Breslau, 1842). In France this line is represented by V. Cousin, *Introduction à l'Histoire de la Philosophie* (Paris, 1828 ; 7th ed. 1872) ; *Histoire Générale de la Philosophie* (12th ed., Paris, 1884).

[1] More precisely, this inadequacy, which cannot here be more exactly developed, and which can be fully brought out only in a system of epistemology, consists in the circumstance that that which is given in experience never meets completely the conceptional demands which, in elaborating the same according to the inner nature of the reason, we set up, at first naïvely and immediately, and later with reflective consciousness. This *antinomism* (or failure to meet the laws of thought) can be escaped by ordinary life, or even by experiential

this reason this material contains the real presuppositions and the logical constraining forces for all rational reflection upon it, and because from the nature of the case these are always asserting themselves anew in the same way, it follows that not only the chief problems in the history of philosophy, but also the chief lines along which a solution is attempted, are repeated. Just this constancy in all change, which, regarded from without, makes the impression that philosophy is striving fruitlessly in ever-repeated circles for a goal that is never attained, proves only this, — that the problems of philosophy are tasks which the human mind cannot escape.[1] And so we understand how the same logical necessity in repeated instances causes one doctrine to give birth to another. Hence progress in the history of philosophy is, during certain periods, to be understood entirely pragmatically, *i.e.* through the internal necessity of the thoughts and through the " logic of things."

The mistake of Hegel's mentioned above, consists, then, only in his wishing to make of a factor which is effective within certain limits, the only, or at least the principal, factor. It would be the opposite error to deny absolutely the " reason in history," and to see in the successive doctrines of philosophy only confused chance-thoughts of individuals. It is rather true that the total content of the history of philosophy can be explained only through the fact that the necessities existing in the nature of things assert themselves over and over in the thinking of individuals, however accidental the special conditions of this latter may be. On these relations rest the attempts made to classify all philosophical doctrines under certain types, and to establish a sort of rhythmical repetition in their historical development. On this basis V. Cousin[2] brought forward his theory of the four systems, Idealism, Sensualism, Scepticism, Mysticism ; so too August Comte[3] his of the three stages, the theological, the metaphysical, and the positive. An interesting and in many ways instructive grouping of philosophical doctrines about the particular main problems is afforded by A. Renouvier in his *Esquisse d'une Classification Systématique des Doctrines Philosophiques* (2 vols., Paris, 1885 f.). A school-book which arranges the philosophical doctrines according to problems and schools has been issued by Paul Janet and Séailles ; *Histoire de la Philosophie ; les problèmes et les écoles* (Paris, 1887).

4. But the pragmatic thread very often breaks off in the history of philosophy. The historical order in particular, in which problems have presented themselves, shows almost a complete absence

---

science, by working with auxiliary conceptions, which indeed remain problematical in themselves, but which, within certain bounds, suffice for an elaboration of the material of experience that meets our practical needs. But it is just in these auxiliary conceptions that the problems of philosophy inhere.

[1] In this way the results of Kant's investigations on " The Antinomy of Pure Reason " (*Critique of Pure Reason*, Transcendental Dialectic, second sec.) might be historically and systematically extended ; cf. W. Windelband, *Geschichte der neueren Philosophie*, II. 95 f.

[2] Cf. Note 12, p. 10.

[3] A. Comte, *Cours de Philosophie Positive* I. 9, with which Vols. V. and VI. are to be compared as the carrying out of the scheme. Similar thoughts are also found in D'Alembert's *Discours Préliminaire* in the *Encyclopédie*.

of such an immanent logical necessity. Here, on the contrary, another factor asserts itself which may best be designated as the *factor contributed by the history of civilisation.* For philosophy receives both its problems and the materials for their solution from the ideas of the general consciousness of the time, and from the needs of society. The great conquests and the newly emerging questions of the special sciences, the movements of the religious consciousness, the intuitions of art, the revolutions in social and political life, — all these give philosophy new impulses at irregular intervals, and condition the directions of the interest which forces, now these, now those, problems into the foreground, and crowds others for the time being aside; and no less do they condition also the changes which questions and answers experience in course of time. Where this dependence shows itself with especial clearness, we have under certain circumstances a philosophical system appearing, that represents exactly the knowledge which a definite age has of itself; or we may have the oppositions in the general culture of the age finding their expression in the strife of philosophical systems. And so besides the constant dependence upon the essential character of the subject-matter — the pragmatic factor — there prevails also a necessity growing out of the history of civilisation, or current state of culture, which warrants a historical right of existence to structures of thought in themselves untenable.

This relation also was first brought to notice in a greater degree than before by *Hegel*, although the "relative truth" which he ascribes to the particular systems has with him at the same time a systematic meaning, owing to his dialectical fundamental thought. On the other hand, the element due to the history of civilisation has been best formulated among his successors by *Kuno Fischer*,[1] who has also availed himself of it in most brilliant manner in his exposition of the subject. He regards philosophy in its historical unfolding as the progressive self-knowledge of the human mind, and makes its development appear as constantly conditioned by the development of the object which in it is attaining self-knowledge. Although this applies to a number of the most important systems, it is yet but one of the factors involved.

The influences from the history of civilisation which condition the statement and solution of philosophic problems, afford an explanation in most cases of an extremely interesting phenomenon which is of great importance for understanding the historical development; viz. *the complication or interweaving of problems.* For when interest is directed chiefly on certain lines of thought, it is inevitable, according to psychological laws, that associations will be formed between different bodies of thought, — associations which are not based on the subject-matter, — and so, that questions which in themselves have nothing to do with each other become blended and made to depend upon each other in their solution. An extremely important and very often recurring example of this is the intermingling of ethical and æsthetic interests in the treatment of theoretical problems. The well-known fact of daily life that men's views are determined by their wishes, hopes, fears, and inclinations, that their theoretical are condi-

---

[1] Kuno Fischer, *Geschichte der neueren Philosophie*, I. 1, Einleitung I.-V. {trans. by J. P. Gordy, *Descartes and his School*, N.Y. 1887].

tioned by their ethical and æsthetic judgments (*Urtheile durch ihre Beurthei-lungen*), — this fact is repeated on a larger scale in their views of the universe, and has even been able to rise so high in philosophy that what had been pre-viously involuntarily practised, was proclaimed (by Kant) an epistemological postulate.

5. Meanwhile the historical process we are tracing owes all its variety and multiplicity of forms to the circumstance that the de-velopment of ideas and the formulation of general beliefs into abstract conceptions are accomplished only through the thinking of individual *personalities*, who, though rooted ever so deeply with their thought in the logical connection and prevalent ideas of a historical period, always add a particular element by their own individuality and conduct of life.　This *individual factor* in the development of the history of philosophy deserves so great atten-tion for the reason that those who have borne the leading part in the movement have sho vn themselves to be marked, independent personalities, whose peculiar nature has been a determining in-fluence, not merely for the selection and combination of problems, but also for working out the conceptions to furnish solutions, both in their own doctrines and in those of their successors.　That history is the kingdom of individualities, of details which are not to be repeated and which have value in themselves, is shown also in the history of philosophy : here, too, great personalities have exercised far-reaching and not exclusively beneficial influences.

It is clear that the above-mentioned complication of problems is brought about by the subjective relations in which individual philosophers stand, in a much greater degree than by the occasions presented in the general conscious-ness of a time, of a people, etc.　There is no philosophical system that is free from this influence of the personality of its founder.　Hence all philosophical systems are creations of individuality, presenting in this respect a certain re-semblance with works of art, and as such are to be understood from the point of view of the personality of their founder.　The elements of every philosopher's *Weltanschauung* grow out of the problems of reality which are ever the same, and out of the reason as it is directed to their solution, but besides this out of the views and ideals of his people and his time ; the form and arrangement, however, the connection and valuation which they find in the system, are condi-tioned by his birth and education, his activity and lot in life, his character and his experience.　Here, accordingly, the universality which belongs to the other two factors is often wanting.　In the case of these purely individual creations, æsthetic charm must take the place of the worth of abiding knowledge, and the impressiveness of many phenomena of the history of philosophy rests, in fact, only upon the magic of their "poetry of ideas" (*Begriffsdichtung*).

In addition, then, to the complication of problems and to the ideas determined by fancy and feeling, which are already enough to lead the general conscious-ness astray, there are in the case of individuals similar, but purely personal, processes to lend to the formation and solution of problems still more the char-acter of artificiality.　We cannot fail to recognise that philosophers have often gone about struggling with questions which have no basis in reality, so that all thought expended upon them was in vain, and that, on the other hand, even in connection with the solution of real problems, unfortunate attempts in the *a priori* construction of conceptions have slipped in, which have been hindrances rather than helps toward the issue of the matter.

The wonderful feature in the history of philosophy remains just this, that out of such a multitude of individual and general complications there has yet been on the whole laid down that outline of universally valid conceptions for viewing the world and judging life, which presents the scientific significance of this development.

6. *Investigation in the history of philosophy has accordingly the following tasks to accomplish:* (1) To *establish with precision* what may be derived from the available sources as to the circumstances in life, the mental development, and the doctrines of individual philosophers; (2) from these facts to reconstruct the *genetic* process in such a way that in the case of every philosopher we may understand how his doctrines depend in part upon those of his predecessors, in part upon the general ideas of his time, and in part upon his own nature and the course of his education; (3) from the consideration of the whole to *estimate* what value for the total result of the history of philosophy belongs to the theories thus established and explained as regards their origin.

With reference to the first two points, the history of philosophy is a *philologico-historical,* with reference to the third element it is a *critico-philosophical science.*

(*a*) To establish its facts the history of philosophy must proceed to a careful and comprehensive examination of the *sources.* These sources, however, vary greatly at different times in their transparency and fulness.

The main sources for investigation in the history of philosophy are of course the *works of the philosophers* themselves. For the *modern period* we stand here upon a relatively safe footing. Since the discovery of the art of printing, literary tradition has become so well established and clear that it offers in general no difficulties of any kind. The writings which philosophers have published since the Renaissance are throughout accessible for the research of to-day. The cases in which questions of genuineness, of the time of origination, etc., give rise to controversies are extremely seldom ; a philological criticism has here but a narrow field for activity, and where it can enter (as is the case in part in reference to the different editions of Kant's works), it concerns solely subordinate, and in the last instance indifferent, points. Here, too, we are tolerably sure of the completeness of the material ; that anything of weight is lost, or still to be expected from later publication, is scarcely to be assumed ; if the sharpened philological attentiveness of the last decades has brought us new material for Spinoza, Leibniz, Kant, Maine de Biran, the philosophical outcome has been only vanishing in comparison with the value of what was already known. At most it has concerned the question of supplementing our knowledge, and this must continue to be its province. The importance of occasional expressions in letters has been specially felt here, for these are adapted to shed more light on the individual factor in the historical development of philosophy.

With the sources of the *Mediæval Philosophy* the case stands less favourably. These have in part (a small part, to be sure) still only a manuscript existence. *V. Cousin* and his school have rendered valuable service in publishing the texts, and in general we may be convinced that for this period also we possess material, which has indeed gaps, but is on the whole adequate for our purpose. On the other hand, our knowledge of the Arabian and Jewish philosophy of the Middle Ages, and so of the influence of those systems on the course of Western Thought, is still very problematical in details ; and this is perhaps the gap most sorely felt in our investigation of the sources for the history of philosophy.

Much worse still is the situation as regards the direct sources for *Ancient Philosophy.* Of the original works, we have preserved, to be sure, the most important: the fundamental portion of the works of Plato and Aristotle, though even these are often doubtful in form. Besides these we have only the writings of later time, such as those of Cicero, Seneca, Plutarch, the Church Fathers, and the Neo-Platonists. By far the greater part of the philosophical writings of antiquity is lost. In their stead we must content ourselves with the fragments which the accident of an incidental mention in the writings of extant authors has kept for us, here too often in a questionable form.[1]

If, nevertheless, success has been attained in gaining a view of the development of the ancient philosophy, clearer than that of the mediæval, presenting a picture whose accuracy extends even to details and is scientifically assured, this is due not only to the unremitting pains of philologists and philosophers in working through their material, but also to the circumstance that beside the remains of the original works of the philosophers there are preserved also, as *secondary sources*, remains of historical records made in antiquity. The best, indeed, of these also is lost: namely, the historical works which arose from the learned collection made by the Peripatetic and Stoic schools at the end of the fourth and in the third century B.C. These works passed later through many hands before they were preserved for us in the extant compilations prepared in the Roman period, as in the *Placita Philosophorum*,[2] going by the name of Plutarch, in the writings of Sextus Empiricus,[3] in the *Deipnosophistæ* of Athenæus,[4] in the treatise of Diogenes Laertius, περὶ βίων δογμάτων καὶ ἀποθεγμάτων τῶν ἐν φιλοσοφίᾳ εὐδοκιμησάντων,[5] in the collections of the Church Fathers, and in the notes of the Commentators of the latest period, such as Alexander Aphrodisias, Themistius, and Simplicius. H. Diels has given an excellent and thorough treatment of these secondary sources of ancient philosophy, *Doxographi Græci* (Berlin, 1879).

Where the condition of the sources is so doubtful as is the case over the entire field of ancient philosophy, critical ascertainment of the facts must go hand in hand with examination of the pragmatic and genetic connection. For where the transmission of the material is itself doubtful we can reach a decision only by taking a view of the connection that shall accord with reason and psychological experience. In these cases it becomes the task of the history of philosophy as of all history, after establishing a base of operations in that which is assured by the sources, to proceed to ascertain its position in those regions with which tradition finds itself no longer directly and surely in touch. The historical study of philosophy in the nineteenth century may boast that it has fulfilled this task, to which it was stimulated by Schleiermacher, by the labours of H. Ritter, — whose *Geschichte der Philosophie* (12 vols., Hamburg, 1829-53) is now, to be sure, antiquated, — Brandis and Zeller for the ancient philosophy; and of J. E. Erdmann and Kuno Fischer for the modern. Among the many complete expositions of the history of philosophy by far the most trustworthy in these respects is J. E. Erdmann's *Grundriss der Geschichte der Philosophie*, 2 vols. (3d ed.), Berlin, 1878 ; [Erdmann's *History of Philosophy*, trans. ed. by W. S. Hough, Lond. and N.Y., 1890].

An excellent bibliography of the entire history of philosophy, assembling the literature in exhaustive completeness and good arrangement, is to be found in Ueberweg's *Grundriss der Geschichte der Philosophie*, 4 vols., 8th ed., ed. by M. Heinze (Berlin, 1894-98). [Ueberweg's *History of Philosophy*, trans. from the 4th ed. by G. S. Morris (N.Y. 1871), contains additions, but of course does not

---

[1] The collections of fragments of particular authors are mentioned under the notices of the individual philosophers. It would be desirable if they were all as excellent as Usener's *Epicurea*. Of the fragments of the Pre-Socratics W. F. A. Mullach has published a careful collection, which, however, is no longer adequate in the present condition of research (*Fragmenta Philosophorum Græcorum*).

[2] Plut. *Moralia*, ed. Dübner, Paris, 1841 ; Diels, *Dox.*, pp. 272 ff. ; [Plutarch's *Morals, Miscellanies, and Essays*, ed. by Goodwin, Boston, 1870 ; trans. also in the Bohn Lib.].

[3] Ed. Bekker, Berlin, 1847.

[4] G. Kaibel, Leips. 1888-90.

[5] Ed. Cobet, Paris, 1850.

give the bibliography of recent works.] Under the general literature may also be mentioned, R. Eucken, *Die Lebensanschauungen der grossen Denker* (Leips. 1890).

(*b*) Explanation of facts in the history of philosophy is either pragmatic (logical), or based on the history of civilisation, or psychological, corresponding to the three factors which we have set forth above as determining the movement of thought. Which of these three modes of explanation is to be applied in individual cases depends solely upon the state of the facts with regard to the transmission of material. It is then incorrect to make either one the sole principle of treatment. The pragmatic method of explanation is dominant with those who see in the entire history of philosophy the preparation for a definite system of philosophy ; so with Hegel and his disciples (see above, p. 10 f.); so from a Herbartian standpoint with Chr. A. Thilo, *Kurze pragmatische Geschichte der Philosophie* (2 pts. ; Coethen, 1876–80). Kuno Fischer and W. Windelband have emphasised in their interpretation of modern philosophy, the importance of considering the history of civilisation and the problems of the individual sciences.

The purely *biographical* treatment which deals only with successive personalities is quite inadequate as a scientific exposition of the history of philosophy. This mode of treatment is represented in recent time by the treatise of G. H. Lewes, *The History of Philosophy from Thales to the Present Day* (2 vols., Lond. 1871), a book destitute of all historical apprehension, and at the same time a party composition in the spirit of the Positivism of Comte. The works of the French historians (Damiron, Ferraz) are inclined to take this form of a separate essay-like treatment of individual philosophers, not losing from sight, however, the course of development of the whole.[1]

(*c*) The most difficult task is to establish the principles according to which the critical philosophical estimate of the individual doctrines must be made up. The history of philosophy, like all history, is a critical science ; its duty is not only to record and explain, but also to estimate what is to count as progress and fruit in the historical movement, when we have succeeded in knowing and understanding this. There is no history without this critical point of view, and the evidence of a historian's maturity is that he is clearly conscious of this point of view of criticism ; for where this is not the case he proceeds in the selection of his material and in his characterisation of details only instinctively and without a clear standard.[2]

It is understood, of course, that the standard of critical judgment must not be a private theory of the historian, nor even his philosophic conviction ; at least the employment of such a standard deprives the criticism exercised in accordance with it of the value of scientific universality. He who is given to the belief that he possesses the sole philosophical truth, or who comes to this field imbued with the customs of the special sciences in which, no doubt, a sure result makes it a very simple[3] matter to estimate the attempts which have led to it, — such a one may well be tempted to stretch all forms that pass before him upon the Procrustes-bed of his system ; but he who contemplates the work of thought in history, with an open historical vision, will be restrained by a respectful reverence from reprimanding the heroes of philosophy for their ignorance of the wisdom of an epigone.[4]

---

[1] A. Weber, *History of Philosophy*, is to be recommended as a good text-book (5th French ed., Paris, 1891). [Eng. tr. by Thilly, N.Y. 1896.]

[2] This applies in every domain of history, in the history of politics and of literature, as well as in that of philosophy.

[3] As an example of this it may be noticed that the deserving author of an excellent *History of the Principles of Mechanics*, Ed. Dühring, has developed in his *Kritische Geschichte der Philosophie* (3d ed., Berlin, 1878) all the caprice of a one-sided judgment. The like is true of the confessional criticism passed by A. Stöckl, *Lehrbuch der Geschichte der Philosophie* (2 vols., 3d ed., Mainz, 1889).

[4] It is impossible to protest enough against the youthful conceit with which it was for a time the fashion in Germany to look down with ridicule or insult from the "achievements of the present" upon the great men of Greek and Ger-

In contrast with this external method of pronouncing sentence, the scientific history of philosophy must place itself upon the standpoint of *immanent criticism*, the principles of which are two : *formal logical consistency* and *intellectual fruitfulness.*

Every philosopher grows into a certain set of ideas, and to these his thinking remains bound, and is subjected in its development to psychological necessity. Critical investigation has to settle how far it has been possible for him to bring the different elements of his thinking into agreement with each other. The contradiction is almost never actually present in so direct a form that the same thing is expressly maintained and also denied, but always in such a way that various positions are put forward which, only by virtue of their logical consequences, lead to direct contradiction and really irreconcilable results. The discovery of these discrepancies is formal criticism ; it frequently coincides with pragmatic explanation, for this formal criticism has been performed in history itself by the successors of the philosopher in question, and has thus determined for them their problems.

Yet this point of view alone is not sufficient. As purely formal it applies without exception to all attested views of a philosopher, but it gives no criterion for decision on the question, in what the philosophical significance of a doctrine really consists. For it is often the case that philosophy has done its work just in conceptions which must by no means be regarded as in themselves perfect or free from contradiction ; while a multitude of individual convictions, which there is no occasion to oppose, must remain unnoticed in a corner, so far as our historical survey is concerned. In the history of philosophy great errors are weightier than small truths.

For before all else the decisive question is : what has yielded a contribution to the development of man's conception of the universe and estimate of life ? In the history of philosophy those structures of thought are the objects of study which have maintained themselves permanent and living as forms of apprehension and norms of judgment, and in which the abiding inner structure of the human mind has thus come to clear recognition.

This is then the standard, according to which alone we can decide also which among the doctrines of the philosophers — concerning, as they often do, so many various things — are to be regarded as properly philosophical, and which, on the other hand, are to be excluded from the history of philosophy. Investigation of the sources has of course the duty of gathering carefully and completely all the doctrines of philosophers, and so of affording all the material for explaining their genesis, whether from their logical content, or from the history of civilisation, or from psychological grounds ; but the purpose of this laborious work is yet only this, that the philosophically indifferent may be ultimately recognised as such, and the ballast then thrown overboard.

It is especially true that this point of view must essentially determine selection and presentation of material in a *text-book*, which is not to give the investigation itself, but to gather up its results.

§ 3. Division of Philosophy and of its History.

It cannot be our purpose here to propose a systematic division of philosophy, for this could in no case possess universal validity historically. The differences which prevail in the course of the historical development, in determining the conception, the task, and the subject-matter of philosophy, involve so necessarily and obviously a change also in the divisions, that this needs no especial illustration. The oldest philosophy knew no division at all. In later antiquity

---

man philosophy ; this was mainly the haughtiness of an ignorance which had no suspicion that it was ultimately living only by the thoughts of those whom it was abusing and despising.

a division of philosophy into logic, physics, and ethics was current. In the Middle Ages, and still more in modern times, the first two of these subjects were often comprised under the title, theoretical philosophy, and set over against practical philosophy. Since Kant a new threefold division into logical, ethical, and æsthetical philosophy is beginning to make its way, yet these various divisions are too much dependent upon the actual course of philosophy itself to make it worth our while to recount them here in detail.

On the other hand, it does commend itself to preface the historical exposition with at least a brief survey of the entire circuit of those problems which have always formed the subject of philosophy, however varied the extent to which they have been studied or the value that has been attached to them, — a survey, therefore, for which no claim is made to validity from a systematic point of view, but which is determined only by the purpose of preliminary orientation.

1. *Theoretical problems.* Such we call those which refer, in part to our knowledge of the actual world, in part to an investigation of the knowing process itself. In dealing with the former class, however, the general questions which concern the actual taken as a whole are distinguished from those which deal with single provinces of the actual. The former, viz. the highest principles for explaining the universe, and the general view of the universe based on these principles, form the problem of *metaphysics,* called by Aristotle first, *i.e.* fundamental, science, and designated by the name now usual, only on account of the position which it had in the ancient collection of the Aristotelian works — " after physics." On account of his monotheistic view of the world, Aristotle also called this branch of knowledge theology. Later writers have also treated *rational* or *natural theology* as a branch of metaphysics.

The special provinces of the actual are Nature and History. In the former, external and internal nature are to be distinguished. The problems presented to knowledge by external nature are called *cosmological,* or, specially, problems of *natural philosophy,* or perhaps *physical.* The investigation of internal nature, *i.e.* of consciousness and its states and activities, is the business of *psychology.* The philosophical consideration of history remains within the borders of theoretical philosophy only if it be limited to the investigation of the laws that prevail in the historical life of peoples ; since, however, history is the realm of man's purposeful actions, the questions of the *philosophy of history,* so far as this deals with the end of the movement of history viewed as a whole, and with the fulfilment of this end, fall under the head of practical problems.

Investigation directed upon knowledge itself is called logic (in the general sense of the word), and also sometimes *noëtic*. If we are occupied with the question how knowledge actually arises, this *psycho-genetic* consideration falls in the province of *psychology*. If, on the other hand, we set up norms or standards according to which our ideas are estimated as regards their worth for truth, we call these *logical* laws, and designate investigation directed upon them as *logic* in the narrower sense. The application of these laws gives rise to *methodology*, which develops the prescriptions for a systematic ordering of scientific activity with reference to the various ends of knowledge. The problems, finally, which arise from the questions concerning the range and limit of man's knowing faculty and its relation to the reality to be known, form the subject-matter of *epistemology* or *theory of knowledge*.

H. Siebeck, *Geschichte der Psychologie*, Vol. I., in two parts (Gotha, 1880–84), incomplete, extending into the scholastic period.

K. Prantl, *Geschichte der Logik im Abendlande*, 4 vols. (Leips. 1855–70), brought down only to the Renaissance.

Fr. Harms, *Die Philosophie in ihrer Geschichte*. I. "Psychologie"; II. "Logik" (Berlin, 1877 and 1881).

[R. Adamson, *The History of Psychology* (in prep.).]

2. *Practical* problems are, in general, those which grow out of the investigation of man's activity, so far as it is determined by ends. Here, too, a psycho-genetic treatment is possible, which falls under psychology. That discipline, on the other hand, which considers man's action from the point of view of the ethical norm or standard, is *ethics* or *moral philosophy*. By *morals* (*Moral*) in the narrower sense is usually understood the proposal and grounding of ethical precepts. Since, however, all ethical action has reference to the community, there are attached to morals or ethics, in the narrower sense, the *philosophy of society* (for which the unfortunate name *sociology* seems likely to become permanent), and the *philosophy of law or right*. Further, in so far as the ideal of human society constitutes the ultimate meaning of history, the *philosophy of history* appears also in this connection, as already mentioned.

To practical problems, in the broadest sense of the word, belong also those which relate to art and religion. To designate philosophical investigation of the nature of the beautiful and of art, the name *æsthetics* has been introduced since the end of last century. If philosophy takes the religious life for its object, not in the sense of itself intending to give a science of the nature of the deity, but in the sense of an investigation with regard to man's religious behaviour, we call this discipline *philosophy of religion*.

Fr. Schleiermacher, *Grundlinien einer Kritik der bisherigen Sittenlehre* (collected works, III., Vol. I., Berlin, 1834). L. v. Henning, *Die Principien der Ethik in historischer Entwicklung* (Berlin, 1825). Fr. v. Raumer, *Die geschichtliche Entwicklung der Begriffe von Staat, Recht, und Politik* (Leips., 3d ed., 1861). E. Feuerlein, *Die philos. Sittenlehre in ihren geschichtlichen Hauptformen* (2 vols., Tübingen, 1857–59). P. Janet, *Histoire de la philosophie morale et politique* (Paris, 1858). W. Whewell, *History of Moral Science* (Edinburg, 1863). H. Sidgwick, *The Methods of Ethics*, 4th ed. (Lond. and N.Y. 1890). [*Outlines of the History of Ethics*, by same author (Lond. and N.Y., 3d ed., 1892). J. Martineau, *Types of Ethical Theory* (2d ed., Oxford and N.Y. 1886).] Th. Ziegler, *Geschichte der Ethik*, 2 vols. (the third not yet appeared; Strassburg, 1881–86). K. Köstlin, *Geschichte der Ethik* (only the beginning, 1 vol., Tübingen, 1887). [J. Bonar, *Philosophy and Economics in their Historical Relations* (Lond. and N.Y. 1893). D. G. Ritchie, *The History of Political Philosophy* (in prep.).]

R. Zimmermann, *Geschichte der Aesthetik* (Vienna, 1858). M. Schasler, *Kritische Geschichte der Aesthetik* (Berlin, 1871). [B. Bosanquet, *The History of Æsthetics* (Lond. and N.Y. 1892). W. Knight, *The Philosophy of the Beautiful* (an outline of the history, Edin. and N.Y. 1891). Gayley and Scott, *A Guide to the Literature of Æsthetics*, Univ. of California, and *Introd. to the Methods and Materials of Literary Criticism* (Bost. 1899) have bibliographies.]

J. Berger, *Geschichte der Religionsphilosophie* (Berlin, 1800). [Pünjer, *History of the Christian Philosophy of Religion* (Vol. I., Edin. and N.Y. 1887). O. Pfleiderer, *The Philosophy of Religion*, trans. by Menzies (Lond. 1887). Martineau, *A Study of Religion* (2 vols., 1888), and *Seat of Authority in Religion* (1890). J. Caird, *Introd. to the Philos. of Religion* (1880). E. Caird, *Evolution of Religion* (2 vols., Lond. and N.Y. 1893).]

The division of the history of philosophy is usually connected with that current for political history, so as to distinguish three great periods, — Ancient, Mediæval, and Modern Philosophy. Yet the sections made in this way are not so favourable for the history of philosophy as they perhaps are for political history. Other points of division must be made, equally important as regards the nature of the development; and, on the other hand, the transition between the Middle Ages and modern times demands a shifting of the point of division on either side.

In consequence of this, the entire history of philosophy will here be treated according to the following plan of division, in a manner to be more exactly illustrated and justified in detail by the exposition itself: —

(1) *The Philosophy of the Greeks:* from the beginnings of scientific thought to the death of Aristotle, — from about 600 to 322 B.C.

(2) *Hellenistic-Roman Philosophy:* from the death of Aristotle to the passing away of Neo-Platonism, — from 322 B.C. to about 500 A.D.

(3) *Mediæval Philosophy:* from Augustine to Nicolaus Cusanus, — from the fifth to the fifteenth century.

(4) *The Philosophy of the Renaissance:* from the fifteenth to the seventeenth century.

(5) *The Philosophy of the Enlightenment:* from Locke to the death of Lessing, — 1689–1781.

(6) *The German Philosophy:* from Kant to Hegel and Herbart, — 1781–1820.

(7) *The Philosophy of the Nineteenth Century.*

PART I.

THE PHILOSOPHY OF THE GREEKS.

Chr. A. Brandis, *Handbuch der Geschichte der griechisch-römischen Philosophie.* 3 pts. in 6 vols. Berlin, 1835–66.

Same author, *Geschichte der Entwickelungen der griechischen Philosophie und ihrer Nachwirkungen im römischen Reiche.* 2 pts. Berlin, 1862–66.

Ed. Zeller, *Die Philosophie der Griechen.* 3 pts. in 5 vols. 1st vol. in 5th, 2 vol. in 4th, 3–5 vols. in 3d ed. Leips. 1879–93. [Trans., with the exception of the portion on the concluding religious period, as six works: *Pre-Socratic Philosophy* (2 vols.), *Socrates and the Socratic Schools, Plato and the Older Academy, Aristotle and the Earlier Peripatetics* (2 vols.), *Stoics, Epicureans, and Sceptics, History of Eclecticism,* chiefly by S. F. Alleyne and O. J. Reichel. Lond. and N.Y., Longmans.]

A. Schwegler, *Geschichte der griechischen Philosophie.* Ed. by K. Köstlin. 3d ed. Freiburg, 1882.

L. Strümpell, *Die Geschichte der griechischen Philosophie.* 2 pts. Leips. 1854–61.

W. Windelband, *Geschichte der alten Philosophie.* 2d ed. Munich, 1894. [*History of Ancient Philosophy*, trans. by H. E. Cushman, N.Y., 1899.]

Ritter et Preller, *Historia philosophiæ græco-romanæ (Græcæ).* In 8th ed. Edited by Wellman. Gotha, 1898. An excellent collection of the most important sources.

[A. W. Benn, *The Greek Philosophers.* 2 vols. Lond., 1883. *The Philosophy of Greece.* Lond. 1898.]

Th. Gomperz, *Griechische Denker.* Vienna, 1897. [Trans. by L. Magnus. *Greek Thinkers.* Lond. and N.Y., 1900.]

IF by science we understand that independent and self-conscious work of intelligence which seeks knowledge methodically for its own sake, then it is among the Greeks, and the Greeks of the sixth century B.C., that we first find such a science, — aside from some tendencies among the peoples of the Orient, those of China and India[1] particularly, only recently disclosed. The great civilised

---

[1] Even if it be conceded that the beginnings of moral philosophy among the Chinese rise above moralising, and especially those of logic in India above incidental reflections on the scientific formation of conceptions, — on which we shall not here pronounce, — these remain so remote from the course of European philosophy, which forms a complete unity in itself, that a text-book has no occasion to enter upon them. The literature is brought together in Ueberweg, I. § 6.

peoples of earlier antiquity were not, indeed, wanting either in an abundance of information on single subjects, or in general views of the universe; but as the former was gained in connection with practical needs, and the latter grew out of mythical fancy, so they remained under the control, partly of daily need, partly of religious poetry; and, as was natural in consequence of the peculiar restraint of the Oriental mind, they lacked, for their fruitful and independent development, the initiative activity of individuals.

Among the Greeks, also, similar relations existed until, at the time mentioned, the mighty upward movement of the national life unfettered the mental powers of this most gifted of all peoples. For this result the democratic development of constitutions which in passionate party struggle tended to bring out independence of individual opinions and judgments, and to develop the significance of personality, proved even more favourable than the refinement and spiritualisation of life which increasing wealth of trade brought with it. The more the luxuriant development of individualism loosened the old bonds of the common consciousness, of faith, and of morals, and threatened the youthful civilisation of Greece with the danger of anarchy, the more pressing did individual men, prominent by their position in life, their insight, and their character, find the duty of recovering in their own reflection the measure that was becoming lost. This ethical reflection found its representatives in the lyric and gnomic poets, especially, however, in the so-called *seven wise men.*[1] It could not fail to occur, also, that a similar movement, in which individual opinions asserted their independence, should trench upon the religious life already so varied, in which the opposition between the old mystery-cults and the æsthetic national mythology stimulated the formation of so many special types.[2] Already in the cosmogonic poetry the poet had dared to portray the heaven of the myths according to his own individual fancy; the age of the seven sages began to read its ethical ideals into the gods of the Homeric poetry, and in the ethico-religious reformation attempted by Pythagoras,[3] coming as it did in the outer form of a return to the old strictness of life, the new content which life had gained came all the more clearly to view.

---

[1] The "seven sages," among whom Thales, Bias, Pittacus, and Solon are usually named, while with regard to the rest tradition is not agreed, must not, with the exception of Thales, be regarded as representatives of science. Diog. Laert. I. 40; Plato, *Protag.* 343.

[2] Cf. E. Rohde (*Psyche*, 2d ed., 1897) for the influence of religious ideas.

[3] *Pherecydes* of Syrus is to be regarded as the most important of these cosmogonic poets; he wrote in prose at the time of the first philosophies, but his mode of thought is still mythical throughout, not scientific. Fragments of his writings collected by Sturz (Leips. 1834).

From such conditions of fermentation the science of the Greeks to which they gave the name philosophy was born. The independent reflection of individuals, aided by the fluctuations of religious fancy, extended itself from the questions of practical life to the knowledge of Nature, and there first won that freedom from external ends, that limitation of knowledge to itself, which constitutes the essence of science.

All these processes, however, took place principally in the outlying parts of Greek civilisation, in the colonies, which were in advance of the so-called Mother-country in mental as in material development. In Ionia, in Magna Græcia, in Thrace, stood the cradles of science. It was only after Athens in the Persian wars had assumed together with the political hegemony the mental as well, which she was to keep so much longer than the former, that Attic soil, consecrated to all the muses, attracted science also. Its advent was at the time of the Sophists; it found its completion in the doctrine and school of Aristotle.

It was in connection with the disinterested consideration of Nature that reflection first rose to the scientific construction of conceptions. The result of this was that Greek science devoted all the freshness of youthful joy and knowledge primarily to the problems of Nature, and in this work stamped out fundamental conceptions, or Forms of thought, for apprehending the external world. In order to turn the look of philosophy inward and make human action the object of its study, there was first need, for one thing, of subsequent reflection upon what had, and what had not, been accomplished by this study of Nature, and, for another thing, of the imperious demands made by public life on science now so far matured as to be a social factor. The effect of this change might for a time seem to be to check the pure zeal for research which had marked the beginnings, but after positive results had been reached in the field of the knowledge of man's inner nature this same zeal developed all the more vigorously, and led to the construction of those great systems with which purely Greek philosophy reached its consummation.

The philosophy of the Greeks divides, therefore, into *three periods :* a *cosmological,* which extends from about 600 to about 450 B.C.; an *anthropological,* which fills out about the second half of the fifth century B.C. (450–400) ; and a *systematic,* which contains the development of the three great systems of Greek science, those of Democritus, Plato, and Aristotle (400–322).

The philosophy of the Greeks forms the most instructive part of the whole history of philosophy from a theoretical point of view, not only because the fundamental conceptions created in it have become the permanent foundations for all further development of thought, and promise to remain such, but also because in it the formal presuppositions contained in the postulates of the thinking Reason itself, attained sharp formulation as set over against the material of knowledge, which, especially at the beginning, was still relatively small in amount. In this the Greek philosophy has its typical value and its didactic importance.

These advantages appear already in the transparency and simplicity of the entire development, which enable us to see the inquiring mind at first turned outward, then thrown back upon itself, and from this point of view returning to a deeper apprehension of reality as a whole.

There is, therefore, scarcely any controversy with regard to this course of the general development of Greek philosophy, though different expositions have located the divisions between the periods at different points. Whether Socrates is made to begin a new period, or is placed together with the Sophists in the period of Greek Enlightenment, depends ultimately only on whether the result (negative or positive), or the object-matter of the philosophising, is regarded as of decisive importance. That, however, Democritus must in any case be separated from the "Pre-Socratics" and assigned to the great systematic period of Greek Philosophy, has been proved by the Author in his survey of the *History of Ancient Philosophy*, ch. V., and the objections which the innovation has encountered have not sufficed to convince him of any mistake.

CHAPTER I.

THE COSMOLOGICAL PERIOD.

S. A. Byk, *Die vorsokratische Philosophie der Griechen in ihrer organischen Gliederung.* 2 Parts. Leips. 1875–77.

[J. Burnet, *Early Greek Philosophy.* Lond. 1892.]

THE immediate background for the beginnings of Greek philosophy was formed by the cosmogonic poetry, which aimed to present in mythical garb the story of the prehistoric ages of the given world, and so, in the form of narratives of the origination of the universe, made use of prevailing ideas as to the constant mutations of things. The more freely individual views developed in this process, the more the time factor in the myth retreated in favour of the emphasising of these abiding relations; and the question finally emerged: "What is then the original ground of things, which outlasts all temporal change, and how does it change itself into these particular things, or change these things back into itself?"

The solution of this question was first attempted in the sixth century by the *Milesian School of natural philosophy*, of which Thales, Anaximander, and Anaximenes are known to us as the three chief representatives. Information of many kinds, which had long been publicly accumulating in the practical experience of the sea-faring Ionians, stood at their disposal, as well as many true observations, often of an acute sort. They kept in touch, also, no doubt, with the experience of the Oriental peoples, especially the Egyptians, with whom they stood in so close relation.[1] Knowledge from these various sources was brought together with youthful zeal. The chief interest fell upon physical questions, particularly upon

---

[1] The influence of the Orient upon the beginnings of Greek philosophy has been overestimated by Glabisch (*Die Religion und die Philosophie in ihrer weltgeschichtlichen Entwicklung*, Breslau, 1852) and Roth (*Geschichte unserer abendländischen Philosophie*, 2 Vols., Mannheim, 1858 ff.). In the case of information upon particular fields such influence is certainly to be recognised; on the other hand, the scientific conceptions are throughout independent works of Greek thought.

the great elementary phenomena, to explain which many hypotheses were thought out. Besides this, interest turned chiefly to geographical and astronomical problems, such as the form of the earth, its relation to the sidereal heavens, the nature of the sun, moon, and planets, and the manner and cause of their motion. On the other hand, there are but feeble indications of a zeal for knowledge applied to the organic world and man.

Such were the objects of experience studied by the first "philosophy." It stood quite far removed from medical science, which, to be sure, was limited to technical information and proficiency in the art, and was handed down as a secret doctrine, guarded in priest-like fashion in orders and schools, such as those of Rhodes, Cyrene, Crotona, Cos, and Cnidus. Ancient *medicine*, which aimed expressly to be an art and not a science (so Hippocrates), came into contact with philosophy when this was an all-embracing science, only at a late period and quite transiently. Cf. Häser, *Lehrbuch der Geschichte der Medicin*, I. (2d ed., Jena, 1875).

So also the beginnings of *mathematics* go along independently beside those of ancient philosophy. The propositions ascribed to the Milesians make the impression of individual pieces of information picked up and put together, rather than of results of genuine research, and are quite out of relation with their doctrines in natural science and philosophy. In the circles of the Pythagoreans, also, mathematical studies were at first evidently pursued for their own sake, to be drawn all the more vigorously into the treatment of general problems. Cf. G. Cantor, *Geschichte der Mathematik*, I. (Leips. 1880).

The efforts of the Milesians to determine the nature of the one world-ground had already in the case of *Anaximander* led beyond experience to the construction of a metaphysical conception to be used for explanation, viz. the ἄπειρον, and thereby drew science away from the investigation of facts to the consideration of conceptions. While *Xenophanes*, the *founder of the Eleatic School*, drew the consequences which result for the religious consciousness from the philosophical conception of the unity of the world, *Heraclitus*, in hard struggle with ideas that were obscure and religiously coloured, analysed destructively the presupposition of an abiding substance, and allowed only a law of change to stand as ultimate content of knowledge. All the more sharply, on the other hand, did the Eleatic School, in its great representative, *Parmenides*, shape out the conception of Being until it reached that regardless boldness of formulation which, in the following generation of the School, was defended by Zeno, and softened down in some measure only by Melissus.

Very soon, however, a series of efforts appeared, which brought anew into the foreground the interest in explanatory natural science that had been thrust aside by this development of the first metaphysical antitheses. In behalf of this interest more comprehensive efforts were made toward an enrichment of knowledge; this time, more than in the case of previous observations, questions and hypotheses from the organic and physiological realms were kept in mind; and the attempt was made to mediate with explanatory theories between the opposing conceptions of Heraclitus and Parmenides.

Out of these needs arose, about the middle of the fifth century, side by side, and with many reciprocal relations, positive and polemical, the theories of *Empedocles, Anaxagoras,* and *Leucippus,* founder of the *Atomistic* School of Abdera. The number of these theories and their well-known dependence upon one another prove that in spite of the distance by which individual men and schools found themselves separated, there was already a great vigour in exchange of thought and in literary activity. The picture of this life takes on a much fuller form as we reflect that tradition, in sifting its material, has obviously preserved only the memory of what was most important, and that each of the names remaining known to us indicates, in truth, an entire circle of scientific activity.

The *Pythagoreans,* during this same period, occupied a peculiar position at one side. They also took up the metaphysical problem given by the opposition between Heraclitus and the Eleatics, but hoped to find its solution by the aid of mathematics, and, by their *theory of numbers,* as whose first literary representative *Philolaus* is known, added a number of most important factors to the further movement of thought. The original purpose or tendency of their league made itself felt in their doctrines, in that, in fixing these, they conceded a considerable influence to considerations of (ethical or æsthetic) worth. They indeed attempted a scientific treatment of ethical questions as little as did the entire philosophy of this period, but the cosmology which they based upon their astronomical ideas, already widely developed with the help of mathematics, is yet at the same time permeated by æsthetic and ethical motives.

Of the **Milesian School** only three names — Thales, Anaximander, and Anaximenes — have been handed down to us. From this it appears that the school flourished in what was then the Ionic capital during the entire sixth century, and perished with the city itself, which was laid waste by the Persians in 494, after the battle of Lade.

Thales, sprung from an old merchant family, is said to have predicted the solar eclipse in 585, and survived the invasion of the Persians in the middle of the sixth century. He had perhaps seen Egypt, and was not deficient in mathematical and physical knowledge. So early an author as Aristotle did not know writings from him.

Anaximander seems to have been little younger. Of his treatise περὶ φύσεως a curious fragment only is preserved. Cf. Neuhäuser (Bonn, 1883). — Büsgen, *Ueber das ἄπειρον des A.* (Wiesbaden, 1867).

It is difficult to determine the period of **Anaximenes.** It falls probably about 560–500. Almost nothing of his work περὶ φύσεως remains.

Aside from that given by Aristotle (in the beginning of the *Metaphysics*) we owe our meagre information concerning the theories of the Milesians chiefly to the *Commentary* of Simplicius. Cf. H. Ritter, *Geschichte der jonischen Philosophie* (Berlin, 1821); R. Seydel, *Der Fortschritt der Metaphysik unter den ältesten jonischen Philosophen* (Leips. 1861).

At the head of the **Eleatic School, Xenophanes,** who at all events was concerned in its establishment, is generally placed. Born about 570 in Colophon, he fled in 546, in consequence of the Persian conquest of Ionia, and gained a living as wandering poet. At last, in Elea, founded by the Ionians who fled into Magna Græcia, he found a permanent dwelling. He died after 480. The fragments of his partly gnomic, partly philosophical, sayings have been collected by Karsten (Amsterdam, 1835). Concerning him see Fr. Kern (Naumburg, 1864, Oldenburg, 1867, Danzig, 1871, Stettin, 1874 and 1877) and J. Freudenthal (Breslau, 1886).

Parmenides, an Eleatic of renowned family, who was not a stranger to the Pythagorean society, wrote about 470. The fragments of his didactic poem have been collected by Peyron (Leips. 1810) and H. Stein (Leips. 1864). [Met. tr. in *Jour. Spec. Phil.,* IV.] The lost treatise of **Zeno** (about 490–430) was probably the first which was separated into chapters and arranged dialectically. He, too, came from Elea.

Melissos, on the contrary, was the Samian general who conquered the Athenians in 442. Concerning his personal connection with the Eleatic school nothing is known. A. Pabst, *De M. Fragmentis* (Bonn, 1889).

The unimportant fragments of the Eleatics are in a measure supplemented by the accounts of Aristotle, Simplicius, and others. The pseudo-Aristotelian work, *De Xenephone, Zenone, Gorgia* (Arist., Berl. ed., 974 ff.), which must be used with great discretion, gives an account in the first chapter probably of Melissos ; in the second, from confusedly intermingling sources, of Zeno ; in the third, of Gorgias.

Heraclitus of Ephesus ("the Obscure"), about 536–470, disgusted with the ever-growing power of the democracy, gave up the high position which was his by birth, and in the moody leisure of the last decade of his life, wrote a treatise which was pronounced difficult of comprehension even by the ancients, while the fragments of it which we possess are often very ambiguous. Collected and edited by P. Schuster (Leips. 1873) and J. Bywater (Oxford, 1877). Cf. Fr. Schleiermacher (*Ges. W.,* III. Abth., Bd. 2, pp. 1–146); J. Bernays (*Ges. Abhandlungen,* Bd. I., 1885); F. Lasalle (2 Bde., Berlin, 1858); E. Pfleiderer (Berlin, 1886). [G. T. W. Patrick, *Heraclitus* in Am. Jour. Psy., I., 1888, contains trans. of the *Fr.*]

The first Dorian in the history of philosophy is **Empedocles** of Agrigentum, about 490–430, a priestly and prophetic personality, much regarded in his character as statesman, physician, and worker of miracles. He had, too, relations with the Sicilian school of orators, of which the names of Korax and Tisias are familiar ; and besides his καθαρμοί (Songs of Purification) has left a didactic poem, the fragments of which have been published by Sturz (Leips. 1805), Karsten (Amsterdam, 1838), and Stein (Bonn, 1852).

Anaxagoras of Klazomene (500 till after 430) settled, toward the middle of the fifth century, in Athens, where he made friends with Pericles. In 434 he was accused of impiety and obliged to leave the city, and founded a school in Lampsacus. Schaubach (Leips. 1827) and Schorn (Bonn, 1829) have collected the fragments of his treatise, περὶ φύσεως. Cf. Breier (Berlin, 1840), Zévort (Paris, 1843).

So little is known of the personality of **Leucippus,** that even in ancient times his very existence was doubted. The great development of the atomistic theory by Democritus (see ch. 3) had completely overshadowed its founder. But traces of Atomism are to be recognised with certainty in the entire structure of thought after Parmenides. Leucippus, if not born in Abdera, yet active there as head of the school out of which Protagoras and Democritus went later, must have been contemporary with Empedocles and Anaxagoras, even though somewhat older. Whether he wrote anything is uncertain. Cf. Diels, *Verh. der Stett. Philol. Vers.* (1886). — A Brieger, *Die Urbewegung der Atome* (Halle, 1884); H. Liepmann, *Die Mechanik der leucipp-demokritischen Atome* (Leips. 1885).

The **Pythagorean Society** first appeared in the cities of Magna Græcia as a religious-political association toward the end of the sixth century. Its founder was **Pythagoras,** of Samos, who, born about 580, after long journeys, which probably led him toward Egypt also, made the aristocratic city of Crotona the starting-point of a reform movement which had for its aim a moral and religious purification. We are first apprised of the internal relations of the society through subsequent narratives (Jamblichus, *De Vita Pythagorica*, and Porphyrius, *De Vita Pythagoræ* published by Kiesling (Leips. 1815–16), whose trustworthiness is doubtful. It seems, however, to be certain that already the old society imposed definite duties upon its members, even for private life, and introduced the practice of working in common at intellectual pursuits, especially at music and mathematics. In consequence of its political position (in regard to which B. Krische, Göttingen, 1830) the external conditions of the society assumed at first a very favourable form, inasmuch as, after the plunder of the democratic Sybaris, 509, Crotona won a kind of hegemonic influence in Magna Græcia. In time, however, the Pythagoreans became the losers in the bitter party struggles of the cities, and often suffered bitter persecution, by which the society was finally destroyed in the fourth century.

To Pythagoras himself, who died about 500, we can trace back no philosophical writings, although the subsequent myth-making process sought so strenuously to make him the idol of all Hellenic wisdom. (E. Zeller in *Vortr. u. Abhandl.*, I., Leips. 1865.) Plato and Aristotle knew only of a philosophy of the *Pythagoreans*. **Philolaus**, who seems to have been somewhat younger than Empedocles and Anaxagoras, appears as the most prominent representative of this philosophy. Almost nothing is known of the circumstances of his life, and the fragments of his treatise (ed. by Boeckh, Berlin, 1819; cf. C. Schaarschmidt, Bonn, 1864) lie under considerable suspicion.

Of the remaining adherents of the society, only the names are known. The latest representatives came into so close relations with the Platonic Academy that, as regards their philosophy, they may almost be said to have belonged to it. Among them **Archytas** of Tarentum, the well-known *savant* and statesman, should be mentioned. Concerning the very doubtful fragments attributed to him, cf. G. Hartenstein (Leips. 1833), Fr. Petersen (Zeitschr. f. Alterthumsk; 1836), O. Gruppe (Berlin, 1840), Fr. Beckman (Berlin, 1844).

The reports concerning the teaching of the Pythagoreans, especially in the later accounts, are clouded by so many additions from foreign sources, that perhaps at no point in ancient philosophy is it so difficult to determine the actual facts in the case as here, even if we sift out the most trustworthy, namely Aristotle and his best taught commentators, notably Simplicius, many dark points and contradictory statements remain, particularly in details. The reason for this lies probably in the fact that in the school, which for a time was widely extended, various trends of thought ran side by side, and that among these the general fundamental thought first brought forward perhaps by Philolaus, was worked out in different ways. It would be of great service to attempt such a separation.

H. Ritter, *Geschichte der pythagoreischen Philosophie* (Hamburg, 1826); Rothenbücher, *Das System der Pythagoreer nach Aristoteles* (Berlin, 1867); E. Chaignet, *Pythagore et la philosophie pythagoricienne* (2 vols., Paris, 1873).

§ 4. The Conceptions of Being.

The fact that things of experience change into one another was the stimulus to the first philosophical reflections, and wonder[1] at this must indeed have arisen early among a people so mobile and with so varied an experience of Nature as the Ionians. To this fact, which furnished the fundamental motive of its reflection, the Ionic philosophy gave liveliest expression in Heraclitus, who seems to have been unwearied[2] in seeking the most pointed formulations for this universal mutability of all things, and especially for the sudden changes of opposites into each other. But while myth gave

---

[1] Cf. upon the philosophical value of the θαυμάζειν, Arist. *Met.* I. 2, 982 b 12.
[2] *Fragm.* (Schust.) 41–44, 60, 63, 67.

to this view the garb of a fabled account of the formation of the
world, science asked for the abiding ground of all these changes,
and fixed this question in the conception of the *cosmic matter*, or
"world-stuff" (*Weltstoff*), which experiences all these transformations, from which all individual things arise, and into which they
become again transformed (ἀρχή). In this conception [1] was tacitly
contained the *presupposition of the unity of the world;* whether the
Milesians [2] already sought to justify this we do not know. It was a
later eclectic straggler [3] who first attempted to justify this *Monism*
by the transformation of all things into one another, and by the
inter-connection of all things without exception.

1. That, however, a single cosmic matter, or world-stuff, lies at
the basis of the entire process of nature, appears in ancient tradition as a self-evident presupposition of the Ionic School. The only
question was to determine what this elementary matter was. The
nearest course was then to seek for it in what was given in experience, and so *Thales* declared it to be *water; Anaximenes, air.* To
this choice they were probably determined only by the mobility,
changeability, and apparent inner vitality [4] of water and air. It is
evident, too, that the Milesians thought little in this connection of
the chemical peculiarities of water and air, but only of the states
of aggregation [5] concerned. While the solid appears in itself dead,
moved only from without, the liquid and volatile make the impression of independent mobility and vitality; and the monistic prepos-
session of this first philosophising was so great that the Milesians
never once thought of asking for a reason or ground of this ceaseless change of the cosmic matter, but instead assumed this as a self-
intelligible fact — a matter of course — as they did all change or
occurrence; at most they described its individual forms. The cosmic matter passed with them for something in itself living: they
thought of it as animated, just as are particular organisms, [6] and for
this reason their doctrine is usually characterised from the standpoint of the later separation in conceptions as *Hylozoism.*

---

[1] Which Aristotle in the *Met.* I. 3, 983 b 8, has defined, not without the
admixture of his own categories.

[2] The expression ἀρχή, which, moreover, bears in itself the memory of the
chronological fancies of the Cosmologists, is said by Simplicius to have been
used first by Anaximander.

[3] Diogenes of Apollonia. Cf. Simpl. *Phys.* (D.) 32ʳ 151, 30, and Arist. *Gen. et
Corr.* I. 6, 322 b 13.

[4] *Schol.* in Arist. 514 a 33.

[5] For ὕδωρ, ὑγρόν is frequently substituted. With regard to the ἀήρ of Anaximenes the accounts are such that the attempt has been made to distinguish his
metaphysical "air" from the empirical: Ritter, I. 217 ; Brandis, I. 144.

[6] Plut. *Plac.* I. 3 (*Doxogr.* D. 278). Perhaps this is intended in the conjec-
ture of Aristotle, *Met.* I. 3, 983 b 22.

2. If we ask, however, why Anaximenes, whose doctrine, like that of Thales, seems to have kept within the bounds of experience, substituted air for water, we learn[1] that he believed air to have a characteristic which water lacked, — a characteristic, too, which his predecessor Anaximander had postulated as indispensable for the conception of primitive matter, viz. that of *infinity*. As motive for this postulate of *Anaximander* there is related the argument that a finite cosmic matter would exhaust itself in the ceaseless succession of productions.[2] But Anaximander had also seen that this demand made by the conception of the ἀρχή could not be satisfied by any matter or substance which we can perceive, and had on this account transferred the cosmic matter beyond experience. He maintained boldly the reality of an original ground of things, possessing all the properties that are necessary, if we are to derive the changes in the world of experience from something itself abiding and raised above change, — even though such a ground might not be found in experience. He drew from the conception of the ἀρχή the consequence, that though no object of experience corresponds to this conception, we must yet, to explain experience, assume such a conception behind it as real and conditioning it. He therefore called the cosmic matter *"the Infinite"* (τὸ ἄπειρον), and ascribed to it all the qualities postulated in the conception of the ἀρχή: that is, that it had never begun to be, and was imperishable, inexhaustible, and indestructible.

The conception of *matter*, thus constructed by Anaximander is, nevertheless, clear only in the respect that it is to unite within it spatial infinity and the quality of being without beginning or end in time, and thus the mark of the all-embracing and all-determining;[3] on the other hand, with reference to its qualitative determination, it cannot be made clear what the philosopher intended. Later accounts give us to understand that he expressly maintained that the original matter was qualitatively undetermined or indefinite (ἀόριστος),[4] while the statements of Aristotle[5] speak more for the assumption of a mixture of all kinds of matter known in experience, — a mixture completely adjusted or equalised, and therefore as a whole indifferent or neutral. The most probable view here is, that Anaximander reproduced in the form of an abstract conception the

[1] Simpl. *Phys.* (D.) 6ʳ 24, 26.

[2] Plut. *Plac.* I. 3 (*Doxogr.* D. 277); Arist. *Phys.* III. 8, 208 a 8.

[3] Arist. *Phys.* III. 4, 203 b 7.

[4] Schol. in Arist. 514 a 33; Herbart, *Einleitung in die Philosophie* (Ges. W., I. 196).

[5] *Met.* XII. 2, 1069 b 18, and especially *Phys.* I. 4, 187 a 20. Cf. also Simpl. *Phys.* (D.) 33ʳ 154, 14 (according to Theophrastus). This much-treated controversy will be spoken of more in detail below (§ 6).

unclear idea of the mythical chaos which was "one" and yet also "all." This he did by assuming as the cosmic matter an infinite, corporeal mass, in which the various empirical substances were so mixed that no definite quality could be ascribed to it as a whole. For this reason, however, the separation of the individual qualities out of this self-moved matter could no longer be regarded as properly a qualitative change in it. With this view the conception of the unity of the world as regards quality would be given up, to be sure, and an essential preparation made for the later development.

3. Still another predicate was given by Anaximander to the Infinite, — τὸ θεῖον, the divine. As a last remembrance of the religious home in which scientific reflection arose, it shows for the first time the inclination of philosophers, constantly recurring in history, to view as "Deity" the highest conception which theory has led them to use for explaining the world, and so to give it at the same time a sanction for the religious consciousness. Anaximander's matter is the first philosophic conception of God, the first attempt, and one which remains still entirely within the physical, to strip the idea of God of all mythical form.

But while the *religious need* thus maintained itself in the determination of metaphysical conception, the possibility of an influence of the results of science upon the religious life was brought nearer, the more these results met and responded to an impulse which hitherto had been dominant only in an obscure and uncertain manner within that life. The transformation which the Greek myths had undergone, as well in the import given them in cosmogonic fancy as in that given to their ethical interpretation, tended everywhere toward a monotheistic culmination (Pherecydes, Solon); and to this movement its final result, a clearly outspoken monism, was now proffered by science.

This relation was brought to expression by *Xenophanes*, not a thinker and investigator, but an imaginative disciple of science, strong in his convictions, who brought the new teaching from East to West and gave it a thoroughly religious colouring. His maintenance of *monotheism*, which he expressed as enthusiastic intuition in the saying,[1] that whithersoever he looked all was constantly flowing together for him into one Nature (μίαν εἰς φύσιν), took on at once, however, that sharp polemic turn against the popular faith, by which he is principally characterised in literature. The scorn, which he poured out with abundant wit over the anthropomorphism of mythology,[2] the anger with which he pursued the poets as the portrayers

---

[1] Timon in Sext. Emp. *Pyrrh. Hyp.* I. 224.   [2] Clem. Alex. *Strom.* V. 601.

of these divine figures provided with all the weaknesses and vices of human nature,[1] — these rest upon an ideal of God which will have the Supreme Being regarded as incomparable with man in both bodily and mental characteristics.   When he passes to positive attributes, Xenophanes becomes more obscure.   On the one hand, the deity as ἓν καὶ πᾶν is identified with the universe, and to this "*World-God*" are then ascribed all the predicates of the Milesian ἀρχή (eternity, existence that has not become what it is, imperishability) ; on the other hand, qualities are ascribed to the deity, some of which are spatial, as the spherical form, while others are psychical functions.   Among these latter the omnipresence of the knowing activity and of the rational guidance of things is expressly mentioned.   In this respect the World-God of Xenophanes appears only as the highest among the rest of "gods and men."

While here a predominantly theological turn of philosophy is already manifested, the exchange of the point of view of metaphysics and natural science taken by Anaximander, for the religious point of view of Xenophanes shows itself in two essential deviations. The conception of the World-God is for the latter an object of religious reverence, and scarcely a means for understanding Nature. The Colophonian's sense for knowledge of Nature is slight, his ideas are in part very childlike, and, as compared with those of the Milesians, undeveloped.   And so for his views, the characteristic of infinity, which Milesian science regarded as necessary in the cosmic matter, could be dispensed with; on the contrary, it seemed to him more in accordance with the dignity of the divine Nature,[2] to think of this as limited within itself, as entirely shut up or complete, consequently as regards its spatial aspect, spherical.   And while the Milesians thought of the original ground of things as ever in motion spontaneously, and as characterised by living variety in its internal structure, Xenophanes struck out this postulate hitherto in use for the explanation of Nature, and declared the World-God to be immovable and perfectly homogeneous in all its parts.   How, indeed, he thought that the variety of individual things whose reality he did not doubt, could be reconciled with this view, must remain uncertain.

4. As was required by the conception of change, the Milesian conception of the World-substance had united without clear discrimination two essential elements: the one that of a substance remaining like itself, the other that of independent or self-subsistent

---

[1] Sext. Emp. *Adv. Math.* IX. 193.
[2] Hippol. *Ref.* I. 14 (*Doxogr.* D. 565).   In other passages, again, it is said that he would have the deity thought neither limited nor unlimited (?).

cnangeability. In the thought of Xenophanes the first element was isolated; the same process took place for the second through *Heraclitus*. His doctrine presupposes the work of the Milesians, from the conclusion of which it is separated by a generation, in this way: their effort to determine or define in conceptions an abiding world-ground has been recognised as hopeless. There is nothing abiding, either in the world or in its constitution taken as a whole. Not only individual things, but also the universe as a whole, are involved in perpetual, ceaseless revolution: *all flows*, and nothing abides. We cannot say of things that they are; they become only, and pass away in the ever-changing play of the movement of the universe. That, then, which abides and deserves the name of deity, is not a thing, and not substance or matter, but motion, the cosmic process, *Becoming* itself.

To meet a strong demand that seems made by this turn to abstraction, Heraclitus found help in the sensuous perception in which this motion presented itself to him: that of *fire*. The co-operation of this in the conversion of things of Nature into each other had been already noticed by the Milesians; to this may have been added ancient Oriental mystical ideas, which contact with the Persians made especially accessible to the Ionians of that day. But when Heraclitus declared the world to be an ever-living fire, and Fire, therefore, to be the essence of all things, he understood by this ἀρχή not a material or substance which survived all its transformations, but just the transforming process itself in its ever-darting, vibrating activity (*züngelnde*), the soaring up and vanishing which correspond to the Becoming and passing away.[1]

At the same time, however, this idea takes on a still firmer form, in that Heraclitus emphasised much more strongly than the Milesians the fact that this change is accomplished in accordance with definite relations, and in a succession that remains always the same.[2] This rhythm of events (which later times have called the uniformity of Nature under law) is therefore the only permanent; it is termed by Heraclitus the destiny (εἱμαρμένη), the order (δίκη), the reason (λόγος) of the world. These predicates, in which physical, ethical,

---

[1] The difficulty of ascribing to such a motion without any substrate, to a mere Becoming, the highest reality and the capacity to produce things, was evidently very much less for undeveloped thought not yet conscious of its categories than for later apprehension. The conception of Becoming as fire, hovering between the symbolic and the real meaning of the term, was supported by the use of language which treats of functions and relations as also substantives. But Heraclitus does not disdain to let the dim idea of a World-substance stand in the background in his metaphors (of the clay kneaded ever anew, of the drink continually stirred).

[2] Further in detail on this point in the following section.

and logical order in the world appear as still identified, prove only the undeveloped state of thought which does not yet know how to separate the different motives. The conception, however, which Heraclitus has grasped with complete clearness, and carried though with all the strength of his austere personality, is that of *order*, a conception, nevertheless, whose validity was for him as much a matter of conviction as of knowledge.

5. In evident opposition to this theory of the Ephesian, the conception of *Being* was worked out by *Parmenides*, the head of the Eleatic School, and the most important thinker of this period. Yet it is not easy to reconstruct his formulation of this conception from the few fragments of his didactic poem, the quite unique character of which consists in the union of dryest abstraction with grand and rich imagery. That there is a Being (ἔστι γὰρ εἶναι), is for the Eleatic a postulate of such cogent evidence that he only states this position without proving it, and that he explains it only by a negative turn of thought which first discloses to us completely the sense in which we are to understand his main thought. "Non-being" (μὴ εἶναι), he adds, or that which "is" not (τὸ μὴ ἐόν), cannot be and cannot be thought. For all thought is in relation to a something that *is*, which forms its content.[1] This view of the correlative nature of Being and consciousness leads so far with Parmenides that the two, thought and Being, are declared to be fully identical. No thought to whose content Being does not belong, — no Being that is not thought: thought and Being are the same.

These propositions, which look so abstractly ontological if we consider only the words, take on quite another meaning when we consider that the fragments of the great Elean leave no doubt as to what he desired to have regarded as "Being" or that which "is." This was *corporeality*, materiality (τὸ πλέον). For him, "being" and "filling space" are the same. This "Being," this function of filling space, is precisely the same in the case of all that "is"; there is, therefore, only the one, single Being which has no internal distinctions. "Non-being," or what *is* not [has not the attribute of Being], means, accordingly, incorporeality, *empty space* (τὸ κενόν). This double meaning of the εἶναι (Being) employed by Parmenides, according to which the word means at one time "the full" and at another time "Reality," leads then to the proposition *that empty space cannot be*.

Now for the naïve, sensuous way of looking at things which lurks even in these principles of Parmenides, the separateness of

---

[1] *Fr.*, ed. Karsten. vv. 94 ff.

things, by virtue of which they present themselves in their plurality and multiplicity, consists in their separation by empty space; and, on the other hand, all that takes place in the corporeal world, *i.e.* all motion, consists in the change of place which the "full" experiences in the "empty" (or the "Void"). If, therefore, the Void is not real or actual, then *the plurality and motion of individual things cannot be real.*

The number and variety of things presented in co-existence and succession by experience had given the Milesians occasion to ask for the common abiding ground of which all these things were metamorphoses. When, however, the conception of cosmic substance or world-stuff has culminated with Parmenides in the conception of Being, there seems so little possibility of uniting these individual things with it, that reality is denied them, and the one unitary Being remains also the *only* being.[1] The conception formed for the purpose of explanation has so developed internally that to maintain it involves the denial of that which was to be explained by it. In this sense the Eleatic doctrine is *acosmism:* the manifoldness of things has sunk in the All-one: the latter alone "is," the former are deception and seeming.

According to Parmenides, however, we are to predicate of the One that it is eternal, has never come into being, is imperishable, and especially (as Xenophanes had maintained) that it is through and through one in kind, one with itself, without any distinctions or differences, *i.e.* completely homogeneous and absolutely unchangeable. He follows Xenophanes also in regarding the One as limited, complete, and definitive. Being is then a well-rounded sphere, perfectly homogeneous within itself, and this only and unitary *worldbody* is at the same time the *world-thought,*[2] simple, excluding all particulars from itself: τὸ γὰρ πλέον ἐστὶ νόημα.

6. All these attempts, in part fantastic, in part regardlessly abstract, were needed in order to gain the presuppositions for the development of the first usable conceptions for apprehending Nature. For important as were the motives of thought that had come to recognition therein, neither the world-stuff or cosmic matter of the Milesians, nor the "Fire-Becoming" of Heraclitus, nor the Being of Parmenides were available for explaining Nature. Now the imperfection of the first had become clear through the contrast which

---

[1] A great rôle in these considerations of the Eleatics is obviously played by the ambiguities in language, by which, on the one hand, the ἕν means both numerical unity and also qualitative unity or simplicity, while the verb εἶναι has not only the function of the copula, but also the meaning of "Reality."

[2] Hence, terms like "materialism" and "idealism" do not apply to this naïve identification of consciousness and its object, the corporeal world.

separated the two latter as by a gulf, and with the recognition of this, occasion was given for the more independent investigators of the next period to separate in their conceptions the two *motifs* (being and becoming), and by setting them over against one another to think out new forms of relation, out of which permanently valuable categories for the knowledge of Nature resulted.

These *mediating attempts* have in common, on the one hand, the recognition of the Eleatic postulate that that which " is " must be thought throughout not only as eternal, without a beginning and imperishable, but also as homogeneous, and as regards its qualities unchangeable; on the other hand, however, they assent also to the thought of Heraclitus that an undeniable reality belongs to Becoming and change (*Geschehen*), and so to the manifoldness of things. Common to them, also, in their adjustment of these two needs of thought is the attempt to assume a *plurality of beings,* each of which should satisfy for itself the postulate of Parmenides; while, on the other hand, by changing their spatial relations, they were to bring about the changeful variety of individual things which experience shows. If the Milesians had spoken of qualitative changes of the cosmic substance or matter, the Eleatic principle had excluded the possibility of it; if, nevertheless, change ought to receive recognition, as with Heraclitus, and be attributed to Being itself it must be reduced to a kind of change which leaves untouched the qualities of the existent. Such a change, however, was thinkable only as a change of place, *i.e.* as *motion.* The investigators of Nature in the fifth century maintained, therefore, with the Eleatics, the (qualitative) unchangeableness of the existent, but against the Eleatics, its plurality and motion;[1] with Heraclitus, they insisted upon the reality of occurrence and change, and against Heraclitus, upon the Being of permanent and unchangeable substances as underlying and producing the same. Their common view is this: there is a plurality of existing beings which, unchangeable in themselves, make the change and variety of individual things comprehensible.

7. This principle seems to have been asserted first and in its most imperfect form by *Empedocles,* — in a form, however, that was widely influential historically. He put forward as " *elements* "[2] the four which are still current in the popular modes of thought, — earth,

---

[1] Later (Plato, *Theaet.* 181 D; Arist. *var. loc.*), ἀλλοίωσις (qualitative change) and περιφορά (change of place) are contrasted as species of κίνησις or μεταβολή. In reality this is done here, though the terms are as yet lacking.

[2] Instead of the later expression στοιχεῖα, we find in Empedocles the more poetic term " roots of all things," ῥιζώματα.

water, air, and fire.[1] Each of these is according to this system, without beginning and imperishable, homogeneous and unchangeable, but at the same time divisible into parts, and in these parts capable of change of place. Out of the mixture of the elements arise individual things, which in turn cease to exist when the mixture is separated into the elements; to the kind of mixture made are due the various qualities of individual things, which are often different from the properties of the elements themselves.

At the same time the note of unchangeableness and a deviation from the Milesian Hylozoism assert themselves in the system of Empedocles to the extent that he could not assign independent capacity of motion to these material elements which experience only changing states of motion and mechanical mixings. On this account he was obliged to seek a *cause of motion* independent of the four elements. As such a cause he designated *love* and *hate*. The outcome, however, of this first attempt to set over against a dead matter, deprived by abstraction of all motion of its own, the force which moves it, as a metaphysically independent something, was very obscure. Love and hate are, with Empedocles, not mere properties, functions, or relations of the elements, but rather independent powers set over against them; but how we are to think the reality of these *moving forces* is not disclosed in any satisfactory way in the fragments.[2] Only this seems certain, that in fixing the dual nature of the principle of motion the thought was also operative that two distinct causes, love and hate, were requisite to account for the good and the evil in the change of things of our experience,[3] — a first indication that determinations of "worth" or value are beginning to be introduced into the theory of Nature.

8. Empedocles thought it possible to derive the special qualities of individual things from the proper mixture of the four elements: whether he attempted so to derive them, and if so, how, we do not indeed know. This difficulty was avoided by *Anaxagoras*, who, from the Eleatic principle that nothing that is can arise or pass away, drew the conclusion that as many elements must be assumed[4]

---

[1] Aside from dependence upon his predecessors, his selection was evidently due to the inclination to regard the different states of aggregation as the original essence of things. No importance seems to have attached to the number four, in this. The dialectical construction which Plato and Aristotle gave for this is quite remote from the thought of the Agrigentine.

[2] If φιλία and νεῖκος are occasionally counted by the later recorders as fifth and sixth ἀρχή of Empedocles, we must not infer from this that he regarded them as substances. His obscure and almost mythical terminology rests, for the most part, upon the fact that conceptions standing for functions are substantives in language.   [3] Arist. *Met.* I. 4, 984 b 32.

[4] He called them σπέρματα (seeds of things), or also simply χρήματα (substances).

as there are simple substances in the things of experience, meaning by simple substances those which on repeated division always separate into parts qualitatively the same with their wholes. Such elementary substances were later, in accordance with his definition, called *homoiomeriai*. At that time, however, when only mechanical division or change of temperature were known as means of investigation, this conception of element (in principle entirely corresponding to the conceptions of the chemistry of to-day) applied to the greater part of the substances given in experience,[1] and on that account Anaxagoras maintained that there were *countless elements* differing in form, colour, and taste. He held that they were present throughout the entire universe in a very finely divided state. Their coming together or compounding (σύγκρισις) constitutes the arising, their separation (διάκρισις) the passing away, of individual things. There is, accordingly, something of every substance present in everything: it is only for our sensuous apprehension that the individual thing takes on the properties of that substance or of those substances which may be present in a preponderating degree.

The elements, as the true being, are regarded now by Anaxagoras also as eternal, without beginning or end, unchangeable, and though movable in space, yet not in motion of themselves. Here, too, then, we must ask for a force which is the cause of motion. Since, however, this force must be regarded as **existent**, a something that is, Anaxagoras hit upon the expedient of assigning it to a special, single sort of matter or elementary substance. This *force-element* or *motive-matter* (*Bewegungsstoff*) is conceived to be the lightest and most mobile of all elements. In distinction from all the others it is that one of the *homoiomeriai* which alone is in motion of itself, and communicates this its own motion to the rest; it moves itself and the rest. To determine the inner nature of this "force-substance," however, two lines of thought unite: the property of originating motion is, for the naive mode of looking at things, the surest sign of the *animate;* this exceptional kind of matter, then, which is self-moved, must be animate matter or "soul-stuff" (*Seelenstoff*), its quality must be animate or psychical.[2] And, secondly, a power is known through its effect: if, now, this motive-matter is the cause of the formation of the world, to bring about which it has separated out the remaining idle elements, then we must be able to know its nature from this which it has accomplished. But the universe, in particular the regular revolution of the stars, makes the impression

---

[1] According to the fragments of Anaxagoras, bones, flesh, and marrow also; on the other hand, the metals.

[2] [The Greek ψυχή and German *Seele* include both these meanings.]

of *beautiful* and *purposive order* (κόσμος). Such a mastering of gigantic masses in a harmonious system, — this undisturbed circling of countless worlds, on which Anaxagoras turned his wondering contemplation, it seemed to him could be the result only of a *mind* arranging the movements according to ends, and ruling them. For this reason he characterised the force-substance as *Reason* (νοῦς) or as " *Thought-stuff.*"

The νοῦς of Anaxagoras is then a stuff or substance, a corporeal element, homogeneous, unproduced, and imperishable, diffused in a finely divided state throughout the universe; different from the other substances, however, not only in degree, as being the finest, lightest, and most mobile, but also in essence, since it alone is self-moved, and by virtue of its own motion moves the other elements in the purposive way which we recognise in the order of the world. This emphasising of the order in the universe is a Heraclitic element in the teaching of Anaxagoras, and the conclusion drawn from the ordered movements to a rational cause of them, acting according to ends, is the first instance of the *teleological explanation of nature.*[1] With this procedure a conception of worth (*Werthbegriff*) — namely, beauty and perfection — is made a principle of explanation in the theoretical field also.

9. The *Atomism* of *Leucippus* developed from the Eleatic conception of Being in a direction opposite to that just traced. While Empedocles maintained that some, and Anaxagoras that all, qualities were metaphysically primitive, the founder of the school of Abdera remained in accord with the position of Parmenides, that no "Being" belongs to any of all the various qualitative determinations exhibited by experience, and that the sole property of Being is the property of filling space, *corporeality*, τὸ πλέον. If now, however, the plurality of things, and the mutations taking place among them as they come and go, were to be made intelligible, then instead of the single world-body, with no internal distinctions which Parmenides had taught, a plurality of such must be assumed, separated from one another, not by other Being, but by that which is not Being, Non-being: *i.e.* by the incorporeal, by *empty space.* This entity, then, which is Non-being [*i.e.* not Being in the true sense], must have in its turn a kind of Being, or of metaphysical reality ascribed to it,[2] and Leucippus regarded it

---

[1] As such he was praised by Plato (*Phæd.* 97 B), and overestimated by Aristotle (*Met.* I. 3, 984 b). Cf., however, § 5. The moderns (Hegel) have added the further over-estimate of seeking to interpret the νοῦς as an immaterial principle. But the fragments (Simpl. *Phys.* (D.) 33ᵛ 156, 13) leave no doubt that this lightest, purest element, which does not mingle with the rest, but only plays about them and moves them as living force, was also a space-filling matter or stuff.　　[2] Plut. *Adv. Col.* 4, 2, 1109.

as the unlimited, the ἄπειρον, in contrast with the limitation which Being proper possesses, according to Parmenides. Leucippus, therefore, shatters in pieces the world-body of Parmenides, and scatters its parts through infinite space. Each of these parts, however, is, like the absolute Being of Parmenides, eternal and unchangeable, without beginning, indestructible, homogeneous, limited, and indivisible. Hence these portions of Being are called *atoms*, ἄτομοι; and for the reasons which had led Anaximander to his concept of the ἄπειρον Leucippus maintained that there were countless numbers of such atoms, infinitely varied in form. Their size must be taken as imperceptibly small, since all things in our experience are divisible. Since, however, they all possess only the one like quality of filling space, differences between them can be only quantitative; differences in size, form, and situation.

Out of such metaphysical considerations grew the concept of the atom, which has proved so fruitful for the theoretical science of Nature just because, as was evident already in the system of Leucippus, it contains the postulate that all qualitative differences exhibited by Nature are to be reduced to quantitative. The things which we perceive, Leucippus taught, are combinations of atoms; they arise when atoms unite, and pass away when they part. The properties which we perceive in these complexes are only seeming or appearance; there exist in truth only the determinations of size, form, arrangement, and situation of the individual atoms which constitute Being.

Empty space is, accordingly, the presupposition as well for the uniting and separating of atoms as for their separateness and shape. All "becoming," or change, is in its essence *motion of atoms in space*. If we ask for the ground of this motion of the atoms,[1] since space as properly not a true Being cannot be allowed as cause, and Atomism recognises nothing as actual except space and the atoms, this ground can be sought only in the atoms themselves; *i.e.* the atoms are of themselves in motion, and this, their independent motion, is as truly without beginning and end as is their being. And as the atoms are indefinitely varied in size and form, and completely independent of one another, so their original motions are infinite in variety. They fly confusedly about in infinite space, which knows no above and below, no within and without, each for itself, until their accidental meeting leads to the formation of things and worlds. The separation between the conceptions of matter and moving force

---

[1] Arist. *Phys.* VIII. 1, 252 a 32, says of the Atomists that they did not ask as to the origin of motion — as a matter of course, for they declared motion itself to be causeless (cf. *Met.* I. 4).

which Empedocles and Anaxagoras, each in his way, had attempted,
was thus in turn abolished by the Atomists. They ascribed to the
particles of matter the capacity, not indeed of qualitative change
(ἀλλοίωσις), but of *independent motion* (κίνησις in the narrower sense,
equivalent to περιφορά), and took up again in this sense the principle
of Milesian hylozoism.

10. In opposition to these pluralistic systems, *Zeno*, the friend
and disciple of Parmenides, sought to defend the Eleatic doctrine by
setting forth the contradictions in which the assumption of a plurality of Beings is involved. As regards size, he pointed out, it follows that the totality of Being must be on the one hand infinitely
small, on the other hand infinitely great: infinitely small, because
the combination of any number whatever of parts, each of which is
to be infinitely small, never yields anything more than an infinitely
small sum;[1] infinitely great, on the contrary, because the boundary which is to separate two parts must itself be an existent something, *i.e.* spatial magnitude, which again is itself separated from
the two parts by a boundary of which the same holds true, and so
on *in infinitum*. From the latter argument, which was called that
from dichotomy (the ἐκ διχοτομίας), Zeno reasoned also that as
regards number, what *is* must be unlimited, while, on the other hand,
this complete Being, not in process of becoming, is to be regarded
also as numerically limited [*i.e.* as complete]. And just as with the
assumption of the "many," so the position that empty space is real
is held to refute itself by a regress *ad infinitum*: if all that is is in
space, and thus space is itself an existing entity, then it must itself
be in a space, and this last likewise, etc. When the concept of the
infinite, to which the Atomists had given a new turn, became thus
prominent, all the enigmas involved in it for the contrasting points
of view of intellect and sense-perception became prominent also, and
Zeno used them to involve in a *reductio ad absurdum* the opponents
of the doctrine of the one, self-limited Being.

This dialectic, however, cut both ways, as was shown in the Eleatic School itself, by the fact that a cotemporary of Zeno, *Melissus*,
who shared his opinions, saw himself forced to declare that the
Being of Parmenides was as unlimited in space as in time. For as
Being can arise neither from other Being nor from Non-being, so
it can be limited neither by existing Being (for then there must be
a second Being), nor by a non-existent (for then this non-existent
must be): a line of argument more consistent from a purely theo-

---

[1] The argument can be directed only against Atomism, and applies to this
weakly.

retical point of view than the position of the master, which had been influenced by determinations of worth.

11. The *Pythagoreans* took a mediating position in these questions : for this, as for their other doctrines, they were happily fitted by their employment with mathematics, and by the manner in which they prosecuted this study. Its chief direction seems to have been arithmetical ; even the geometrical knowledge ascribed to them (as the well-known proposition named after Pythagoras) amounts to a linear representation of simple relations between numbers ($3^2 + 4^2 = 5^2$, etc.). It was not, however, in the general relations of constructions in space only that the Pythagoreans found numbers to be the determining principles; the same was found to be true also in such phenomena of the corporeal world as they were chiefly engaged with. Their theoretical investigations concerning music taught them that harmony was based upon simple numerical relations of the length of the strings (octave, third, fourth), and their knowledge of astronomy, which was far advanced, led them to the view that the harmony prevailing in the motions in the heavenly bodies had, like the harmony in music,[1] its ground in an order, in accordance with which the various spheres of the universe moved about a common centre at intervals fixed by numbers. Suggestions so various as these mentioned seem to have united to evoke in a man like *Philolaus* the thought, that the permanent Being which philosophy was seeking was to be found in *numbers*. In contrast with the changing things of experience mathematical conceptions possess as regards their content the marks of a validity not subject to time — they are eternal, without beginning, imperishable, unchangeable, and even immovable; and while they thus satisfy the Eleatic postulate for Being, they present, on the other hand, fixed relations, — that rhythmical order which Heraclitus had demanded. Thus, then, the Pythagoreans found the abiding essense of the world in the mathematical relations, and in particular in numbers, — a solution of the problem more abstract than the Milesian, more capable of being represented to perception or imagination than the Eleatic, clearer than the Heraclitic, more difficult than those offered by cotemporary mediating attempts.

The Pythagorean *doctrine of numbers*, as carried out by them, was attached partly to the numerous observations they had made on the arithmetical relations, partly to analogies which they discovered or sometimes artificially introduced, between numerical and philosophical problems. The definite nature of each individual number and

---

[1] Out of this analogy arose the fantastic idea of the harmony of the spheres.

the endlessness of the number series must indeed have at first suggested that reality belongs as well to the limited as to the unlimited,
and by transferring this thought into the geometrical sphere the
Pythagoreans came to recognise, in addition to the elements as the
limited, a Reality as belonging also to space as the unlimited void.
They thought of the elements, however, as determined by the forms
of the simple solids: fire by the tetrahedron, earth by the cube,
air by the octahedron, water by the icosahedron, and a fifth material,
æther, which they added as the celestial element to the four terrestrial elements assumed by Empedocles, by the dodecahedron.[1] In
these conceptions the prevailing idea was this: *corporeality*, or the
essential quality of bodies, consists in the mathematical limitation
of the unlimited, in the *shaping out of space into forms.* Mathematical forms are made the essence of physical reality.

The Pythagoreans further believed that in the antithesis between
the limited and the unlimited they recognised the antithesis found
in numbers between the odd and the even;[2] and this antithesis was
again identified with that between the perfect and the imperfect,
the good and the bad,[3] in this last case not without the influence of
old ideas connected with the religious faith of the oracles. Their
Weltanschauung becomes thus *dualistic:* over against the limited,
odd, perfect, and good stands the limitless, even, imperfect, and bad.
As, however, both principles are united in the number one,[4] which
has the value of an even as well as of an odd number, so in the
world as a whole these antitheses are adjusted to form a harmony.
The world is harmony of numbers.

Some of the Pythagoreans,[5] moreover, sought to trace out through
the various realms of experience that fundamental antithesis, in the
assumption of which all the school were agreed, and so a table of ten
pairs of opposites came into existence: viz. limited and unlimited —
odd and even — one and many — right and left — male and female
— at rest and in motion — straight and curved — light and dark —

---

[1] While the main line of the Pythagoreans thus followed Empedocles, a later,
Ecphantus, conceived of this limitation of space in the sense of Atomism.

[2] The reason presented for this, viz. that even numbers permit of bisection
to infinity (?), is indeed very questionable and artificial (Simpl. *Phys.* D. 105ʳ
455, 20).

[3] Nor must we here overlook the factor which had already asserted itself with
Xenophanes and Parmenides, viz. that to the Greek the conception of measure
was one that had a high ethical worth; so that the infinite, which derides all
measure, must to him appear imperfect, while the definite or limited (πεπερασ-
μένον) was necessarily regarded as more valuable.

[4] Arist. *Met.* I. 5, 986 a 19.

[5] Or men standing in close relations with Pythagoreanism, such as the physician Alcmæon, a perhaps somewhat older contemporary of Philolaus. Cf.
Arist. *Met.* I. 5, 986 a 22.

good and bad — square and oblong or with unequal sides. This is evidently a collection put together without system, to fill out the sacred number ten, but an attempt at an articulation may at least be recognised.

In accordance, then, with this or a similar scheme the Pythagoreans exerted themselves to make an order of things corresponding to the system of numbers, by assigning the fundamental conceptions in every department of knowledge to various numbers, and on the other hand by adjudging to every individual number, but especially to those from one to ten, determining significance in the various spheres of reality. The fantastic nature of the symbolic interpretation into which they fell in doing this must yet not cause us to overlook the fact that the attempt was therewith made to recognise an *abiding order of things* which could be grasped and expressed in *conceptions*, and to find the ultimate ground of this order in *mathematical relations.*

Nor did it escape the notice of the Pythagoreans themselves, notably of the later members of the school, that numbers could not be called the principles (ἀρχαί) of things in the same way in which the term is applied to the various "stuffs," or kinds of matter, to the elements, etc., that things have not arisen out of them, but are *formed according to them;* and perhaps they best and most effectively express their thoughts when they say that all things are *copies or imitations of numbers.* With this conception the world of mathematical forms was thought as a higher, more original reality, of which the empirical reality was held to be only a copy: to the former belonged abiding Being; the latter was the contrasted world of Becoming and change.

§ 5. Conceptions of Cosmic Processes.[1]

E. Hardy, *Der Begriff der Physis in griechischen Philosophie*, I. Berlin, 1884.

As the fact of change — that is, the cosmic processes — furnished the most immediate occasion for reflection upon the abiding Being, so, on the other hand, the various conceptions of Being had as their ultimate aim only to make the processes of Nature intelligible. This task was indeed occasionally forgotten, or set aside, in the development of the conceptions of Being, as by the Eleatics; but immediately afterward the further progress of thought proved to be determined all the more by the renewed attention given to

[1] [*Geschehen.* I have translated this word variously by "change," "occurrence," "event," "taking place," "coming to pass," "becoming," etc. The last, which is ordinarily used for the Greek γίγνομαι seems hardly broad enough. The German means any natural process or event.]

Becoming and change, and by the need of so thinking Being that Becoming and change could not only be reconciled with it, but also be made intelligible by it. Hand in hand, then, with ideas of Being, go those of Becoming, the two in constant relation to one another.

1. To the Ionians the living activity of the world was something so much a matter of course that they never thought of asking for a cause of it. *Naïve Hylozoism* could have in view only the explanation of a *particular* occurrence or cosmic process. *Explanation,* however, consists in reducing what is striking — not a matter of course or intelligible in itself — to such simpler forms of occurrence as seem to need no explanation, inasmuch as they are most familiar to our perception. That things change their form, their qualities, their working upon one another, seemed to the *Milesians* to require explanation. They contented themselves in this with conceiving these changes as condensation or rarefaction of the cosmic matter. This latter process did not seem to them to need a farther explanation, though Anaximenes at least did add, that these changes in the state of aggregation were connected with changes in temperature — condensation with cooling, rarefaction with growing warm. This contrast gave rise to the arrangement of the states of aggregation in a series corresponding to the degree of rarefaction or condensation of the primitive matter:[1] viz. fire, air, water, earth (or stone).

The Milesians used these ideas not only to explain individual phenomena of Nature, particularly the meteorological processes so important for a sea-faring people, but also to explain the development of the present state of the world out of the prime matter. Thus Thales conceived water as in part rarefying to form air and fire, and in part condensing to form earth and stone; Anaximenes, starting from air, taught an analogous process of world-formation. As a result of these views it was assumed that the earth — resting on water, according to the first, on air, according to the second — occupied the centre of the sphere of air revolving about it, and this sphere of air was yet again surrounded by a sphere of fire, which either broke through or shone through in the stars.

In setting forth this process of *world-origination*, which was perhaps still regarded by Thales and Anaximander as a process occurring once for all, the Milesians attached themselves closely to the cosmogonic poetry.[2] Not until later does the consideration seem to

---

[1] Hence it is intelligible that there were also physicists (not known to us by name) who would regard the world-stuff as an intermediate stage between air and water, or between air and fire.

[2] Hence, also, the designation of the world-stuff as ἀρχή (beginning).

have gained prevalence, that if to change of form a change back to the original form corresponds, and if, at the same time, matter is to be regarded as not only eternal but eternally living, it is necessary to assume a ceaseless process of world-formation and world-destruction, a *countless number of successive worlds.*[1]

2. Although these essential constituents characterise also the physical theories of *Anaximander,* he was led beyond them by his metaphysical conception of the ἄπειρον. The infinite, self-moved matter which was intended by this obscure conception was indeed, as a whole, to have no definite properties. It was held, however, to *contain qualitative opposites within itself,* and in its process of evolution to *exclude* them from itself, so that they became separate.[2] Anaximander remained then a Hylozoist in so far as he regarded matter as self-moved; he had seen, however, that the differences must be put into it if they were to come forth out of it on occasion of its self-motion. If, then, as regards his doctrine of Being, he approached the later theory of a plurality of primitive substances, and abandoned the doctrine that the primitive matter was changeable in quality, he was yet entirely at one with the other Milesians as regards his conception of the causelessness of the cosmic process, and thought that by the union of the two opposites, the warm and the cold, which he conceived as the first to come out from the ἄπειρον, he could explain water. This done, he could proceed with his cosmogony along the oceanic path taken by Thales.

But besides these physical and metaphysical determinations, the only fragment[3] preserved from him, giving his own words, represents the perishing of things as an expiation for injustice, and so presents the first dim attempt to present the world-process as *ethical necessity,* and to conceive of the shadows of transitoriness, which rest even on the bright picture of Hellenic life, as retribution for sin. However doubtful the particular interpretation of this utterance, there is yet without doubt voiced in it the need of giving to physical necessity the worth of an ethical order. Here Anaximander appears as a predecessor of *Heraclitus.*

3. The order of events which Heraclitus thought he could establish as the only constant amid the mutation of things, had two essential marks, the *harmony of opposites* and the *circuit completed by*

---

[1] This doctrine was supported, probably by Anaximander, certainly by Anaximenes. It is repeated in Heraclitus and Empedocles.

[2] The decisive passages for this very controverted question (Ritter, Seydel, Zeller) are Arist. *Phys.* I. 4, 187 a 20, and Simpl. *Phys.* (D.) 33ʳ 154, 14 (after Theophrastus) ; also the continuation of the passage in the following note.

[3] Simpl. *Phys.* (D.) 6ʳ 24, 18. Cf. Th. Ziegler, *Arch. f. Gesch. d. Philos.,* I. 16 ff.

matter in its successive changes in the universe. The observation that everything in the world is in process of constant change was exaggerated by Heraclitus to the claim that everything is continually changing into its opposite. The "other" was for him *eo ipso* the opposed. The "flux of things" became transformed in his poetic rhetoric into a ceaseless strife of opposites, and this strife (πόλεμος) he declared to be the father of things. All that seems to be for a shorter or longer time is the product of opposed motions and forces which in their operation maintain themselves in equilibrium. The universe is thus at every moment a unity divided in itself and again re-united, a strife which finds its reconciliation, a want that finds its satisfaction. The essence of the world is the invisible harmony in which all differences and oppositions are solved. The world is Becoming, and Becoming is unity of opposites.

These antitheses, according to the view of Heraclitus, present themselves particularly in the two processes taking place in contrary directions, through which, on the one hand, fire becomes changed into all things, and, on the other hand, all things change back into fire. The same stages are passed through in both processes: on the "*way downward*" fire passes over, by condensation, into water and earth, on the "*way upward*" earth and water, by rarefaction, pass over into fire; and these two ways are alike. Change and counter-change run on side by side, and the semblance of a permanent thing makes its appearance where for a time there is as much counter-change upon the one way as there is change upon the other. The fantastic forms in which Heraclitus put these views envelop the essential thought of a sequence of changes taking place in conformity to law, and of a continual compensation of these changes. The world is produced from the fire in ever-repeated rhythm and at fixed intervals of time, and then again flashes up in fire, to arise from it anew, a Phœnix.[1]

In this ceaseless transformation of all things nothing individual persists, but only the order, in which the exchange between the contrary movements is effected, — the *law of change*, which constitutes the meaning and worth of the whole. If in the struggle between opposites it seems as though something new were constantly arising, this new is at the same time always a perishing product. The Becoming of Heraclitus produces no Being, as the Being of Parmenides produces no Becoming.

---

[1] In details his physical, and especially his astronomical, ideas are weak. Metaphysical inquiry is more important with him than explanatory investigation. He shares this with his opponent, Parmenides.

4. In fact, the doctrine of *Being* held by the *Eleatics* excluded with plurality and change, events or cosmic processes, also. According to their metaphysics an event or occurrence is incomprehensible, it is impossible. This metaphysics tolerates no physics. Parmenides denies to time, as to space, independent reality (ἄλλο παρὲκ τοῦ ἐόντος): for him there is only timeless Being with no distinctions. Although Parmenides added to the first part of his didactic poem, which presents the doctrine of Being, a second part which treats physical problems, this is yet done with the protest in advance that he is here presenting not truth, but the "opinions of mortals."[1] ᴀt the basis of all these ordinary opinions lies the false presupposition, previously rejected, that in addition to Being there is still another, Non-being. All becoming, all plurality and motion, rest on the interaction of these opposites, which are then further designated as light and darkness, warmth and cold. A *Weltanschauung* is then portrayed in poetic imagery, in which fire shapes the dark empty space into corporeal structures, a mode of representation which in part reminds us of Heraclitus, and in part accords with the astronomical teaching of the Pythagoreans. The all-ruling Fire-power (δαίμων), as inexorable necessity (δίκη), with the help of love (ἔρως) forces together what is akin, working from the centre of the world outward. Appropriation of the doctrines of others and polemic against them appear in motley mixture, agreeably to the purpose of the whole. Over this tissué thus interwoven hovers a poetic breath of plastic formative power, but original research and clear conceptions are lacking.

5. Ideas more definite, and more usable for explaining the particular, are found among the successors, who transformed the Eleatic conception of Being into the conceptions of element, homoiomeriæ, and atom, expressly for this purpose. They all declare that by occurrence or coming to be nothing else is to be understood than the motion of unchangeable corporeal particles. *Empedocles* and *Anaxagoras* seem still to have sought to connect with this the denial of empty space, — a principle which they received from Parmenides. They ascribed to their substances universal divisibility, and regarded parts as capable of displacement in such a way that as these parts mixed and reciprocally interpenetrated, all space should be always filled out. The motion in the world consists, then, in this

---

[1] The hypothetical exposition of how the world would have to be thought if, in addition to Being, Non-being, plurality, and becoming were also regarded as real, had, on the one hand, a polemic purpose; and on the other, it met the want of his disciples, who probably demanded of the master an explanation of his own of the empirical world.

displacement of the parts of matter, each of which is always crowding and displacing the other. Things at a distance from one another
cannot act upon one another, except as parts of the one flow out and
penetrate into the other. This action is the more possible in proportion as the effluxes of the one body resemble in their spatial
form the pores of the other. So at least Empedocles taught, and
the assumption of an *infinite divisibility of substances* is attested in
the case of Anaxagoras also. Another picture of occurrence more
akin to the present way of thinking is that presented by *Leucippus*.
The atoms which impinge upon each other in empty space act upon
each other by pressure and impact, group themselves together, and
so form greater or smaller things or masses which are not separated
and destroyed until some impact or pressure of other masses comes
from without. All occurrence and coming to be consists in this
process in which atom-complexes are successively formed and
shattered.

The fundamental form of world-motion in all three systems, however, is that of the vortex, of circular rotation (δίνη). According to
Empedocles it is brought about by the forces of love and hate acting
among the elements; according to Anaxagoras it is begun by the
Reason-stuff acting according to ends, and then continues with
mechanical consistency; according to Leucippus it is the result
always occurring from the collision of several atoms. The principle
of *mechanism* was with Empedocles still enveloped in myth, with
Anaxagoras it first made a half-successful attempt to break through
the covering, and was completely carried through only by Leucippus.
What hindered the first two from reaching this position was the
introduction of considerations of worth into their explanatory
theory. The one was for tracing the good and the evil back to corresponding powers of mind, which were, to be sure, not ascribed to
any being, but mythically hypostatised; the other believed that he
could explain the order of the whole only from the assumption that
purposive, rationally considered impulse had originated the motions.
Yet both came so near the position of Leucippus as to demand a
teleological explanation for the *beginning* only of the vortex-motion;
the farther course of the motions, and thus *every individual occurrence*, they explained, as did Leucippus, *purely mechanically*, by the
pushing and crowding of the particles of matter after these are once
in motion in the manner determined. They proceeded so consistently in this that they did not exclude from this mechanical
explanation even the origination and functions of organisms, among
which, moreover, plants are regarded as being as truly animate as are
animals. Anaxagoras is reproached for this by Plato and Aristotle,

and an expression of Empedocles has been handed down,[1] according to which he taught that the animals had arisen here and there, without any rule, in odd and grotesque forms, and that in the course of time only those fitted for life maintained themselves. The principle of the survival of the fittest, which plays so great a part in the biology of to-day, *i.e.* in Darwinism, is here already clearly formulated.

On the ground of these ideas, an interesting contrast discloses itself in the case of the three investigators, as regards their attitude toward cosmogonic theories. For Empedocles and for Leucippus, namely, the process of world-formation and world-dissolution is a perpetual one; for Anaxagoras, on the contrary, it is one that takes place once for all. Between the first two there is again the difference that Empedocles, like Heraclitus, teaches that the world arises and perishes in periodic alternation; while Atomism, on the contrary, holds that a countless number of worlds come into being and pass away. According to the principles of Empedocles, to be more explicit, there are four different states of the elements; their complete intermixture, in which love alone rules, and hate is excluded, he calls σφαῖρος[2] (sphere) ; when hate penetrates, this homogeneous world-sphere becomes separated into the individual things, until the elements are completely parted from one another; and out of this separate condition love brings them again together, until full union is again attained. Neither in the case of complete mixture, nor in that of complete separation, are there individual things; in both cases the Eleatic acosmism makes its appearance. A world of individual things in motion exists only where love and hate struggle with one another in mingling and separating the elements.

It is otherwise with Leucippus. Some of the atoms that dart about irregularly in the universe strike together here and there. From the various impulses to motion which the individual particles bring with them, where such aggregations occur, there results, according to *mathematical necessity* (ἀνάγκη), a whirling movement of the whole, which draws into itself neighbouring atoms and atom complexes, and sometimes even whole "worlds," and so gradually

---

[1] Arist. *Phys.* II. 8, 198 b 29. Moreover, we find an expression already attributed to Anaximander, which teaches a transformation of organisms by adaptation to changed conditions of life : Plut. *Plac.* V. 19, 1 (*Dox.* D. 430, 15) For man, also, the oldest thinkers claimed no other origin than that of growth out of the animal world : so Empedocles in Plut. *Strom.* fr. 2. (*Dox.* D. 579, 17).

[2] Evidently not without suggestion from the Eleatic world-sphere, which this absolute, fully adjusted mingling of all elements, taught by Empedocles, much resembles.

extends. Meanwhile such a system in process of revolution is differentiating itself, since, by the rotation, the finer, more movable atoms are driven to the periphery, the more inert and massy are gathered in the centre; and so like finds its way to like, not by inclination or love, but through their like conformity to the law of pressure and impact. So there arise at various times and in different places in the boundless universe, various worlds, each of which continues in motion within itself, according to mechanical law, until it perhaps is shattered in pieces by collision with another world, or is drawn into the revolution of a greater. So, the Atomists maintained, the sun and moon were at one time worlds by themselves, which subsequently fell into the greater vortex of which our earth is the centre. How near in principle this whole conception is to the natural science of to-day is obvious.

The *teleological point of view* taken by Anaxagoras excludes, on the contrary, a plurality of worlds in time as well as a plurality of worlds in space. The ordering mind, which introduces the purposive motion of the elements, forms just this *one world* only, which is the most perfect.[1] Anaxagoras, therefore, quite in the manner of the cosmogonic poetry, describes how the beginning of the world was preceded by a chaotic primitive condition, in which the elements were intermingled without order and without motion. Then came the νοῦς, the "Reason-stuff" (*Vernunftstoff*), and set it into ordered motion. This vortex-motion began at one point, the pole of the celestial vault, and extended gradually throughout the entire mass of matter, separating and dividing the elements, so that they now perform their mighty revolution in a uniformly harmonious manner. The teleological motive of the doctrine of Anaxagoras is due essentially to his admiration of the order in the *stellar world*, which, after it has performed the rotations started by the νοῦς, moves on without disturbance always in the same track. There is no ground for assuming that this teleological cosmology directed attention to the adaptation to ends in living beings, or even to the connected system of Nature as beneficent to man; its gaze was fixed on the beauty of the starry heavens; and what is related of the views of Anaxagoras on terrestrial things, on organisms, and on man, keeps quite within the setting of the mechanical mode of explanation in vogue among his contemporaries. What he said, too, with regard to the presence of life on other heavenly bodies, might just as well have come from the Atomists.

---

[1] This motive, fully carried out, is found in Plato, *Tim.* 31, with unmistakable reference to the opposition between Anaxagoras and the Atomists.

Accordingly, although Anaxagoras conceived of the νοῦς as also the principle of animation, and thought of the particles of this substance as mingled in greater or lesser number with organic bodies, yet the central point in this conception is that of the authorship of the astronomical world-order. The other side, the moment or factor of the cause of animate life, is much more energetically emphasised in the transformation which a younger eclectic natural philosopher, *Diogenes of Apollonia*, undertook to effect in the conception of Anaxagoras by connecting it with the hylozoistic principle of Anaximenes. He designated air as ἀρχή [first principle, primitive element], fitted it out, however, with the characteristics of the νοῦς, — omniscience and force acting according to ends, — named this "rational air" also πνεῦμα [spirit], and found this formative principle in man and other organisms as well as in the universe. A rich physiological knowledge enabled him to carry through in detail this thought as applied to the structure and functions of the human body. With him teleology became the dominant mode of apprehending also the *organic world*.

His fragments have been collected by Schorn (Bonn, 1829) and Panzerbieter (Leips. 1830). Cf. K. Steinhart in Ersch und Grüber's *Encyclopädie*.

6. All these doctrines, however, presuppose the conception of *motion* as one that is intelligible of itself and in need of no further explanation. They thought they had explained qualitative change when they had pointed out as its true essence motion, whether between the parts of a continuously connected matter, or in empty space. The opposition, therefore, which the Eleatic School brought to bear upon all these doctrines was directed first of all against this conception of motion, and *Zeno* showed that this could by no means be taken so simply, but was rather full of contradictions which incapacitated it for serving as principle of explanation.

Among Zeno's famous proofs of the impossibility of motion,[1] the weakest is that which proceeds from the *relativity of the amount of motion*, by showing that the movement of a wagon is variously estimated if it is observed either from wagons also in motion but in different directions and at varying rates of speed, or again from two wagons one of which is moving and one standing still. The three other proofs, on the contrary, which made use of the analysis into discrete parts, infinitely many and infinitely small, of the space passed through by motion, and the time occupied by it, were stronger, and for a long time were not overcome. The first proof was with reference to the *impossibility of passing through a fixed space*. This was regarded as proved by the infinite divisibility of the line, since the infinite number of points which must be attained before reaching the goal permitted no beginning of motion. The same thought appears, somewhat varied, in the second argument, which seeks to prove the *impossibility of passing through a space which has movable boundaries*. The argument (known as that of

---

[1] Arist. *Phys.* VI. 9, 239 b. 9. Cf. Ed. Wellmann, *Zenon's Beweise gegen die Bewegung und ihre Widerlegungen* (Frankfurt a. O. 1870).

Achilles and the tortoise) is, that since the pursuer in every interval or subdivision of time must first reach the point from which the
pursued simultaneously starts, it follows that the latter will always
be in advance, though by an interval which becomes constantly
smaller and approaches a minimum.   The third argument has reference to *the infinitely small extent of the motion performed in any
instant.*   According to this argument, called *"the resting arrow,"* the
moved body *is* in every instant in some one point of its track; its
movement in this instant is then equal to zero; but from ever so
many zeros no real magnitude arises.

Together with the above-mentioned difficulties (ἀπορίαι) with
regard to space and plurality, these argumentations of Zeno set
forth an extremely skilfully projected system of refuting the
mechanical theories, especially Atomism, — a refutation which was
intended to serve at the same time as indirect proof of the correctness of the Eleatic conception of Being.

7. The number-theory of the *Pythagoreans,* too, was determined by
Eleatic conceptions in so far as its procedure was, in the main, to
demonstrate mathematical forms to be the fundamental relations
of reality.   When, however, they termed the actual world of reality
an imitation of the mathematical forms, they thereby ascribed a sort
of reality, even though of a derivative and secondary character, to
individual things, and to what takes place among them.   They were
also the less inclined to withdraw from answering cosmological and
physical questions as they were able to bring to philosophy the
brilliant results of their astronomical investigation.   They had come
to a knowledge of the spherical form of the earth and of the heavenly bodies; they were aware also that the change of day and night
depends upon a movement of the earth itself.   At first, indeed, they
thought of this movement as a circuit performed about a central fire
to which the earth presented always the same side, a side unknown
to us.[1]   On the other hand, they assumed that about this same central fire there moved in concentric circles, outside the earth's track,
successively the moon, the sun, the planets, and finally the heaven
containing the fixed stars.   They brought into this system, however,
in a way, the metaphysical dualism which they had maintained between the perfect and the imperfect, inasmuch as they regarded the

---

[1] Already in Plato's time the hypothesis of the central fire was given up by
the younger Pythagoreans, Ecphantus, Hicetas of Syracuse (and with it that
of the " counter-earth," which had hitherto been assumed as placed between the
central fire and the earth, invented merely to fill out the number ten), and
instead the earth was located in the centre of the universe and provided with a
rotation on its axis.   With this latter assumption that of a resting position of
the heaven of the fixed stars was connected.

heaven of the stars, on account of the sublime uniformity of its motions, as the realm of perfection; the world "beneath the moon," on the contrary, on account of the unrest of its changing formations and motions, they regarded as that of imperfection.

This way of looking at things runs parallel to that of Anaxagoras, and leads, though in another way, to the interweaving and complication of theory with considerations of worth [ethical or æsthetic values]. *It was in connection with astronomical insight that the thought of an order of Nature in conformity to law dawned as clear knowledge upon the Grecian mind.* Anaxagoras reasons from this to an ordering principle. Pythagoreanism finds in the heavens the divine rest of unchangeableness (*Sichgleichbleibens*) which it misses upon the earth. Here we have a meeting of the ancient religious ideas and the very different result yielded thus far by the scientific work of the Greeks. This latter, seeking a Permanent in the mutation of occurrence, found such a permanence only in the great, simple relations, in the revolution of the stars, which abides ever the same. In the terrestrial world, with its whole change of manifold, constantly intersecting motions, this uniformity remained still hidden from Greek science: she regarded this terrestrial world rather as a domain of the imperfect, the lower, which wants the sure order of that other world. In a certain sense this may be looked upon as the ultimate result of the first period, a result which had a determining influence for after time.

What the attitude of the Pythagoreans was to the question concerning a periodic change of origination and annihilation of the world is uncertain. A plurality of co-existing worlds is excluded in their system. In their theory of world-formation and in their particular physical doctrines they concede so prominent a place to fire that they come very near to Heraclitus. Aristotle even places one of the contemporaries of Philolaus, *Hippasus* of Metapontum, in immediate connection with Heraclitus (*Met.* I. 3).

Their assumption of æther as a fifth element out of which the spherical shells of the heavens were formed, in addition to the four elements of Empedocles, is doubtless connected with the separation which they made between heaven and earth. It is not less difficult to decide whether they derived the elements from a common ground, and if so, how: according to many passages it would seem as if they had spoken of a progressive "attraction," *i.e.* in this case (cf. above, p. 46), mathematical shaping out or forming of empty space by the ἔν (one), the original number, which is exalted above limitation and the unlimited. Yet it seems, too, that in regard to these questions various views were held within the school side by side.

§ 6. The Conceptions of Cognition.

M. Schneidewin, *Ueber die Keime erkenntnisstheoretischer und ethischer Philosopheme bei den vorsokratischen Denkern*, Philos. Monatshefte, II. (1869), pp. 257, 345, 429.

B. Münz, *Die Keime der Erkenntnisstheorie in der vorsophistischen Periode der griechischen Philosophie.* Vienna, 1880.

The question, what things *really* are, or what is the intrinsic nature of things, which is already contained in the Milesian conception of the ἀρχή, presupposes that the current, original and naïve mode of thinking of the world has been shaken, although this presupposition has not come to clear recognition in consciousness. The question proves that reflective thought is no longer satisfied with the ideas which it finds current, and that it seeks truth behind or above them. Those ideas are given, however, through sense-perception and through the involuntary elaboration of this in thought, — an elaboration that has been transmitted from generation to generation, until it has became consolidated and fixed and embodied in language, and so forms a part of the thinker's data. When the individual with his reflection transcends these ideas so given — and it is in this that philosophical activity ultimately consists — he does it on the ground of logical needs which assert themselves as he reflects on the given. His philosophising, then, even though he takes no account of this fact, grows out of discrepancies between his experience and his thought — out of the inadequacy exhibited by what is presented to his perception or imagination, when set over against the demands and presuppositions of his understanding. However unconscious of this its inner ground naïve philosophising may be at the outset, attention cannot fail to be turned in time to the diver. sity in the sources of the conflicting ideas within.

1. The first observations, therefore, which the Grecian philosophers made on human knowledge concern this *contrast between experience and reflection.* The farther the explanatory theories of science became separated from the way of looking at things which belongs to daily life, the clearer it became to their authors that those theories sprang from another source than that of the customary opinions. To be sure they have not as yet much to say on this point. They set opinion (δόξα) over against truth, and this often means only that their own doctrines are true and the opinions of others false. So much only is certain to them, that they owe their own views to reflection, while the mass of mankind — concerning whose intellectual activity it is just the older philosophers, Heraclitus, Parmenides, Empedocles, who express themselves in an extremely depreciatory manner — persist in the illusion of the senses. Only through thinking (φρονεῖν, νοεῖν, λόγος), then, is the truth found ; the senses, if alone, give fraud and a lie.[1] So strong has reflection become in itself that it not only proceeds to consequences which to the common thinking have become absolutely

---

[1] Heracl. *Frag.* (Schust.) 11, 123 ; Parmen. *Frag.* (Karsten) 54 ff.

paradoxical, but also maintains expressly that it is itself the sole source of truth as opposed to opinions.

This, to be sure, works oddly when we notice that completely opposite illustrations of this same assertion are given by *Heraclitus* and *Parmenides* in close succession. The former finds the deceit caused by the senses, and the error of the multitude, to consist in the illusory appearance of the Being of permanent things, which is presented to men by sense-perception; the Eleatic, on the contrary, is zealous against the senses, because they would fain persuade us that there are in truth motion and change, becoming and arising, plurality and variety. Precisely this double form in which this same claim is put forward shows that it is not the result of an investigation, but the expression of a demand made on other grounds.

Moreover, this proposition fits very differently into the general theories of the two great metaphysicians. The flux of all things, with its restless change of individual phenomena, as taught by Heraclitus, makes it easy to comprehend also the possibility of the emergence of false ideas, and the seeming of permanence and Being had besides a special explanation in the counter-course or opposition (ἐναντιοτροπία) of the two "ways," for this causes the illusion of permanence or Being to arise where there is just as much change in one direction as in the other [*i.e.* from primitive fire into things and *vice versa*]. On the contrary, it is quite impossible to see where the seat of illusion and error was to be sought in the one world-sphere of Parmenides, everywhere the same, which was held to be at the same time the one, true world-thought. The search could be only among individual things and their changing activities, which were themselves declared to be illusion, non-existent. Nevertheless there is no support to be found in the literature preserved, for supposing that this so simple a thought[1] which would have over-thrown the entire Eleatic system, ever occurred to the investigators of that time. In any case, the Eleatics contented themselves with the assertion that all particular existence and all change were deception and illusion of the senses.

The same *naïve denial of that which they could not explain* seems to have been employed also by the successors of the Eleatics in the matter of the qualitative attributes of individual things. *Empedocles* at least maintained that all things were mixtures of the elements. The task that logically grew out of this was to show how the other qualities arise from the mixture of the properties of the

---

[1] First carried out in Plato, *Sophist*, 237 A.

elements. But this he did not perform; so far as our knowledge extends, he did not at all set himself this task; he probably regarded these particular qualities as not being (objectively), and as a deception of the senses, just as all qualities whatever were such in the view of Parmenides. And so the oldest view of the Atomists, as supported by *Leucippus*, may well have gone just to this point, maintaining that in individual things only the form, arrangement, situation, and motion of the constituent atoms were real, and that the other properties were a deceitful product of the senses, which here, too, found no further explanation.[1]

These difficulties were perhaps jointly influential in the mind of *Anaxagoras* when he regarded all qualities as original, and not as having *become* what they are, and accordingly postulated countless elements. But for him arose the opposite difficulty of showing how it could come about, if all was regarded as contained in all, every quality in every thing, that only some of these qualities seemed to be present in individual things. He explained this in part from the consideration that many of the constituent parts are imperceptible because of their minuteness; hence it is only by thought that we can learn the true qualities of things.[2] Besides this, however, he seems to have followed up the thought, found already in Anaximander's idea of the ἄπειρον, that a complete mingling of definite qualities yields something indefinite. So, at least, he described the primitive mixture of all substances which preceded the formation of the world as completely devoid of quality,[3] and a similar thought seems to have permitted him to regard the four elements of Empedocles not as primitive substances, but rather as already mixtures.[4]

The *rationalism* common to the pre-Sophistic thinkers assumes, among the *Pythagoreans*, the particular form of affirming that knowledge consists in *mathematical* thought. This, though in itself a narrowing, is yet, on the other hand, a great step in advance, inasmuch as there is here given for the first time a positive definition of "thought" as contrasted with "perception." Only through number, taught *Philolaus*,[5] is the essential nature of things to be known; that is, it is when the definite mathematical relations lying at their basis are recognised that things are properly conceived or

---

[1] It is extremely improbable that the solution of the problem through the subjectivity of the sense-qualities, which is found in Democritus, was presented already by Leucippus, and therefore before Protagoras, who is universally regarded as the founder of this theory.

[2] Sext. Emp. *Adv. Math.* VII. 90 f.

[3] *Frag.* (Schorn) 4. From this passage the true light may, perhaps, be thrown upon the sense in which Anaximander designates the ἄπειρον as ἀόριστον.

[4] Arist. *De Gen. et Corr.* I. 1, 314 a 24.

[5] *Frag.* (Mull.) 13.

understood. This had been the experience of the Pythagoreans in music and in astronomy, and this was the object of their desire and effort in all other fields. When, however, they ultimately came to the result that this requirement could be completely met only in the knowledge of the perfect world of the stars, they concluded from this that science (σοφία) relates only to the realm of order and perfection, that is, to heaven, and that in the realm of the imperfect, of change not subject to order, *i.e.* on earth, only practical ability (ἀρετή) is of avail.[1]

Another positive characteristic of the "thinking" which the earlier investigators had set over against "perceiving," without closer specification, appears obscurely in the reasonings of *Zeno*, viz. conformity to *logical* laws. At the basis of all his attacks against plurality and motion lie the *principle of contradiction* and the presupposition that that can not be actual of which the same thing must be affirmed and also denied. This principle and presupposition were applied with clearness and certainty, though not abstractly expressed. The Eleatic theory of the world, so highly paradoxical, forced its supporters to enter into polemic more than did others, and the accounts as to Zeno's treatise, which, as it seems, was also logically well arranged and divided, offer a notable evidence of the developed technique of refutation to which the school attained in consequence. To be sure, this formal training which prevailed in Eleatic circles does not seem to have led as yet to the abstract statement of logical laws.

2. The setting over against each other of "thinking" and "perceiving" arose, then, from an estimation of their relative epistemological value (*erkenntnisstheoretischen Werthbestimmung*) [*i.e.* from the postulate that one of these two forms of mental activity is worth more epistemologically for attaining truth]. In decided contradiction with this, however, stand the *psychological* principles with which these same investigators sought to apprehend the origin and process of knowing. For although their thinking was directed first and chiefly toward the outer world, man's mental activity came under their attention in so far as they were obliged to see in this activity one of the formations, or transformations, or products of motion, of the universe. The mind or soul and its action are then at this time considered scientifically only in *connection with the entire course of the universe,* whose product they are as truly as are all other things; and since among the men of this period the general principles of explanation are everywhere as yet conceived corpore-

ally it follows that we meet also a thorough-going *materialistic psychology*.[1]

Now mind or soul is in the first place *moving force*. Thales ascribed such a soul to magnets, and declared that the whole world was full of souls. The essential nature of individual souls was therefore sought at first in that which had been recognised as the moving principle in the whole. Anaximenes found it in air, Heraclitus and likewise Parmenides (in his hypothetical physics) in fire, Leucippus in the fiery atoms,[2] and Anaxagoras in the world-moving, rational substance, the νοῦς. Where, as in the system of Empedocles, a corporeal moving principle was lacking, the mixed substance which streams through the living body, the blood, was regarded as soul. Diogenes of Apollonia found the essence of the soul in the air mixed with the blood.[3] With the Pythagoreans, too, the individual soul could not be considered as the same with the ἔν (One) which they conceived as moving principle of the world, nor regarded as a part of it; instead, they taught that the soul was a number, and made this very vague statement more definite by say-ing that it was a harmony, — an expression which we can only interpret[4] as meaning a harmony of the body; that is, the living, harmonious activity of its parts.

If now to this moving force, which leaves the body in death, were ascribed at the same time those properties which we to-day designate as " psychical," we find a clear characterisation of the specifically theoretical interest by which this oldest science was filled, in the fact that among these attributes it is that of ideation, of " knowing," which is almost exclusively the object of attention.[5] Of feelings and volitions there is scarcely incidental mention.[6] But as the

---

[1] Besides those characterisations of the soul, which resulted from their gen-eral scientific theory, we find in the tradition in case of several of these men (Heraclitus, Parmenides, Empedocles, and the Pythagoreans) still other doc-trines which are not only not connected with the former, but are even in con-tradiction to them. A conception of the body as prison of the soul (σῶμα = σῆμα), personal immortality, recompense after death, transmigration of souls, —all these are ideas which the philosophers took from their relations to the mysteries and retained in their priestly teaching, however little they accorded with their scientific teachings. Such expressions are not treated above.

[2] In like manner, some of the Pythagoreans declared the motes which the sunlight discloses in the air to be souls.

[3] Since, with reference to this, he recognised the distinction between venous and arterial blood, he meant by his πνεῦμα what the chemistry of to-day calls oxygen.

[4] Acc. to Plato, *Phædo*, 85 ff., where the view is rejected as materialistic.

[5] The νοῦς of Anaxagoras is only knowing ; air with Diogenes of Apollonia is a great, powerful, eternal, intelligent body. Being with Parmenides is at the same time νοεῖν, etc. Only φιλότης and νεῖκος with Empedocles are mythically hypostasised impulses, and these, too, have nothing to do with his psychological views.

[6] With this is connected the fact that in general we cannot once speak of

individual soul in so far as it is moving force was held to be a part of the force which moves the entire universe, so also the *"knowing"* of the individual could be conceived only as a part of the knowing activity of the world.[1] This is clearest in the systems of Heraclitus and Anaxagoras; each individual has so much knowledge as there is contained in him of the general World-reason,—fire with Heraclitus,[2] the νοῦς with Anaxagoras. In the case of Leucippus and of Diogenes of Apollonia the ideas are similar.

This physical conception, which with Anaxagoras especially is purely quantitative, was given a turn by Heraclitus, in which the epistemological postulate again forces its way to the front, and asserts itself in the interest of a deeper insight and a profounder view. The World-reason in which the individual participates in his knowledge is everywhere the same; the λόγος of Heraclitus[3] and the νοῦς of Anaxagoras, as homogenous Reason, are distributed through the whole universe as moving force. Knowing, then, is that which is *common* to all. It is therefore the law and order to which every one has to unite himself. In dreams, in personal opinion, each one has his own world; knowing is common (ξυνόν) to all. By means of this characteristic, viz. that of universally valid law, the conception of knowing acquires a *normative significance,*[4] and subjection to the common, to the law, appears as a duty in the intellectual realm as well as in the political, ethical, and religious.[5]

---

attempts at ethical investigation in this period. For single moralising reflections or admonitions cannot be regarded as beginnings of ethics. On the only exception cf. below, note 5.

[1] The expression "World-soul" was first used by Plato, or at the earliest by Philolaus (in the fragment which has certainly been much questioned just for this reason, Mull. 21). The idea is certainly present in Anaximenes, Heraclitus, Anaxagoras, and perhaps also among the Pythagoreans.

[2] Hence the paradoxical expression, the dryest soul is the wisest, and the warning to guard the soul from the wet (intoxication).

[3] Cf., for this and the following, M. Heinze, *Die Lehre vom Logos in der griechischen Philosophie* (Oldenburg, 1872).

[4] *Frag.* (Schust.) 123.

[5] This is the only conception in the development of pre-Sophistic thought, in the case of which we can speak of an attempt to propound a scientific principle of *ethics.* If Heraclitus had in mind a universal expression for all moral duties in speaking of this subordination to law, or at least hit upon such, he attached it at once to the fundamental thoughts of his metaphysics, which declared this law to be the abiding essence of the world. Yet attention has above (§ 4) been called to the fact that in the conception of the world-order which hovered before him, he did not as yet separate consciously the different motives (especially the physical from the ethical), and so ethical investigation does not as yet work itself clear from the physical to an independent position. The same is true of the Pythagoreans, who expressed the conception of order by the term "harmony" (which also might be adopted from Heraclitus), and therefore designated virtue as "harmony." To be sure, they used the term "harmony" for the soul, for health, and for many other things.

3. If now we ask how under these assumptions the fact was explained that "knowledge" comes into the individual man, *i.e.* into his body, we find that the only answer offered by Heraclitus and the whole company of his successors is, "through the door of the *senses.*" When a man is awake, the World-reason streams into his body through the opened senses (sight and hearing are of course chiefly noticed[1]), and, therefore, he knows. This comes about, to be sure, only if there is besides, in the man himself, so much reason or soul that the motion coming from without is met by an inner motion;[2] but upon this interaction, effected through the senses, between the outer and the inner reason knowledge rests.

A *psychological* distinction, then, between perceiving and thinking, which, as regards their respective epistemological values, are so abruptly opposed, Heraclitus does not know how to state. Parmenides,[3] however, was just as little in a position to make such a distinction.[4] Rather, he expressed more sharply still the *dependence upon bodily relations* in which the thinking of the individual man is involved, when he said that every one so thought as the conditions constituted by the mixture of substances in the members of the body permitted, and when he found in this a confirmation of his general thought of the identity of corporeality and thinking in general.[5] Still more express is the testimony[6] that Empedocles declared thinking and perceiving to be the same, that he thought change in thinking as dependent upon change of the body, and that he regarded the constitution of the blood as of decisive importance for the intellectual capacity of the man.

These two last-named thinkers did not hesitate, moreover, to make their conception more plain to the imagination by means of physiological hypotheses. Parmenides taught in his hypothetical physics

---

[1] Also smell (Empedocles) and taste (Anaxagoras). Only the Atomists, and in particular Democritus, seem to have given value to the sense of touch.

[2] Arist. *De An.* I. 2, 405 a 27.

[3] Theophr. *De Sens.* 3 f.

[4] So, too, it is reported (Theophr. *De Sens.* 25) of Alcmæon, the Pythagoreanising physician, that he declared thought or consciousness (ὅτι μόνος ξυνίησι) to be the characteristic which distinguishes man from the other animals. But a more precise determination is lacking here also unless, in accordance with the expression, we think of something similar to the Aristotelian κοινὸν αἰσθητήριον. With this would agree the circumstance that the first attempts to localise the particular psychical activities in particular parts of the body seem to have been made in the circles of the Pythagoreans and of the physicians who stood in near relations to them ; localising, *e.g.*, thought in the brain, perception in the individual organs and in the heart, and the emotions also in the latter organ. From them Diogenes of Apollonia, and after him Democritus, seem to have taken these beginnings of a physiological psychology.

[5] *Frag.* (Karst.) vv. 146–149.

[6] Arist. *De An.* I. 2, 404 b 7 ; III. 3, 427 a 21 ; *Met.* III. 5, 1009 b 17 ; Theophr. *De Sens.* 10 f.

that like is always perceived by like, warmth without by the warmth in man, the cold without by the cold even in the dead body. Empedocles, with the aid of his theory of effluxes and pores, carried out the thought that every element in our body perceives the same element in the outer world, so as to teach that each organ is accessible to the impress of those substances only whose effluxes fit into its pores; *i.e.* he derived the specific energy of the sense organs from relations of similarity between their outer form and their objects, and carried this out for sight, hearing, and smell, with observations which in part are very acute.[1]

This view, that like is apprehended by like, was opposed by Anaxagoras, — on what ground it is not certain.[2] He taught that perception is only of opposite by opposite, warmth without by the cold in man, etc.[3] At all events, his doctrine also is a proof that these *metaphysical rationalists* maintained all of them in their *psychology* a *crass sensationalism.*

---

[1] Theophr. *De Sens.* 7.

[2] Perhaps we have here a remembrance of Heraclitus, who also explained perception from the ἐναντιοτροπία, — motion against motion, — and with whom opposition was the principle of all motion.

[3] Theophr. *De Sens.* 27 ff. It is interesting that Anaxagoras inferred from this that every perception is joined with pain (λύπη).

CHAPTER II.

THE ANTHROPOLOGICAL PERIOD.

G. Grote, *History of Greece*, VIII. (London, 1850), pp. 474–544.

C. F. Hermann, *Geschichte und System der platonischen Philosophie*, I. (Heidelberg, 1839), pp. 179–231.

Blass, *Die attische Beredsamkeit von Gorgias bis zu Lysias.* Leips. 1868.

H. Köchly, *Sokrates und sein Volk*, 1855, in "Akad. Vorträgen und Reden," I. (Zürich, 1859), pp. 219 ff.

H. Siebeck, *Ueber Sokrates' Verhältniss zur Sophistik*, in "Untersuchungen zur Philosophie der Griechen," 1873, 2 Aufl. (Freiburg i. B. 1888).

W. Windelband, *Sokrates* in "Præludien" (Freiburg i. B. 1884), pp. 54 ff.

[H. Jackson, Art. *Sophists*, in *Enc. Brit.*]

THE farther development of Greek science was determined by the circumstance that in the powerful, universal upward movement of the mental and spiritual life which the nation achieved after the victorious result of the Persian wars, science was torn away from the restraints of close schools in which it had been quietly pursued, and brought out upon the stage of *publicity*, where all was in vehement agitation.

The circles in which scientific research was fostered had widened from generation to generation, and the doctrines which at first had been presented in smaller societies and spread abroad in writings that were hard to understand, had begun to filter through into the general consciousness. The *poets*, as Euripides and Epicharmus, began already to translate into their language scientific conceptions and views; the knowledge gained by investigation of Nature had already been made *practically effective*, as by Hippodamus in his architecture. Even *medicine*, which had formerly been only an art practised according to traditions, became so permeated with the general conceptions of natural philosophy, and with the special doctrines, information, and hypotheses of physiological research which in the course of time had occupied an ever-broader space in the systems of science, that it became encumbered with an excessive growth of etiological theories,[1] and first found in Hippocrates the reformer who reduced this tendency to its proper measure and gave back to the physician's art its old character in contrast to scientific doctrine.[2]

Moreover, the Greek nation, matured by the stern experience which had been its lot within and without, had entered upon the age of manhood. It had lost its naïve faith in old tradition, and had learned the value of knowledge and ability for practical life. Of science, which up to this time had followed in quiet the pure impulse of investigation — the noble curiosity which seeks knowledge for its own sake — the state now demanded light on the questions which disturbed it, counsel and help in the doubt into which the luxuriance of its own development in culture had plunged it. In the feverish emulation of intellectual forces which this greatest period in the world's history brought with it, the thought everywhere gained recognition that in every walk in life the man of knowledge is the most capable, the most useful, and the most successful. In every department of practical activity, the fruitful innovation of independent reflection, of individual judgment, took the place of the old life controlled by custom. *The mass of the people was seized with the burning desire to make the results of science its own.* It was especially true, however, that at this time family tradition, habituation, personal excellence of character and address were no longer sufficient, as formerly, for the man who wished to play a political part. The variety of transactions and the attendant difficulties, as well as the intellectual status of those with whom and upon whom he would work, made a *theoretical schooling for the political career* indispensable. Nowhere was this movement so powerful as in *Athens*, then the capital of Greece, and here also these desires found their fullest satisfaction.

For the supply followed the demand. The men of science, *the Sophists* (σοφισταί), stepped forth out of the schools into public life, and taught the people what they themselves had learned or discovered. They did this, indeed, partly out of the noble impulse to teach their fellow-citizens,[3] but it was none the less true that this teaching became their *business*. From all parts of Greece men of the different schools flocked toward Athens to expound their doc-

---

[1] This innovation in medicine began among the physicians who stood in near relation to Pythagoreanism, especially with Alcmæon. As a literary instance of it, the writing which goes falsely under the name of Hippocrates, περὶ διαίτης, serves. Cf. H. Siebeck, *Gesch. d. Psych.* I. 1, 94 ff.

[2] Cf. principally his writings περὶ ἀρχαίης ἰητρικῆς and περὶ διαίτης ὀξέων.

[3] Cf. Protagoras in Plato, *Prot.* 316 d.

trines, and from so expounding them in the capital as well as in the smaller cities, to gain honour and wealth.

In this way it happened that in a short time not only the *social position of science*, but its own inner nature, its tendency and the questions for its solution, were fundamentally changed. It became a social power, a determining factor in political life, as in the case of Pericles; but just by this means it came into a state of *dependence upon the demands of practical, and in particular, of political life.*

These demands showed themselves principally in the facts that the democratic polity demanded of politicians first of all the capacity for public speaking, and that in consequence the instruction of the Sophists was especially sought as a preparation for public life, and converged more and more upon this object. Men of science became *teachers of eloquence.*

As such, however, they lost sight of the goal of nature-knowledge, the vision of which had formerly hovered before the eyes of science. At the most they presented transmitted doctrines in the most graceful and pleasing form possible. But their own investigations, if they were not confined to a formal routine, were necessarily directed toward *man's thinking and willing,* — the activities which public speaking was designed to determine and control, — toward the manner in which ideas and volitions arise, and the way in which they contend with one another and maintain their mutual rights. In this way Greek science took an essentially *anthropological* or *subjective* direction, studying the inner activities of man, his ideation and volition, and at the same time lost its purely theoretical character and acquired a preponderantly *practical significance.*[1]

But while the activity of the Sophists found itself brought face to face with the manifold character of human thought and will, while the teachers of eloquence were presenting the art of persuasion and pursuing the path upon which every opinion could be helped to victory, every purpose to its achievement, the question rose before them whether above and beyond these individual opinions and purposes which each one feels within himself as a necessity and can defend against others, there is anything whatever that is right and true in itself. The question *whether there is anything universally valid,* is the problem of the anthropological period of Greek philosophy, or of the Greek Enlightenment.

For it is likewise the problem of the time, — of a time in which religious faith and the old morality were wavering, a time when the

---

[1] Cicero's well-known expression (*Tusc.* V. 4, 10) with regard to Socrates holds good for the entire philosophy of this period.

respect which authority had commanded sank more and more, and all tended towards an anarchy of individuals who had become self-governing. Very soon this internal disintegration of the Greek spirit became clearly evident in the disorders of the Peloponnesian war, and with the fall of Athenian supremacy the flower of Grecian culture withered.

The dangers of this condition were at first decidedly increased by philosophy. For while the Sophists were perfecting the scientific development of the formal art of presentation, verification, and refutation which they had to teach, they indeed created with this rhetoric, on the one hand, the beginnings of an independent *psychology*, and raised this branch of investigation from the inferior position which it had taken in the cosmological systems to the importance of a fundamental science, and developed, on the other hand, the preliminaries for a systematic consideration of the *logical* and *ethical norms*. But as they considered what they practised and taught, — viz. the skill to carry through any proposition whatever,[1] — the *relativity* of human ideas and purposes presented itself to their consciousness so clearly and with such overwhelming force that they disowned inquiry as to the existence of a universally valid truth in the theoretical, as well as in the practical sphere, and so fell into a *scepticism* which at first was a genuine scientific theory, but soon became a frivolous play. With their self-complacent, pettifogging advocacy, the Sophists made themselves the mouth-piece of all the unbridled tendencies which were undermining the order of public life.

The intellectual head of the Sophists was *Protagoras;* at least, he was the only one who was the author of any conceptions philosophically fruitful and significant. Contrasted with him, *Gorgias*, who is usually placed at his side, appears only as a rhetorician who occasionally attempted the domain of philosophy and surpassed the artifices of the Eleatic dialectic. *Hippias* and *Prodicus* are only to be mentioned, the one as the type of a popularising polyhistor, and the other as an example of superficial moralising.

To the disordered activity and lack of conviction of the younger Sophists, Socrates opposed faith in reason and a conviction of the existence of a universally valid truth. This conviction was with him of an essentially practical sort; it was his *moral disposition*, but it led him to an investigation of *knowledge*, which he anew set over against opinions, and whose essence he found in *conceptional thought*.

Socrates and the Sophists stand, accordingly, on the ground of

---

[1] Cf. the well-known τὸν ἥττω λόγον κρείττω ποιεῖν, Aristoph. *Nub.* 112 ff., 893 ff.; Arist. *Rhet.* II. 24, 1402 a 23.

the same common consciousness of the time, and discuss the same problems; but where the Sophists with their skill and learning remain caught in the confusion of the opinions of the day and end with a negative result, there the plain, sound sense, and the pure and noble personality of Socrates find again the ideals of morality and science.

The strong impression which the teaching of Socrates made forced the Sophistic activity into new lines. It followed him in the attempt to gain, through scientific insight, sure principles for the ethical conduct of life. While the old schools had for the most part become disintegrated, and had diverted their activity to the teaching of rhetoric, men who had enjoyed intercourse with the Athenian sage now founded new schools, in whose scientific work Socratic and Sophistic principles were often strangely intermingled, while the exclusively anthropological direction of their investigation remained the same.

Among these schools, called for the most part " Socratic," though not quite accurately, the *Megarian*, founded by *Euclid*, fell most deeply into the unfruitful subtleties of the later Sophists. Connected with this is the *Elean-Eretrian* School, the most unimportant. The fundamental contrast, however, in the conception of life which prevailed in the Greek life of that day, found its scientific expression in the teachings of those two schools whose opposition permeates all ancient literature from that time on: namely, the *Cynic* and the *Cyrenaic*, the precursors of the Stoic and Epicurean. The first of these schools numbers among its adherents, besides its founder *Antisthenes*, the popular figure of *Diogenes*. In the latter, which is also called the Hedonistic School, the founder, *Aristippus*, was succeeded by a grandson of the same name, and later by *Theodorus*, *Anniceris*, *Hegesias*, and *Euemerus*.

The wandering teachers known as the Sophists came in part from the earlier scholastic societies. In the second half of the fifth century these had for the most part disappeared, and had given place to a freer announcement of opinions attained, which was not unfavourable to special research, particularly physiological research, as in the case of **Hippo, Cleidemus,** and **Diogenes** of Apollonia, but which was attended by a crippling of general speculation. Only the school of Abdera and the Pythagorean School survived this time of dissolution. A society of Heracliteans which maintained itself in Ephesus appears soon to have fallen away into the pursuits of the Sophists, as in the case of **Cratylus.**[1]

From the Atomistic School came **Protagoras** of Abdera (about 480–410). He was one of the first, and rightly the most renowned, of these wandering teachers. Active at various times in Athens, he is said to have been convicted of impiety in that city, to have fled because of this, and to have met his death in flight. Of his numerous treatises, grammatical, logical, ethical, political, and religious in their character, very little has been preserved.

---

[1] In Plato (*Theæt.* 181 A) they are called οἱ ῥέοντες: cf. Arist. *Met.* IV. 5, 1010 a 13.

Gorgias of Leontini (483–375) was in Athens in 427 as an envoy from his native city, and there gained great literary influence. In old age he lived in Larissa in Thessaly. He came from the Sicilian school of orators, with which Empedocles also had been connected.[1]

Concerning **Hippias** of Elis, with the exception of some opinions (among which are those criticised in the Platonic dialogue *Hippias Major*), it is known only that he made great parade of his "much knowledge." Of **Prodicus** of Iulis, a town on the island of Ceos, the familiar allegory "Hercules at the Cross-roads" is preserved by Xenophon, *Memor.* II. 1, 21. The remaining Sophists, known for the most part through Plato, are without intrinsic importance. We know only that this or that characteristic affirmation is put in the mouth of one or another.

In forming a conception of the Sophistic doctrine we have to contend with the difficulty that we are made acquainted with them almost exclusively through their victorious opponents, Plato and Aristotle. The first has given in the *Protagoras* a graceful, lively delineation of a Sophist congress, redolent with fine irony, in the *Gorgias* a more earnest, in the *Theaetetus* a sharper criticism, and in the *Cratylus* and *Euthydemus* supercilious satire of the Sophists' methods of teaching. In the dialogue the *Sophist*, to which Plato's name is attached, an extremely malicious definition of the theories of the Sophists is attempted, and Aristotle reaches the same result in the book on the fallacies of the Sophists (Ch. I. 165 a 21).

The history of philosophy for a long time repeated the depreciatory judgment of opponents of the Sophists, and allowed the word σοφιστής (which meant only a "learned man," or, if you will, a "professor") to bear the disparaging meaning which they had given it. Hegel rehabilitated the Sophists, and thereupon it followed, as often happens, that they were for a time over-estimated, as by Grote.

M. Schanz, *Die Sophisten* (Göttingen, 1867).

Socrates of Athens (469–399) makes an epoch in the history of philosophy, even by his external characteristics, by his original personality, and his new style of philosophising. He was neither *savant* nor wandering teacher, belonged to no school and adhered to none. He was a simple man of the people, the son of a sculptor, and at first busied himself with the chisel. In his ardent desire for knowledge he absorbed the new doctrines with which the streets of his native city re-echoed, but did not allow himself to be dazzled by these brilliant rhetorical efforts, nor did he find himself much advanced by them. His keen thought took note of their contradictions, and his moral earnestness was offended by the superficiality and frivolity of this constant effort after culture. He held it to be his duty to enlighten himself and his fellow-citizens concerning the emptiness of this pretended knowledge, and, through earnest investigation, to follow after truth. So, a philosopher of this opportunity and of daily life, he worked unremittingly among his fellow-citizens, until misunderstanding and personal intrigue brought him before the court which condemned him to the death that was to become his greatest glory.

The accounts concerning him give a clear and trustworthy picture of his personality. In these accounts Plato's finer and Xenophon's coarser portrayal supplement each other most happily. The first in almost all his writings brings out the honoured teacher with dramatic vividness. Of the second we have to consider the *Memorabilia* ('Απομνημονεύματα Σωκράτους) and the *Symposium*. As regards his teaching, the case is more difficult, for here the presentations of both Xenophon and Plato are partisan writings, each laying claim to the famous name for his own doctrine (in the case of Xenophon a mild Cynicism). The statements of Aristotle are authoritative on all essential points, because of the greater historical separation and the freer point of view.

E. Alberti, *Sokrates* (Göttingen, 1869); A. Labriola, *La Dottrina di Socrate* (Naples, 1871); A. Fouillée, *La Philosophie de Socrate* (Paris, 1873).

Euclid of Megara founded his school soon after the death of Socrates. The two Eristics (see below), **Eubulides** of Miletus, **Alexinus** of Elis, **Diodorus Cronus** of Caria (died 307), and **Stilpo** (380–300), are to be mentioned as

---

[1] In regard to these relationships cf. H. Diels, *Berichte der Berl. Akademie.* 1884, pp. 343 ff.

belonging to this school, which had only a brief existence, and later became incorporated with the Cynics and Stoics. The same is true of the society which **Phædo**, the favourite pupil of Socrates, founded in his home at Elis, and which **Menedemus** soon after transplanted to Eretria. Cf. E. Mallet, *Histoire de l'école de Megare et des écoles d'Elis et d'Erétrie* (Paris, 1845).

The founder of the Cynic School (named after the gymnasium Cynosarges) was **Antisthenes** of Athens, who, like Euclid, was an older friend of Socrates. The singular **Diogenes** of Sinope is rather a characteristic by-figure in the history of civilisation than a man of science. In this connection **Crates** of Thebes may also be mentioned. Later this school was blended with that of the Stoics.

F. Dümmler, *Antisthenica* (Halle, 1882) ; K. W. Göttling, *Diogenes der Kyniker, oder die Philosophie des griechischen Proletariats* (Ges. Abhandl. I. 251 ff.).

Aristippus of Cyrene, a Sophist and wandering teacher, somewhat younger than Euclid and Antisthenes, and united only for a little time with the Socratic circle, founded his school in old age, and seems to have left to his grandson the systematic development of thoughts, which, for himself, were rather a practical principle of life. The above-named successors (Theodorus, etc.) extend into the third century, and form the transition to the Epicurean School, which took up the remnants of the Hedonistic into itself.

A. Wendt, *De Philosophia Cyrenaica* (Göttingen, 1841).

§ 7. The Problem of Morality.

The reflections of the Gnomic poets and the sentences of the so-called seven wise men had already, as their central point, the admonition to observe moderation. In like manner the pessimistic complaints which we meet among poets, philosophers, and moralists of the fifth century are directed for the most part against the unbridled license of men, their lack of discipline and of obedience to law. The more serious minds discerned the danger which the passionate seething and foaming of public life brought with it, and the political experience that party strife was ethically endurable only where it left the order of the laws untouched, made subjection to law appear as the supreme duty. Heraclitus and the Pythagoreans expressed this with complete clearness, and knew how to attach it to the fundamental conceptions of their metaphysical theories.[1]

We meet here with two assumptions which even among these thinkers appear as self-evident presuppositions. The first is the *validity of laws*. The naïve consciousness obeys the command without asking whence it comes or by what it is justified. Laws have actual existence, those of morals as well as those of the courts; they are here once for all, and the individual has to follow them. No one in the pre-Sophistic period thought of examining the law and asking in what its claim to valid authority consists. The second assumption is a conviction which is fundamental in the moralising of all peoples and all times : viz. that obedience to the law brings *advantage*, disregard of it, *disadvantage*. As the result of

---

[1] Cf. above, p. 63, note 5.

this thought admonition takes on the character of persuasive counsel,[1] which is directed to the shrewdness of the one admonished as well as to the desires slumbering within him.

With the Greek Enlightenment confidence in both of these presuppositions began to waver, and accordingly morality became for it a problem.

1. The impulse to this came from the *experiences of public life.* The frequent and sudden change of constitutions was indeed adapted to undermine the authority of law. It not only took away the halo of unconditional, unquestioned validity from the individual law, but it accustomed the citizen of the democratic republic especially to reflect and decide upon the ground and validity of laws as he consulted and voted. Political law became a subject for discussion, and the individual set himself with his judgment above it. If, now, besides noting this mutation in time, attention is also given to the variety exhibited not only in the political laws, but also in the usages prescribed by customary morality in the different states and among different peoples, the consequence is that the worth of universal validity for all men can no longer be attributed to laws. At least this holds good in the first place for all *laws made by man;* in any case, therefore, for political laws.

In the face of these experiences the question arose whether there is anything whatever that is valid everywhere and always, any law that is independent of the difference between peoples, states, and times, and therefore authoritative for all. *Greek ethics began thus with a problem which was completely parallel to the initial problem of physics.* The essence of things which remains ever the same and survives all changes the philosophers of the first period had called Nature (φύσις):[3] it is now asked whether there is also determined by this unchanging *Nature* (φύσει) a law that is exalted above all change and all differences, and in contrast with this it is pointed out that all existing prescriptions valid only for a time, and within a limited territory, are given and established by *human institution or statute* (θέσει or νόμῳ).

This contrast between Nature and institution or statute is the most characteristic work of the Greek Enlightenment in the forma-

---

[1] A typical example of this is the allegory of Prodicus, in which the choosing Hercules is promised golden mountains by Virtue as well as by Vice, in case he will intrust himself to her guidance.

[2] Hippias in Xen. *Mem.* IV. 4, 14 ff.

[3] Περὶ φύσεως is the title borne by the writings of all the older philosophers. It is to be emphasised that the constitutive mark of the concept φύσις was originally that of remaining ever like itself. The contrary of this is then the transient, that which occurs a single time.

tion of conceptions. It dominates the entire philosophy of the period, and has from the beginning not only the meaning of a principle of genetic explanation, but the significance of a *norm* or standard *for the estimation of worth.* If there is anything universally valid, it is that which is valid " by Nature" for all men without distinction of people and time; what has been established by man in the course of history has only historical worth, worth for a single occasion. That only is justly authorised which Nature determines, but human institution goes beyond this. The "law" (νόμος) tyrannises over man and forces him to much that is contrary to Nature.[1] Philosophy formulated in its conceptions that opposition between a natural, "divine" law and the written law, which formed the theme of the *Antigone* of Sophocles.

Out of this antithesis came the problems, on the one hand, to establish in what this law of Nature, everywhere the same, consists; on the other, to understand how, in addition to this, the institutions of historical law arise.

The first problem Protagoras did not avoid. In the mythical presentation of his thought which Plato has preserved,[2] he taught that the gods gave to all men in equal measure a *sense of justice,* and *of ethical respect* or *reverence* (δίκη and αἰδώς), in order that in the struggle of life they might be able to form permanent unions for mutual preservation. He found, therefore, the φύσις of practical life in *primary ethical feelings* which impel man to *union in society and in the state.* The carrying out of this thought in its details and the definition of the boundary between this which is valid by Nature (φύσει) and the positive determinations of historical institution are unfortunately not preserved to us.

There are, however, many indications that the theory of the Sophists proceeded from such fundamental conceptions to a wide-reaching *criticism of existing conditions,* and to the *demand* for profound *revolutions* in social and political life. The thought was already at that time forcing its way forward, that all distinctions between men before the law rest only upon institution, and that Nature demands *equal right for all.* Lycophron desired to do away with the nobility. Alcidamas[3] and others[4] combated slavery from this point of view. Phaleas demanded equality of property as well as of education for all citizens, and Hippodamus was the first to

---

[1] Hippias in Plat. *Prot.* 337 C.
[2] Plat. *Prot.* 320 ff. Cf. A. Harpff, *Die Ethik des Protagoras* (Heidelberg, 1884).
[3] Arist. *Rhet.* I. 13, 1373 b 18. Cf. also *Orat. Attic.* (ed. Bekker) II. 154.
[4] Arist. *Pol.* I. 3, 1253 b 20.

project the outlines of an ideal state, constituted according to reason. Even the thought of a political equality of women with men came to the surface in this connection.[1]

If now positive legislation deviates from these demands of Nature, its rationale is to be sought only in the *interests* of those who make the laws. Whether this takes the form assumed in the opinion of Thrasymachus[2] of Chalcedon, who held that it is those in power who by means of the law force the subjects to do what is for their (the masters') advantage, or whether it wears the contrary form as developed by Callicles,[3] that laws have been erected by the great mass of the weak as a bulwark against the power of strong person-alities which would be superior to the individual, and that according to the view of Lycophron[4] all those who do no harm to others thus mutually assure for themselves life and property,—in all these cases the ground of the laws lies in the interests of those who make them.

2. If personal interest is therefore the ground for setting up laws, it is also the sole *motive for obeying them.* Even the moralist wishes to convince man that it is for his interest to accommodate himself to the law. From this it follows, however, that obedience to the law is under obligation to extend only so far as it is the *indi-vidual's interest.* And there are cases where the two do not coincide. It is not true that only subordination to law makes a man happy; there are great criminals, so Polus works out the thought,[5] who have attained the happiest results by the most frightful misdeeds. Experience contradicts the claim that only right doing leads to happiness; it shows rather that a shrewd conduct of life, restrained by no regard for right and law, is the best guaranty of good for-tune.[6]

Through such considerations the scepticism which had originally, as it seems,[7] been directed only toward the validity of political law, gradually attacked that of the moral laws as well. What Polus, Callicles, and Thrasymachus propound in the Platonic dia-logues, the *Gorgias* and the *Republic,* with regard to the concep-tions of the *just* and *unjust* (δίκαιον and ἄδικον) has reference in equal measure to the moral and to the political law. This double reference is effected through the middle ground of the characteristics

---

[1] The persiflage in the *Ecclesiazusæ* of Aristophanes can refer only to this.
[2] Plat. *Rep.* 338 C.
[3] Plat. *Gorg.* 483 B.
[4] Arist. *Pol.* III. 9, 1280 b 11.
[5] In Plat. *Gorg.* 471.
[6] Cf. the praise of ἀδικία by Thrasymachus in Plat. *Rep.* 344 A.
[7] This is especially true of Protagoras, perhaps also of Hippias.

of penal justice, and proves that the law of Nature is set over against, not only the civil law, but also the requirements of morals.

In both respects the naturalism and radicalism of the younger Sophists pushed on to the extreme consequences. The weak may subject himself to the law; he is, though, but the stupid man, serving the uses of others by so doing;[1] the strong, however, who is at the same time the wise, does not allow himself to be led astray by the law; he follows solely the *impulse of his own nature.* And this is the right, if not according to human law, yet according to the higher law of Nature. She shows in all living beings that the stronger should rule the weaker; only for the slave is it becoming to recognise a command above himself. The free man should not bridle his desires, but let them have full development; according to human law it may be a disgrace to do injustice, according to the dictates of Nature it is a disgrace to suffer injustice.[2]

In such forms the *individual's natural disposition, the constitution of his impulses, was proclaimed as law of Nature,* and exalted to be the *supreme law of action ;* and *Archelaus,* a disciple of Anaxagoras, belonging to the Sophistic period, proclaimed that the predicates good and bad, "just" and "shameful" (δίκαιον — αἰσχρόν), spring not from Nature, but from Institution. *All ethical judging is conventional.*[3]

3. *Religious* ideas were also involved in this overthrow as a matter of course, and all the more since after their theoretical value had been taken away, at least in educated circles, by the cosmological philosophy typified by Xenophanes, they had retained recognition only as allegorical methods of presenting ethical conceptions. In this latter line of thought the school of Anaxagoras had been active for a time, especially a certain Metrodorus of Lampsacus. It was only a consequence of the ethical *relativism* of the Sophists when *Prodicus* taught that men had made to themselves gods out of all that brought them blessing, and when *Critias* declared belief in the gods to be an invention of shrewd statecraft.[4] If such claims still excited indignation among the masses and the powers of the official priesthood,[5] it was easy for Protagoras in the presence of these questions to wrap himself in the mantle of his scepticism.[6]

4. The position of *Socrates* with reference to this whole movement presents two sides : on the one hand, he brought the principle

---

[1] Thrasymachus in Plat. *Rep.* 343 C.
[2] Callicles in Plat. *Gorg.* 483 A and 491 E.
[3] Diog. Laert. II. 16.
[4] Sext. Emp. *Adv. Math.* IX. 51–54.
[5] As is shown by the condemnation of Diagoras of Melos (Aristoph. *Av.* 1073)
[6] D. g. Laert. IX. 51.

underlying the movement to its clearest and most comprehensive expression; on the other hand, he set himself in the most vigorous manner against its outcome, and both these sides of his activity, contrary as they seem to be and much as this external opposition had to do with the tragic fate of the man, stand, nevertheless, in the most exact and rigidly consistent connection; for just by grasping the principle of the Enlightenment in all its depth, and formulating it in its full force, did Socrates succeed in developing from it a positive result of wide-reaching power.

For him, also, the time for following traditional customs without question is past. Independent judgment of individuals has taken the place of authority. But while the *Sophists* gave their attention to the *analysis of the feelings and impulses* which lie at the basis of the actual decisions of individuals, and ultimately saw themselves forced to adjudge to all these motives the equal right of an unfolding in accordance with the necessity of Nature, Socrates, on the contrary, reflected upon precisely that element which was the decisive factor in the culture of his time: namely, the practical, political, and social significance which knowledge and science had achieved. Just through the process in which individuals had achieved independence, through the unfettering of personal passions, it had become evident that in all fields *man's ability rests upon his insight*. In this Socrates found that *objective standard for the estimation* of men and their actions which the Sophists had sought in vain in the machinery of feelings and desires.

Ability, then, or excellence (*Tüchtigkeit, ἀρετή*) is insight. He who acts according to feelings, according to presuppositions that are not clear, according to customs that have been handed down, may indeed occasionally hit the right thing, but he does not know it, he is not sure of the issue; he who is entirely involved in delusion and error as to the matter in hand is certain to make mistakes; he only will be able to act right who has the right knowledge of things and of himself.[1] Scientific knowledge (*ἐπιστήμη*) is therefore the basis of all qualities which make man able and useful, of all single ἀρεταί.

This insight consists, on the one hand, in an *exact knowledge of the things* to which the action is to relate. Man should understand his business; as we find the able man in every business to be the one who has learned it thoroughly and knows the objects with which he has to work, so should it be also in civil and political life; here, too,

---

[1] These fundamental thoughts of Socrates are reproduced by Xenophon and Plato in countless turns and variations. In Xenophon the passage, *Mem.* III. ch. 9. is most important for comparison; in Plato, the dialogue *Protagoras.*

only insight should be trusted.[1] The individual excellences differentiate themselves accordingly with reference to the objects which the knowledge concerns in the individual case;[2] common to all, however, is not only knowledge in general, but also *self-knowledge.* Hence Socrates declared it to be his principal vocation to educate himself and his fellow-citizens to earnest self-examination; the γνῶθι σεαυτόν was the watch-word of his teaching.[3]

5. These considerations, which Socrates developed out of the principles by which practical ability or excellence is determined, became transferred by the aid of the *ambiguity in the word* ἀρετή,[4] to ethical excellence also, or *virtue,* and so led to the fundamental doctrine that *virtue consists in knowledge of the good.*[4] So far the course of thought followed by Socrates is clear and free from doubt. The sources become less clear when we ask what the man who was so strenuous to reach clearly defined conceptions intended by the *good.* According to Xenophon's exposition, the good (ἀγαθόν) must have coincided everywhere, for his master, with the profitable or useful (ὠφέλιμον). Virtue would then be the knowledge of what was suited to the end in view, or useful, in each particular instance. This interpretation is the easiest to attach to that analogy between moral virtue and the various kinds of excellence shown in daily life, which Socrates really taught, and the presentation given in the earliest Platonic dialogues, in particular the *Protagoras* attributes to Socrates this standpoint of *individual advantage.* Insight or discernment (here called prudence, φρόνησις) is a measuring art, which weighs exactly the benefit and the harm that will result from the action, and so chooses what is most to the purpose. In further agreement with this view is the fact that in exact contrast with the Sophists, who demanded a free and uncramped development of the passions, Socrates emphasised no virtue so much, and exhibited none so fully in his own life, as that of self-control (σωφοσύνη).

But according to this interpretation the Socratic conception of the good would be indefinite in its content; decision must be made from case to case as to what suits the end in view, or is useful, and

---

[1] Hence, too, the anti-democratic position, so fatal for his personal destiny, taken by Socrates, who demanded expressly that the most difficult and most responsible art, that of governing, should be practised only by those of the most complete discernment, and who on this account absolutely rejected the appointment of state officials by lot or popular choice.

[2] Socrates did not attempt a system of the individual excellences; on the other hand, he did give by way of example definitions of courage (cf. the Platonic *Laches*), piety (Plat. *Euthyphro*, Xen. *Mem.* IV. 6, 3), justice (*Mem* IV. 6, 6), etc.

[3] As defined by his theoretical philosophy; see § 8.

[4] The same ambiguity which has given occasion to countless difficulties lies in the Latin *virtus ;* so, too in ἀγαθόν, *bonum,* good.

instead of the good we should again always have what is *good for something.*[1] It may be regarded as certain that Socrates strove to transcend this relativism, and also that by reason of the anthropological basis of his thinking he did not get beyond this position in the formulation of his conceptions.   His doctrine that it is better to suffer wrong than to do wrong, his strict conformity to law, in accordance with which he scorned to avoid the execution of an unjust sentence and preserve himself by flight for further life and activity, his admonition that the true meaning of life consists in εὐπραξία, in continual right-doing, in man's ceaseless labour for ethical improvement, in the participation in all that is good and beautiful (καλοκἀγαθία), especially, however, his *erotic, i.e.* his doctrine that friendship and the relation of attachment between teacher and taught should consist only in a mutual striving to become good or constantly better through their life in common and their mutual furtherance of each other's aims, — all this goes far beyond the con-ception presented by Xenophon.   It can be united with the stand-point of utility only if we attribute to Socrates the distinction between the true welfare of the soul, on the one hand, and earthly gain, on the other, which Plato makes him set forth in the *Phœdo,* but of which we elsewhere find but slight traces, since the historic Socrates, even according to Plato's *Apology,* maintained a completely sceptical position with regard to personal immortality, and did not know the sharp Platonic separation between immateriality and cor-poreality.   Socrates teaches, indeed, even according to Xenophon, that man's true fortune is to be sought, not in outward goods nor in luxurious life, but in virtue alone : if, however, this virtue is to consist only in the capacity to recognise the truly useful and act accordingly, the doctrine moves in a circle as soon as it maintains that this truly useful is just virtue itself.   In this circle Socrates remained fast ; the objective determination of the conception of the good which he sought he did not find.

6. However indefinite the answer to the question as to what should properly form the content of that knowledge of the good which constitutes virtue, Socrates was at all events convinced — and this proved much more important — that *this knowledge is in itself sufficient to cause one to do the good, and so bring happi-ness.*   This proposition, which may serve as a type of a rationalis-tic conception of life, contains two pregnant presuppositions, one *psychological,* viz. pronounced *intellectualism,* the other ethical, viz. pronounced *eudœmonism.*

---

[1] Xen. *Mem.* III. 8, 5.

The fundamental assumption which Socrates thus makes is indeed the expression of his own reflective, judicious nature. Every man, he says, acts in the manner that he considers best suited for his end, most beneficial and most useful; no one does that which he knows to be unfit for the end in view, or even fit in a lesser degree. If, then, virtue is knowledge of what is to the purpose, it follows immediately that the virtuous man acts in accordance with his knowledge, therefore to the purpose, rightly, in the way that is beneficial to him. No one does wrong knowingly and purposely : he only does not act rightly who has not right insight. If it sometimes seems as if some one acted wrongly in the face of better insight — "against his better judgment" — it must be that he was not clearly and surely in possession of this better knowledge, for otherwise he would have purposely injured himself, which is absurd.

In this a fundamental difference between Socrates and the Sophists becomes evident: the latter maintained the originality of the will, and on that account its warrant from Nature ; for Socrates, to will a thing and to regard a thing as good, profitable, and useful are the same thing. Knowledge determines the will without opposition ; man does what he holds to be best. True as it may be that Socrates was in error in this opinion, and that the truth lies in the mean between him and the Sophists, this his intellectualistic conception of the will came to exercise a decisive influence over all ancient ethics.

Sin is, then, error. He who does a bad act does it from a mistaken judgment, regarding the bad, *i.e.* the injurious, as the good ; for every one believes that he is doing the good, *i.e.* the advantageous. Only because the case stands thus is there any meaning in instructing men ethically ; only for this reason is virtue capable of being taught. For all teaching addresses itself to man's knowledge. Because man can be taught what the good is, therefore — and by this means alone — he can be brought to the stage of right action. Were virtue not knowledge, it would not be capable of being taught.

From this standpoint Socrates raised the customary morality taught by the popular moralising to a scientific plane. All his keenness, his subtlety, and dialectical dexterity were employed[1] to prove against the Sophists that not only the surest, but even the only sure way of attaining to permanent happiness, lies in obeying ethical prescriptions under all circumstances, *in subordination to law and morals.* So he gives back to Authority her right. The prin-

---

[1] Compare in Plato the refutation of Thrasymachus in the first book of the *Republic*, which may be regarded as Socratic in its principles, but which in part is very weakly supported, both in form and in matter.

ciple of the Enlightenment tolerates no unquestioning subjection to
the existing state of things and requires examination of the laws;
but *these laws sustain the examination,* they evince themselves to be
requirements made by insight into what is for the best; and because
it has now been recognised that it is the right course to obey them,
unconditional obedience must be rendered.[1]   Far from being in conflict with the institutions of law and morals, Socrates is rather the
one who undertook to prove their *reasonableness and thereby their
claim to universal validity.*[2]

F. Wildauer, *Socrates' Lehre vom Willen.*   Innsbruck, 1877.
M. Heinze, *Der Eudämonismus in der griechischen Philosophie.*   Leips.
1883.

7. In addition to the psychologico-ethical presuppositions that
the will is always directed toward what is recognised as good,
and that therefore virtue, as knowledge of the good, draws after it
of itself the appropriate action, we find in the argumentations of
Socrates the further opinion that this appropriate action of the
virtuous man actually attains its end and makes him happy. *Happiness or well-being* (εὐδαιμονία) *is the necessary result of virtue.* The
intelligent man knows, and hence does, what is good for him; he
must then, through his doing, become happy also. This assumption applies, however, only to a perfect intelligence which would
be absolutely certain of the effects that an intended action would
have in the connected series of the world's events.

---

[1] In details, as might be expected from the nature of the case, this rehabilita-
tion of the popular morals falls into trivial moralising, especially as Xenophon
portrays it. But while Socrates hoped precisely by this means to render the
right service to his people, it proved to be just the point where he came to the
ground between two stools: with the Sophists and their adherents, he passed for
a reactionary ; on the other hand, the men who, like Aristophanes, saw precisely in the questioning of the authority of law and morals in general, the dangerous cancer of the time, without investigation classed him who wished to
place this authority on a basis of reason, among those who were undermining
it. So it was that it could come about that Socrates appeared in the *Clouds* of
Aristophanes as the type of Sophistic teaching which he combated.
[2] It is hence quite alien to the principles of Socrates to demand or *even to
allow* for every *individual act* a special examination of the grounds of the political or ethical command. If, for example, it has once been recognised as right
to obey the ordinances of the government under all circumstances, this obedience
must then be rendered, even if the ordinance evidently commands the unreasonable and the unjust; cf. Plato's *Crito.* If, as was true of Socrates himself, a man
is convinced that his life is under divine guidance, and that where his insight
does not suffice, a higher voice warns him through his feeling, — at least, warns
him away from what is wrong, — then he must obey this voice. Cf. on the
δαιμόνιον, § 8.   The essential thing always is that a man give an account to himself of his doing, but the grounds on which he acts in so doing may even consist
in such maxims as *exclude an examination in individual cases.*

The transmitted expressions of Socrates, in fact, make the impression that he was convinced that man could possess that insight which by its operation upon his action and its consequences is adapted to bring about happiness, and that he might gain this insight through philosophy: that is, through unremitting earnest examination of himself, of others, and of the relations of human life. Investigations as to how far the world's course, which man cannot foresee, may cross and destroy the operation even of the best planned and most intelligent conduct of life, are not to be pointed out in the teaching of Socrates. When we consider the slight degree of confidenc. which he otherwise had in human knowledge, as soon as this attempted to venture beyond establishing ethical conceptions and practical requirements, we can explain the above conviction only on the following basis — he did not fear that the *providential guidance*, which was for him indeed an object not of knowledge, but of faith, would frustrate the beneficial consequences of right action.

8. Socrates had defined virtue, the fundamental ethical conception, as insight, and this in turn as knowledge of the good, but had given to the concept of the good no universal content, and in a certain respect had left it open. This made it possible for the most diverse conceptions of life to introduce their views of the ultimate end (τέλος) of human existence into this open place in the Socratic concept; and so this first incomplete work in the formation of ethical conceptions at once afforded the material for a number of particular structures.[1] The most important of these are the *Cynic* and the *Cyrenaic*. Both present the attempt to define the true intrinsic worth of the life of the individual in a universal manner. Both wish to show in what man's *true happiness* consists, how man must be constituted and how he must act in order to attain this with certainty; both call this constitution or disposition through which participation in happiness is gained, *virtue*. The eudæmonistic side of the Socratic ethics is here developed in an entirely one-sided manner, and though universal validity is vindicated for the conception proposed, the point of view of the *individual's happiness* forms so exclusively the standard that the worth of all relations of public life even is estimated by it. In Cynicism, as in Hedonism, the Greek spirit is proceeding to appropriate the fruit which the conditions

---

[1] So indeed in the case of Xenophon and Æschines; the philosophising cobbler Simon, too, seems to have have been thus dependent on Socrates. What the Megarian and the Elean-Eretrian schools accomplished in this respect is too indefinitely transmitted to us, and is too closely in contact with Cynicism, to deserve separate mention.

of life brought about by civilisation yield for the fortune of the individual. The criticism of the social conditions and authorities, begun by the Sophists, has won a fixed standard through the mediating aid of the Socratic conception of virtue.

The doctrine of virtue taught by *Antisthenes*[1] takes at the beginning a high and specious turn at the point where the doctrine finds itself hopelessly entangled in the Socratic circle. He declines to define more closely the contents of the concept of the good, and declares virtue itself to be not only the highest, but the only good, understanding, however, by virtue essentially only the *intelligent conduct of life.* This alone makes happy, not indeed through the consequences which it brings about, but *through itself.* The contentment that dwells within the right life itself is accordingly completely independent of the world's course : virtue is itself sufficient for happiness ; the wise man stands free in the presence of fate and fortune.

But this Cynic conception of virtue as sufficient in itself is, as is shown by its further development, in nowise to be interpreted as meaning that the virtuous man should find his fortune in doing good for its own sake amid all the whims of fate. Cynicism did not rise to this height, however much it may sound like it when virtue is celebrated as the only sure possession in the vicissitudes of life, when it is·designated as the only thing to be striven for, and baseness, on the contrary, as the only thing to be avoided. This doctrine is a postulate derived with great logical consistency from the Socratic principle that virtue necessarily makes happy (cf. above, 7), and from this postulate Antisthenes sought in turn to define the real contents of the concept of virtue.

If, namely, virtue is to make happy with certainty and under all circumstances, it must be that conduct of life which makes man *as independent as possible of the course of events.* Now every want and every desire is a bond which makes man dependent upon fortune, in so far as his happiness or unhappiness is made to consist in whether a given wish is fulfilled or not by the course of life. We have no power over the outer world, but we have power over our desires. We expose ourselves the more to alien powers, the more we desire, hope, or fear from them ; every desire makes us slaves of the outer world. Virtue, then, which makes man independent, can consist only in suppression of desires, and restriction of wants to the smallest conceivable measure. *Virtue is freedom from wants,*[2] — from the standpoint of eudæmonism certainly the most

---

[1] Principally preserved in Diog. Laert. VI.   [2] X.n. *Symp.* 4. 34 ff.

consistent conclusion, and one that must have appealed especially to men of a humble position in life such as we find the Cynics to be in part.

By carrying out this thought in a radical manner the Cynics came to occupy a purely negative attitude toward civilisation. By aiming to reduce the measure of the virtuous wise man's wants to what was absolutely inevitable, and to regard all other strivings as pernicious or indifferent, they rejected all the goods of civilisation and attained the *ideal of a state of Nature,* — an ideal stripped of all higher worth. Taking up earlier Sophistic theories and developing them farther, they taught that the wise man accommodates himself only to what Nature peremptorily demands, but despises all that appears desirable or worthy of obedience merely as the result of human opinion or institution.   Wealth and refinement, fame and honour, seemed to them just as superfluous as those enjoyments of the senses which went beyond the satisfaction of the most elementary wants of hunger and love.   Art and science, family and native land, were to them indifferent, and Diogenes owed his paradoxical popularity to the ostentatious jest of attempting to live in civilised Greece as if in a state of Nature, solely φύσει.

In this way the philosophising proletarian forced himself to despise all the good things of civilisation, from the enjoyment of which he found himself more or less excluded.   On the other hand, he recognised none of the laws to which civilised society subjected itself, as binding in themselves, and if there is any truth at all in the coarse anecdotes which antiquity relates on the subject, this class took pleasure in scoffing openly at the most elementary demands of morals and decency.   This forced and, in part, openly affected naturalism knows nothing any longer of δίκη and αἰδώς (justice and reverence), which the older Sophistic teaching had allowed to remain as natural impulses, and elicits a conception of virtue which supposes that greed and lust complete the essential qualities of the natural man.

Yet the Cynics were not so bad as they made themselves. Diogenes even preserved a remnant of respect for mental training, as the only thing which could free man from the prejudices of conventional institutions and lead to freedom from wants by insight into the nothingness of the pretended goods of civilisation.   He also conducted the education of the sons of Xeniades, a Corinthian Sophist, according to the principles of the Cynic naturalism, and not without success.

On the whole, this philosophy is a characteristic sign of the time, the mark of a disposition which, if not hostile, was yet indifferent

to society and had lost all comprehension of its ideal goods ; it enables us to see from within how at that time Greek society was dis-
integrating into individuals.   When Diogenes called himself a
cosmopolitan, there was in this no trace of the ideal thought of a
community of all men, but only the denial of his adherence to any
civilised community ; and if Crates taught that the plurality of gods
exists only in the opinion of men, and that, "according to Nature,"
there is but one God, there is in the Cynic doctrine no trace to warrant the conclusion that this monotheism was for them an especially
clear idea or even an especially deep feeling.

9. In complete contrast with this system stands *Hedonism*, the
philosophy of *regardless enjoyment.*   Starting as did the Cynics
from the incompleteness of the Socratic doctrine, Aristippus struck
out in the opposite direction.   He was quick to give to the concept
of the good, a clear and simple content, — that of *pleasure* ($\dot{\eta}\delta o\nu\dot{\eta}$).
This latter conception at first does duty under the general psycholo-
gical meaning of the feeling of contentment which grows out of
the fulfilment of every striving and wish.[1]   Happiness is then the
state of pleasure which springs from the satisfied will.   If this is
the only thing to be considered, it is a matter of indifference what
the object of will and of gratification is ; all depends on the
degree of pleasure, on the strength of the feeling of satisfaction.[2]
This, however, in the opinion of Aristippus, is present in the highest
degree in the case of sensuous, bodily enjoyment which relates to
the immediate present, to the satisfaction of the moment.   If, then,
virtue is knowledge directed toward happiness, it must enable man
to enjoy as much and as vigorously as possible.   *Virtue is ability
for enjoyment.*

Every one, to be sure, may and can enjoy ; but only the man of
education, of intelligence, of insight — the wise man — understands
how to enjoy *rightly*.   In this we must consider not only the
intelligent appraisal ($\phi\rho\acute{o}\nu\eta\sigma\iota\varsigma$), which knows how to select, among
the various enjoyments that present themselves in the course of
life, those which will afford the pleasure that is highest, purest,
least mixed with pain ; we must consider also the inner self-posses-
sion of the man who is not blindly to follow every rising appetite,
and who, when he enjoys, is never to give himself entirely up to
the enjoyment, but is to stand above it and control it.   The enjoyment which makes man the slave of things is, indeed, as the Cynics

---

[1] Besides this, also, Xenophon not infrequently puts the $\dot{\eta}\delta\acute{v}$ into the mouth
of Socrates.

[2] This, too, is a completely correct consequence from the eudæmonistic principle.

say, to be rejected; but to delight in pleasure and yet not give one's self up to it is harder than to renounce it, as they do. Of this, however, man becomes capable through right insight only.[1]

On this ground the Cyrenaics, in particular the younger Aristippus (called μητροδίδακτος, "mother-taught," because his grandfather's wisdom was transmitted to him through his mother Arete), set on foot systematic investigations as to the origin of the πάθη, the feelings and impulses. In a physiological psychology which was connected with that of Protagoras (cf. below, § 8), they traced the varieties in feeling back to states of motion in the body: to rest corresponded indifference, to violent motion pain, to gentle motion pleasure. Besides such explanatory theories, however, this philosophy of *bonvivants* extended to an unprejudiced general theory of things. For them, too, as *Theodorus* taught, all ethical and legal prescriptions were ultimately merely institutions that were valid for the mass of men; the educated man of enjoyment gives himself no trouble about them, and enjoys things when they come into his possession. Theodorus, who bears the surname "the Atheist," put aside also all religious scruples which are opposed to devotion to sensuous enjoyment, and the school also exerted itself in this interest to strip the halo from religious faith, so far as possible, as is proved by the well-known theory of *Euemerus*, who in his ἱερὰ ἀναγραφή undertook to trace belief in the gods back to the worship of ancestors and veneration of heroes.

Thus the Cyrenaics ultimately agreed with the Cynics in this, that they, too, regarded all that is fixed νόμῳ, *i.e.* by the social convention of morals and law, as a limitation of that right to enjoyment which man has by nature (φύσει), and which the wise man exercises without troubling himself about historical institutions. The Hedonists gladly shared the refinement of enjoyment which civilisation brought with it; they found it convenient and permissible that the intelligent man should enjoy the honey which others prepared; but no feeling of duty or thankfulness bound them to the civilisation whose fruits they enjoyed. This same condition of recognising no native land, this same turning aside from the feeling of political responsibility, which among the Cynics grew out of despising the enjoyments of civilisation, resulted for the Cyrenaics from the egoism of their enjoyment. Sacrifice for others, patriotism, and devotion to a general object, Theodorus declared to be a form of foolishness which it did not become the wise man to share, and even Aristippus rejoiced in the freedom from

---

[1] Cf. Diog. Laert. II. 65 ff.

connection with any state, which his wandering life afforded him.[1] The philosophy of the parasites, who feasted at the full table of Grecian beauty, was as far removed from the ideal meaning of that beauty as was the philosophy of the beggars who lay at the threshold.

In the meantime, the principle of the expert weighing of enjoyments contains an element which necessarily leads beyond that doctrine of enjoyment for the moment which Aristippus preached, and this advance was made in two directions. Aristippus himself had already admitted that in the act of weighing, the pleasure and pain which would in future result from the enjoyment must be taken into account; *Theodorus* found that the highest good was to be sought rather in the cheerful frame of mind ($\chi\alpha\rho\acute{\alpha}$) than in the enjoyment of the moment, and *Anniceris* came to see that this could be attained in a higher degree through the spiritual joys of human intercourse, of friendship, of the family, and of civil society than through bodily enjoyments. This knowledge that the enjoyments afforded by the intellectual and spiritual aspects of civilisation are ultimately finer, richer, and more gratifying than those of bodily existence, leads directly over into the doctrine of the Epicureans. But, on the other hand, the Hedonistic school could not fail ultimately to see that the painless enjoyment to which it aimed to educate the man of culture is but a rare lot. In general, found *Hegesias*, he is to be accounted as already happy who attains the painless state, is free from actual discomfort. With the great mass of men discomfort, the pain of unsatisfied desires, preponderates: for them it would be better, therefore, not to live. The impressiveness with which he presented this brought him the surname $\pi\epsilon\iota\sigma\iota\theta\acute{\alpha}\nu\alpha\tau\sigma\varsigma$, — he persuaded to death. He is the first representative of *eudæmonistic pessimism;* with this doctrine, however, eudæmonism refutes itself. He shows that if happiness, satisfaction of wishes, and enjoyment are to be the meaning and end of human life, it misses this end, and is to be rejected as worthless. Pessimism is the last but also the annihilating consequence of eudæmonism, — its immanent criticism.

§ 8. The Problem of Science.[2]

P. Natorp, *Forschungen zur Geschichte des Erkenntnissproblems bei den Alten.* Berlin, 1884.

The Sophists were teachers of political eloquence. They were obliged in the first instance to give instruction on the nature and

---

[1] Xen. *Mem.* II. 1, 8 ff.

[2] [*Wissenschaft.* Science, as used in this section, is nearly equivalent to "scientific knowledge." Sometimes the subjective aspect of the term is prominent, and sometimes the objective.]

right use of language. And while they were transforming rhetoric from a traditional art to a science, they applied themselves in the first place to linguistic researches, and became creators of grammar and syntax. They instituted investigations as to the parts of the sentence, the use of words, synonyms, and etymology. Prodicus, Hippias, and Protagoras distinguished themselves in this respect; as to the fruit of their investigations, we are only imperfectly informed.

1. Our knowledge of their *logical* acquisitions, which with the exception of a few allusions are lost, is in a still more unfortunate condition. For, as a matter of course, the teachers of rhetoric treated also the train of thought in discourse. This train of thought, however, consists in proof and refutation. It was then inevitable that the Sophists should project a theory of proof and refutation, and there is explicit testimony to this in the case of Protagoras.[1] Unfortunately, there is no more precise information as to how far the Sophists proceeded with this, and as to whether they attempted to separate out the logical Forms from those elements which belong to the content of thought. It is characteristic that the little information which we have concerning the logic of the Sophists relates almost without exception to their emphasising of the *principle of contradiction*. To the essential nature of the advocate's task, refutation was more closely related than proof. *Protagoras* left a special treatise [2] concerning *Grounds of Refutation*, perhaps his most important writing, and formulated the law of the contradictory opposite, so far, at least, as to say that there are with reference to every object two mutually opposing propositions, and to draw consequences from this. He thus formulated, in fact, the procedure which Zeno had practically employed, and which also played a great part in the disciplinary exercises of the Sophists, indeed the greatest part.

For it was one of the main arts of these "Enlighteners" to perplex men as to the ideas previously regarded as valid, to involve them in contradictions, and when the victims were thus confused, to force them if possible, by logical consequences, real or manufactured, to such absurd answers as to make them become ridiculous to themselves and others. From the examples which Plato [3] and Aristotle [3] have preserved, it is evident that this procedure was not

---

[1] Diog. Laert. IX. 51 ff.

[2] It is probable that Καταβάλλοντες (*sc.* λόγοι) and Ἀντιλογίαι are only two different titles of this work, the first chapter of which treated truth.

[3] Plato in the *Euthydemus* and in the *Cratylus*, Aristotle in the book "*On the Sophistic Fallacies.*"

always any too purely logical, but was thoroughly sophistical in the present sense of the word. The examples show that these people let slip no ambiguity in speech, no awkwardness in popular expression, if out of it they might weave a snare of absurdity. The witticisms which result are often based merely upon language, grammar, and etymology; more rarely they are properly logical; quite often, however, coarse and dull. Characteristic here, too, are the *catch-questions*, where either an affirmative or negative answer, according to the customs and presuppositions of the ordinary mean- ings of the words, gives rise to nonsensical consequences, unforeseen by the one answering.[1]

Plato has portrayed two brothers, *Euthydemus* and *Dionysidorus*, who practised this art of logomachy or *eristic*, which had great success among the Athenians who were great talkers and accus- tomed to word-quibbling. Aside from them, it was prosecuted principally by the *Megarians*, among whom the head of the school, *Euclid*, busied himself with the theory of refutation.[2] His adhe- rents, *Eubulides* and *Alexinus*, were famous for a series of such catches, which made a great sensation and called forth a whole lit- erature.[3] Among these there are two, the "Heap" and the "Bald- head,"[4] the fundamental thought in which is to be traced back to Zeno, and was introduced by him into the arguments by which he wished to show that the composition of magnitudes out of small parts is impossible. In like manner, Zeno's arguments against motion were amplified, even if not deepened or strengthened,[5] by another Megarian, *Diodorus Cronos*. Unwearied in finding out such *aporiœ*, difficulties, and contradictions, this same Diodorus invented also the famous argument ($\kappa\upsilon\rho\iota\epsilon\acute{\upsilon}\omega\nu$) which was designed to destroy the conception of possibility: only the actual is possible; for a possible which does not become actual evinces itself thereby to be impossible.[6]

In another manner, also, the Sophists who were affiliated with the *Eleatics*, show an extreme application of the principle of contradic- tion, and a corresponding *exaggeration of the principle of identity.* Even Gorgias seems to have supported his opinion that all state- ments are false, upon the assumption that it is incorrect to predicate

---

[1] As a typical example, "Have you left off beating your father?" or "Have you shed your horns?"
[2] Diog. Laert. II. 107.
[3] Cf. Prantl, *Gesch. der Log*, I. 33 ff.
[4] Which kernel of grain by being added makes the heap? Which hair falling out makes the bald head?
[5] Sext. Emp. *Adv. Math.* X. 85 ff.
[6] Cic. *De Fato*, 7, 13.

of any subject anything else than just this subject itself; and the Cynics, as well as Stilpo the Megarian, made this thought their own. There remain, accordingly, only such purely identical judgments as, good is good, man is man, etc.[1] As a logical consequence of this, judging and talking are made as impossible as were plurality and motion according to the Eleatic principle. As in the metaphysics of Parmenides, the ghost of which appears occasionally both among the Megarians and the Cynics (cf. below, No. 5), the lack of conceptions of relation permitted no combination of unity with plurality and led to a denial of plurality, so here the lack of conceptions of logical relation made it appear impossible to assert of the subject a variety of predicates.

2. In all these devious windings taken by the researches of the Sophists concerning the knowing activity, the *sceptical direction* is manifesting itself. If on such grounds the logical impossibility of all formation of synthetic propositions was maintained, this showed that knowledge itself was irreconcilable with the abstract principle of identity, as it had been formulated in the Eleatics' doctrine of Being. The doctrine of Parmenides had itself become ensnared past help in the dichotomies of Zeno. This came to most open expression in the *treatise* of *Gorgias*,[2] which declared Being, Knowledge, and Communication of Knowledge to be impossible. There is nothing; for both Being, which can be thought neither as eternal nor as transitory, neither as one nor as manifold, and Non-being are conceptions that are in themselves contradictory. If, however, there were anything, it would not be knowable; for that which is *thought* is always something else than that which actually *is*, otherwise they could not be distinguished. Finally, if there were knowledge, it could not be taught; for every one has only his own ideas, and in view of the difference between the thoughts and the signs which must be employed in their communication, there is no guaranty of mutual understanding.

This *nihilism*, to be sure, scarcely claimed to be taken in earnest; even the title of the book, περὶ φύσεως ἢ περὶ τοῦ μὴ ὄντος (*Concerning Nature, or concerning that which is not*), appears like a grotesque farce. The Rhetorician, trained to formal dexterity, who despised all earnest science and pursued only his art of speaking,[3] indulged in the jest of satirising as empty the entire labour of philos-

---

[1] Plat. *Theæt.* 201 E. Cf. *Soph.* 251 B.

[2] Extracts are found partly in the third chapter of the pseudo-Aristotelian treatise *De Xenophane, Zenone, Gorgia* (cf. p. 30), in part in Sext. Emp. VII. 65–86.

[3] Plat. *Meno.* 95 C.

ophy, and doing this ironically in the style of Zeno's pinching-mill of contradictions. But just the facts that he did this, and that his work found applause, show how among the men who occupied themselves in instructing the people, and in the circles of scientific culture itself, faith in science was becoming lost at just the time when the mass of the people was seeking its welfare in it. This despair of truth is the more comprehensible, as we see how the serious scientific investigation of Protagoras attained the same result.

E. Laas, *Idealismus und Positivismus.* I. Berlin, 1880.
W. Halbfass. *Die Berichte des Platon und Aristoteles über Protagoras.* Strassb. 1882.
Sattig, *Der Protagoreische Sensualismus* (Zeitschrift für Philosophie, vols. 86–89).

3. The germ of the doctrine of *Protagoras* is found in his effort to explain the ideas of the human mind *psycho-genetically.* Insight into the origin and development of ideas was absolutely necessary for the practical aspect of a system of ethics, and particularly for the cultivation of rhetoric. The statements, however, which the metaphysicians had occasionally uttered, were in nowise sufficient for the purpose, constructed as they were from general presuppositions and permeated by them ; on the contrary, the observations in physiological psychology which had been made in the more recent circles of investigators who were more given to natural science, offered themselves as fit for the purpose. Thinking and perceiving had been set over against each other from the point of view of their relative worth ; this determining element now disappeared for Protagoras, and so there remained for him only the view of the psychological identity of thinking and perceiving, — a view to which even those metaphysicians had committed themselves as soon as they attempted to explain ideation from the world-process (cf. § 8). In consequence of this he declared that *the entire psychical life consists only in perceptions.*[1] This *sensualism* was then illustrated by the great mass of facts which physiological psychology had assembled in connection with the teaching of the physicians that were scientific investigators, and by the numerous theories which had been brought forward with special reference to the process of the action of the senses.

All these, however, had in common the idea that *perception* rests in the last instance upon *motion*, as does every process by which things come to be or occur in the world. In this even Anaxagoras

---

[1] Diog. Laert. IX. 51.

and Empedocles were at one with the Atomists, from whose school Protagoras, as a native of Abdera, had probably gone out. This agreement extended still farther to the assumption, made on all sides, that in perception there was not only a condition of motion in the thing to be perceived, but also a like condition in the percipient organ. Whatever view might be taken as to the metaphysical essence of that which was there in motion, it seemed to be acknowledged as undoubted that every perception presupposed this double motion. Empedocles had already anticipated the doctrine that the inner organic motion advances to meet the outer.[1]

On this foundation[2] the Protagorean *theory of knowledge* is built up. If, that is to say, perception is the product of these two motions directed toward one another, it is obviously *something else than the perceiving subject*, but just as obviously it is *something else than the object which calls forth the perception.* Conditioned by both, it is yet different from both. This pregnant discovery is designated as the doctrine of the *subjectivity of sense-perception.*

Nevertheless, in the case of Protagoras this appears with a peculiar restriction. Since, like all earlier thinkers, he evidently could not assume a consciousness without a corresponding existent content of consciousness, he taught that from this double motion there was a twofold result: viz. *perception* (αἴσθησις) in the man, and *content of perception* (τὸ αἰσθητόν) in the thing. Perception is therefore indeed the *completely adequate knowledge of what is perceived,* but no knowledge of the thing. Every perception is then in so far true as, at the instant when it arises, there arises also in connection with the thing the represented content, as αἰσθητόν, but no perception knows the thing itself. Consequently every one knows things not as they are, but as they are in the moment of perception for him, and for him only; and they are in this moment with reference to him such as he represents them to himself. This is the meaning of the Protagorean *relativism,* according to which things are for every individual such as they *appear* to him; and this he expressed in the famous proposition that *man is the measure of all things.*

According to this, therefore, every opinion which grows out of perception is true, and yet in a certain sense, just for this reason, it is

---

[1] Whether these two motions were already designated by Protagoras as active and passive (ποιοῦν and πάσχον), as is the case in Plato's presentation (*Theæt.* 156 A), may remain undecided. At all events, such anthropological categories in the mouth of the Sophist are not surprising.

[2] With regard to such preparatory ideas, there is no ground to trace this theory of the motions which advance to meet one another, to direct connection with *Heraclitus.* Its Heraclitean element, which Plato very correctly saw, was sufficiently maintained by those direct predecessors who reduced all Becoming and change to relations of motion.

also false. It is valid only for the one perceiving, and for him even only at the moment when it arises. All *universal validity* forsakes it. And since, according to the view of Protagoras, there is no other kind of ideas, and therefore no other knowledge than perception, there is for human knowledge nothing whatever that is universally valid. This view is *phenomenalism* in so far as it teaches in this entirely definite sense a knowledge of the phenomenon, limited to the individual and to the moment ; it is, however, *scepticism* in so far as it rejects all knowledge which transcends that.

How far Protagoras himself drew practical consequences from this principle that every one's opinion is true for himself, we do not know. Later Sophists concluded that, according to this, error would not be possible; everything, and again nothing, belongs to everything as attribute. In particular they concluded that no actual contradiction is possible ; for since every one talks about the content of his perception, different assertions can never have the same object. At all events, Protagoras refused to make any positive statement concerning what *is;* he spoke not of the actual reality that moves, but only of motion, and of the phenomena which it produces for perception.

Moreover, the attempt was now made, whether by Protagoras himself, or by the Sophistic activity dependent upon him, to trace differences in perception, and so also in the phenomenon, back to differences in this motion. It was principally the velocity of the motion which was considered in this connection, though the form also was probably regarded.[1] It is interesting to note further that under the concept of perception not only sensations and perceptions, but also the sensuous feelings and desires, were subsumed; it is noteworthy especially because to these states also an αἰσθητόν, a momentary qualification of the thing which produced the perception, was held to correspond. The predicates of agreeableness and desirability receive in this way the same valuation epistemologically as do the predicates of sensuous qualification. What appears agreeable, useful, and desirable to any one is agreeable, useful, and desirable for him. The individual state of consciousness is here, too, the measure of things, and no other universally valid determination of the worth of things exists. In this direction the Hedonism of Aristippus was developed out of the Protagorean doctrine ; we know, teaches Aristippus, not things, but only their

---

[1] Doubtless we have here asserting itself the development of the Pythagorean theory of knowledge out of the Atomistic school, to which this reduction of the qualitative to the quantitative was essential (cf. above, § 5), even though the Sophist declined from principle to enter into such metaphysical theories as Atomism.

worth for us, and the states ($\pi\acute{a}\theta\eta$) into which they put us. These, however, are rest and indifference, violent motion and pain, or gentle motion and pleasure. Of these only the last is worth striving for (cf. above, § 7, 9).

4. Thus all courses of Sophistic thought issued in giving up truth as unattainable. *Socrates, however, needed truth,* and on this account he believed that it was to be attained if it were honestly sought for. Virtue is knowledge; and since there must be virtue, there must be knowledge also. Here for the first time in history the *moral consciousness* appears with complete clearness as an *epistemological postulate.* Because morality is not possible without knowledge, there must be knowledge; and if knowledge is not here and now existent, it must be striven for as the lover seeks for the possession of the loved object. Science is the yearning, struggling love for knowledge, — $\phi\iota\lambda o\sigma o\phi\acute{\iota}a$, philosophy (cf. Plat. *Symp.* 203 E).

Out of this conviction grow all the peculiarities of the Socratic[1] doctrine of science,[2] and in the first place the bounds within which he held knowledge to be necessary and therefore possible. It is only a knowledge of the relations of human life that is necessary for the ethical life; only for these is a knowing necessary, and only for these is man's knowing faculty adequate. Hypotheses as to metaphysics and the philosophy of Nature have nothing to do with man's ethical task, and they are left unconsidered by Socrates, so much the rather as he shared the view of the Sophists that it was impossible to gain a sure knowledge concerning them. Science is possible only as practical insight, as knowledge of the ethical life.

This view was formulated still more sharply by the Sophistic successors of Socrates under the influence of his eudæmonistic principle. For both Cynics and Cyrenaics science had worth only so far as it affords to man the right insight which serves to make him happy. With Antisthenes and Diogenes science was prized not in itself, but as a means for controlling the desires and for knowing man's natural needs; the Cyrenaics said the causes of perception ($\tau\grave{a}\ \pi\epsilon\pi o\iota\eta\kappa\acute{o}\tau a\ \tau\grave{a}\ \pi\acute{a}\theta\eta$) are for us as much matters of indifference as they are unknowable; knowledge which leads to happiness has to do only with our states, which we know with certainty. Indifference toward metaphysics and natural science

---

[1] Cf. Fr. Schleiermacher, *Ueber den Werth des Sokrates als Philosophen* (Ges. W. III., Bd. 2, pp. 287 ff.).

[2] [*Wissenschaftslehre. Wissenschaft,* "scientia," "science," has here both its subjective and objective sense; knowledge as mental act, and knowledge as a body of truth. Hence *Wissenschaftslehre* means both "doctrine of science," *i.e.* science of knowledge, and "scientific doctrine" *i.e.* philosophy. — Tr.]

is with Socrates, as with the Sophists, the result of employment with the inner nature of man.

5. It will remain a noteworthy fact for all time that a man who so narrowed for himself the intellectual horizon of scientific research as did Socrates, should yet determine within this the *essential nature of science* itself, in a manner so clear and so authoritative for all the future. This achievement was due essentially to his *opposition to the relativism of the Sophists,* — an opposition that was a matter both of instinct and of positive conviction. They taught that there are only *opinions* (δόξαι) which hold good for individuals with *psycho-genetic necessity*; he, however, sought a *knowledge* that should be *authoritative for all* in like manner. In contrast with the change and multiplicity of individual ideas he demanded the one and abiding which all should acknowledge. He sought the *logical "Nature"* (φύσις) as others had sought the cosmological or ethical "Nature" (cf. § 7, 1), and found it in the *concept* or general notion. Here, too, the view propounded was rooted in the demand, the theory in the postulate.

The ancient thinkers, also, had had a feeling that the rational thinking to which they owed their knowledge was something essentially other than the sensuous mode of apprehending the world in vogue in everyday life, or than traditional opinion; but they had not been able to carry out this distinction in relative worth either psychologically or logically. Socrates succeeded in this because here, too, he defined the thing in question by the work which he expected it to perform. The idea that is to be more than opinion, that is to serve as knowledge for all, must be what is common in all the particular ideas which have forced themselves upon individuals in individual relations: subjective universal validity is to be expected only for the objectively universal. Hence, if there is to be knowledge, it is to be found only in that in which all particular ideas agree. This universal in the object-matter which makes possible the subjective community of ideas is the concept (λόγος), and *science* [scientific knowledge] is accordingly *conceptional thinking,* — abstract thought. The universal validity which is claimed for knowledge is only possible on condition that the scientific concept brings out into relief the common element which is contained in all individual perceptions and opinions.

Hence the goal of all scientific work is the *determination of the essential nature of conceptions,* — *definition.* The aim of investigation is to establish τί ἕκαστον εἴη, what each thing is, and to come to ideas of an abiding nature as over against changing opinions.

This doctrine was in some measure prepared for by the investigations of the Sophists concerning the meaning of words, synonyms, and etymological relations. In the latter respect, the hypotheses of the Sophists in the beginnings of the philosophy of language (cf. Plato's *Cratylus*) extended to the question whether a natural or only a conventional relation obtains between words and their meanings (φύσει ἢ θέσει). Prodicus, whom Socrates mentions with commendation, seems to have been specially successful in fixing the meanings of words.

Among the later Sophists the Socratic demand for fixed conceptions became forthwith fused with the Eleatic metaphysics, and with its postulate of the identity of Being with itself. Euclid called virtue, or the good, the only Being: it remains the same, changeless in itself, and only the names by which men call it differ. Antisthenes, indeed, explained the concept by the definition that it is this which determines the timeless Being of the thing; [1] but he conceived this identity of the existent with itself, raised above all relations, in so bold a manner that he thought of every truly existing entity as capable of being defined only through itself. Predication is impossible. There are none but analytic judgments (cf. above, No. 1). Accordingly only the composite can have its essential elements determined in conceptions; the simple is not to be defined.[2] There is, then, no possibility of understanding the simple by conceptions; it can only be exhibited in a sensuous presentation. The Cynics came thus from the Socratic doctrine of the conception to a sensualism which recognised as simple and original only that which can be grasped with the hands and seen with the eyes, and this is the ground of their opposition to Plato.

6. *The searching out of conceptions* (for his purpose, indeed, only ethical conceptions) was accordingly for Socrates the essence of science, and this determined in the first place the outer form of his philosophising. The conception was to be that which is valid for all: it must then be found in *common thinking.* Socrates is neither a solitary hypercritic nor an instructor who teaches *ex cathedra,* but a man thirsting for the truth, as anxious to instruct himself as to teach others. His philosophy is a philosophy of the *dialogue;* it develops itself in conversation which he was ready to begin with every one who would talk with him.[3] To the ethical conceptions which he alone was seeking for, it was indeed easy to find access from any object whatever of everyday business. The common element must be found in the mutual exchange of thoughts; the διαλογισμός was the way to the λόγος. But this "conversation" encountered many difficulties: the inertia of the customary mode of thinking, the idle desire for innovation, and the paradoxical statements which were characteristic of the Sophists, the pride belonging to seeming knowledge and thoughtless imitation. Into such a condition of things Socrates made his entrance by introducing himself as one eager to learn. By skilful questions he drew out the views of others, disclosed the defects in these views with remorseless consistency, and finally led the Athenian, proud of his culture, into the state of mind where he recognised that *insight into one's*

---

[1] λόγος ἐστὶν ὁ τὸ τί ἦν ἢ ἔστι δηλῶν: Diog. Laert. VI. 3.

[2] Plat. *Theæt.* 202 B.

[3] This factor united with the influence of Zeno's dialectic to stamp upon the succeeding philosophical literature the form of the dialogue.

own ignorance, is the beginning of all knowledge. Whoever stood this test and still remained with him was taken into partnership in a serious effort to determine, in common thinking, the essential meaning of conceptions. Undertaking the direction of the conversation, Socrates brought his companion step by step to unfold his own thoughts in clearer, less contradictory statements, and so caused him to bring to definite expression what was slumbering in him as an imperfect presentiment. He called this his *art of mental midwifery*, and that preparation for it his *irony.*

7. The *maieutic method* has, however, still another essential meaning. In the process of conversation the common rational quality comes to light, to which all parts are subject in spite of their diverging opinions. The conception is not to be made, it is to be found; it is already there, it requires only to be *delivered* from the envelopes of individual experiences and opinions in which it lies hidden. The procedure of the Socratic formation of conceptions is, therefore, *epagogic* or *inductive:* it leads to the generic conception by the comparison of particular views and individual sensuous presentations; it decides every individual question by seeking to press forward to determine a general conception. This is accomplished by bringing together analogous cases, and by searching out allied relations. The general conception thus gained is then employed to decide the special problem proposed, and this *subordination of the particular under the general* is thus worked out as the *fundamental relation of scientific knowledge.*

The inductive method of procedure as employed by Socrates, according to Xenophon and Plato, is, to be sure, still marked by a childlike simplicity and imperfection. It lacks as yet caution in generalisation and methodical circumspection in the formation of conceptions. The need for the general is so lively that it satisfies itself at once with hastily gathered material, and the conviction of the determining validity of the conception is so strong that the individual questions proposed are decided forthwith in accordance with it. But however great the gaps may be in the arguments of Socrates, the significance of these arguments is by no means lessened. His doctrine of induction has its value not for *methodology*, but for *logic*, and for the *theory of knowledge.* It fixes in a way that is decisive for all the future that it is the *task of science* to strive to *establish general conceptions from comparison of facts.*

8. While Socrates thus defined the essential nature of science as conceptional thought, — thinking in conceptions, — he also fixed *the bounds within which science can be employed:* this task is, in his opinion, to be fulfilled only within the domain of practical life.

Science is, as regards its form, the formation of conceptions, and *as regards its content ethics.*

Meanwhile the whole mass of ideas concerning Nature and all the connected questions and problems still persist, and though for the most part they are a matter of indifference for the moral life, nevertheless they cannot be entirely put aside. But after Socrates renounced the task of attaining insight into such questions through conceptions, it was all the more possible for him to form an idea of the universe that should satisfy his scientifically grounded ethical needs.

So it comes that Socrates puts aside, indeed, all natural science, but at the same time professes a *teleological view of Nature,* which admires the wisdom in the arrangement of the world, the adaptation in things,[1] and which, where understanding ceases, trusts Providence in faith. With this faith Socrates kept himself as near as possible to the religious ideas of his people, and even spoke of a plurality of gods, although he indeed inclined to the ethical monotheism which was preparing in his time. But he did not come forward in such matters as a reformer : he taught morality, and if he expounded his own faith, he left that of others untouched.

Out of this faith, however, grew the conviction with which he limited the rationalism of his ethics, — his confidence in the δαιμόνιον. The more he pressed toward clearness of conceptions and complete knowledge of ethical relations, and the more true to himself he was in this, the less could he hide from himself that man in his limitation does not completely succeed in this task, that there are conditions in which knowledge is not sufficient for certain decision, and where feeling enters upon its rights. Under such conditions Socrates believed that he heard within himself the *daimonion,* a counselling and for the most part warning voice. He thought that in this way the gods warned from evil in difficult cases, where his knowledge ceased, the man who otherwise served them.

So the wise man of Athens set faith and feeling beside ethical science.

---

[1] It is not probable that Socrates experienced any strong influence from Anaxagoras in this respect, for the latter's teleology relates to the harmony of the stellar universe, not to human life, while the considerations which are ascribed to Socrates, especially by Xenophon, make utility for man the standard for admiration of the world. Much more closely related to Socratic faith are the religious views of the great poets of Athens, especially the tragedians.

CHAPTER III.

THE third, completing period of Greek science harvested the fruit of the two preceding developments. It appears essentially as a *reciprocal inter-penetration of cosmological and anthropological bodies of thought*. This union appears in but a very slight degree as a necessity found in the nature of the case, still less as a demand of the time; rather, it is in its essentials the work of great personalities and of the peculiar direction taken by their knowledge.

The tendency of the time was rather toward a practical utilisation of science: it was in accord with this tendency when research separated into special investigations on mechanical, physiological, rhetorical, and political problems, and when scientific instruction accommodated itself to the ideas of the ordinary man. Not only for the mass of the people, but for scholars as well, general questions of cosmology had lost the interest which in the beginning was directed toward them, and the fact that they were sceptically abandoned because of the Sophistic theory of knowledge is nowhere presented in the form of renunciation or lamentation.

If, therefore, Greek philosophy turned with renewed force from the investigation of human thinking and willing — researches with which it had busied itself during the time of the Enlightenment — back to the great problems of metaphysics, and reached its greatest height along this path, it owes this achievement to the personal thirst for knowledge on the part of the three great men who brought in this most valuable development of ancient thought, and stand as its representatives, — *Democritus*, *Plato*, and *Aristotle*.

The creations of these three heroes of Greek thought differ from the doctrines of all their predecessors by reason of their *systematic* character. Each of the three gave to the world an all-embracing system of science complete in itself. Their teachings gained this character, on the one hand, through the all-sidedness of their problems, and on the other, through the conscious unity in their treatment of them.

While each of the earlier thinkers had seized upon but a limited circle of questions, and in like manner had shown himself informed only in certain departments of actual reality, while especially no one had as yet shown interest in both physical and psychological investigation, these three men directed their work *in like measure to the entire compass of scientific problems.* They brought together what experience and observation had won; they examined and compared the conceptions which had been formed from these, and they brought that which up to this time had been isolated, into fruitful union and relation. This all-sidedness of their scientific interest appears in the compass and varied character of their literary activity, and the great amount of material elaborated is in part explained only through the vigorous *co-operation of their extended schools,* in which a division of labour in accordance with inclination and endowment was allowed.

But this work thus shared in common did not result in a mass of unrelated material. This was guarded against by the fact that each of these three men undertook and conducted the *working over* of the entire material of knowledge with a *unity of purpose and method* derived from the principle which formed his fundamental thought. This, indeed, led at more than one point to a one-sided conception, and to a kind of violation of individual domains, and thereby to the inter-weaving of problems in ways which do not stand criticism. But on the other hand, just by means of the adjustment which must take place in this process between the forms of cognition in different departments of knowledge, the formation of metaphysical conceptions was so furthered, abstract thought was so refined and deepened, that in the short time of scarcely two generations the *typical outlines of three different conceptions of the world* were worked out. Thus the advantages and the disadvantages of philosophical system-building appear in like measure in the case of these men of genius who were the first founders of systems.

The *systematising of knowledge so that it should become an all-inclusive philosophical doctrine* was achieved with increasing success by Democritus, Plato, and Aristotle, and with the last first found the form of an *organic articulation of science* into the individual disciplines. With this Aristotle concluded the development of Greek philosophy and inaugurated the age of the special sciences.

The course of this development was more particularly this: the two opposing systems of Democritus and Plato arose from the application to cosmological and metaphysical problems, of the principles gained through the doctrines of the Sophists and of Socrates; from the attempt to reconcile these opposites proceeded the concluding doctrine of Aristotle.

The essential feature in the work of Democritus and Plato was that they used the insight into the theory of knowledge, gained by the philosophy of the Enlightenment, to *ground metaphysics anew.* Their common dependence upon the doctrines of the cosmological period and upon the Sophistic teaching, in particular upon the theory of Protagoras, stamps upon the two doctrines a certain parallelism and a partial relationship, — a relationship the more interesting, the deeper the contrast between the two in other respects. This contrast, however, is due to the fact that the *Socratic teaching* had no effect upon Democritus, while its influence on Plato was decisive; hence the ethical factor is as preponderant in the system of the latter as it is unimportant in that of the former. Thus in parallel lines from the same source developed the *materialism of Democritus and the idealism of Plato.*

From this contrast is explained, too, the difference in their working. The purely theoretical conception of science which prevails with Democritus did not suit the age; his school soon disappeared. Plato, on the contrary, whose scientific teaching furnished at the same time the basis for a principle of life, had the pleasure of forming in the *Academy* an extensive and lasting school. But this school, the so-called *Older Academy*, following the general tendency of the time, soon ran out partly into special investigation, partly into popular moralising.

Out of it rose then the great form of *Aristotle*, the most influential thinker that history has seen. The powerful concentration with which he caused the entire content of thought in Greek science to crystallise about the *conception of development* (ἐντελέχεια) in order to adjust the opposition discovered between his two great predecessors, made him the philosophical teacher of the future, and his system the most perfect expression of Greek thought.

Democritus of Abdera (about 460–360) was educated in the scientific association of his home and by journeys lasting many years, led the life of a quiet, unassuming investigator in his native city during the turmoil of the Sophistic period, and remained far from the noisy activity of Athens. He did not impart any special ability, political or otherwise, by his teaching, but was essentially disposed to theoretical thought, and particularly inclined to the investigation of Nature. With gigantic learning and comprehensive information he united great clearness of abstract thought and apparently a strong inclination to simplify problems schematically. The number of his works proves that he stood at the head of an extended school, of which some unimportant names are preserved, yet nothing is more characteristic of the way in which his age turned aside from research that was not interesting to it than the indifference with which his system of the mechanical explanation of Nature was met. His doctrine was forced into the background for two thousand years by the teleological systems, and prolonged its existence only in the Epicurean school, while even there it was not understood.

Antiquity honoured Democritus as a great writer also, and for this reason the almost complete loss of his works is all the more to be lamented, as aside from the numerous titles only very unimportant and in part doubtful fragments are extant. The most important writings seem to have been, theoretically, the Μέγας and Μικρὸς διάκοσμος, περὶ νοῦ and περὶ ἰδεῶν; practically, περὶ εὐθυμίης and ὑποθῆκαι. W. Kahl (Diedenhofen, 1889) has begun to work through the sources which had been collected by W. Burchard (Minden, 1830 and 1834) and Lortzing (Berlin, 1873). P. Natorp has edited the *Ethics* (Leips. 1893).

Cf. P. Natorp, *Forschungen zur Geschichte des Erkenntnissproblems im Alterthum* (Berlin, 1884); G. Hart, *Zur Seelen- und Erkenntnisslehre des Demokrit* (Leips. 1886).

Plato of Athens (427–347), of distinguished family, had most successfully assimilated the artistic and scientific culture of his time when the personality of Socrates made so decisive an impression upon him that he abandoned his attempts at poetry and devoted himself entirely to the society of the master. He was his truest and most intelligent, and yet at the same time his most independent disciple. The execution of Socrates occasioned his acceptance of Euclid's invitation to Megara; then he journeyed to Cyrene and Egypt, returned for a time to Athens, and here began to teach through his writings, and perhaps also orally. About 390 we find him in Magna Græcia and Sicily, where he became connected with the Pythagoreans and took part also in political action. This brought him into serious danger at the court of the ruler of Syracuse, the elder Dionysius, whom he sought to influence with the help of his friend Dion; he was delivered as prisoner of war to the Spartans and ransomed only by the help of a friend. This attempt at practical politics in Sicily was twice repeated later (367 and 361), but always with unfortunate results.

After the first Sicilian journey, he founded his school in the grove *Akademos,* and soon united about him a great number of prominent men for the purpose of common scientific work. Yet the bond of this society was to be sought still more in a friendship based upon community of ethical ideals. His teaching activity at the beginning had, like that of Socrates, that character of a common search for truth which finds expression in the dialogue. It was not until his old age that it took on more the form of the didactic lecture.

This life finds its æsthetic and literary embodiment in Plato's *works,*[1] in which the process itself of philosophising is set forth with dramatic vividness and plastic portraiture of personalities and their views of life. As works of art, the *Symposium* and the *Phædo* are most successful; the grandest impression of the system, as a whole, is afforded by the *Republic.* With the exception of the *Apology* of Socrates, the form is everywhere that of the dialogue. Yet the artistic treatment suffers in Plato's old age, and the dialogue remains only as the schematic setting of a lecture, as in the *Timæus* and the *Laws.* For the most part, Socrates leads the conversation, and it is into his mouth that Plato puts his own decision when he comes to one. Exceptions to this are not found until in the latest writings.

The mode of presentation is also on the whole more artistic than scientific. It exhibits extreme vividness and plasticity of imagination in perfect language, but no strictness in separating problems or in methodical investigation. The contents of any individual dialogue is to be designated only by the prominent subject of inquiry. Where abstract presentation is not possible or not in place Plato takes to his aid the so-called myths, allegorical presentations which utilise motives from fables and tales of the gods in free, poetic form.

The transmission of his works is only in part certain, and it is just as doubtful in what order they originated and what relation they bear to one another.

The following are among the most important names of those who have worked over these questions since Schleiermacher in his translation (Berlin, 1804 ff.) gave an impulse in that direction: J. Socher (Munich, 1820), C. Fr. Hermann

---

[1] Translated into German by Hier. Müller, with introductions by K. Steinhart. 8 vols. Leips. 1850–1866. As ninth volume of the series *Platon's Leben,* by K. Steinhart. Leips. 1873. [English by Jowett, third ed. 5 vols. Oxford, 1893.] Among more recent editions, in which the paging of that of Stephanus (Paris, 1578), employed in citations, is always repeated, are to be noted those of J. Bekker (Berlin, 1816 f.), Stallbaum (Leips. 1850), Schneider and Hirschig (Paris: Didot, 1846 ff.), M. Schanz (Leips. 1875 ff.).

(Heidelberg, 1839), E. Zeller (Tübingen, 1839), Fr. Suckow (Berlin, 1855), Fr. Susemihl (Berlin, 1855–56), E. Munk (Berlin, 1886), Fr. Ueberweg (Vienna, 1861), K. Schaarschmidt (Bonn, 1866), H. Bonitz (Berlin, 1875), G. Teichmüller (Gotha, 1876 ; Leipsic, 1879 ; Breslau, 1881), A. Krohn (Halle, 1878), W. Dittenberger (in *Hermes*, 1881), H. Siebeck (Freiburg i. B. 1889). [H. Jackson in *Jour. Phil.*, X., XI., and XIII.; Archer-Hind's editions of *Phædo* and *Timæus ;* reviewed critically by P. Shorey in *Am. Jour. Philol.*, IX. and X.]

[On Plato's philosophy, in addition to the above, W. Pater, *Plato and Platonism* (Lond. and N.Y. 1893) ; J. Martineau, in *Types of Ethical Theory* (Lond. and N.Y. 1886), also in *Essays ;* Art. *Plato* in *Enc. Brit.*, by L. Campbell ; R. L. Nettleship, *The Theory of Education in P.'s Rep.*, in *Hellenica ;* J. S. Mill in *Essays and Discussions.*]

The writings which are considered genuinely Platonic are (*a*) youthful works, which scarcely go beyond the Socratic standpoint: *Apology, Crito, Euthyphro, Lysis, Laches* (perhaps also *Charmides, Hippias Minor,* and *Alcibiades,* I.) ; (*b*) writings to establish his position with regard to the Sophistic doctrines: *Protagoras, Gorgias, Euthydemus, Cratylus, Meno, Theætetus ;* (*c*) main works intended to present his own doctrine : *Phædrus, Symposium, Phædo, Philebus,* and the *Republic,* whose working out, begun early and completed in successive strata, as it were, extended into the last years of the Philosopher's life ; (*d*) the writings of his old age : *Timæus,* the *Laws,* and the fragment of *Critias.* Among the doubtful writings the most important are the *Sophist, Politicus,* and *Parmenides.* These probably did not originate with Plato, but with men of his school who were closely related with the Eleatic dialectic and eristic. The first two are by the same author.

Cf. H. v. Stein, *Sieben Bücher zur Geschichte des Platonismus* (Göttingen, 1861 ff.); G. Grote, *Plato and the Other Companions of Socrates* (Lond. 1865); A. E. Chaignet, *La vie et les écrits de Platon* (Paris, 1873); E. Heitz, (*O. Müller's Gesch. der griech. Lit.*, 2. Aufl., II. 2, 148–235).

Plato's school is called the **Academy**, and the time of its development, which reaches to the end of ancient thought, and which was aided by the continued possession of the academic grove and the gymnasium existing there, is usually divided into three or five periods : (1) the Older Academy, Plato's most immediate circle of scholars and the succeeding generations, extending to about 260 B.C.; (2) the Middle Academy, which took a sceptical direction, and in which an older school of Arcesilaus and a younger school of Carneades (about 160) are distinguished ; (3) the New Academy, which with Philo of Larissa (about 100) turned back to the old dogmatism, and with Antiochus of Ascalon (about twenty-five years later) turned into the paths of Eclecticism. Concerning the two (or four) later forms cf. Part II. ch. 1. Later the Neo-Platonic school took possession of the Academy. Cf. Part II. ch. 2.

To the **Older Academy** belonged men of great erudition and honourable personality. The heads of the school were **Speusippus**, the nephew of Plato, **Xenocrates** of Chalcedon, **Polemo** and **Crates** of Athens ; beside these, **Philip** of Opus and **Heracleides** from Pontic Heraclea are to be mentioned among the older, and **Crantor** among the younger members. Less closely related with the school were the astronomers **Eudoxus** of Cnidos and the Pythagorean **Archytas** of Tarentum. R. Heinze, *Xenocrates* (Leips. 1892).

Aristotle of Stagira towers far above all his associates in the Academy (384–322). As son of a Macedonian physician, he brought with him an inclination toward medical and natural science, when, at eighteen years of age, he entered the Academy, in which as literary supporter and also as teacher, at first of rhetoric, he early played a comparatively independent part, without acting contrary to a feeling of reverent subordination to the master, by so doing. It was not until after Plato's death that he separated himself externally from the Academy, visiting, with Xenocrates, his friend Hermias, the ruler of Atarneus and Assus in Mysia, whose relative Pythias he afterwards married. After an apparently transient stay at Athens and Mitylene, he undertook, at the wish of Philip of Macedon, the education of the latter's son Alexander, and conducted it for about three years with the greatest results. After this, he lived for some years in his native city, pursuing scientific studies with his friend Theophrastus, and together with him, in the year 335, founded in Athens his own school, which had its seat in the *Lyceum,* and (probably on account of its shady walks) was called the **Peripatetic** School.

After twelve years of the greatest activity, he left Athens on account of political disturbances and went to Chalcis, where he died in the following year, of a disease of the stomach. Cf. A. Stahr, *Aristotelia*, I. (Halle, 1830).

Of the results of the extraordinarily comprehensive literary activity of Aristotle only the smallest part, but the most important part from the point of view of science, is extant. The dialogues published by himself, which in the eyes of the ancients placed him on a level with Plato as an author also, are lost with the exception of a few fragments, and so also are the great compilations which with the aid of his scholars he prepared for the different branches of scientific knowledge. Only his *scientific didactic writings*, which were designed as text-books to be made the foundation of lectures in the Lyceum, are extant. The plan of execution in his works varies greatly ; in many places there are only sketchy notes, in others complete elaborations ; there are also different revisions of the same sketch, and it is probable that supplementary matter by different scholars has been inserted in the gaps of the manuscripts. Since the first complete edition prepared in ancient times (as it appears, on the occasion of a new discovery of original manuscripts) by Andronicus of Rhodes (60–50 B.C.) did not separate these parts, many critical questions are still afloat concerning it.

Cf. A. Stahr, *Aristotelia*, II. (Leips. 1832); V. Rose (Berlin, 1854); H. Bonitz (Vienna, 1862 ff.); J. Bernays (Berlin, 1863); E. Heitz (Leips. 1865 and in the second ed. of O. Müller's *Gesch. der griech. Lit.*, II. 2, 236–321); E. Vahlen (Vienna, 1870 ff.).

This text-book collection,[1] as it were, is arranged in the following manner : (*a*) Logical treatises : the *Categories*, on the *Proposition*, on *Interpretation*, the *Analytics*, the *Topics* including the book on the Fallacies — brought together by the school as "*Organon*" ; (*b*) Theoretical Philosophy : *Fundamental Science* (*Metaphysics*), the *Physics*, the *History of Animals*, and the *Psychology ;* to the three last are attached a number of separate treatises ; (*c*) Practical Philosophy: the *Ethics* in the Nicomachean and Eudemian editions and the *Politics* (which likewise is not complete) ; (*d*) Poietical or Poetical Philosophy : the *Rhetoric* and the *Poetic.*

Fr. Biese, *Die Philosophie des Aristoteles* (2 vols., Berlin, 1835–42); A. Rosmini-Serbati, *Aristotele Exposto ed Esaminato* (Torino, 1858); G. H. Lewes, *Aristotle, a Chapter from the History of Science* (Lond. 1864) ; G. Grote, *Aristotle* (published from his literary remains, Lond. 1872).

[Trans. of the *Psychology* by E. Wallace (Camb. 1882) ; of the *Ethics*, by Peters (Lond. 1881), Welldon (Lond. and N.Y.), Williams (Lond. 1876), Chase (Lond. 1877), Hatch (Lond. 1879); of the *Poetics*, by Wharton (Camb. 1883) ; of the *Politics*, by Welldon (Camb. 1888), Jowett (2 vols., Oxford, 1885–88) ; of the *Rhetoric*, by Welldon (Lond. and N.Y. 1886) ; also tr. of all of the above and of the *Metaphysics, Organon,* and *History of Animals* in the Bohn Library. Editions of the *Politics* with valuable introduction by Newman (Oxford, 1887, 2 vols.); of the *Ethics*, by A. Grant. Cf. also Art. in *Enc. Brit., Aristotle* by A. Grant ; T. H. Green in *Works ;* A. C. Bradley, *A.'s Theory of the State*, in *Hellenica*. E. Wallace, *Outlines of A.'s Phil.* is convenient for the student.]

§ 9. Metaphysics grounded anew in Epistemology and Ethics.

The great systematisers of Greek science exercised a swift but just criticism upon the Sophistic doctrine. They saw at once that among the doctrines of the Sophists but a single one possessed the worth of lasting validity and scientific fruitfulness — *the perception theory of Protagoras.*

---

[1] Of the newer editions, that of the Berlin Academy (J. Bekker, Brandis, Rose, Usener, Bonitz), 5 vols., Berlin, 1831–70, is made the basis of citations. The Parisian edition (Didot) is also to be noticed (Dübner, Bussemaker, Heitz) 5 vols., Paris, 1848–74.

1. This, therefore, became the starting-point for Democritus and for Plato; and both adopted it in order to transcend it and attack the consequences which the Sophist had drawn from it. Both admit that perception, as being itself only a product of a natural process, can be the knowledge of something only which likewise arises and passes away as transitory product of the same natural process. Perception then gives only opinion (δόξα); it teaches what appears in and for human view (called νόμῳ in Democritus with a genuine Sophistic mode of expression), not what *truly* or really (ἐτεῇ with Democritus, ὄντως with Plato) is.

For Protagoras, who regarded perception as the only source of knowledge, there was consequently no knowledge of what is. That he took the farther step of denying Being altogether and declaring the objects of perception to be the sole reality, behind which there is no Being to be sought for, — this "positivist" conclusion is not to be demonstrated in his case : the doctrine of "nihilism" ("there is no Being") is expressly ascribed by tradition only to Gorgias.

If, nevertheless, from any grounds whatever, a universally valid knowledge (γνησίη γνώμη with Democritus, ἐπιστήμη with Plato) was to be again set over against opinions, the sensualism of Protagoras must be abandoned and the position of the old metaphysicians, who distinguished *thought* (διάνοια), as a higher and better knowledge, from perception, must be taken again (cf. § 6). Thus Democritus and Plato both in like manner transcend Protagoras by acknowledging the relativity of perception, and looking to "thought" again for knowledge of what truly is. Both are outspoken *rationalists.*[1]

2. This new metaphysical rationalism is yet distinguished from the older rationalism of the cosmological period, not only by its broader psychological basis, which it owed to the Protagorean analysis of perception, but also in consequence of this, by another *valuation of perception itself from the standpoint of the theory of knowledge.* The earlier metaphysicians, where they could not fit the contents of perception into their conceptional idea of the world, had simply rejected them as deceit and illusion. Now this illusion had been explained (by Protagoras), but in such a way that while surrendering its universal validity the content of perception might yet claim at least the value of a *transient and relative reality.*

This, in connection with the fact that scientific knowledge was

---

[1] Cf. Sext. Emp. *Adv. Math.* VIII. 56. The doctrine of Democritus with regard to "genuine" knowledge is most sharply formulated in Sext. Emp. *Adv. Math.* VII. 139. Plato's attack upon the Protagorean sensualism is found principally in the *Theætetus,* his positive rationalistic attitude in the *Phædrus, Symposium, Republic,* and *Phædo.*

directed toward the abiding "true" Being, led to a *division in the
conception of reality*, and with this the fundamental need of explanatory thought came to clear, explicit consciousness, — a need which
unconsciously lay at the basis of the beginnings of science. To the
two kinds of knowledge — so Democritus and Plato taught — correspond *two different kinds of reality :* to perception a changing,
relative, transient reality or actuality; to thought a reality homogeneous, absolute and abiding. For the former Democritus seems
to have introduced the expression phenomena; Plato designates it
as the world of generation, γένεσις : the other kind of reality Democritus calls τὰ ἐτεῇ ὄντα ; Plato, τὸ ὄντως ὄν or οὐσία [that which *really*
is, or essence].

In this way perception and opinion gain a correctness which is
analogous to that of scientific thought. Perception cognises changing reality as thought cognises abiding reality. To the two modes
of cognition correspond two domains of reality.[1]

But between these two domains there exists for this reason the
same *relation, as regards their respective values*, as obtains between
the two kinds of cognition. By as much as thought, the universally
valid act of consciousness, is above perception, the knowledge valid
only for individuals and for the particular, by so much is the true
Being higher, purer, more primitive, raised above the lower actuality
of phenomena and the changing processes and events among them.
This relation was especially emphasised and carried out by Plato
for reasons hereafter to be unfolded. But it appears also with Democritus, not only in his theory of knowledge, but also in his ethics.

In this way the two metaphysicians agree with the result which
the Pythagoreans (cf. § 5, 7, and § 6, 1) had likewise won from
their premises, viz. the distinction of a higher and lower kind of
reality. Nevertheless, in the presence of this similarity we are not
to think of a dependence; in nowise in the case of Democritus,
who was a complete stranger to the astronomical view of the Pythagoreans, and scarcely in the case of Plato, who indeed later adopted
the astronomical theory, but whose idea of the higher reality (the
doctrine of Ideas) has an entirely different content. The case
rather is that the common, fundamental motive which came from
the conception of Being propounded by Parmenides, led in these
three quite different forms to the division of the world into a
sphere of higher and one of lower reality.

3. The *pragmatic parallelism* in the motives of the two opposed
systems of Democritus and Plato reaches a step farther, although

---

[1] Best formulated in Plat., *Tim.* 27 D ff., especially 29 C.

but a short step. To the world of perception belong, without doubt, the specific qualities of the senses, for these disclose their relativity in the fact that the same thing appears differently to different senses. But after we have abstracted these qualities, that which remains as an object for the knowledge of the truly actual, is primarily the *form* which things have, and both thinkers designated as the true essential nature of things the pure *forms* (ἰδέαι).

But it almost seems as though here they had nothing in common but the name, striking as this fact is; for if Democritus understood by the ἰδέαι, which he also called σχήματα, his atom-forms, while Plato understood by his ἰδέαι or εἴδη the conceptions corresponding to logical species (*Gattungsbegriffe*), then the apparently like statement that the truly existent consists in "forms" has a completely different meaning in the two authors. For this reason we must here, too, remain in doubt as to whether we should see a parallel dependence upon *Pythagoreanism*, which, to be sure, had previously found the essence of things in mathematical forms, and whose influence upon the two thinkers may be assumed without encountering any difficulties in the assumption itself. At all events, however, if a common suggestion was present, it led to quite different results in the two systems before us, and though in both of them knowledge of mathematical relations stands in very close relation to knowledge of true reality, these relations are yet completely different with the respective thinkers.

4. The relationship thus far unfolded between the two rationalistic systems changes now suddenly to a sharp opposition as soon as we consider the motives from which the two thinkers transcended the Protagorean sensualism and relativism, and observe also the consequences which result therefrom. Here the circumstance becomes of decisive importance, that *Plato was the disciple of Socrates*, while Democritus experienced not even the slightest influence from the great Athenian sage.

With Democritus the demand which drives him to transcend the position of Protagoras grows solely out of his theoretical need and develops according to his personal nature, — the demand, namely, that there is a knowledge, and that this, if it is not to be found in perception, must be sought for in thought; the investigator of Nature believes, as against all the Sophistic teaching, in the possibility of a theory that shall explain phenomena. Plato, on the contrary, sets out with his postulate of the Socratic conception of virtue. Virtue is to be gained only through right knowledge; knowledge, however, is cognition of the true Being: if, then, this is not to be found in perception, it must be sought for through thought. For

Plato philosophy grows, according to the Socratic principle,[1] out of the ethical need. But while the Sophistic friends of Socrates were endeavouring to give to the knowledge that constituted virtue some object in the form of a general life-purpose, the good, pleasure, etc., Plato wins his metaphysical position with one stroke, by drawing the inference that this knowledge in which virtue is to consist must be the cognition of what is truly real, the οὐσία, — as opposed to opinions which relate to the relative. In his case the knowledge in which virtue is to consist demands a metaphysics.

Here, then, the ways are already parting. Knowledge of the truly real was for Democritus, as for the old metaphysicians, essentially an idea of the unchangeably abiding Being, but an idea by means of which it should be possible to understand the derivative form of reality which is cognised in perception. His rationalism amounted to an *explanation of phenomena*, to be gained through thought; it was *essentially theoretical rationalism*. For Plato, on the contrary, knowledge of the truly real had its ethical purpose within itself; this knowledge was to constitute virtue, and hence it had no other relation to the world given through perception than that of sharply defining its limits. True Being has for Democritus the theoretical value of explaining phenomena; for Plato, the practical value of being the object of that knowledge which constitutes virtue. His doctrine is, as regards its original principle, *essentially ethical rationalism*.

Democritus, therefore, persevered in the work undertaken in the school of Abdera, — the construction of a metaphysics of Nature. With the help of the Sophistic psychology he developed *Atomism* to a comprehensive system. Like Leucippus, he regarded empty space and the atoms moving in it as the true reality. He then attempted not only to explain from the motion of these atoms all qualitative phenomena of the corporeal world as quantitative phenomena, but also to explain from these motions all mental activities, including that knowing activity which is directed toward true Being. Thus he created the *system of materialism*.

Plato, however, was led to the entirely opposite result by his attachment to the Socratic doctrine, which proved to be of decisive importance for his conception of the essential nature of science.

5. Socrates had taught that knowledge consists in *general conceptions*. If, however, this knowledge, in contrast with opinions, was to be knowledge of what truly, actually is, there must belong to the content of these conceptions that higher Being, that true essential

---

[1] Set forth most clearly in the *Meno*, 96 ff.

reality which, it was held, could be grasped only by thought, in contrast with perception. The "forms" of true reality, knowledge of which constitutes virtue, are the *species* or *class-concepts* (*Gattungsbegriffe*), εἴδη. With this consideration, the Platonic conception of the "Idea" first gains its complete determination.

So understood, Plato's *doctrine of Ideas* presents itself as the summit of Greek philosophy. In it are combined all the different lines of thought which had been directed toward the physical, the ethical, the logical first principle (ἀρχή or φύσις). The Platonic Idea, the species or class-concept, is firstly the abiding Being in the change of phenomena; secondly, the object of knowledge in the change of opinions; thirdly, the true end in the change of desires.

But this οὐσία, from the nature of its definition, is not to be found within the sphere of what may be perceived, and everything corporeal is capable of being perceived. The Ideas are then something essentially different from the corporeal world. True reality is incorporeal. The division in the conception of reality takes on accordingly a fixed form; the lower reality of natural processes or generation (γένεσις), which forms the object of perception, is the corporeal world; the higher reality of Being, which thought knows, is the incorporeal, the immaterial world, τόπος νοητός. Thus the Platonic system becomes *immaterialism,* or, as we call it after the meaning given by him to the word "Idea," *Idealism.*

6. In the Platonic system, accordingly, we find perhaps the most extensive interweaving and complication of problems which history has seen. The doctrine of Democritus, on the contrary, is ruled throughout by the one interest of explaining Nature. However rich the results which this latter doctrine might achieve for this its proper end, — results which could be taken up again in a later, similarly disposed condition of thought, and then first unfold their whole fruitfulness, — at first the other doctrine must surpass this, all the more in proportion as it satisfied all needs of the time and united within itself the entire product of earlier thought. More points of attack for immanent criticism are perhaps offered by the Platonic system than by that of Democritus; but for Greek thought the latter was a relapse into the cosmology of the first period, and it was Plato's doctrine that must become the system of the future.

§ 10. The System of Materialism.

The systematic character of the doctrine of Democritus consists in the way in which he carried through in all departments of his work the fundamental thought, that scientific theory must so far gain knowledge of the true reality, *i.e.* of the atoms and their motions in space, as to be able to explain from them the reality which appears in phenomena, as this presents itself in perception. There is every indication (even the titles of his books would show this) that Democritus took up this task by means of investigations covering the entire compass of the objects of experience, and in this connection devoted himself with as great an interest to the psychological as to the physical problems. So much the more must we regret that the greater part of his teachings has been lost, and that what is preserved, in connection with accounts of others, permits only a hypothetical reconstruction of the main conceptions of his great work, a reconstruction which must always remain defective and uncertain.

1. It must be assumed in the first place that Democritus was fully conscious of this task of science, viz. that of explaining the world of experience through conceptions of the true reality. That which the Atomists regard as the Existent, viz. space and the particles whirring in it, has no value except for theoretical purposes. It is only thought in order to make intelligible what is perceived; but for this reason the problem is so to think the truly real that it may explain the real which appears in phenomena, that at the same time this latter reality may "remain preserved"[1] as something that "is" in a derived sense, and that the truth which inheres in it may remain recognised. Hence Democritus knew very well that thought also must seek the truth in perception, and win it out of perception.[2] His rationalism is far removed from being in contradiction with experience, or even from being strange to experience. Thought has to infer from perception that by means of which the latter is explained. The motive which lay at the foundation of the mediating attempts following the Eleatic paradox of acosmism became with Democritus the clearly recognised principle of metaphysics and natural science. Yet unfortunately nothing is now known as to how he carried out in detail the methodical relation between the two modes of cognition, and how the process by which knowledge grows out of perception in the particular instance was thought by him.

More particularly, the theoretical explanation which Democritus

---

[1] The very happy expression for this is διασώζειν τὰ φαινόμενα. Cf. also Arist. *Gen. et Corr.* I. 832, 5 a.

[2] Hence, the expressions in which he recognised the truth in the phenomenon; *e.g.* Arist. *De An.* I. 2, 404 a 27, and the like. To attempt, however, to construe out of this a "sensualism" of Democritus, as has been attempted by E. Johnson (Plauen, 1868), contradicts completely the accounts with regard to his attitude toward Protagoras.

gave for the contents of perception consists, as with Leucippus, in the *reduction of all phenomena to the mechanics of atoms.* What appears in perception as qualitatively determined, and also as involved in qualitative change (ἀλλοιούμεμον), exists " in truth " only as a quantitative relation of the atoms, of their order, and their motion. The task of science is then to *reduce all qualitative to quantitative relations,* and to show in detail what quantitative relations of the absolute reality produce the qualitative characteristics of the reality which appears in phenomena. Thus, the *prejudice in favour of what may be perceived or imaged (anschaulich)*, as if spatial form and motion were something simpler, more comprehensible in themselves, and less of a problem than qualitative character and alteration, is made the principle for the theoretical explanation of the world.

Since this principle is applied with complete systematic rigour to the whole of experience, Atomism regards the *psychical life* with all its essential elements and values as also a *phenomenon,* and the form and motion of the atoms which constitute the true Being of this phenomenon must be stated by the explanatory theory. Thus matter in its form and motion is regarded as that which alone is truly real, and the entire mental or spiritual life as the derived, phenomenal reality. With this the system of Democritus first assumes the character of conscious, outspoken *materialism.*

2. In the properly *physical* doctrines, the teaching of Democritus presents, therefore, no change in principle as compared with that of Leucippus, though there is a great enrichment by careful detailed investigation. He emphasised still more sharply than his predecessor, where possible, the thought of the mechanical necessity (ἀνάγκη, which he also occasionally called λόγος), in accordance with which all occurrence or change whatever takes place, and further defined this thought as involving that no operation of atoms upon one another is possible except through impact, through immediate contact, and further, that this operation consists only in the change of the state of motion of the atoms which are also unchangeable as regards their form.

The atom itself as that which " is," in the proper sense of the word, has accordingly only the characteristics of abstract corporeality, viz. the filling of a limited space, and the quality of being in motion in the void. Although all are imperceptibly small, they yet exhibit an endless variety of forms (ἰδέαι or σχήματα). To form, which constitutes the proper fundamental difference in the atoms, belongs in a certain sense also size; yet it is to be observed that the same stereometrical form, *e.g.* the sphere, may appear in different sizes. The larger the atom, the greater its mass; for the essential quality of what is, is indeed materiality, space-claiming. For this reason Democritus asserted weight or lightness to be a function of size,[1] evidently yielding to the mechanical analogies of daily life. In connection with these terms (βαρύ and κοῦφον), however, we are not to think of the falling motion, but solely of the *degree of mechanical movability* or of *inertia*.[2] Hence it was also his opinion that as the atom-complexes whirled about, the lighter parts were forced outward, while the more inert with their inferior mobility were gathered in the middle.

The same properties communicate themselves as metaphysical qualities to things which are composed of atoms. The form and size of things is produced by the simple summation of the form and size of the component atoms; though in this case, the inertia is not dependent solely upon the sum total of the magnitudes of the atoms, but upon the greater or less amount of empty space that remains between the individual particles when they are grouped together. The inertia depends therefore upon the less or greater degree of *density*. And since the ease with which particles may be displaced with reference to one another depends upon this interruption of the mass by empty space, the properties of *hardness* and softness belong also to the true reality that is known by thought.

All other properties, however, belong to things not in themselves, but only in so far as motions proceeding from things act upon the organs of perception; they are "states of perception as it is in process of qualitative change." But these states are also conditioned throughout by the things in which the perceived properties appear, and here the arrangement and the situation which the atoms have taken with reference to each other in the process of composition are of principal importance.[3]

While, then, form, size, inertia, density, and hardness are properties of things ἐτεῆ, *i.e.* in truth, all that is perceived in them by the individual senses as colour, sound, smell, taste, exists only νόμῳ or θέσει, *i.e.* in the phenomenon. This doctrine, when taken up anew in the philosophy of the Renaissance (cf. Part IV. ch. 2) and later, was

---

[1] As the most extensive exposition for this and for the following topic Theophr. *De Sens.* 61 ff. (*Dox.* D. 516) is to be compared.

[2] It is scarcely to be decided now whether the motion of their own, which Atomism ascribed to all the atoms as primitive and causeless, was thought of by Democritus as conditioned already by the size or mass, so that the greater had, even from the beginning, possessed less velocity. At all events, these determinations held good for him within the sphere of the mechanical operation of the atoms on one another. What is larger can be pushed with greater difficulty; what is smaller can be pushed more easily.

[3] Cf. Arist. *Gen. et Corr.* I. 2, 315 b 6.

designated as distinguishing between the *primary and secondary qualities of things,* and it is desirable to introduce this expression here, since it corresponds throughout to the metaphysical and epistemological sense in which Democritus made the Protagorean doctrine useful for his own purpose. While the Sophist would make all properties secondary and relative, Democritus admitted this only for the qualities perceived by special senses, and set over against these the quantitative determinations as primary and absolute. He therefore designated also as "genuine knowledge" the insight into the primary qualities to be won through thought, while, on the contrary, perception which is directed toward the secondary qualities he termed "obscure knowledge" (γνησίη — σκοτίη γνώμη).

3. The secondary qualities appear accordingly as dependent upon the primary; they are not, however, dependent upon these alone, but rather upon the action of these upon the percipient agent. But in the atomistic system that which perceives, the *mind or soul,* can consist only of atoms. To be more explicit, it consists, according to Democritus, of the same atoms which constitute also the essence of *fire:* namely, the finest, smoothest, and most mobile. These are indeed scattered also through the whole world, and in so far animals, plants, and other things may be regarded as animate, as having souls, but they are united in largest numbers in the human body, where in life a fire-atom is placed between every two atoms of other sorts, and where they are held together by breathing.

Upon this presupposition, then, analogous, as we see, to the older systems, Democritus built up his explanation of phenomena from the true essence of things. That is, perception, and with it the secondary qualities, arises from the action of things upon the fire-atoms of the soul. The reality which appears is a necessary result of the true reality.

In carrying out this doctrine Democritus took up and refined the theories of perception advanced by his predecessors. The effluxes (cf. above, § 6, 3) which proceed from things to set in motion the organs and through them the fire-atoms, he called *images* (εἴδωλα), and regarded them as infinitely small copies of the things. Their impression upon the fire-atoms is perception, and the similarity between the content of this perception and its object was held to be secured thereby. Since impact and pressure are the essence of all the mechanics of the atoms, *touch* is regarded as the most primitive sense. The special organs, on the contrary, were regarded as capable of receiving only such images as corresponded to their own formation and motion, and this theory of the *specific energy of the sense organs* was worked out very acutely by Democritus. From this it followed also that in case there were things whose effluxes could not act upon any one of the organs, these would remain imperceptible for the ordinary man, and for these perhaps "other senses" might be accessible.

This *theory of images* appeared very plausible to ancient thought. It brought to definite expression, and indeed to a certain extent explained, the mode of representing things which is still common for the ordinary consciousness, as if our perceptions were "copies" of things existing outside of us. If one did not ask further how things should come to send out such miniature likenesses of themselves into the world, he might think that he understood, by means of this theory, how our "impressions" can resemble things without. For this reason this theory at once attained the predominance in physiological psychology, and retained its position until after the beginnings of modern philosophy, where it was defended by Locke.

Its significance, however, for the conceptions in the system of Democritus, lies in this, that it was regarded as describing that motion of the atoms in which perception consists. It remained hidden from this materialism, which was such from principle, as well as from all its later transformations, that perception as a psychical activity is something specifically different from any and every motion of atoms, however determined. But in seeking out the individual forms of motion from which the individual perceptions of the special senses arise, the philosopher of Abdera caused many a keen observation, many a fine suggestion, to become known.

4. It is interesting now that the same fate befell the materialistic psychology of Democritus as had befallen the pre-Sophistic metaphysicians (cf. § 6): it, too, was obliged in a certain respect to obliterate again the epistemological contrast between perception and thought. Since, that is, all psychical life is regarded as motion of the fire-atoms,[1] and since the motion of atoms in the connected system of the universe is conditioned by contact and impact, it follows that *thought*, which knows the truly real, can be explained only from an *impression* which this truly real makes upon the fiery atoms, — explained therefore itself only through the efflux of such *images*. As a psychological process, therefore, thought is the same as perception, viz. impression of images upon fire-atoms; the only difference is that in the case of perception the relatively coarse images of the atom-complexes are active, while thought, which apprehends true reality, rests upon a contact of the fire-atoms with the finest images, with those which represent the atomic structure of things.

---

[1] Arist. *De An.* I. 2, 405 a 8.

Odd and fantastic as this sounds, the indications are yet all in favour of the supposition that Democritus drew this conclusion from the presuppositions of his materialistic psychology. This psychology knew no independent, internal mechanism of ideas or conscious states, but only an arising of ideas through the motion of atoms. Hence it regarded ideas that were evidently deceptive as also "impressions," and sought for these the exciting images. Dreams, *e.g.* were traced back to εἴδωλα which had either penetrated into the body in the waking state and on account of their weak motion had previously produced no impression, or had first reached the fiery atoms in sleep, evading the senses. A mysterious ("magnetic," or "psychic," we should say to-day) action of men upon one another appeared comprehensible on this hypothesis, and an objective basis was given to faith in gods and demons by assuming giant forms in infinite space from which corresponding images proceeded.

In correspondence with this Democritus seems to have thought of "genuine knowledge" as that motion of the fire-atoms which is produced by the impression of the smallest and finest images, — those which represent the atomic composition of things. This motion is, however, the most delicate, the finest, the gentlest of all — that which comes nearest to rest. With this definition the *contrast between perception and thought was expressed in quantitative terms* — quite in the spirit of the system. The coarse images of things as wholes set the fiery atoms into relatively violent motion and produce by this means the "obscure insight" which presents itself as perception; the finest images, on the contrary, impress upon the fiery atoms a gentle, fine motion which evokes the "genuine insight" into the atomic structure of things, *i.e.* thought. In consideration of this, Democritus commends the thinker to turn away from the world of the senses, quite in contrast with the mode of thought which would develop truth out of perception. Those finest motions assert their influence only where the coarser are kept back; and where too violent motions of the fiery atoms take place, the result is false ideation, the ἀλλοφρονεῖν.[1]

5. This same quantitative contrast of strong and soft, violent and gentle motion, was laid by Democritus at the *basis of his ethical theory* also.[2] In so doing he stood with his psychology completely upon the *intellectualistic* standpoint of Socrates in so far as he transposed the epistemological values of ideas immediately into ethical values of states of will. As from perception only that

---

[1] Theophr. *De Sens.* 58 (*Dox.* D. 515).

[2] The resemblance with the theory of Aristippus (§ 7, 9) is so striking, that the assumption of a causal connection is scarcely to be avoided. Yet it may be that we should seek for this rather in a common dependence upon Protagoras, than in the interaction of Atomism and Hedonism upon each other.

obscure insight follows which has for its object the phenomenon and not the true essence, so also the pleasure which arises from the excitation of the senses is only relative (νόμῳ), obscure, uncertain of itself, and deceitful. The true happiness, on the contrary, for which the wise man lives "according to nature" (φύσει), the εὐδαιμονία, which is the end (τέλος) and measure (οὖρος) of human life, must not be sought in external goods, in sensuous satisfaction, but only in that gentle motion, that tranquil frame (εὐεστώ), which attends upon right insight, upon the gentle movement of the fiery atoms. This insight alone gives to the soul measure and harmony (ξυμμετρία), guards it from emotional astonishment (ἀθαυμασία), lends it security and imperturbability (ἀταραξία, ἀθαμβία), — the ocean-calm (γαλήνη) of the soul that has become master of its passions through knowledge. True happiness is rest (ἡσυχία), and rest is secured only by knowledge. Thus Democritus gains as the cap-stone of his system his personal ideal of life, — that of pure knowledge, free from all wishes; with this ideal, this systematic materialism culminates in a noble and lofty theory of life. And yet there is in it also a tendency which characterises the morals of the age of the Enlightenment: this peace of mind resting upon knowledge is the happiness of an individual life, and where the ethical teachings of Democritus extend beyond the individual, it is friendship, the relation of individual personalities to one another, that he praises, while he remains indifferent as regards connection with the state.

§ 11. The System of Idealism.

The origin and development of the Platonic *doctrine of Ideas* is one of the most difficult and involved, as well as one of the most effective and fruitful, processes in the entire history of European thought, and the task of apprehending it properly is made still more difficult by the literary form in which it has been transmitted. The Platonic dialogues show the philosophy of their author in process of constant re-shaping: their composition extended through half a century. Since, however, the order in which the individual dialogues arose has not been transmitted to us and cannot be established absolutely from external characteristics, pragmatic hypotheses based on the logical connections of thought must be called to our aid.

1. In the first place there is no question that the opposition between Socrates and the Sophists formed the starting-point for Platonic thought. Plato's first writings were dedicated to an affectionate and in the main, certainly, a faithful presentation of the Socratic doctrine of virtue. To this he attached a polemic

against the Sophistic doctrines of society and knowledge marked by increasing keenness, but also by an increasing tendency toward establishing his own view upon an independent basis. The Platonic criticism of the Sophistic theories, however, proceeded essentially from the Socratic postulate. It admitted fully, in the spirit of Protagoras, the relativity of all knowledge gained through perception, but it found just in this the inadequacy of the Sophistic theory for a true science of ethics.[1] The knowledge which is necessary for virtue cannot consist in opinions as they arise from the changing states of motion in subject and object, nor can it consist of a rational consideration and legitimation of such opinions gained by perception;[2] it must have a wholly different source and wholly different objects. Of the corporeal world and its changing states — Plato held to this view of Protagoras in its entirety — there is no science, but only perceptions and opinions; it is accordingly an *incorporeal world* that forms the object of science, and this world must exist side by side with the corporeal world as independently as does knowledge side by side with opinion.[3]

Here we have for the first time the claim of an *immaterial reality*, brought forward expressly and with full consciousness, and it is clear that this springs from the ethical need for a knowledge that is raised above all ideas gained by sense-perception. The assumption of immateriality did not at first have as its aim, for Plato, the explanation of phenomena : its end was rather to assure an object for ethical knowledge. The idealistic metaphysics, therefore, in its first draft[4] builds entirely upon a new foundation of its own, without any reference to the work of earlier science that had been directed toward investigating and understanding phenomena; it is an *immaterial Eleatism*, which seeks true Being in the Ideas, without troubling itself about the world of generation and occurrence, which it leaves to perception and opinion.[5]

To avoid numerous misunderstandings[6] we must, nevertheless, expressly point out that the Platonic conception of immateriality (ἀσώματον) is in nowise coincident with that of the spiritual or psychical, as might be easily assumed from the modern mode of thinking. For the Platonic conception the particular psychical

---

[1] On this point, the *Theætetus* brings together the whole criticism of the Sophistic doctrine.

[2] δόξα ἀληθὴς μετὰ λόγου, *Theæt.* 201 E. (Probably a theory of Antisthenes.)

[3] Arist. *Met.* I. 6, 987 a 32 ; XIII. 4, 1078 b 12.

[4] As set forth in the dialogues *Phædrus* and the *Symposium.*

[5] Investigations as to theoretical and natural science are first found in the latest dialogues.

[6] To which the Neo-Pythagorean and Neo-Platonic transformation of the doctrine of Ideas gave occasion. Cf. Pt. II. ch. 2, § 18.

functions belong to the world of Becoming, precisely as do those of
the body and of other corporeal things; and on the other hand, in
the true reality the "forms" or "shapes" of corporeality, the Ideas
of sensuous qualities and relations, find a place precisely as do those
of the spiritual relations. The identification of spirit or mind and
incorporeality, the division of the world into mind and matter, is un-
Platonic. The incorporeal world which Plato teaches is not yet the
spiritual.

Rather, the Ideas are, for Plato, *that incorporeal Being which is
known through conceptions.* Since, that is, the conceptions in which
Socrates found the essence of science are not given as such in the
reality that can be perceived, they must form a "second," "other"
reality, different from the former, existing by itself, and this immaterial reality is related to the material, as Being to Becoming, as the
abiding to the changing, as the simple to the manifold — in short,
as the world of Parmenides to that of Heraclitus. The object of
ethical knowledge, cognised through general conceptions, is that
which "is" in the true sense: the ethical, the logical, and the physical ἀρχή (ground or first principle) are the same. This is the point
in which all lines of earlier philosophy converge.

2. If the Ideas are to be "something other" than the perceptible world, knowledge of them through conceptions cannot be found
in the content of perception, for they cannot be contained in it.
With this turn of thought, which corresponds to the sharper separation of the two worlds, the Platonic doctrine of knowledge becomes
much more rationalistic than that of Democritus, and goes also
decidedly beyond that of Socrates; for while the latter had developed the universal out of the opinions and perceptions of individuals
inductively, and had found it as the common content in these opinions and perceptions, Plato does not conceive of the process of
induction in this analytical manner, but sees in perceptions only the
suggestions or promptings with the help of which the soul *bethinks
itself* of the conceptions, of the knowledge of the Ideas.

Plato expressed this rationalistic principle in the form that *philosophical knowledge is recollection* (ἀνάμνησις). He showed in the
example of the Pythagorean proposition[1] that mathematical knowledge is not extracted from sense-perception, but that sense-perception offers only the opportunity on occasion of which the soul
recollects the knowledge already present within her, that is, knowledge that has purely rational validity. He points out that the pure
mathematical relations are not present in corporeal reality; on the

---

[1] *Meno,* 80 ff.

contrary, the notion of these relations arises in us when similar figures of perception offer but the occasion therefor, and he extended this observation, which is completely applicable to mathematical knowledge, to the sum total of scientific knowledge.

That this reflection upon what is rationally necessary should be conceived of as recollection is connected with the fact that Plato, as little as any of his predecessors, recognises a creative activity of the consciousness, which produces its content. This is a general limit for all Greek psychology; the content for ideas must somehow be given to the "soul"; hence, if the Ideas are not given in perception, and the soul nevertheless finds them in herself on occasion of perception, she must have already *received* these Ideas in some way or other. For this act of reception, however, Plato finds only the mythical representation,[1] that before the earthly life the souls have *beheld* the pure forms of reality in the incorporeal world itself, that the perception of similar corporeal things calls the remembrance back to those forms forgotten in the corporeal earthly life, and that from this awakes the *philosophical impulse,* the *love of the Ideas* (ἔρως), by which the soul becomes raised again to the knowledge of that true reality. Here, too, as in the case of Democritus, it is shown that the entire ancient rationalism could form no idea of the process of thought except after the analogy of sensuous perception, particularly that of the sense of sight.

What Socrates in his doctrine of the formation of conceptions had designated as induction, became transformed, therefore, for Plato, into an intuition that proceeds by recollecting (συναγωγή), into reflection upon a higher and purer perception (*Anschauung*). This pure perception, however, yields a plurality of ideas corresponding to the multiplicity of objects which occasion such perceptions, and from this grows the further task for science to know also the *relations of the Ideas to each other.* This is a second step of Plato's beyond Socrates, and is specially important for the reason that it led shortly to the apprehension of the *logical relations between conceptions.* It was principally the relations of the subordination and co-ordination of concepts to which Plato became attentive. The division of the class-concepts or logical genera into their species played a great part in his teaching.[2] The possibility or impossibility of the union of particular conceptions is brought more exactly into

---

[1] *Phædr.* 246 ff.

[2] Cf. *Phileb.* 16 C. Yet this dividing process is not anywhere especially prominent in the writings that are certainly Platonic. It is handled with the pedantry of a school in the *Sophist* and *Politicus.* Antiquity preserved "definitions" and "divisions" from the Platonic school. In *Athenæus,* II. 59 C, is an instance of mockery, by a comic poet, at this academical concept-splitting.

consideration,[1] and as a methodical aid he recommended the hypothetical method of discussion, which aims to examine a tentatively proposed conception by developing all the possible consequences that would follow from the possibility of its union with conceptions already known.

These logical operations taken as a whole, by means of which the Ideas and their relations to one another (κοινωνία) were to be found, Plato denoted by the name *dialectic*. What is found in his writings concerning it has throughout a methodological character, but is not properly logical.

3. The doctrine of knowledge as recollection stood, however, in closest connection with Plato's conception of the *relation of Ideas to the world of phenomena*. Between the higher world of οὐσία and the lower world of γένεσις, between what *is* and what is in process of Becoming, he found that relation of similarity which exists between archetypes (παραδείγματα) and their copies or images (εἴδωλα). In this, too, a strong influence of mathematics upon the Platonic philosophy is disclosed: as the Pythagoreans had already designated things as imitations of numbers, so Plato found that individual things always correspond to their class-concepts only to a certain degree, and that the class-concept is a logical ideal which none of its empirical examples comes up to. He expressed this by the conception of *imitation* (μίμησις). It was thus at the same time established that that second world, that of the incorporeal Ideas, was to be regarded as the higher, the more valuable, the more primitive world.

Yet this mode of representing the matter gave rather a determination of their respective values than a view that was usable for metaphysical consideration: hence Plato sought for still other designations of the relation. The logical side of the matter, according to which the Idea as class-concept or species represents the total unitary extent or compass, of which the individual things denote but a part, appears in the expression *participation* (μέθεξις), which means that the individual thing but partakes in the universal essence of the Idea; and the changing process of this partaking is emphasised by the conception of *presence* (παρουσία). The class-concept or species is present in the thing so long as the latter possesses the qualities which dwell in the Idea. The Ideas come and go, and as these now communicate themselves to things and now again withdraw, the qualities in these things which are like the Ideas are successively changed to the eye of perception.

The precise designation of this relation was, for Plato, an object

---

Phædo, 102 ff.

of only secondary interest, provided only the difference between the world of Ideas and the corporeal world, and the dependence of the latter upon the former, were recognised.[1] Most important and sufficient for him was the conviction that by means of conceptions that knowledge which virtue needs of what truly and really *is*, could be won.

A. Peipers, *Ontologia Platonica.* Leips. 1883.

4. But the logico-metaphysical interest which Plato grafted upon the Socratic doctrine of knowledge carried him far beyond the master as regards the contents of this doctrine. The general characteristics which he developed for the essence of the Ideas applied to *all class-concepts*, and the immaterial world was therefore peopled with the archetypes of the entire world of experience. So many class-concepts, so many Ideas; for Plato, too, there are countless "forms." In so far criticism[2] was right in saying that Plato's world of Ideas was the world of perception thought over again in conception.

In fact, according to the first draft of the Platonic philosophy, there are Ideas of everything possible, of things, qualities, and relations; of the good and the beautiful as well as of the bad and the ugly. Since the Idea is defined methodologically, in a purely formal way, as class-concept, every class-concept whatever belongs to the higher world of pure forms; and in the dialogue *Parmenides*,[3] not only was Plato's attention called by a man schooled in the Eleatic Sophistic doctrine to all kinds of dialectical difficulties which inhere in the logical relation of the one Idea to its many copies, but he was also rallied, spitefully enough, with the thought of all the foul companions that would be met in his world of pure conceptual forms.

Plato's philosophy had no principle that could serve as a weapon against such an objection, nor is there in the dialogues any intimation that he had attempted to announce a definite criterion for the *selection* of those class-concepts that were to be regarded as Ideas, as constituents of the higher incorporeal world. Nor do the examples which he adduces permit such a principle to be recognised; we can only say that it seems as if in course of time he continually emphasised more strongly the attributes expressing worth (as the good and the beautiful), the mathematical relations (greatness and smallness, numerical determinations, etc.), and the types of species in the organic world, while, on the contrary, he no longer reckoned

---

[1] *Phædo,* 100 D.   [2] Arist. *Met.* I. 9, 990 b 1.   [3] *Parm.* 130 C.

among the Ideas mere concepts of relation, especially negative notions and things made by human art.[1]

5. Our knowledge of the *systematic connection and order* which Plato intended to affirm in the realm of Ideas remains ultimately as obscure as that in regard to the preceding point. Urgent as he was to establish co-ordination and subordination among the conceptions, the thought of a logically arranged pyramid of conceptions which must culminate in the conception that was most general and poorest in content seems not to have been carried out. A very problematical attempt to set up a limited number (five) of most general conceptions[2] is presented in the *Sophist* (254 ff.). But these attempts, which tend toward the Aristotelian doctrine of the categories, are not to be traced back with certainty to Plato himself.

With him we find, rather, only the doctrine presented in the *Philebus*, as well as in the *Republic*, that the *Idea of the Good* is the highest, embracing, ruling, and realising all others. Plato defines this Idea as regards its content as little as did Socrates; he determined it only by means of the relation, that it should represent in its content the highest *absolute end of all reality*, of the incorporeal as of the corporeal. The subordination of the other Ideas to this highest Idea is accordingly not the *logical* subordination of a particular under the general, but the *teleological* of the means to the end.

In the latest period of his philosophising, concerning which we have only intimations in the *Laws* and in critical notices of Aristotle,[3] and in the teachings of his nearest successors, the imperfection of this solution of the logical problem seems to have led Plato to the unfortunate thought of developing the *system of Ideas* according to the method of the *Pythagorean number-theory*. The Pythagoreans also, to be sure, had the purpose of attaching the abiding arrangements of things symbolically to the development of the number series. But that was only a makeshift, because they had as yet no idea of the logical arrangement of conceptions: hence, when Plato, in connection with his other thoughts, fell back upon this makeshift, designated the Idea of the Good as the ἕν, the One, and attempted to derive from it the duality (δυάς) of the Infinite or Indefinite, and the Measure (ἄπειρον and πέρας, = even and odd; cf. § 4, 11), and from this, further, the other Ideas in such a way as to present a series of the conditioning and the conditioned, neither

---

[1] Cf. also Arist. *Met.* XII. 3, 1070 c 18.

[2] Being, rest, motion, sameness (ταὐτότης) and otherness (ἑτερότης), *i.e.* the division of Being into the resting (οὐσία), ever the same with itself, and the moved (γένεσις), in process of constant change.

[3] Cf. A Trendelenburg, *Platonis de Ideis et Numeris Doctrina* (Leips. 1826).

this deplorable construction nor the fact that men like Speusippus, Xenocrates, Philippus, and Archytas undertook to carry it out in detail, would be worth more particular mention, were not this just the point to which the speculation of the Neo-Pythagoreans and the Neo-Platonists became attached. For by this gradation which Plato thus began within the οὐσία the world of true reality, the *division in the conception of reality,* which had developed out of the opposition between perception and thought, became *multiplied,* and thus dualism was again abolished. For when to the One, or the Idea of the Good, was ascribed the highest absolute reality, and to the various strata of the world of Ideas, a reality of constantly decreasing worth in proportion as they were removed from the One in the system in numbers, there arose from this a *scale of realities* which extended from the One down to the lowest reality, — that of the corporeal world. Fantastic as this thought may be, it yet evinced its force and influence in the development of thought, even to the threshold of modern philosophy. Its power, however, lies doubtless in all cases in its amalgamation of attributes of worth with these various grades of reality.

6. While as metaphysics, the doctrine of Ideas fell into such serious difficulties, it was carried out in an extremely happy, simple, and transparent manner in that domain which formed its proper home, —that of ethics. For the systematic elaboration of this, however, Plato needed a *psychology,* and that, too, of another sort than the psychology which had arisen in previous science, out of the presuppositions of natural philosophy, and with the aid of individual perceptions or opinions. When, in contrast with this, he developed his psychology from the postulates of the doctrine of Ideas, the result was of course a purely metaphysical theory which stood and fell with its postulate, yet it was at the same time, by reason of the import of the doctrine of Ideas, a first attempt to understand the psychical life from within, and in accordance with its internal character and articulation.

The conception of the *soul* or mind was in itself a difficulty[1] in the dualism of the doctrine of Ideas. For Plato, also, "soul" was on the one hand the living element, that which is moved of itself and moves other things, and on the other hand, that which perceives, knows, and wills. As principle of life and of motion, the soul belongs, therefore, to the lower world of Becoming, and in this it remains when it perceives and directs its desires toward objects of the senses. But this same soul, nevertheless, by its true knowledge

---

[1] *Phædo,* 76 ff., 105, *Phædr.* 245, *Laws,* X. 896.

of the Ideas, becomes partaker in the higher reality of abiding Being. Hence it must be assigned a *position between the two worlds* — not the timeless, unchanged essence of the Ideas, but a vitality which survives change; *i.e. immortality*. Here, for the first time, personal immortality is brought forward by Plato as a part of philosophic teaching. Of the proofs which the *Phædo* adduces for this, those are most in accord with the spirit of the system which reason from the soul's knowledge of Ideas to its relationship with eternity; in correspondence with the form of the system is the dialectic false conclusion that the soul cannot be or become dead, because its essential characteristic is life; the most tenable of the arguments is the reference to the unity and substantiality which the soul evinces in ruling the body.

In consequence of this intermediate position the soul must bear in itself the traits of both worlds; there must be in its essence something which corresponds to the world of Ideas, and something which corresponds to the world of perception. The former is the *rational nature* (λογιστικόν or νοῦς), the seat of knowledge and of the virtue which corresponds to it; in the latter, the irrational nature, Plato made a further distinction of two elements, — the nobler, which inclines towards the Reason, and the lower, which resists it. The nobler he found in the ardent, spirited Will (*Spirit*, θύμος), the lower in the sensuous desire (*Appetite*, ἐπιθυμία). Thus Reason, Spirit, and Appetite are the three forms of activity of the soul, the classes or species (εἴδη) of its states.

These fundamental psychological conceptions which had thus grown out of considerations of ethical worth are employed by Plato to set forth the moral destiny of the individual. The fettering of the soul to the body is at once a consequence and a punishment of the sensuous appetite. Plato extends the immortal existence of the soul equally beyond the two boundaries of the earthly life. The sin for the sake of which the soul is ensnared in the world of sense is to be sought in a pre-existent state;[1] its destiny in the hereafter[1] will depend upon how far it has freed itself in the earthly life from the sensuous appetite, and turned to its higher vocation — knowledge of the Ideas. But inasmuch as the ultimate goal of the soul appears to be to strip off the sensuous nature, the three forms of activity are designated also as *parts of the soul*. In the *Timæus* Plato even portrays the process of the formation of the soul out of these parts, and retains immortality for the rational part only.

---

[1] These doctrines are depicted in the form of mythical allegories which make use of motives from the popular faith and from the Mystery-cults. V. *Phædr.* 246 ff.; *Gorgias*, 523 ff.; *Rep.* 614 ff.; *Phædo*, 107 ff.

It is already clear from these changing determinations that the relation of these three fundamental forms of the psychical life to the none too strongly emphasised unity of the soul's nature was not clearly thought out; nor is it possible to give to these conceptions formed from the ethical need the significance of purely psychological distinctions, such as have since been made.[1]

7. But at all events there followed in this way, from the doctrine of the two worlds, a negative *morals* that would fly from the world, and in which the withdrawal from the world of sense and the spiritualisation of life were praised as ideals of wisdom. It is not only the *Phædo* that breathes this earnest disposition in its portrayal of the death of Socrates; the same ethical theory prevails in such dialogues as the *Gorgias*, the *Theœtetus*, and, in part, the *Republic.* But in Plato's own nature the heavy blood of the thinker was associated with the light heart-beat of the artist, and thus while his philosophy lured him into the realm of bodiless forms, the whole charm of Hellenic beauty was living and active within him. Strongly as he therefore combated root and branch the theory of Aristippus, which would fain regard man's strivings as satisfied with sensuous pleasure, it was nevertheless his opinion that the Idea of the Good becomes realised even in the world of sense. Joy in the beautiful, pleasure in the sensuous imitation of the Idea, painless because free from the element of wishing, the development of knowledge and practical artistic skill, the intelligent understanding of the mathematical relations which measure empirical reality, and the appropriate ordering of the individual life, — all these were valued by him as at least preparatory stages and participations in that highest good which consists in knowledge of the Ideas, and of the highest among them, the Idea of the Good. In the *Symposium* and in the *Philebus* he has given expression to this his estimate of the goods of life.

This same thought, that ethical values and standards must illumine the whole circuit of human life, was used in another form by Plato in that presentation of the system of the virtues which he developed in the *Republic.* Here he showed that each part of the soul has a definite task to fulfil, and so a perfection of its own to reach : the rational part, in *wisdom* (σοφία), the spirited (θυμοειδές) in *energy of will* (courage, ἀνδρία), the appetitive (ἐπιθυμητικόν) in

---

[1] That the question here for Plato was essentially that of the gradation of the psychical from the point of view of relative worth, is shown not only in the employment made of these distinctions in ethics and politics, but also in such remarks as those which designated this triple division as characteristic for the different organic beings (plant, animal, man), or for the different peoples, inhabitants of southern countries, of northern countries, and the Greeks.

self-control (moderation, σωφροσύνη) ; that, however, in addition to all these, as the virtue of the soul as a whole, there must be the right relation of these parts, complete *uprightness* (justice, δικαιοσύνη).

The true significance, however, of these *four cardinal virtues*, is first unfolded upon a higher domain, that of politics.

8. The tendency of the doctrine of Ideas, directed as it was toward the general and the universal, exhibited its most perfect operation in the aspect now to be noticed, viz. that the ethical ideal of the Platonic philosophy lay not in the ability and happiness of the individual, but in the ethical perfection of the *species*. True to the logical principle of the doctrine of Ideas, that which truly *is* in the ethical sense, is not the individual man, but mankind, and the form in which this truly existent humanity appears is the organic union of individuals in the *state*. The ethical ideal becomes for Plato the *political*, and in the midst of the time which saw the dissolution of Greek political life, and in opposition to those doctrines which proclaimed only the principle of individual happiness, he raised the conception of the state to an all-controlling height.

He considered the state, however, not from the side of its empirical origin, but in reference to its task, viz. that of presenting in large the ideal of humanity, and of educating the citizen to that particular virtue which makes him truly happy. Convinced that his project could be realised, with force if necessary, he wove into its fabric not only features which he approved of the then-existing Greek political life, in particular those of the aristocratic Doric constitutions, but also all the ideals for whose fulfilment he hoped from the right formation of public life.

K. F. Hermann, *Ges. Abhandlungen*, 122 ff. ; E. Zeller, *Vorträge und Abhandlungen*, I. 62 ff.

If the *ideal state* is to present man in large, it must consist of the three parts which correspond to the three parts of the soul, — the *teaching class*, the *warrior class*, and the *working class*. It belongs to the first class alone, that of the cultured (φιλόσοφοι), to guide the state and to rule[1] (ἄρχοντες), to give laws and to watch over their observance. The virtue proper to this class is wisdom, insight into that which is for the advantage of the whole, and which is demanded by the ethical aim of the whole. To support this class there is the second class, that of the public officials (ἐπίκουροι; guardians, φύλακες), which has to evince the virtue of the fearless performance of duty (ἀνδρία) as it maintains the order of the state within and without.

---

[1] Hence the λογιστικόν is called also ἡγεμονικόν.

It is, however, obedience which holds the desires in check, self-control (σωφροσύνη), that becomes the great mass of the people, the artisans and farmers (γεωργοὶ καὶ δημιουργοί), who have to care for providing for the external means of the states by their labour and industry.[1] Only when each class thus does its duty and maintains its appropriate virtue does the nature of the state correspond to the ideal of justice (δικαιοσύνη).

The principle of *aristocracy in education*, which is of decisive importance in the Platonic ideal of the state, appears most clearly in the provision that for the great mass of the third class only the ordinary ability of practical life is claimed, and in that this is regarded as sufficient for their purpose, while the education, which the state has the right and duty to take in hand itself in order to train its citizens for its own ends, is given only to the two other classes. By means of a constantly repeated process of selection continued from birth to the late years, the government causes the two upper classes to be continually renewed, strata by strata; and in order that no individual interest may remain to hold back these classes, who are properly the organs of the whole body, in the fulfilment of their task, they are to renounce family life and private property. Their lot is that of education by the state, absence of family relations, community of life and of goods. He who is to live for the ends of the whole, for the ethical education of the people, must not be bound to the individual by any personal interest. To this thought, which found its historic realisation in the sacerdotal state of the mediæval hierarchy, is limited whatever of communism, community of wives, etc., men have professed to discover in the Platonic teaching. The great Idealist carries out to its extreme consequences the thought that the end of human life consists in moral education, and that the entire organisation of a community must be arranged for this sole end.

9. With this a new relation between the world of ideas and the world of phenomena was discovered, and one which corresponded most perfectly to the spirit of the Platonic system: the Idea of the Good disclosed itself as the task, as the *end* (τέλος), which the phenomenon of human life in society has to fulfil. This discovery became of decisive importance for the final form taken by Plato's metaphysical system.

For, as first projected, the doctrine of Ideas had been precisely as incompetent as the Eleatic doctrine of Being to explain empirical reality. The class-concepts were held to give knowledge of the

---

[1] Hence the third part of the soul is called also the φιλοχρήματον.

absolute reality,[1] which, purely for itself, simple and changeless, without origin and imperishable, forms a world by itself, and, as in-corporeal, is separated from the world where things arise. Hence, as was demonstrated in the dialogue the *Sophist*,[2] in a keen polemic against the doctrine of Ideas, this doctrine formed no principle of motion, and therefore no explanation of facts, because it excluded from itself all motion and change.

But however little Plato's interests may have been directed toward this end, the conception of the Idea as true Being ultimately demanded, nevertheless, that the phenomenon should be regarded, not only as something other, something imitative, something that participated, but also as something dependent. It demanded that the *Idea be regarded as cause of occurrence and change* (αἰτία). But that which is itself absolutely unchangeable and immovable, and excludes every particular function from itself, cannot be a cause in the mechanical sense, but only in the sense that it presents the *end* for the sake of which the occurrence takes place. Here for the first time the relation between the two worlds of Being and Becoming (οὐσία and γένεσις) is fully defined; all change and occurrence exists for the sake of the Idea;[3] the Idea is the *final cause* of phenomena.

This foundation of *teleological metaphysics* Plato gives in the *Philebus* and in the middle books of the *Republic,* and adds at once a further culminating thought by introducing as the final cause of all occurrence, the world of Ideas as a whole, but in particular the high-est Idea, to which all the rest are subordinate in the sense of means to end, — the *Idea of the Good.* This, referring to Anaxagoras, he designates as the *World-reason* (νοῦς), or as the *deity*.[4]

Side by side with this *motif* taken from Anaxagoras, another of a Pythagorean nature appears with increasing force in a later form of the doctrine of Ideas, a *motif* in accordance with which the imperfection of the phenomenon is pointed out as in contrast with the true Being. This inadequacy, however, could not be derived from Being itself, and just as Leucippus, in order to understand plurality and motion, had declared that in addition to the Being of

---

[1] *Symp.* 211 B, αὐτὸ καθ' αὑτὸ μεθ' αὑτοῦ μονοειδὲς ἀεὶ ὄν.

[2] Page 246 ff. The doctrine there criticised, that of the ἀσώματα εἴδη, can in accordance with the individual verbal coincidences be only the Platonic; just this is a factor in the decision against the genuineness of the dialogue. Schleier-macher's hypothesis of a Megarian doctrine of Ideas, thought out to rescue the genuineness, has not shown itself tenable.

[3] *Phileb.* 54 C.

[4] Yet we are not to think in this case of personality, or of a spiritual being, but of the absolute ethical end or purpose of the world, the conception of the ἀγαθόν finding an exact definition as little as with Socrates. It is rather presup-posed as being the simplest, the most comprehensible in itself.

Parmenides the Not-being was also "real," or "actual," and existent, so Plato saw himself forced, with like logical consistency, for the purpose of explaining phenomena and the inadequacy which they show with reference to the Ideas, to assume beside the world of Being or of cause, *i.e.* the world of Ideas and the Idea of the Good, a *secondary or accessory cause* (ξυναίτιον) in that which has not the attribute of Being. Indeed, the parallelism in the two thinkers goes so far that this secondary cause, which is not Being (τὸ μὴ ὄν), is for Plato precisely the same as for Leucippus and Philolaus, viz. *empty space.*[1]

Space was then for Plato the "nothing" out of which the world of phenomena is formed for the sake of the Idea of the Good, or of the deity. This process of formation, however, consists in *taking on mathematical form;* hence Plato taught in the *Philebus* that the world of perception was a "mixture" of the "unlimited" (ἄπειρον), *i.e.* space, and of "limitation" (πέρας), *i.e.* the mathematical forms;[2] and that the cause of this mixture, the highest, divine world prin-ciple, was the Idea of the Good. Space assumes mathematical for-mation in order to become like the world of Ideas.

The importance which mathematics had possessed from the outset in the development of Plato's thought finds thus at last its metaphys-ical expression. The mathematical structures are the intermediate link, by means of which empty space, which *is* not, is able to imitate in phenomena the pure "forms" of the world of Ideas. Hence mathematical knowledge (διάνοια), as well as purely philosophical knowledge (ἐπιστήμη), has to do with an abiding essence (οὐσία), and is therefore comprised together with this, as rational knowledge (νόησις), and set over against knowledge of phenomena (δόξα). But occupying thus an intermediate place, it takes only the position of a last stage in the preparation for the wisdom of the "rulers," as set forth in the system of education in the *Republic.*

10. The metaphysical preliminaries were now given for what Plato ultimately projected in the *Timæus;* viz. *a sketch or rough draught of the philosophy of Nature,* for which, of course, true to his epistemological principle, he could not claim the worth of certainty, but only that of probability.[3] Since, that is, he was not in a position

---

[1] Under the influence of the Aristotelian terminology, this secondary cause has been designated as "matter" (ὕλη), and it is only recently that modern researches have made it clear that the Platonic "matter" is simply space. Cf. H. Siebeck, *Untersuchungen z. Philos. d. Gr.* (2 Aufl., Freiburg i. B. 1889).

[2] It is probable that in this case Plato transposed the *numbers* into the world of Ideas itself, but looked upon their representation in *geometrical* structures as the "limitation" added to space.

[3] The Platonic Physics is then hypothetical in like manner with that of Parmenides. Here, too, it would seem that regard for the demands of his dis-

to carry through dialectically, and establish in conceptions this project of explaining occurrence from the world's end or purpose, Plato gave an exposition of his *teleological view of Nature* in mythical form only, — a view intended only as an opinion, and not as science.

This view, nevertheless, takes a position sharply *opposed to the mechanical explanation of Nature*, and, as this latter is set forth, we can scarcely suppose that Plato had any other doctrine in mind than that of Democritus. In opposition to the theory which makes all kinds of worlds arise here and there from the "accidental" (meaning "purposeless" or "undesigned") meeting of "that which is in unordered, lawless motion," and perish again, he sets forth his own theory that there is only this one, most perfect and most beautiful cosmos, unitary in nature and unique as regards its kind, and that its origin can be traced only to a reason acting according to ends.

If, then, it is desired to form a theory concerning this origin, the ground of the world of phenomena must be sought in the telic relation of this world to the Ideas. This relation Plato expressed by the idea of a "*world-forming God*" (δημιουργός, demiurge) who formed or shaped out that which is not Being, *i.e.* space, "with regard to the Ideas." In this connection the Not-being is characterised as the indefinite plasticity which takes up all corporeal forms into itself (δεξαμένη), and yet at the same time forms the ground for the fact that the Ideas find no pure representation in it. This counter-working of the accessory cause, or of the individual accessory causes, Plato designates as *mechanical necessity* (ἀνάγκη). He takes up then the conception of Democritus as a particular *moment* into his physics, in order to explain by it what cannot be understood teleologically. Divine activity according to ends and natural necessity are set over against each other as explaining principles, on the one hand for the perfect, and on the other hand for the imperfect in the world of phenomena. Ethical dualism passes over from metaphysics into physical theory.

---

ciples was united with a polemical purpose. Hence there is found mingled in the *Timæus*, a dependence upon Democritus and a combating of his views, an attitude like that of Parmenides toward Heraclitus. Yet the distinction is not to be forgotten, that the Eleatic denied the reality of the world of phenomena, while Plato denied only that it could be known scientifically, *i.e.* through conceptions. In presenting his view, however, Plato goes into questions of astronomy, mechanics, chemistry, organic life, physiological psychology, finally even into those of medicine. He gives, therefore, a kind of compendious exposition of his opinions in matters of natural science, opinions which in detail are extraordinarily fantastic, and as compared with the exact ideas even of his time, inadequate ; and yet taken in their whole connection, in their relation to their central principle, they have exercised an effect extending far beyond the design of their author.

The characteristic fundamental thought of the Platonic as contrasted with the Atomistic physics is, that while Democritus conceived of the movements of the whole as mechanical resultants of the original states of motion of the individual atoms, Plato, on the contrary, regarded the *ordered motion of the universe as a whole*, as the primitive unit, and derived every individual change or occurrence from this purposively determined whole. From this thought sprang the strange construction of the conception of the *world-soul*, which Plato characterised as the single principle of all motions, and thus also of all determinations of form, and likewise of all activities of perception and ideation in the world.[1] In fantastic, obscure exposition he brought forward as the mathematical "division" of this world-soul, his astronomical theory, which was in the main closely connected with that of the younger Pythagoreans, but which was less advanced than theirs in its assumption that the earth stood still. The main criterion in this process of division was the distinction between that which remains like itself (ταὐτόν) and that which changes (θάτερον), — a contrast in which we easily recognise the Pythagorean contrast between the perfect stellar world and the imperfect terrestrial world.

A similar continuation of Pythagorean doctrine is contained in the Platonic *Timæus*, with reference also to the purely mathematical construction of the corporeal world. Here, too, the four elements are characterised according to the simple, regular, geometrical solids (cf. p. 46). But it is expressly taught that these *consist of triangular surfaces*, and those, too, of a right-angled sort, which are in part equilateral, in part so formed that the shorter side is half the length of the hypothenuse. The *limiting surfaces* of these solids, — tetrahedron, cube, etc., — may be thought of as composed of such right-angled triangles, and Plato would have the essence of space-filling, *i.e.* density or solidity of bodies, regarded as consisting in this composition of these limiting surfaces. By thus conceiving of physical bodies as purely mathematical structures, the metaphysical thought of the *Philebus* found expression also in physics, — the thought, namely, that the phenomenal world is a limitation of space formed in imitation of the Ideas. These triangular surfaces, which were, moreover, conceived of as being indivisible, have a suspicious similarity with the atomic forms (σχήματα) of Democritus.

---

[1] In this respect the *Timæus*, quite as does Democritus, characterises psychical differences by differences of motion, tracing, for example, right ideation to the ταὐτόν, merely individual perception to the θάτερον, etc. "Soul" is for the Greeks at the same time principle of motion and of perception, and just that (κινητικόν and αἰσθητικόν, Arist. *De An.* I. 2, 403 b 25), and even Plato makes the second characteristic dependent upon the first.

§ 12. The Aristotelian Logic.

The breadth of plan which appeared in the systems of the two great antipodal thinkers, Democritus and Plato, and in accordance with which their doctrines were methodically developed, made it indispensable that there should be not only a division of labour, but a separation of problems. The titles of the writings of Democritus make it probable that he proceeded clearly and definitely in this respect also. Plato, to be sure, conceived his literary activity essentially from the artist's point of view, but it is evident that in his activity as a teacher he did not fail to make that arrangement of problems for separate treatment which we miss in his dialogues. In his school the division of philosophy into dialectic, physics, and ethics became dominant.

If by dialectic in this connection we are to understand essentially the doctrine of Ideas in its metaphysical development, *Aristotle* made the great step in advance of prefacing the investigation of the subject-matter in all three departments with a preliminary study of the *essential nature of science*, a doctrine of the forms and laws of scientific thought. Even with the Sophists and Socrates reflection had begun upon the question, in what scientific activity properly consists, and the sharpened attention given to the inner processes had made it possible for the abstracting thinker to separate the general forms of the thought-process itself from the particular contents to which this process relates at different times. All these beginnings and attempts — for even with Plato it did not go beyond this — were comprehended by Aristotle in his *Logic*, and developed into a complete system in which we have before us the ripe self-knowledge of Greek science.

1. The immediate aim of the Aristotelian logic is, according to the express declarations of the philosopher, entirely *methodological*. The way is to be shown by which the goal of scientific cognition can be reached in all departments of knowledge. As in rhetoric the art of persuasion is taught, so in logic we are to learn the art of scientific investigation, cognition, and proof. For this reason Aristotle did not reckon logic, which was his greatest creation, among the philosophical disciplines themselves, but treated it in his lectures as a propædeutic, and for this reason his school regarded this study as the general instrument (ὄργανον) for all scientific work.

But this preparatory study itself was made a science by Aristotle. Instead of bringing forward rules of practical value in individual cases, as may well have been the case with the Sophists, instead of the general fixing of a principle which had been the service of

Socrates, he offers an examination of the thinking activity on all sides, a comprehensive examination of its regular forms.   He fulfils the methodological task by *formal logic.*

But in so doing it becomes evident that the knowledge of the forms of right thinking can be gained only from understanding the task of thought, and that in turn this task can be disclosed only from a definite idea of the general relation of knowledge to its object.   Thus the Aristotelian logic is connected in the most intimate manner with the metaphysical presupposition which lie at the basis of his treatment of the other disciplines also.   In its principle, it is thoroughly *epistemological.*

2. As such, however, it has its roots in the Socratic-Platonic doctrine of Ideas.   That which truly *is*, is the *general* or *universal*, and knowledge of this is the *conception*.   In this respect Aristotle always remained a Platonist.   What he combated in the system of his great predecessor [1] was only the *Eleatic assumption of absence of relation*, — absence of relation between general and particular, between Ideas and phenomena, between conceptions and perceptions; an absence of relation which, in spite of all his efforts, Plato had not overcome, even in the later phase of his teaching. Even as the final cause of occurrence the Ideas remained a world by themselves beside ($\pi\alpha\rho\acute{\alpha}$) the phenomena.   This tearing apart ($\chi\omega\rho\acute{\iota}\zeta\epsilon\iota\nu$) of essence and phenomenon, of Being and Becoming, is, in addition to special dialectical objections,[2] the object of the chief reproach which Aristotle brings against the doctrine of ideas. While Plato had made two different worlds out of the general which is known by the conception, and the particular which is perceived, the entire effort of Aristotle is directed toward removing again this division in the conception of reality, and discovering that relation between Idea and phenomenon which shall make conceptional knowledge able to explain what is perceived.

Out of this grows as the primary task for logic, that of recognising the true *relation between the general and the particular*, and hence this fundamental form of abstract or conceptional thought, which had been already recognised as fundamental by Socrates, stands in the centre of the Aristotelian logic.

---

[1] Principally in *Met.* I. 9, and XIII. 4.

[2] Of these, two are principally worthy of mention in passing.   The one argues, from the logical subordination which obtains among the Ideas, that everything that we perceive must be subsumed under a number of Ideas ; the other calls attention to the difficulty that the resemblance, which, according to this system exists between the Idea and the phenomenon, makes necessary still a higher general above both, etc., *in infinitum* ($\check{\alpha}\nu\theta\rho\omega\pi\sigma s$ — $\alpha\dot{v}\tau\acute{\alpha}\nu\theta\rho\omega\pi\sigma s$ — $\tau\rho\acute{\iota}\tau\sigma s$ $\check{\alpha}\nu\theta\rho\omega\pi\sigma s$).

The importance of this same relation grows out of still another course of thought. If Aristotle found any previous works that were preparatory for his theory of science, they consisted in the considerations of the Sophists with regard to the art (principally rhetorical) of *proof* and refutation. If now Aristotle asked how one can prove anything scientifically, *i.e.* in a manner universally valid and relating to true knowledge, he found that this could consist only in the *deduction of the particular from the general.* To prove scientifically means to state the grounds for the validity of what is asserted, and these are to be found only in the more general under which the particular is subsumed.

From this resulted the peculiar complication which constitutes the Aristotelian conception of science. The general, the Idea, is, as the true Being, the *cause* of occurrence and change. It is that, therefore, out of which and through which the perceived particular is to be *comprehended, conceived,* or *explained.* Science has to set forth how the perceived particular follows from the general which is known in conceptions. On the other hand, the general is in thought the *ground* by means of which and from which the particular is *proved.* Accordingly, conceiving or comprehending and proving are the same thing, viz. *deduction of the particular from the general.*

The scientific theory of Aristotle is accordingly concentrated in the conception of *derivation* or *deduction* (ἀπόδειξις). Scientific explanation of phenomena from true Being is the same logical process as scientific proof: namely, the deduction or derivation of what is given in perception from its general ground. Explaining and proving are therefore denoted by the same word, "deduction," and the right proof is that which takes as its ground the actual or real general cause of that which is to be proved.[1] It is, therefore, the task of science to exhibit the *logical necessity* with which the particular insight (of perception) follows from the general insight (of conception), and the particular phenomenon from the general cause.

This characterisation of the task of science, thus developed from metaphysical presuppositions, experienced an essential change in the progress of its author's investigations.

3. The most immediate task of logic, according to this, is to establish more exactly what *deduction* — *i.e.* on the one hand, *proof;*

---

[1] This definition of the conception of *scientific proof* is obviously directed against the *rhetorical* proof of the Sophists. In the art of persuasion, all proofs are welcome, however external they may remain to the true nature of the case, provided only they are formally sufficient to bring the hearer to assent. Scientific proof, however, should proceed from the inner, logical necessity of the case, and should therefore give at the same time insight into the true cause of what is to be proved.

on the other hand, *explanation* — properly is, or to set forth those forms in which thought cognises the *dependence of the particular upon the general.* This theory was given by Aristotle in the *Analytics*, the logical groundwork, which treats synthetically, in the first part, of the syllogism, in the second of deduction, proof, and conception. For in the process of analysing those activities of thought in which all deduction consists, there results as simple fundamental form the deduction of one proposition, one statement from another : *i.e.* the *inference or syllogism* (συλλογισμός).

The *doctrine of the syllogism* became thus the central point of the Aristotelian logic. To this points all that he taught (apparently only in the most general outlines) concerning the forms of thought which lie at the basis of the syllogism : out of it come all the points of view in his methodology.

The outlines of this doctrine, which form the basis of traditional logic even to this day, are the following. The syllogism is the deduction of a judgment from two other judgments. Since in a judgment one concept (the predicate) is affirmed of another concept (the subject), this affirmation can be grounded only by establishing the desired connection between the two by means of a third concept, the middle term (μέσον). This third concept must then stand in some relations with the other two, and these relations must be expressed in two judgments, which are called the premises (προτάσεις) of the syllogism. Inference, or drawing the conclusion, consists in the process of thought which, from the relations that one and the same concept (the middle term) sustains to two other concepts, discovers the relation of these two concepts to each other.

Agreeably to its general presuppositions, the Aristotelian doctrine of the syllogism fixed its attention upon but one of the possible relations existing between concepts, — the relation of the *subordination* of the particular under the general. The only question for this theory is always whether the one *concept* (the subject) should be subordinated to the other (the predicate) or not. The doctrine of the syllogism has to do only with the knowledge of those forms of thought according to which it is to be decided, with the help of an intermediate concept, *whether a subordination of one concept under another occurs or not.* This question Aristotle answered in an absolutely exhaustive manner ; in this consists both the abiding worth of his doctrine of the syllogism and also the limits of its significance.

In correspondence with the fact just noted, Aristotle treats in his *theory of the judgment* essentially only the two elements which come into consideration for this end : first, Quantity, which determines the kind of subordination of the subject to the predicate as regards extent, and yields the distinctions of general, particular, and singular judgments; and second, Quality, according to which this subordination is either affirmed or denied, and, therefore, the relation either of connection or of separation is asserted as existing between the respective extents of the two concepts.

The kinds or figures (σχήματα) of the syllogism are, therefore, essentially fixed by the manner in which the relations of subordination between the concepts, which are given in the premises, determine the subordination sought in the conclusion, — a relation which finds its external expression in the position of the middle term in the two premises, since this is either the subject of one premise and predicate of the other, or predicate of both, or subject of both. As the most valuable and primitive of these three figures, however, Aristotle consistently designated the first, because in it the principle of subordination is purely and clearly expressed, since the subject of the conclusion is subordinated to the middle term, and together with this, as falling within its compass, is subordinated to the predicate of the major.[1]

4. But by defining inference, and so deduction, proof, and explanation in this way, it followed that only propositions of a lesser degree of generality could be deduced from those of higher generality by means of this activity so essential to science. That is, by means of inference, we can never prove anything equally general with the premises, to say nothing of proving anything more general. The peculiar restriction of the ancient idea of the nature of thought, according to which thought can only apprehend and take apart what is given but can never produce anything new, makes its appearance in this feature of the Aristotelian logic. From this, however, it follows immediately that the deducing, proving, and explaining science may, indeed, in the individual case, be able to take that which has served as premise in the syllogism, and deduce it again as the conclusion of a still more general syllogism, but must, nevertheless, ultimately proceed from premises which are themselves capable of no further deduction, proof, and comprehension, of no reduction to middle terms. The truth of these ultimate premises is, therefore, *immediate* (ἄμεσα), not to be deduced, proved or comprehended. All deduction needs something primitive; all proof, a ground that cannot be proved; all explaining, something given which cannot be explained.

---

[1] The details cannot be developed here. Cf. in general, F. Kampe, *Die Erkenntnisstheorie des Aristoteles* (Leips. 1870); R. Eucken, *Die Methode der aristotelischen Forschung* (Berlin, 1872).

The apodictic, proving, and explaining activity of science has, therefore, a limit; the ultimate grounds of proof are not to be proved; the ultimate causes used in explaining are not to be explained. Hence if science is to fulfil its task, which consists in explaining the particular by means of the general, it must first press forward from the particular on to the general, in the case of which proving and explaining are forbidden by the nature of the case, because as immediately certain it asserts itself as not to be deduced and not to be proved. Hence the processes of deducing, proving, and explaining, in which the ultimate task of science consists, must be preceded by the searching out of the starting-points for deduction, of the ultimate grounds of proof, and of the highest principles of explanation. The activity of thought involved in this last process Aristotle calls *dialectic*, and has laid down its principles in the *Topics*.

This procedure of *searching out the grounds* is not, in the nature of the case, attended by the same " apodictic certainty," as is that of deducing consequences from the grounds, when the latter are once established. Investigation proceeds from the particular given in perception, and from the ideas current in customary opinion (ἔνδοξον), to find the general, from which the particular can then be proved and explained. *Investigation*, therefore, follows a direction the reverse of that taken by deduction; the latter is deductive, the former inductive,' *epagogic*. The latter proceeds, proving and explaining, from general to particular; the former, searching and testing, from particular to general.[1] Only the completed science is "apodictic"; science, in its process of coming into being, is epagogic.

In all these investigations and the contrasts that appear in them, the chief question for Aristotle is that with regard to judgments; but in connection with this he treats also *concepts*. As a judgment is proved or deduced, by being concluded from more general judgments, by means of the middle term, so a *concept is deduced or derived* by being formed from a more general concept (the next higher class or *genus*, γένος) by adding a particular characteristic mark or *difference* (διαφορά). This deduction of the concept is *definition* (ὁρισμός). As, however, the deduction of propositions ultimately presupposes most general premises, which cannot be further

---

[1] This relation of contrariety between deduction and inquiry Aristotle expressed in the statements that that which, as regards the nature of the thing, is the original (πρότερον τῇ φύσει), and therefore the general, is for human knowledge the later, that which must be acquired (ὕστερον πρὸς ἡμᾶς) ; and that, on the contrary, that which is for us the most immediate (πρότερον πρὸς ἡμᾶς), the particular, is, according to the true essence, the derivative, the later (ὕστερον τι φύσει).

proved, so, too, definition of lower concepts goes back ultimately to most general concepts which withdraw from all attempts at deduction and explanation.   These concepts, also, as well as the highest premises of proof, must be sought inductively;[1] and it seems as though Aristotle looked upon the propositions of highest generality as the elucidations of these most general concepts.

5. Among the text-books which Aristotle left, the two main logical treatises, the *Analytics* and the *Topics*, are those which are most nearly complete by far.[2] This may explain the fact that the logical demands which the Philosopher makes of science are developed so clearly and surely, while, on the other hand, his system as carried out in the form known to us, fulfils in but a lesser measure the expectations thus raised.

For evidently we should expect that a sure statement could be made as to what the Philosopher declared to be those immediately certain, highest propositions or concepts which were to be the result of investigation, and the starting-point of proof and explanation. If, however, we ask for these, we find ourselves in great embarrassment as regards the teaching of Aristotle.   Of general propositions there is but a single principle, the *principle of contradiction*,[3] which he set forth as an unprovable major premise, or highest principle for all proofs, partly in the purely logical setting that affirmation and denial of the same combination of concepts reciprocally exclude each other, partly in the metaphysical form that a thing cannot be the same and also not be the same.   But aside from this he prefers to call attention to the fact that every department of knowledge has its own ultimate presuppositions, and does not state these more exactly.

If, however, we seek for the highest concepts, — aside from the reference made here also to the particular nature of individual disciplines, — we have the choice between the four "principles" (ἀρχαί), or "causes," of the *Metaphysics*, and the "categories," which are designated as the fundamental forms of predication concerning what is, — a choice not decided by Aristotle.   In both cases we find ourselves already in the midst of the material as opposed to the formal elements of his teaching.

---

[1] Over against determination (πρόσθεσις), as the deduction of one concept from the higher by adding a new mark, stands therefore abstraction (ἀφαίρεσις) as process of formation of class-concepts, — a process which, by continually taking away individual characteristics, gains a concept poorer in contents, but wider in its extent.   Formation of concepts is, accordingly, with Aristotle, again completely analytic, while with Plato it had been intuitive.   Aristotle was the first to free himself from the optical analogy, in accordance with which the knowing process of thought had been conceived even by Democritus and Plato.

[2] In the case of the *Topics*, this completeness seems even to have been attained.   [3] *Met.* IV. 3 ff.

§ 13. The System of Development.

The impression of something completely new, which the logic of Aristotle makes, as contrasted with all that had previously appeared in Greek science, rests principally upon the capacity for *abstract thought*, presupposed in so high a degree by this separation of the general Forms of thought from every possible content — a separation that evinced his genius. This genius for the formation of conceptions by abstraction was evinced by Aristotle in all departments of his scientific work, and if the "Father of logic" became the philosophic teacher for two thousand years, he owes this success, first of all, to the sureness, clearness, and consistency with which he formed and defined his conceptions. He fulfilled the task set by Socrates, and in so doing created the language of science. The fundamental part of the scientific conceptions and expressions everywhere in use, even to the present time, goes back to his formulations.

With this inclination to abstraction is connected the further fact that Aristotle solved *the fundamental problem of Greek philosophy* — viz. how behind the changing multiplicity of phenomena a unitary and abiding Being is to be thought — by means of a *concept of relation*, that of *development*. His two great predecessors had still been seeking to assign a particular content to the conception of true Being. Democritus had regarded the atoms and their motion, Plato the Ideas and their final causation, as the causes of phenomena, — causes different from the phenomena themselves. Aristotle, however, determined the true reality — that which is — *as the essence which unfolds in the phenomena themselves*. He renounced the attempt to think out as the cause of phenomena something different from them (a second world), and taught that the Being of things which is known in conception possesses no other reality than the sum total of the phenomena in which it *realises* itself. So regarded, Being (οὐσία) takes on the character of the *essence* (τὸ τὶ ἦν εἶναι), which constitutes the one, only ground of its individual formations, but is real or actual only in these themselves, and *all phenomenal appearance* or coming into being becomes the *realisation of the essence*. This is the concept of relation by means of which Aristotle overcame the opposition of the Heraclitic and Eleatic metaphysics.

1. In particular, the process of development presents itself to Aristotle as the *relation of Form and Matter* (εἶδος, μορφή — ὕλη). Plato [1] had declared the world of phenomena to be a mixture of the

---

[1] The main outlines of the Aristotelian metaphysics develop in the simplest way from that phase of the Platonic metaphysics which is presented in the *Philebus* (cf. above, § 11, 9). Cf. J. C. Glaser, *Die Metaphysik des Aristoteles* (Berlin, 1841).

"unlimited" and of "limitation"; Aristotle holds to the observation that, in everything of the phenomenal world, formed matter lies before us. But for him this matter is, indeed, in itself indefinite, and yet not purely indifferent, empty space, but a corporeal substratum (ὑποκείμενον); for him, this form is not merely the mathematical limit, but the form determined as to its contents by the essence. The matter or material substratum is the possibility of that which, in the complete thing, has become actual or real by means of the form. In matter, therefore, the essential nature (οὐσία) is given only *potentially* (δυνάμει). First, and only by means of the form, does it exist in *reality* or *actuality* (ἐνεργείᾳ, *actu*). *Occurrence*, however, or the natural process, is that process in which the essence passes over from mere possibility, through form, into *actualisation*. The essence has not any second, higher reality beside and apart from the phenomena; it exists only in the succession of its phenomenal manifestations, by means of which it realises its own possibility. The universal is real or actual only in the particular; the particular *is* only because in it the universal realises itself.

With this transformation of the doctrine of Ideas, Aristotle solves the fundamental problem of the theoretical philosophy of the Greeks, viz. that of so thinking Being or what "*is*" that Becoming, or the process of Nature (*das Geschehen*), may be explained from it. From the Hylozoism of the Milesians on to the opposing theories of his two great predecessors, all standpoints of Greek metaphysics are contained as elements in this doctrine of Aristotle. The Being cognised in conception is the general essence, which realises itself in its particular phenomenal manifestations from potentiality on through form, and the process of this realisation is motion. Being is that which comes to existence in the processes of Nature. This self-realisation of the essence in the phenomena, Aristotle calls *entelechy* (ἐντελέχεια).

2. The central point of the Aristotelian philosophy lies, therefore, in this *new conception of the cosmic processes as the realisation of the essence in the phenomenon*, and the respect in which it is opposed to the earlier explanation of Nature consists therefore in *carrying through in conceptions the teleology* which Plato had only set up as postulate, and developed in mythical, figurative form. While the earlier metaphysics had looked upon the mechanical process of pressure and impact as the typical fundamental relation of the cosmic processes, Aristotle regarded as this typical relation the development of organisms and man's building or forming activity. From these two departments he took his examples when

he wished to elucidate the metaphysical character of the cosmic processes.[1]

Nevertheless, the relation of form and matter is not completely the same in these two kinds of purposive processes, and the difference between the two asserts itself everywhere in the carrying out of the Aristotelian fundamental thought. In the case of organic processes, matter and form are the two sides, separable only through abstraction, of one and the same reality identical from beginning to end; even in the germ which in the process of development brings the essence to its unfolding, the matter is already shaped internally by the form. In the case of artistic construction, on the contrary, the material which contains possibility exists at first by itself, and the work of the artist with its end in view is added later to produce the shape by means of motion.

In the latter case, therefore, the development is to be regarded under *four principles*. These are the *Matter*, the *Form*, the *End*, and the *Cause* of what comes to pass or comes to be.

In the former case, on the contrary, the three other principles, as set over against the Matter, are but different expressions for the same thing, since the Form constitutes the Cause and the Result of the process.

We find, accordingly, that when applied to the task of science, this fundamental relation of form and matter is carried out in a twofold way: on the one hand, *individual things* are regarded as self-realising forms; on the other hand, things in *relation to one another* are regarded, the one as matter, the other as form. These two applications of the fundamental principle go through the entire Aristotelian system side by side, and in the general principles of the system they sometimes so collide, that it is only by their separation that apparent contradiction can be cleared away.

3. The former point of view yields the result, that for the Aristotelian conception of the world, in contrast with both that of Democritus and that of Plato, the truly real is the *individual thing*, determined in itself by its form. To it, therefore, belongs primarily the name of *essence* or *substance* (οὐσία). But the essence develops and realises itself in individual determinations, which are partly its states (πάθη), partly its *relations* to other things[2] (τὰ πρός τι). Hence knowledge has these which belong to the thing (τὰ συμβεβηκότα) to predicate of it, while the individual thing itself cannot be predicated of anything else, *i.e.* in the proposition it can be only

---

[1] Aside from its discussion in the *Metaphysics*, this question is chiefly treated in the *Physics*.

[2] *Met.* XIV. 2, 1089 b 23.

subject and never predicate.[1] Of these modes in which substance manifests itself, or of the predicates that are possible with regard to it, Aristotle enumerates as *categories,* quantity (ποσόν), quality (ποιόν), relation (πρός τι), determination in space and time (ποῦ, ποτέ), action (ποιεῖν), and passion or passivity (πάσχειν) ; and in addition, also, position (κεῖσθαι) and condition (ἔχειν). This collection (making ten categories inclusive of substance), in which, perhaps, grammatical observations co-operated, is designed to present the *highest classes* or *genera* under which the contents of all possible ideas are to be subsumed. Yet Aristotle made no methodical use of this collection, and his doctrine of the categories acquired, there-fore, no importance in his metaphysics, aside from the above-noted relation of substance to its determinations.

When we consider how sharply Aristotle shaped out the scientific conception of substance in its logical and metaphysical character, it may appear strange at the first glance that he has announced neither a methodical principle nor a real principle applying to the nature of the thing, according to which it would be possible to de-cide what these truly existing individual things, in his sense of the word, are. It is clear only that, on the one hand, he did not regard as essence everything whatever that occasionally appears in ex-perience as a thing separate from others, and, on the other hand, that he ascribed this character to organic individuals, to individual men. It would be in the spirit of his teaching to suppose that he could have spoken of an " essence " only where an inner determina-tion of form constitutes the ground of the coherence of individual characteristics, where, therefore, the knowledge of this essence solves the problem of science — viz. to determine existent reality by the general conception — in so far as the abiding individual thing forms the class-concept for all its particular modes of appear-ing which show themselves in perception.

But the Socratic-Platonic view of the problem of science brought with it the consequence that Aristotle defined yet again the essence of the individual thing as that through which the individual thing belongs to its *class* or *species.* If substance, as contrasted with its perceptible phenomena and attributes, presents the universal, on the other hand the species (γένος, or again Platonically, εἶδος) is the universal that realises itself in the individual substances. Here, too, the same relation is repeated ; the species exists only in so far as it realises itself in individual things as their truly existing essence, and the individual thing exists only as the species comes to its phe

---

[1] *Analyt. Post.* I. 22, 83 a 24.

nomenal manifestation in it. Just for this reason the species also have the claim to the metaphysical significance of being essences (οὐσίαι). By this means the conception of substance with Aristotle contains a peculiarly changeable double meaning. The substances proper are individual things as determined in conception, but as a second kind of substances (δεύτεραι οὐσίαι) [1] we have the species which constitute the essence of individual things, just as these latter constitute the essence of perceptible phenomena.

Scientific knowledge is directed partly toward the conception of the individual thing, partly toward the conception of the species. Each of these realises itself in phenomena, and here there is found much which, as belonging directly to the conception (συμβεβηκότα in the narrower sense), can be deduced from it, but also much which, as foreign to the conception, appears in the particular only incidentally, as a consequence of the matter in which the conception realises itself; and of this which is conceptionally indifferent or "*accidental*" (συμβεβηκότα in the usual sense of the word) there is, according to the presuppositions of the Aristotelian doctrine, no "theory," no scientific knowledge. Hence Aristotle also — and in this lies a characteristic limit of the ancient study of Nature — disclaimed on principle any scientific insight into the necessity of law, with which even the most individual and most particular follow from the general. This individual instance he declared rather to be something really accidental, not to be explained by conception, and limited scientific consideration to that which is valid universally (καθ' ὅλου), or at least *for the most part* (ἐπὶ τὸ πολύ).

4. In this we see decidedly a holding fast to the tradition of the doctrine of Ideas: the same attitude discloses itself also in another direction. If, that is, the relation of matter and form is affirmed between the different things or classes of things, each of which is in itself already actual as formed matter, this relation becomes *relative* in so far as the same thing which in contrast with a lower is to be regarded as form, appears as matter when contrasted with the higher. In this aspect the conception of development becomes the principle of an *ordering of things according to their metaphysical values*, considering these things as rising in uninterrupted succession from the lowest formations of matter to the highest forms. In this scale every class of things is assigned its metaphysical dignity by means of the test that it is regarded as form of the lower and as the material of the higher.

---

[1] So, at least, they are called in the treatise on categories, the genuineness of which is, to be sure, not entirely uncontested; yet the designation is quite in the line of Aristotle's teaching taken as a whole.

This system of individual things, and of their classes, has both a lower and an upper limit, the former in mere matter, the latter in pure form. Wholly unformed *matter* (πρώτη ὕλη) is, of course, in itself, as mere possibility, not actual; it never exists without being somehow actualised as form. Yet it is not merely that which is not Being (the Platonic μὴ ὄν, or empty space), but the accessory cause, which evinces itself as such through real effects (τὸ οὗ οὐκ ἄνευ, *sine qua non*). Its reality is shown in the fact that the forms do not completely realise themselves in individual things, and that from it side-workings (παραφυάς) proceed which are without connection with the purposefully active form, or even in contradiction with it. It is, therefore, from matter that the fact is explained that the forms realise themselves only potentially (κατὰ τὸ δυνατόν): from matter arises that which is conceptionally indeterminate (συμβεβηκός), or the accidental (αὐτόματον), — the lawless and purposeless in Nature. Hence the Aristotelian doctrine distinguishes, in its explanation of Nature, as did Plato in the *Philebus*, between *final causes* (τὸ οὗ ἕνεκα) and *mechanical causes* (τὸ ἐξ ἀνάγκης): the former are the forms which realise themselves in matter; the latter reside in matter, out of which proceed side-workings and counter-workings. Thus the cosmic processes are regarded by Aristotle ultimately under the *analogy of the plastic artist,* who finds in the hard material a limit to the realisation of his formative thought. This material is, indeed, so far related to the Idea, that the Idea can present itself in it, at least in general, and yet it is in so far a foreign, and thus an independent, element, that it in part opposes itself as a *retarding principle* to the realising of the forms. Ancient philosophy did not overstep this *dualism* between the purposive activity of the form and the resistance of matter; with the demand of the teleological view of the world it united the naive honesty of experience, recognising the necessity, purposeless and contrary to design, which asserts itself in the phenomena of the actual world.

5. It is, on the contrary, self-evident in the case of pure form, since its conception is immediately connected with that of true actuality, that it possesses in itself the highest actuality without needing any matter whatever. The assumption of such a *pure Form* is necessary according to the system of Aristotle, for the reason that matter, as the merely possible or potential, has in itself alone no principle of motion or of generation. We cannot, indeed, speak of a beginning of motion in time in this system of development, which centres about the conception of self-realising essence, since *motion must be as eternal as Being* itself, to the essential characteristics of which it belongs; but yet we must point out that property in Being

which is the *cause* of motion. This is, however, everywhere the action of the form upon the matter, in which, with reference to individual things, Aristotle distinguishes two elements, viz. an impulse to be formed inherent in matter, and the purposive motion proceeding from the form itself. But in so far as the form is itself moved, it must be regarded in turn as matter for a higher form; and, since the same thing is true of the latter, and so on, motion would not be understood if the chain of its causes did not have a first link in the pure Form which is itself not moved. The *first mover* (πρῶτον κινοῦν) is itself unmoved. Hence, in the case of its action upon matter, only the first of the two elements above mentioned comes into consideration. It operates, not by means of its own activity, but only by means of the fact that its absolute actuality excites in matter the impulse to form itself according to it (the prime mover), not as a mechanical, but as a *pure, final cause* (κινεῖ ὡς ἐρώμενον, οὐ κινού‚ μενον).

The prime mover, or the *pure Form*, means, then, in the Aristo‚ telian metaphysics, quite the same thing as the Idea of the Good in the Platonic, and for it alone Aristotle employs all the predicates of the Platonic Idea. It is eternal, unchangeable, immovable, wholly independent, separated (χωριστόν) from all else, incorporeal, and yet at the same time the cause of all generation and change. It is the *perfect Being* (ἐνέργεια) in which all possibility is at the same time actuality; of all that exists it is the highest (τὸ τί ἦν εἶναι τὸ πρῶτον) and best — the *deity*.[1]

The highest Being or Essence, thus determined according to its relations, is also characterised by Aristotle as regards its content. Such an activity, related to no possibility, resting purely within itself (*actus purus*), is thought, and thought alone; not, of course, that mental process which applies itself to individual things and their changing phenomena, but the *pure thought*, which is employed with itself and its eternal nature; that thought which presupposes nothing else as an object, but has itself for its constant, unchanging content, the thought of thought (νόησις νοήσεως), — *self-consciousness*.

In these conceptions, so determined, dwells a significance of mighty import for the world's history. On the one hand, mono-

---

[1] The exposition of this course of thought from which the later, so-called *cosmological proof for the existence of God* essentially arose, is found principally in the twelfth book of the *Metaphysics*. In his popular dialogues Aristotle amalgamated it with determinations of worth, by giving it the following form: the distinction between the imperfect and the more perfect which things of experience show presupposes the reality of a most perfect. Cf. Schol. in Arist. 487 a 6.

theism was herewith conceptionally formulated and scientifically grounded; on the other hand, it passed over from the pantheistic form, which it had with Xenophanes, and even still with Plato, into the *theistic* form, since God is conceived of as a self-conscious being different from the world. But besides this *transcendence*, the doctrine that *God is the absolute mind or spirit* (*Geist*) involves at the same time the metaphysical advance that the *immaterial*, the incorporeal pure Being, is made equivalent to the spiritual. *Spiritual monotheism* is the ripe fruit of Grecian science.

This divine spirituality is conceived of in a purely intellectualistic manner; its essential nature is solely thought directed upon itself. All doing, all willing, is directed toward an object, distinct from the doer or the willer. The divine mind, as pure form, needs no object; he is sufficient for himself, and his knowledge of himself (θεωρία), which has no other goal than itself, is his eternal blessedness. He acts upon the world, not through his motion or activity, but through the longing for him which the world has. The world, and what takes place in it, arises from the *longing of matter after God.*

6. Matter (the merely potential) is that which is moved without itself moving anything; God (the solely actual) is that which moves without itself being moved; between the two is the entire series of things, which suffer motion as well as call it forth; and these, taken as a whole, are designated by Aristotle as *Nature* (φύσις; equivalent to "world" according to present usage). Nature is, accordingly, the *connected system of living beings viewed as a unity*, in which matter developing ever higher, from form to form, through all the multitude of its particular shapes, approaches the resting Being of the deity, and imitating this, potentially takes it up into itself.

But in this connection, the *graded scale of things*, in the exposition of which the Aristotelian *philosophy of Nature* consists, shows a two-fold standard for estimating relative worth. The scale is therefore developed in two different series, which find their union only at the end in a manner which is, indeed, consistent with the fundamental conceptions of the system, but which is, nevertheless, in itself surprising.

In the conception of the deity, according to Aristotle, there meet, as chief characteristics, that of Being, resting within itself, and remaining like itself (ἀίδιον), and that of spirituality or rationality (νοῦς). Hence the individual "forms" of Nature take a higher rank in proportion as they contain the one or the other of these elements which constitute the highest worth. In the one line, the series of phenomena ascends from the unordered change of the terrestrial world to the ever-uniform revolution of the stars; in the other line, we are led from the merely mechanical change of place to the activities of the soul and its most valuable development, rational knowledge; and both series have the same terminus, inasmuch as the stars that are in most uniform motion are conceived of as the highest intelligences, the most rational spirits.

7. In relation to the first of these two aspects Aristotle, taking up the astronomical views of Plato, adopted the old Pythagorean antithesis between the earthly and the heavenly world, and it is to be ascribed to the victorious influence of his philosophy that the maturer ideas of the later Pythagoreans did not prevail in antiquity, in spite of their recognition by those learned in astronomy in the following period. As the whole universe has the most perfect form, everywhere the same, — that of the sphere, — so among all motions the most perfect is the *circular motion,* which returns into itself. This belongs to the *œther,* the celestial element, out of which the *stars* are formed, and the transparent hollow spheres, in which the stars move with ever-unchanged uniformity. Farthest out, and in an absolute changelessness that comes nearest the divine Being, is the heaven of the fixed stars, beneath that the planets, the sun, and the moon, whose apparent deviation from the circular movement was explained by a complicated theory of hollow spheres placed one within another, the theory which Eudoxus, an astronomer sustaining a close relation to the Academy, and his disciple Callippus had propounded.[1] The stars themselves were, however, for Aristotle beings of superhuman intelligence, incorporate deities. They appeared to him as the purer forms, those more like the deity, and from them a purposive, rational influence upon the lower life of earth seemed to proceed, — a thought which became the root of mediæval astrology.

The lower " forms " of terrestrial life, on the other hand, are the *four elements* (of Empedocles), which are characterised by the tendency to *rectilinear* motion. But rectilinear motion involves at once the opposition of two tendencies, — the centrifugal, which belongs to Fire; and the centripetal, which belongs to Earth. The first of the two tendencies is also attributed in a lesser degree to Air, and the latter in a lesser degree to Water, and so the central mass, our earth,

---

[1] Schiaparelli, *Le Sfere Omocentriche di Eudosso, Callippo, ed Aristotele* (Milan, 1876). Cf. also O. Gruppe, *Die kosmischen Systeme der Griechen* (Berlin, 1851). As a principle of method, the following prescription for the proposal of these questions has been preserved from the Old Academy, typical of the mathematico-metaphysical presupposition of the speculative explanation of Nature ; viz. to discover the uniformly ordered motions of the stars by means of which their apparent motions may be explained (διασῴζειν). Simpl. in Arist. *De Cœlo* (Karst.), 119.

in a state of rest as a whole, is composed in such a way that about the earthy material is disposed at first Water and then Air, while Fire strives toward the celestial outer world. The *changing combinations*, however, into which the four elements enter, constitute the imperfect, that which cannot be conceived, that which is *accidental* in the terrestrial world. Here the side-working and counter-working of matter are stronger than in the celestial region where the mathematical determinateness of undisturbed circular motion realises itself.

8. In the changes of the terrestrial world, *mechanical, chemical,* and *organic* processes are built up upon each other in such a way that the higher always presupposes the lower as its condition. Without change of place (φορά or κίνησις in the narrowest sense), change of qualities (ἀλλοίωσις) is not possible, and the organic transformation which consists in growth and decay (αὔξησις — φθίσις) is not possible without both the preceding. The higher form is, however, never merely a product of the lower, but is something self-subsistent, by means of which those lower forms can be employed only in a purposive manner.

From this develops an important principle in which Aristotle is opposed to Democritus, — a principle which the former esteemed very highly in regard to detailed research in natural science, and used a great deal, even with express mention. Aristotle [1] protests against the attempt to reduce all qualitative to quantitative determinations, — an attempt ultimately accepted even by Plato. He combats the contrasting from an epistemological and metaphysical point of view, of secondary and primary qualities ; to the former he accords not a less but rather a higher reality than to the latter, and in the succession of "forms" the inner conceptional character or determination is evidently of more worth for him than the outer determination which is capable of mathematical expression.[2] The attempt of Democritus to raise to the rank of a principle for explaining the world the reduction of all qualitative to quantitative differences, found its victorious opponent in Aristotle and his doctrine of the "entelechies," the inner Forms of things. The keen logician saw that it is never possible to develop qualities analytically from quantitative relations, and that, on the contrary, the quality (by whichever sense it may be perceived) is something new, which presupposes the entire body of quantitative relations as its occasion only.

---

[1] Cf. especially the third book of the treatise *De Cœlo.*

[2] For this reason Aristotle also characterises the elements not only by the different tendencies of their motions, but also by primitive qualities ; and he develops them out of a meeting of the contrasted pairs, warm and cold, dry and moist. *Meteor.* IV. 1, 378 b 11.

9. With logical consistency the same view is applied by Aristotle to the relation of the psychical and bodily activities; the latter are but the matter for which the former furnish the forms. There is, with Aristotle, no such dependence of psychical upon corporeal functions as Democritus, in accordance with the procedure of the older metaphysics, and even Plato, in part (in the *Timœus*), had taught. For Aristotle the *soul* is rather the *entelechy of the body, i.e.* the Form which realises itself in the motions and changes of the organic body. The soul is the cause of bodily formation and motion, a cause acting from ends; itself incorporeal, it is yet actual or real only as the power moving and controlling the body.

But the psychical life itself is also, according to Aristotle, built up as it were in successive grades or strata, each of which, in turn, presents matter for the higher. The first Form of organic life is the *vegetative soul* (θρεπτικόν), which "forms" the mechanical and chemical changes to the purposive functions of assimilation and propagation. The soul of *plants* is restricted to this purely physiological significance of a vital force; to this is added in the whole animal kingdom,[1] the *animal soul*, whose constitutive characteristics are spontaneous motion in space (κινητικόν κατὰ τόπον) and sensation (αἰσθητικόν).

The purposive, spontaneous motion of the animal body proceeds from *desire* (ὄρεξις), which arises from the *feelings* of pleasure and pain, in the form of an effort to procure or shun. But these presuppose everywhere the *idea of their object*, and are at the same time bound together with the thought that this object is worthy to be striven for or to be shunned. The view of the dependence of all desire upon ideas, peculiar to all Greek psychology, is so strong with Aristotle, that he even sets forth these relations expressly, according to the logical function of judgment and inference. In the practical sphere, also, there is affirmation and denial,[2] there is the process of drawing a conclusion from a general aim to a particular mode of action.

The proper seat, or home, as it were, of the entire animal life of ideation is found in *sensation*. In the physiological psychology which treats this subject[3] Aristotle has used in comprehensive

---

[1] Aristotle's *History of Animals* (cf. J. B. Meyer, Berlin, 1855) treats in exemplary manner, and with admirable care of detailed investigation, anatomical, physiological, morphological, and biological problems, and also the questions of system. The parallel work on plants is indeed lost, but in compensation we have the work of his friend and disciple Theophrastus.

[2] *Eth. Nic.* VI. 2, 1139 a 21.

[3] Besides the sections which treat this subject, in the treatise on the Soul, the smaller treatises attached to this are also to be compared, viz: on *Perception*, on *Memory*, on *Dreams*, etc.

manner all the particular information and theories which his predecessors, especially Democritus, possessed on this point; but he
overcame the common inadequacy of all earlier doctrines by conceding a much greater importance to the self-activity of the soul in the
process in which perception arises. Not satisfied to adopt the old
theory that perception consists in a co-operation of object and subject, he pointed to the *unity of consciousness* (*Einheitlichkeit, μεσότης*),
with which the animal soul unites what is given in the individual
perceptions of the individual senses to form collective perceptions,
or perceptions that perceive the object as a whole, and in so doing
grasps also the relations of number, situation, and motion. Thus
above the individual senses we must assume the *common sense*
(*κοινὸν αἰσθητήριον*),[1] which is also the seat of recollection, both of
the involuntary or memory (*μνήμη*) and the voluntary (*ἀνάμνησις*),
by virtue of the circumstance that in it the perceptions remain as
imaginative representations (*φαντασίαι*); at the same time, however,
it is also the seat of our knowledge of our own states.[2]

10. Vegetative and animal souls, however, form in *man* but the
matter for the realisation of the Form peculiar to him, — the *reason*
(*νοῦς — διανοεῖσθαι*). By its operation, impulse (*ὄρεξις*) becomes will
(*βούλησις*); imaginative representation becomes knowledge (*ἐπιστήμη*). It comes as a something new and higher ("from without,"
θύραθεν) to all the psychical activities which develop from perception
even among the beasts. Aristotle expressed this relation by designating the pure rational activity itself as the *active reason* (*νοῦς
ποιητικός*), and, on the contrary, as *passive reason* (*νοῦς παθητικός*),
the material of perceptions, which arises from the bodily existence,
furnishes possibilities and occasions for reason, and is subsequently
worked over and formed by it.

Accordingly the "passive" reason signifies the *individual phase*
(*Erscheinungsweise*) given in the natural disposition of the individual man, and determined by the occasions of his personal experience,
— the "active" reason, on the contrary, signifying the pure reason
considered as a unity in its nature and principles (*principielle Einheitlichkeit*), common to all individuals. The latter is imperishable,
as it is without beginning, while the former passes away with the

---

[1] With regard to physiological localisation Aristotle found the psychical
activity to be attached to the vital warmth (*ἔμφυτον θερμόν*), which as animating
breath (*πνεῦμα*) is mingled with the blood, and his school developed this doctrine still further. Cf. H. Siebeck, *Zeitschrift für Völkerpsychologie*, 1881, pp.
364 ff. In consequence of this he regarded the heart as the seat of the common
sense and so supplanted the better insight with which Alcmæon, Diogenes of
Apollonia, Democritus, and Plato had recognised the importance of the brain.

[2] This beginning for a doctrine of *inner perception* is found in Arist. *De. An.*
III. 2, 425 b 12.

individuals in whom it appears. Personal immortality is put in question by this conclusion just as in the Platonic *Timœus*, where it was claimed only for the "rational" "part" of the soul, *i.e.* that part which is everywhere alike and impersonal. It is clear that we have here no longer to do with empirical psychology, but with such doctrines as have been taken from the systematic connection of the whole work, and grafted upon psychology in consequence of ethical and epistemological postulates.

11. In the conception of the reason as the Form peculiar to the human soul, Aristotle found the key to the solution of that feature of the *ethical* problem which even Plato had sought in vain, *i.e.* that of the content of the Good. Man's *happiness* or *well-being* (εὐδαιμονία), which in Aristotle's system also is regarded as the supreme end of all endeavour (τέλος), is, indeed, dependent in part upon external fortune; it is not complete until this has afforded its good things; but ethics has to do only with that which stands in our power (τὰ ἐφ᾽ ἡμῖν), only with the happiness which man gains by his own activity (πρακτὸν ἀγαθόν). Every being, however, becomes happy by the unfolding of his own nature and of his own peculiar activity — *man*, therefore, through *reason*. The *virtue* of man is, accordingly, that habitude or permanent state of mind (ἕξις) through which he is made capable of the practice of rational activity; it develops out of the endowments of his natural disposition, and has for its fruit, satisfaction, pleasure.

As in the animal soul impulse and perception were to be distinguished as different expressions, so, too, the reason develops itself, partly as rational action, partly as rational thought; as perfection, on the one hand, of the character or disposition (ἦθος), on the other, of the faculty of intelligence (αἰσθάνεσθαι in the broadest sense of the word). Thus there result, as the excellence or ability of the rational man, the *ethical* and the *intellectual* or *dianoetic virtues*.

12. The ethical virtues grow out of that training of the will by which it becomes accustomed to act according to right insight (φρόνησις — ὀρθὸς λόγος). It enables man, in his decisions, to follow practical reason, *i.e.* insight into what is correct or proper. With this doctrine Aristotle transcends the principles of Socrates, — with evident regard to the facts of the ethical life: not that he assigned to the will a psychological independence as over against knowledge; the point, rather, is, that he gave up the opinion that the determination of the will arising from rational insight must of itself be stronger than the desire arising from defective knowledge. Since experience often shows the reverse of this, man must gain by

practice that self-control (ἐγκράτεια) by means of which he follows under all circumstances that which is rationally known, even against the strongest desires.[1]

While to ethical virtue in general belong natural disposition, insight, and habitude, the individual virtues are distinguished by the different relations of life to which they refer. A systematic development of these is not given by Aristotle, but we have, rather, a comprehensive and delicate treatment of the individual virtues. The general principle is that rational insight always finds the *right mean* between the unreasonable extremes to which the natural impulsive life leads. Thus courage is the right mean between cowardice and rashness. A particularly detailed exposition is given to friendship[2] as the common striving for all that is good and beautiful, and also to justice as the basis of the political community.

13. For Aristotle, like Plato, was convinced that the moral excellence of man, since it always relates to activities which prosper in the life of a community, can find its fulfilment only in the life of a community; for him, too, there is ultimately no perfect moral life outside the *state*, the essential end of which was considered by Aristotle, also, to be the ethical training of its citizens. As, nevertheless, in the case of the individual man, virtue ought to develop out of the natural disposition, so the political relations also are treated by Aristotle from the point of view, that the historically given relations are to be used for the highest possible fulfilment of that highest end.

Every constitution is right if the government has the ethical weal of the community as its highest goal; every constitution has failed if this is not the case. The good of the state, therefore, does not depend upon the external form, which is defined by the number of those who rule.[3] The rule of a single individual may be right as a kingdom (βασιλεία), bad if a despotism (τυραννίς); the rule of few may be good if an aristocracy of culture and disposition, if an oligarchy of birth or property, bad; the rule of all as a republic of law and order (πολιτεία) may be good, as mob-rule (δημοκρατία), bad. With profound political intelligence, Aristotle brings together in these expositions the experiences of Grecian history, and on the ground of these enters upon the *philosophy of*

---

[1] In the polemic against the Socratic doctrine which Aristotle brings forward in this line, *Eth. Nic.* III. 1–8, are developed the first beginnings of the problem of freedom.

[2] In the eighth book of the *Nicomachæan Ethics*.

[3] A point of view which the dialogue the *Statesman*, passing under Plato's name, had already emphasised, while Plato himself in the *Republic* constructed the "bad" constitutions from psychological analogies of a predominance of the lower parts of the soul.

history in giving intimations as to the necessity with which individual forms of constitutions pass over into one another and develop out of one another.

After these presuppositions we can understand that Aristotle could not think of projecting in detail the constitution of an ideal state in Plato's manner. He contented himself with a critical emphasising of those elements which had proved requisite in individual constitutions for fulfilling the general task of the state. In this connection he agrees with the Platonic demand for a public system of education; the ethical community must itself take the care of fitting for their place the elements of which it will in future consist, and it is the task of education (in the treatment of which the fragment of the *Politics* breaks off) to lead man out of his rude state of nature with the help of the noble arts, to ethical and intellectual culture.

14. To the practical activity of the reason (λογιστικόν), in the broader sense of the word, Aristotle reckoned also "making" (ποιεῖν) in addition to "acting" (πρᾶξις); yet, on the other hand, he made so great distinction between this creative activity, which presents itself in *art*, and the action directed toward the ends of daily life, that he occasionally set the science of art, poietic philosophy, as a third independent science, side by side with the theoretical and practical. Of this poietic philosophy, there is preserved besides the *Rhetoric* only the fragment of his theory of the art of poetry, under the name of the *Poetic*. This sets out, indeed, from principles relating to the nature of art in general, but in its particular subject offers only the outlines of a theory of tragedy. In this, such peculiar relations of this science of art to the two other principal parts of philosophy appear, that it becomes difficult to subordinate this branch under either of the other two.

Art is imitative production, and the arts are distinguished as well by the objects which they imitate as by the material with which they imitate. The objects of poetic art are men and their actions; its means are language, rhythm, and harmony. Tragedy, in particular, represents an important action as performed immediately by speaking and acting persons.[1]

But the purpose of this imitative representation is an *ethical* one: the passions of man, in particular in the case of tragedy, *fear* and *sympathy*, are to be so excited, that by their excitation and enhancement *purification* of the soul (κάθαρσις) from these passions is brought about.

---

[1] *Poet.* 6, 1449 b 24.

On the doctrine of the *Catharsis*, which became so important for the later theory of art, and on the literature concerning it, cf. A. Döring, *Die Kunstlehre des Aristoteles* (Jena, 1876).

The attainment of this end is, however, accomplished in such a way, that in artistic representation the particular is brought to our view, not as a particular, but in its universal nature or essence. Art, like science, has for its object the universal in its particular realisation; it offers a kind of knowledge, and with this the pleasure which attends upon knowledge.[1]

15. The highest perfection of its development finally is achieved by the rational nature of man in *knowledge*. The *dianoëtic* virtues are the highest, and those which bring complete happiness. The activity of the *theoretical reason* (ἐπιστημονικόν) is directed to the immediate apprehension of the highest truths, *i.e.* of the conceptions and judgments which the inductive search of scientific investigation only leads up to without being able to prove, and from which all deduction must take its beginning (cf. § 12, 4).

But knowledge of these, the full unfolding of the "active reason" in man, is again designated by Aristotle as a "*beholding*" (θεωρία); and with this beholding of the highest truth man gains a participation in that *pure thought*, in which the essence of the deity consists, and thus, also, in the eternal *blessedness* of the divine self-consciousness. For this "beholding" which exists only for its own sake and has no ends of will or deed, this wishless absorption in the perception of the highest truth, is the blessedest and best of ...

---

[1] *Poet.* 9, 1451 b 5.

PART II.

THE HELLENISTIC–ROMAN PHILOSOPHY.

As regards the general literature, the same works serve for this part that were cited at the beginning of Part I.

WITH the age of Aristotle, Grecian civilisation stepped out from its national restrictions and into the great general movement in which the peoples of antiquity that dwelt about the Mediterranean, through interchange and adjustment of their ideas, became fused into one common civilisation. This process began through the union of Oriental with Greek thought, in the Hellenistic states of Alexander's successors. It found its external completion in the Roman Empire, its internal completion in Christianity. Hellenism, Romanism, and Christianity were the three stages in which the world's future civilisation developed from antiquity.

The intellectually determining element in this union was Greek science, and herein consists its significance for the world's history. It became, like Greek art, the common possession of ancient civilisation. To it were joined step by step the highest movements in the inner life of the peoples, and it became the forming power for all the longings and impulses that lived within their souls. It was with the fall of its political independence, with its absorption into the Empire, that the Greek nation bought the accomplishment of its task of civilisation; by their dispersal over the world the Greeks became the teachers of the world.

But in connection with this entrance into more extended relations, Greek science experienced a separation of the different elements which were united in it. Together with the purely theoretical interest in which it had originated, and which had found so clear an expression in the personality and teaching of Aristotle, a practical interest had in time developed, which sought in science the conviction that should govern life. In Plato's philosophy the two were inseparately fused together, but now these two tendencies of science became separated.

Scientific thought, which had come to a knowledge of its own processes in the Aristotelian logic, had arrived at the consciousness of fundamental conceptions, with the aid of which it could use the abundance of phenomena. The principal opposing theories of the interpretation of the world had developed in the great systems, and in this way a fixed frame or setting was formed for the scientific treatment of detail. But beginning, as it did, with so slightly extended a knowledge of detail, the more successful Greek science was in the development of principles, the more it now experienced a crippling, at once of metaphysical interest and metaphysical force.

In consequence of this, however, the theoretical tendency of science was toward details, and the fundamental scientific character of the Hellenistic-Roman time is *erudition* and the *development of the special sciences*. The individual man of science, by entrance into one of the great schools, gained a firm support of collective opinion, and a ruling principle for the treatment of separate questions and subjects which interested him. And indifference toward general metaphysical theories was the greater, the more it appeared that fruitful investigation in special provinces, extension of knowledge of facts, and comprehension of special departments of science were possible, independently of the strife of metaphysical systems. The separation of problems, which had been completed typically in the Aristotelian teaching and school, led necessarily to specialisation, and the purely theoretical interest in knowledge for its own sake developed, during the Hellenistic-Roman period, essentially in the individual sciences. The great *savants* of later antiquity stand, it is true, in loose relations with one school or another, but they always show themselves indifferent to metaphysics. So it happens that during this time production, so far as the theoretical principles of philosophy were concerned, was extremely small, while investigation into mathematics, natural science, grammar, philology, literary and general history, had rich and comprehensive results to record. With the great mass of those names which are reckoned as " philosophers," whether heads of schools or associates in the schools, and which are continued in the schematic treatment of the " *History of Philosophy*," only literary-historical notices are connected, as that they worked specially in this or that department ; or it may be personal information, of no importance to philosophy, as that they attached themselves to this or that one among the earlier teachers, — almost never do we find any formation of new and original conceptions. So far as theoretical knowledge was concerned, this period turned the old problems of the Greeks hither and thither, and moved along the track which it found already laid down.

So much the more powerfully, during these centuries of appropriation and elaboration, did the *practica significance of philosophy* unfold itself. The need of a scientific doctrine of the ends of human life, of such a wisdom as should guarantee the happiness of the individual, could but become more urgent as the ideal structure of Greek life fell in pieces, as the religion of the people sank ever more and more to an external tradition, as the crumbling political life, robbed of its independence, no longer awakened devotion, and the individual in his inner life felt thrown back upon himself. Thus *wisdom for the conduct of life* became the fundamental problem of the philosophy which followed that of the Greeks, and the narrowing in the statement of the philosophical problem which Socrates, and after him the Cynic and Cyrenaic schools of Sophistic thought, had begun, is the general character of the succeeding period.

This did not exclude general theoretical doctrines and their sharply championed contests from assuming airs of great importance during this period; but, on the one hand, they met with no original interest for their own sake, and consequently developed only in the directions which were determined by the real end in view, *i.e.* that of wisdom for the conduct of life; on the other hand, they were lacking in originality, they were throughout only the old traditions shifted about, conditioned by the fundamental practical thoughts. Even such comprehensive systems as the Stoic and the Neo-Platonic work only with the conceptions of Greek philosophy, in order to gain a theoretical basis for their practical ideal. The key to their theoretical doctrines lies always in the fundamental practical conviction, and in so far they are all of them characteristic types of the mingling of problems.

With this predominance of practical importance is connected the fact that the dependence of philosophy upon the general movement of civilisation, which had already with the Sophists made its entrance into the quiet circle of disinterested investigation, became in the Hellenistic-Roman period a permanent phenomenon, and this appears most decisively in the changing attitude of this philosophy toward *religion*.

The development which Greek philosophy had taken, and the ever more sharply pronounced opposition to the religion of the people into which it had come, brought with it the result that the special task of that wisdom for the conduct of life which the post-Aristotelian philosophy sought, was to find a *compensation for religious faith*. The cultured world, which had lost the support afforded by religion, and was obliged to give up that of the state also, sought it in philosophy. As a result, the point of view of the Hellenistic-Roman wisdom for the conduct of life was primarily that of *individual morality*, and the philosophy which busied itself with this had, consequently, a thoroughly *ethical* stamp. The sharpness of the opposition of this individualistic ethics to religion appears most clearly among the Epicureans. But in the other schools, also, the doctrines of the deity have a purely ethical, or perhaps a theoretical interest, but none that is specifically religious.

This essentially ethical development of philosophy reached its completion in Greece, especially, indeed, in Athens, which, amid all the spread of Greek culture eastward and westward, formed for centuries the centre of scientific life. But soon new centres particularly for erudite detailed investigation, arose in the great libraries and museums, in Rhodes, in Pergamum, in Alexandria, in Tarsus, in Rome, and later, in Antioch and Byzantium. Of these, *Alexandria* became especially important, where not only did elaborative erudition experience so typical a development, that the entire direction of this period is generally called "literary-historical" in accordance with it, but where, also, the philosophical direction of the time experienced its decided change.

For as time went on philosophy could not remain indifferent to that deep feeling of dissatisfaction which had seized the ancient world in the midst of all the glory of the Roman Empire. This huge empire offered to the peoples which it had welded together into a mighty unit, no compensation for the loss of their national independence; it granted them neither inner worth nor outer fortune. The draught from the life of earth had become insipid to ancient peoples, and they thirsted after religion. So they groped after the different cults and religious practices which individual peoples had brought with them, and the religions of the Orient became mixed with those of the Occident.

Into this movement philosophy was the more drawn, the more it became clear that it could not satisfy the cultured man by the presentation of its ethical ideal of life,— could not secure for him the promised happiness. It followed then — at first, in Alexandria — that the mingling, surging flood of religious ideas emptied itself into philosophy, which now sought to build up upon a scientific basis, not only an ethical conviction, but a religion as well. Philosophy employed the conceptions of Greek science to clarify and put in order religious ideas, to give to the importunate demand of religious feeling an idea of the world that should be satisfactory to it, and so created the *systems of religious metaphysics*, in more or less intimate connection with the contending religions.

Accordingly, in the Hellenistic-Roman philosophy there are two distinct periods to be distinguished, the *ethical* and the *religious*. The last century B.C. is to be designated as the time in which the one gradually passed over into the other.

CHAPTER I.

THE ETHICAL PERIOD.

THE two schools of the great masters of Attic philosophy, the *Academic* and the *Peripatetic*, followed the tendency of the time which separated science into the two branches, ethical philosophy and learned investigation. While in the first generation of the Academy — that contemporary with Aristotle — a Pythagoreanising metaphysics had predominated, this made room in the next period for popular moralising (cf. p. 101). In the Lyceum, indeed, *Theophrastus*, and after him, *Strato*, held fast to the development and re-shaping of the Aristotelian metaphysics, but the associates of Theoprastus, *Dicœarchus*, *Aristoxenus*, and others, as well as Theophrastus himself, turned to literary-historical studies and to natural science. Later, the Peripatetics had a great share in the Alexandrian erudition, and the history of philosophy especially found in them its most industrious workers. But in philosophy itself they played only the conservative rôle of defending the system of their school against the attacks of the others, especially upon the ethical domain, and the new edition of the Aristotelian works by *Andronicus* gave new stimulus for a zealous reproduction of his teaching. Paraphrases, commentaries, excerpts, and interpretations formed the chief occupation of the later Peripatetics.

The Academy and Lyceum were, however, injured in their working by the two schools which were founded toward the end of the fourth century, and which owed their great success to the fact that they formulated the tendency of the time toward the practical wisdom of life with the clearness and impressiveness of one-sidedness : namely, the *Stoic* and the *Epicurean*.

The first was founded in the Στοὰ ποικίλη by *Zeno*, a native of *Citium* in Cyprus, and had, both in his time and in that of his successor, *Cleanthes*, more likeness to Cynicism than in the time of its third head, *Chrysippus*, who succeeded in turning the school into a more scientific course. *Epicurus*, on the contrary, founded a society which made the Hedonistic principle, in a refined and intellectualised form, its centre, but developed only a slight degree of scientific vitality. While numerous adherents were won to its social-ethical principle then established, and to the view of the world connected with it, as these were continued through antiquity and especially in the Roman world, the school remained decidedly more unfruitful scientifically than the others, as well in the special sciences as in philosophy. Its doctrines have been presented in an interesting manner by the Roman poet, *Lucretius.*

These four schools continued side by side in Athens for centuries, and in the time of the Empire they were still maintained in various chairs of instruction, and formed there a sort of university; but only in the Academy, and here only with great gaps, can a succession of heads of the school be traced; while the tradition in the case of the Stoa and the Epicureans breaks off with the first century B.C., and for the Lyceum soon after that time.

At first, however, these *four schools* contended with each other in the liveliest fashion during the third and second centuries B.C., and it was especially in ethical questions, and in metaphysical, physical, and logical questions only in so far as connected with the ethical, that they sought to bear away the palm from one another.[1]

But, moving along side by side with the dogmatic doctrines during the whole period was another tendency, which, like the Stoic and Epicurean philosophy, originated in the teaching of the Sophists: namely, *Scepticism.* It did not, indeed, take on the form of an association in a school, but it, too, was *brought together into a systematic form,* and found an *ethical culmination.* Such a concentration, in accord with the spirit of the times, of the negative results of the teaching of the Sophists, was achieved by *Pyrrho,* whose doctrines were set forth by *Timon.* This Sophistical scepticism had the triumph of obtaining possession of Plato's grove for a time; for, if the *Middle Academy* did not make this doctrine fully its own, it made it a weapon for combating Stoicism and grounding its own ethics. In this phase of the development of the Academy appear the two heads of the school, *Arcesilaus* and *Carneades,* who were separated by about a century. In after time, when the Academy again rejected Scepticism, this doctrine met with sympathy principally among the *empirical physicians,* among whom, even at the end of this period, *Ænesidemus* and *Agrippa* are to be mentioned. A complete collection of the doctrines of the Sceptics, made at a much later time, is preserved in the works of *Sextus Empiricus.*

---

[1] Cicero in his philosophical dialogues gives vivid pictures of these school controversies. with a dextrous use of the original sources.

But the deeper significance of this Scepticism was that it brought to expression the fundamental frame of mind which had seized the entire ancient civilisation as it had once seized that of Greece, — a frame of mind at variance with the true ideal import and content of that civilisation; and the same lack of the spirit of decided conviction found only another form in the *Eclecticism* which began to develop in the second half of the second century. With the extension of the schools in the great relations of the life of the Roman Empire, the school-spirit disappeared, polemic was crippled, and the need of adjustment and fusion made itself felt instead. The teleological view of the world, especially, formed the basis upon which Platonism, Aristotelianism, and Stoicism could agree in a common opposition against Epicureanism.

The tendency toward such a fusion, toward *syncretism,* first awoke in the Stoic school, and found its most efficient supporters in *Panœtius* and *Posidonius,* who supplemented the doctrine of the Stoa on all sides by borrowing Platonic and Aristotelian elements. In opposition to them stood the *New Academy,* which, after *Philo of Larissa* had made an end of the sceptical episode in the development of the school, made the attempt, through *Antiochus,* to unite philosophy, then so disunited, upon those doctrines in which Plato and Aristotle agree.

Less important, because more devoid of principles, but not, therefore, the less significant historically, was that sort of eclecticism which the *Romans* employed in taking up Greek philosophy. This consisted in piecing together, from an essentially practical point of view, the different school systems which met their approval. This was the case with *Cicero, Varro,* and in part with the school of the *Sextians.*

Of the **Peripatetic** School (the Lyceum), the co-founder himself is primarily to be noticed, **Theophrastus** of Erebus in Lesbos (about 370–287), a somewhat younger friend of Aristotle, who through his teachings and writings won great regard for the school. Of his works, the botanical, also a fragment of the *Metaphysics,* extracts from his *Characters,* from the treatise concerning perception, from his history of physics, and some isolated fragments are preserved (edited by F. Wimmer, Breslau, 1842–62).

With him appear **Eudemus** of Rhodes, **Aristoxenus** of Tarentum, who studied music historically and theoretically (*Elemente der Musik,* German by R. Westphal, Leips. 1883), **Dicæarchus** of Messina, a learned polyhistor who wrote a history of Grecian civilisation (βίος Ἑλλάδος), and **Strato** of Lampsacus, who was head of the school (287–269) and had as surname "The Physicist."

Among the Peripatetic doxographers, Hermippus, Sotion, Satyrus, Heracleides Lembus (in the second century B.C.), and among the later commentators, Alexander of Aphrodisias (about 200 A.D. in Athens) are to be mentioned.

The **Middle Academy** begins with **Arcesilaus** of Pitane in Æolia (about 315–241), whose teachings were recorded by his pupil Lacydes, and ends with **Carneades** (in Rome, 155) and his successor Clitomachus, who died 110. Nothing remains of their writings. The sources are, beside Diogenes Laertius, principally Cicero and Sextus Empiricus.

Just as indirect and general in its character is our knowledge of the **New Academy**. **Philo** of Larissa was still in Rome in 87. His successor, **Antiochus** of Ascalon, was heard by Cicero in Athens in 78. To the supporters of eclectic Platonism in this first, essentially ethical form belong among others **Arius Didymus**, who inclined strongly to Stoicism (in the time of Augustus), and **Thrasyllus** (under Tiberius), who prepared an edition of the works of Democritus and Plato, arranged according to subjects. An extensive literature of paraphrase and commentary connected with Plato's works also developed in the Academy.

When we consider the personality of the **Stoic** School, we are struck by the frequency of the descent of its members from the Hellenistic mixed races of the Orient. Thus the founder, **Zeno** (about 340–265), came from his Cyprian home as a merchant to Athens, and there, taken captive by philosophy, is said to have absorbed the doctrines of the different schools, to found his own in the year 308. His principal pupil was **Cleanthes** of Assos in Troas, from whose writings a monotheistic hymn to Zeus is preserved, Stob. *Ecl.* I. 30 (Wachsmuth, p. 25). The scientific head of the school was **Chrysippus** (280–209) of Soli or Tarsus in Cilicia. He is said to have written an extraordinary amount, but, aside from the titles, only very unimportant fragments of his works are preserved. Cf. G. Bagnet (Loewen, 1822). Among the literary-historical *savants* of the Stoic School, **Diogenes** of Babylon and **Apollodorus** are to be mentioned ; Aristarchus and Eratosthenes stood in close relation to the school.

Panætius (180–110), who was strongly influenced by the Academic scepticism and who maintained a close relation with the Roman statesmen, began the syncretistic development of the Stoa, which was completed by **Posidonius** of Syrian Apamea (about 135–50). The latter was one of the greatest polyhistors of antiquity, especially in the geographico-historical domain. He taught in Rhodes, and was heard by many young Romans, among whom was Cicero.

Concerning the Stoics of the time of the Empire, cf. the following chapter. Sources for the Stoic doctrines are Cicero and Diogenes Laertius, Book VII., in part also the extant writings of the Stoics of the time of the Empire, and the discoveries at Herculaneum.

D. Tiedmann, *System der stoischen Philosophie* (3 vols., Leips. 1776) ; P. Weygoldt, *Die Philosophie der Stoa* (Leips. 1883) ; P. Ogereau, *Essai sur le Système Philosophique des Stoiciens* (Paris, 1885) ; L. Stein, *Die Psychologie der Stoa* (2 vols., Berlin, 1886–88) ; [Capes, *Stoicism*, Lond. 1880].

Epicurus (341–270), born in Samos, the son of an Athenian schoolmaster, had already made attempts at teaching in Mitylene and in Lampsacus, before founding in Athens, in 306, the society which is named after his "gardens" (κῆποι, *horti*, as also the other schools were named after the places where they assembled). He was much loved as a teacher, on account of his companionable qualities. Of his numerous writings lightly thrown off, the proverbs (κύριαι δόξαι), three didactic letters, parts of his treatise περὶ φύσεως (in the discoveries at Herculaneum), and besides only scattered fragments are preserved ; collected and arranged systematically by H. Usener, *Epicurea* (Leips. 1887).

Among the great mass of his followers, antiquity brings into prominence his closest friend Metrodorus of Lampsacus ; also Zeno of Sidon (about 150) and Phædrus (about 100 B.C.). **Philodemus** of Gadara in Coele-Syria has become a somewhat more distinct figure to us since a part of his writings has been found at Herculaneum (*Herculanensium voluminum quæ supersunt*, first series, Naples, 1793 ff. ; second, 1861 ff.) ; the most valuable, περὶ σημείων καὶ σημειώσεων (cf. Fr. Bahusch, Lyck, 1879 ; H. v. Arnim, *Philodemea*, Halle, 1888).

The didactic poem of Tit. **Lucretius** Carus (98–54), *De Natura Rerum*, in six books, has been edited by Lachmann (Berlin, 1850) and Jac. Bernays (Leips. 1852) ; [Eng. ed. with tr. of the poem by Munro, Lond. 1886. Cf. *The Atomic Theory of Lucretius*, by J. Masson, Lond. 1884].

Further sources are Cicero and Diogenes Laertius, in the tenth book.

Cf. M. Guyau, *La Morale d'Epicure* (Paris, 1878) ; P. v. Gizycki, *Ueber das Leben und die Moralphilosophie des Epikur* (Berlin, 1879) ; W. Wallace, *Epicureanism* (Lond. 1880) ; [Wallace, Art. *Ep.* in *Enc. Brit.* ; W. L. Courtney, *Ep.* in *Hellenica*].

Scepticism, as accords with the nature of the case, makes its appearance, not as a close school, but in looser form.[1] It remains doubtful whether the systematiser of Scepticism, **Pyrrho** of Elis (perhaps 365–275), had any intimate relations with the Socratic-Sophistic school of his native city. A certain Bryso, who passes for the son of Stilpo, is looked upon as an intermediate link. He accompanied Alexander on his journey to Asia, together with a follower of Democritus, Anaxarchus by name. The Sillograph, Timon of Phlius (320–230, the latter part of the time at Athens) from Pyrrho's standpoint derides philosophers. Fragments of his writings in C. Wachsmuth, *De Timone Phliasio* (Leips. 1859). Cf. Ch. Waddington, *Pyrrhon* (Paris, 1877).

The external relations of later Scepticism are very obscure and uncertain. **Ænesidemus** from Cnossus taught in Alexandria, and composed a treatise, Πυρρώνειοι λόγοι, of which nothing remains. His life falls probably in the first century B.C., yet it has also been set almost two centuries later. Of Agrippa, nothing in detail can be established. The literary representative of Scepticism is the physician **Sextus Empiricus**, who lived about 200 A.D., and of his writings there are extant his *Outline Sketches of Pyrrhonism* (Πυρρώνειοι ὑποτυπώσεις), and the investigations comprehended under the name *Adversus Mathematicos*, of which Books VII.–XI. contain the exposition of the sceptical doctrine, with many valuable historical notices (ed. by J. Bekker, Berlin, 1842).

Cf. K. Stäudlin, *Gesch. und Geist des Skepticismus* (Leips. 1794–95); N. Maccoll, *The Greek Sceptics* (London, 1869); L. Haas, *De Philosophorum Scepticorum Successionibus* (Würzburg, 1875); [Owen, *Evenings with the Sceptics* (Lond. 1881); A. Seth, Art. *Scepticism*, in *Enc. Brit.*].

Among the Romans, the admission of philosophy at first encountered violent resistance; but by the beginning of the first century B.C. it was the general custom for the young Romans of superior rank to study in Athens or Rhodes, and to hear the lectures of the heads of schools, for the same end as that for which the Athenians had formerly heard the Sophists. The literary activity of Marcus Tullius **Cicero** (106–43) must be judged from the point of view of his purpose, which was to awaken among his countrymen an inclination for general scientific culture and a comprehension of its meaning, and from this standpoint his work is to be highly prized. Skill in composition and grace of form excuse the lack of proper philosophising ability, which is shown in a selection of doctrines based on no philosophical principle. The main treatises are *De Finibus, De Officiis, Tusculanæ Disputationes, Academica, De Natura Deorum, De Fato, De Divinatione.* Cf. Herbart, *Ueber die Philosophie des Cicero;* in Works, XII. 167 ff. [Trans. of the above writings of Cicero in the Bohn. Lib.]

His friend, M. Terentius **Varro** (116–27), the well-known polyhistor and prolific writer, was more learned, but of his labours toward the history of philosophy only occasional notes are extant.

Quintus Sextus and a *son* of the same name and **Sotion** of Alexandria are named as Sextians. Sotion seems to have been the intermediate link in which the Stoic morals were brought into union with the Alexandrian Pythagoreanism, and given that religious turn which characterises them in the time of the Empire. Some of their *Sentences*, discovered in a Syrian translation, have been edited by Gildemeister (Bonn, 1873).

On the literary conditions of this whole period cf. R. Hirzel, *Untersuchungen zu Cicero's philosophischen Schriften* (3 vols., Leips. 1877–83).

§ 14. The Ideal of the Wise Man.

The fundamental ethical tendency of the philosophising of this entire period is still more precisely characterised by the fact that it is throughout *individual ethics* that forms the centre of investigation in this time of epigones. The elevation to the ideals of ethical

---

[1] Hence all reckonings by the successions of heads of the school, attempted in order to fix the chronology of the later Sceptics, are illusory.

community, in which morals culminated with both Plato and Aristotle, was a glorification that had become foreign to its time, of
that through which Greece had become great, viz. the thought
of an active, living state. This had lost power over the hearts of
men, and even in the schools of Plato and Aristotle it found so
little sympathy that the Academicians, as well as the Peripatetics,
brought into the foreground the question of individual happiness
and virtue. What is preserved from the treatise of the Academi-
cian Crantor, *On Grief*,[1] or from the works of Theophrastus under
the title of *Ethical Characters,* stands wholly upon the footing of a
philosophy that esteems the right appreciation of the good things
of life to be its essential object.

In the endless discussions on these questions in which the schools
engaged in the following centuries, the successors of the two great
thinkers of Attic philosophy found themselves in an attitude of
common opposition to the new schools. Both had pursued through
the entire circuit of empirical reality the realisation of the Idea of
the Good, and in spite of all the idealism with which Plato
especially strove to transcend the world of the senses, they had
not failed to appreciate the relative value of this world's goods.
Highly as they prized virtue, they yet did not exclude the view that
for the complete happiness of man[2] the favour of external fortune,
health, prosperity, etc., are requisite also, and they denied especially the doctrine of the Cynics and Stoics that virtue is not
only the highest (as they admitted), but also the sole good.

At all events, however, they too laboured to determine the right
conduct of life which promised to make man happy, and while
individual members of the schools pursued their special researches,
the public activity, especially that of the heads of the schools
in their polemic with their opponents, was directed to the end of
drawing the *picture of the normal man.* This it was that the time
desired of philosophy : "Show us how the man must be constituted
who is sure of his happiness, whatever the fortune of the world
may bring him!" That this normal man must be called the able,
the virtuous, and that he can owe his virtue only to insight, to
knowledge, that he therefore must be the "wise" man, — this is
the presupposition arising from the Socratic doctrine, which is
recognised as self-evident by all parties during this entire period;
and therefore all strive to portray the *ideal of the wise man, i.e.*
of the man whom his insight makes virtuous, and so, happy.

---

[1] Cf. F. Kayser (Heidelberg, 1841).
[2] This Aristotelian view was completely assented to by Speusippus and Xenocrates of the Older Academy.

1. The most prominent characteristic in the conception of the "wise man," as determined in this period, is, therefore, *imperturbability* (ataraxy, ἀταραξία). Stoics, Epicureans, and Sceptics are unwearied in praising this *independence of the world* as the desirable quality of the wise man: he is free, a king, a god; whatever happens to him, it cannot attack his knowledge, his virtue, his happiness; his wisdom rests in himself, and the world does not trouble him. This ideal, as thus portrayed, is characteristic of its time; the normal man, for this period, is not he who works and creates for the sake of great purposes, but he who knows how to free himself from the external world, and find his *happiness in himself alone.* The inner isolation of individuals, and indifference toward general ends, find here sharp expression: the *overcoming of the outer world* conditions the happiness of the wise man.

But since he has no power over the world without him, he must overcome it *within himself;* he must become master of the effects which it exercises upon him. These effects, however, consist in the feelings and desires which the world and life excite in man; they are disturbances of his own nature — emotions, or passions (πάθη, *affectus*). Wisdom is shown, therefore, in the relation which man maintains to his *passions*.[1] It is essentially freedom from passions or emotions, *emotionlessness* (apathy, ἀπάθεια, is the Stoic expression). To rest unmoved within one's self, this is the blessing of this "wisdom."

The terms with which this doctrine is introduced in the case of Epicurus and Pyrrho point immediately to a dependence upon Aristippus and Democritus. It corresponds to the gradual transformation which took place in the Hedonistic school (cf. § 7, 9) that *Epicurus*,[2] who made its principle his own, and likewise designated *pleasure* as the *highest good*, nevertheless preferred the permanent *frame of satisfaction* and *rest* to the enjoyment of the moment. The Cyrenaics also had found the essence of pleasure in gentle motion; but — Epicurus held — that is still a "pleasure in motion"; and the state of painless rest, free from all wishes (ἡδονὴ καταστηματική), is of higher value. Even the zest and spirit of enjoyment has become lost; the Epicurean would indeed gladly enjoy

---

[1] The ancient conception of the passions (*Affect*), extending into modern time (Spinoza), is accordingly wider than that of the present psychology. It is best defined by the Latin translation "*perturbationes animi*," "emotions," and includes all states of feeling and will in which man is dependent upon the outer world.

[2] As intermediate links, the younger followers of Democritus, strongly tinctured with Sophistic doctrine, are named; especially a certain *Nausiphanes*, whom Epicurus heard.

all pleasure, but it must not excite him or set him in motion. Peace of soul (γαληνισμός, cf. § 10, 5) is all that he wishes, and he anxiously avoids the storms which threaten it, *i.e.* the passions.

Epicurus therefore recognised the logical consistency with which the Cynics had characterised *absence of wants* as virtue and happiness; but he was far from seriously renouncing pleasure, as they did. The wise man must, to be sure, understand this also, and act accordingly, as soon as it becomes requisite in the course of things. But his satisfaction will be greater in proportion as the compass of the wishes which he finds satisfied is fuller. Just for this reason, he needs the *insight* (φρόνησις) which not only makes it possible to estimate the different degrees of pleasure and pain as determined through the feelings, which are to be expected in a particular case, but also decides whether and how far one should give place to individual wishes. In this aspect Epicureanism distinguished three kinds of wants: some are natural (φύσει) and unavoidable, so that, since it is not possible to exist at all without their satisfaction, even the wise man cannot free himself from them; others, again, are only conventional (νόμῳ), artificial, and imaginary, and the wise man has to see through their nothingness and put them from him; between the two, however (here Epicurus opposes the radically one-sided nature of Cynicism), lies the great mass of those wants which have their natural right, but are not indeed indispensable for existence. Hence the wise man can in case of necessity renounce them; but since the satisfaction of these gives happiness, he will seek to satisfy them as far as possible. Complete blessedness falls to his lot who rejoices in all these good things in quiet enjoyment, without stormy striving.

On the same ground, Epicurus prized mental joys higher than physical enjoyments which are connected with passionate agitation. But he seeks the joys of the mind, not in pure knowledge, but in the æsthetic refinement of life, in that intercourse with friends which is pervaded by wit and sentiment and touched with delicacy, in the comfortable arrangement of daily living. Thus the wise man, in quiet, creates for himself the blessedness of self-enjoyment, independence of the moment, of its demands and its results. He knows what he can secure for himself, and of this he denies himself nothing; but he is not so foolish as to be angry at fate or to lament that he cannot possess everything. This is his "ataraxy," or impassiveness: an enjoyment like that of the Hedonists, but more refined, more intellectual, and — more *blasé*.

2. *Pyrrho's* Hedonism took another direction, inasmuch as he sought to draw the practical result from the sceptical teachings of

the Sophists. According to the exposition of his disciple, Timon, he
held it to be the task of science to investigate the constitution
of things, in order to establish man's appropriate relations to them,
and to know what he may expect to gain from them.[1] But according to Pyrrho's theory it has become evident that we can never
know the true constitution of things but at the most can know
only states of feelings (πάθη) into which these put us (Protagoras,
Aristippus). If, however, there is no knowledge of things, it
cannot be determined what the right relation to them is, and
what the success that will result from our action. This scepticism
is the negative reverse side to the Socratic-Platonic inference. As
there, from the premise that right action is not possible without
knowledge, the demand had been made that knowledge must be
possible, so here the argument is, that because there is no knowledge, right action is also impossible.

Under these circumstances all that remains for the wise man is
to resist as far as possible the seducements to opinion and to action,
to which the mass of men are subject. All action proceeds, as
Socrates had taught, from our ideas of things and their value; all
foolish and injurious actions result from incorrect opinions. The
wise man, however, who knows that nothing can be affirmed as to
things themselves (ἀφασία), and that no opinion may be assented to
(ἀκαταληψία),[2] restrains himself, as far as possible, from judgment,
and thereby also from action. He withdraws into himself, and in
the *suspension* (ἐποχή)[3] of judgment, which preserves him from
passion and from false action, he finds imperturbability, rest within
himself, *ataraxy*.

This is the Sceptical virtue, which also aims to free man from the
world, and it finds its limit only in the fact that there are, nevertheless, relations in which even the wise man, withdrawn within
himself, must act, and when nothing else remains for him than to act
according to that which appears to him, and according to tradition.

3. A deeper conception of the process of overcoming the world in
man was formed by the *Stoics*. At the beginning, to be sure, they
professed quite fully the Cynic indifference toward all goods of the
outer world, and the self-control of the virtuous wise man remained
stamped upon their ethics also as an ineradicable feature; but they

---

[1] Euseb. *Præp. Ev.* XIV. 18, 2. The doctrine of Pyrrho is shown by this to
be in exact coincidence with the tendency of the time; it asks, " What are we
to do, then, if there is no knowledge ? "

[2] An expression which was probably formed in the polemic against the Stoic
conception of κατάληψις; cf. § 17.

[3] The Sceptics were called also the ἐφεκτικοί [" Suspenders "] with reference
to this term, characteristic for them.

soon dulled the edge of the radical naturalism of the Cynics by a penetrating psychology of the impulsive life, which shows a strong dependence upon Aristotle. They emphasise, still more than the Stagirite, the unity and independence of the individual soul, as contrasted with its particular states and activities, and so, with them, *personality* first becomes a determinative principle. The leading-power, or governing part of the soul (τὸ ἡγεμονικόν), is, for them, not only that which makes perceptions out of the excitations of the individual organs in sensation, but also that which by its assent[1] (συγκατάθεσις) transforms excitations of the feelings into activities of the will. This consciousness, whose vocation is to apprehend and form its contents as a unity, is, according to its proper and true nature, reason (νοῦς); the states, therefore, in which consciousness allows itself to be hurried along to assent by the violence of excitement contradict, in like measure, its own nature and reason. These states (*affectus*) are, then, those of passion (πάθη) and disease of the soul; they are perturbations of the soul, contrary to Nature and contrary to reason.[2] Hence the wise man, if he cannot defend himself from those excitations of feeling in presence of the world, will deny them his assent with the power of reason; he does not allow them to become passions or emotions, his virtue is the *absence of emotions* (ἀπάθεια). His overcoming of the world is his overcoming of his own impulses. It is not until we give our assent that we become dependent upon the course of things; if we withhold it, our personality remains immovable, resting upon itself. If man cannot hinder fate from preparing for him pleasure and pain, he may, nevertheless, by esteeming the former as not a good, and the latter as not an evil, keep the proud consciousness of his self-sufficiency.

Hence, in itself, virtue is for the Stoics the sole good, and on the other hand, vice, which consists in the control of the reason by the passions, is the sole evil, and all other things and relations are regarded as in themselves indifferent (ἀδιάφορα).[3] But in their

---

[1] This assent, to be sure, even according to the Stoics, rests upon the judgment; in the case of passion, therefore, upon a false judgment, but it is yet at the same time the act of the will which is bound up with the judgment. Cf. § 17.

[2] Diog. Laert. VII. 110: τὸ πάθος — ἡ ἄλογος καὶ παρὰ φύσιν ψυχῆς κίνησις ἢ ὁρμὴ πλεονάζουσα. The psychological theory of the emotions was developed especially by Chrysippus. Zeno distinguished, as fundamental forms, pleasure and pain, desire and fear. As principles of division among the later Stoics there seem to have been used, partly characteristics of the ideas and judgments which call out the emotion, and partly the characteristics of the states of feeling and will which proceed from it. Cf. Diog. Laert. VII. 111 ff.; Stob. *Ecl.* II. 174 f.

[3] By reckoning even life in this division, they came to their well-known defence or commendation of suicide (ἐξαγωγή). Cf. Diog. Laert. VII. 130; Seneca, *Ep.* 12, 10.

doctrine of goods they moderate the rigour of this principle by the distinction of the desirable and that which is to be rejected (*προηγ-μένα* and *ἀποπροηγμένα*). Strongly as they emphasised in this connection that the worth (*ἀξία*) which belongs to the desirable is to be distinguished strictly from the Good of virtue, which is a good in itself, there yet resulted from this, in opposition to the Cynic one-sidedness, an at least secondary appreciation of the good things of life. For since the desirable was valued for the reason that it seemed adapted to further the Good, and, on the other hand, the demerit of that which was to be rejected consisted in the hindrances which it prepares for virtue, the threads between the self-sufficient individual and the course of the world, which the Cynic paradoxical theory had cut, were thus more and more knit together again. The mean between what is desirable and what is to be rejected, the absolutely indifferent, survived ultimately only in that which could be brought in no relation whatever to morality.

As these distinctions, by repression of the Cynic element, gradually made Stoicism more viable and, so to speak, better able to get on in the world, so we may see a like modification, by means of which it became more usable pedagogically, in the later removal of the abrupt contrast which at the beginning was made between the virtuous wise and the vicious fools (*φαῦλοι, μωροί*). The wise man, so it was said at the beginning, is wise and virtuous entirely, and in everything the fool is just as entirely and universally foolish and sinful; there is no middle ground. If man possesses the force and soundness of reason, with which he controls his passions, then he possesses with this one virtue all the individual particular virtues [1] at the same time, and this possession, which alone makes happy, cannot be lost; if he lacks this, he is a plaything of circumstances and of his own passions, and this radical disease of his soul communicates itself to his entire action and passion. According to the view of the Stoics, therefore, the few sages stood as perfect men over against the great mass of fools and sinners, and in many declamations they lamented the baseness of men with the Pharisaic pessimism which thus gratifies its self-consciousness. But over against this first opinion, which looked upon all fools as to be rejected alike, the consideration presented itself that among these fools there were always noticeable differences with regard to their departure from the ideal virtue, and thus between wise men and fools there was inserted the conception of the man who is progressive and in a state of *improvement* (*προκόπτων*). The Stoics, indeed,

---

[1] The Stoics also made the Platonic cardinal virtues the basis for their systematic development of their doctrine of the virtues. Stob. *Ecl.* II. 102 ff.

held fast to the view that no gradual transition takes place from this process of improvement to true virtue, and that the entrance into the condition of perfection results rather from a sudden turn about. But when the different stages of ethical progress (προκοπή) were investigated and a state was designated as the highest stage, in which apathy is indeed attained, but not yet with full sureness and certainty,[1] — when this was done, the rigorous boundary lines were in some measure effaced.

4. Yet in spite of these practical concessions, the withdrawal of the individual personality within itself remained ultimately an essential characteristic in the Stoic ideal of life; on the other hand, this which these Greek epigones in common regarded as the mark of wisdom, was nowhere so valuably supplemented as among the Stoics. Scepticism, so far as we can see, never desired such a positive supplementation — consistently enough; and *Epicureanism* sought it in a direction which expressed in the sharpest form the restriction of ethical interest to individual happiness. For the positive content of the wise man's peace of soul, hidden from the storms of the world, is, for Epicurus and his followers, at last only *pleasure.* In this they lacked, indeed, that spirited joy of the sensuous nature with which Aristippus had exalted the enjoyment of the moment and the joys of the body to be the supreme end, and we find, as already mentioned, that in their doctrine of the highest good the *blasé*, critically appreciative epicurism of the cultivated man, is declared to be the content of the ethical life. To be sure, in his psycho-genetic explanation Epicurus reduced all pleasure without exception to that of the senses, or, as they said later, to that of the flesh;[2] but, combating the Cyrenaics, he declared[3] that just these derivative and therefore refined joys of the mind were far superior to those of the senses. He recognised very properly that the individual, upon whose independence of the outer world all hinges, is much surer and much more the master of mental than of material enjoyments. The joys of the body depend on health, riches, and other gifts of fortune, but what is afforded by science and art, by the intimate friendship of noble men, by the calm, self-contented and free from wants, of the mind freed from passions, — this is the sure possession of the wise man, almost or wholly untouched by the change of fortune. The *æsthetic self-enjoyment of the cultured man* is hence the highest good for the Epicureans.

---

[1] Cf. the account (probably with regard to Chrysippus) in Seneca, *Ep.* 75, 8 ff.

[2] Athen. XII. 546 (Us. *Fr.* 409); Plut. *Ad. Col.* 27, 1122 (Us. *Fr.* 411); id. *Contr. Epic. Orat.* 4, 1088 (Us. *Fr.* 429).   [3] Diog. Laert. X. 137.

Thus, to be sure, the coarse and sensuous in Hedonism fell away, and the Gardens of Epicurus were a nursery of fair conduct of life, finest morals, and noble employments; but the principle of individual enjoyment remained the same, and the only difference was that the Greeks, in the old age of the national life, together with their Roman disciples, enjoyed in a more refined, intellectual, and delicate manner than did their youthful and manly ancestors. Only the content had become more valuable, because it was the content presented to enjoyment by a civilisation more richly developed and deeply lived out; the disposition with which life's cup was smilingly emptied, no longer in hasty quaffing, but in deliberate draughts, was the same egoism, devoid of all sense of duty. Hence the inner indifference of the wise man toward ethical tradition and rules of the land, which we find here also, though with greater caution; hence, above all, the putting aside of all metaphysical or religious ideas that might disturb the wise man in this self-complacent satisfaction of enjoyment, and burden him with the feeling of responsibility and duty.

5. To this, the *Stoic* ethics forms the strongest contrast. Already, in the thought reminding us of Aristotle (§ 13, 11), that the soul exercises its own proper nature in the rational power with which it refuses assent to impulses, we may recognise the peculiar antagonism which the Stoics assumed in the human psychical life. For just what we now are likely to call the natural impulses, viz. the excitations of feeling and will called forth by things of the outer world through the senses, and referring to these things, — just these seemed to them, as above mentioned, that which was contrary to nature (παρὰ φύσιν). Reason, on the other hand, was for them the "nature," not only of man, but of the universe in general. When, for this reason, they adopt the Cynic principles in which the moral is made equivalent to the natural, the same expression contains in this latter case a completely changed thought. As a part of the World-reason the soul excludes from itself, as an opposing element, the determination by sensuous impulses to which the Cynics had reduced morality: the demands of Nature, identical with those of reason, are in contradiction with those of the senses.

Accordingly, the positive content of morality among the Stoics appears as *harmony with Nature*, and thus, at the same time, as a *law* which claims normative validity as it confronts the sensuous man (νόμος).[1] In this formula, however, "Nature" is used in a

---

[1] With this is completed an interesting change in Sophistic terminology in which (§ 7, 1) νόμος and θέσις had been made equivalent to one another, and set over against φύσις; with the Stoics νόμος = φύσις.

double sense.[1] On the one hand is meant universal Nature, the creative, cosmic power, the world-thought acting according to ends (cf. § 15), the λόγος; and agreeably to this meaning, man's morality is his subordination to the law of Nature, his willing obedience to the course of the world, to the eternal necessity, and in so far as this World-reason is designated in the Stoic doctrine as deity, it is also obedience to God and to the divine law, as well as subordination to the world-purpose and the rule of Providence. The virtue of the perfect individual, who, as over against other individual beings and their action upon him through the senses, ought to withdraw within himself, his own master, and rest within himself, appears thus under obligation to something universal and all-ruling.

Nevertheless, since according to the Stoic conception the ἡγεμονικόν, the life-unity of the human soul, is a consubstantial part of this divine World-reason, the life in conformity with Nature must be also that which is adapted to *human nature*, to the essential nature of man; and this, too, as well in the more general sense that morality coincides with genuine, complete humanity and with the reasonableness which is valid in like measure for all, as also in the special meaning, that by fulfilling the command of Nature, each person brings to its unfolding the inmost germ of his own individual essence. Uniting these two points of view, it seemed to the Stoics that a rationally guided consistency in the conduct of life was the ideal of wisdom, and they found the supreme task of life in this, that the virtuous man has to preserve this complete harmony with himself [2] in every change of life, as his true strength of character. The political doctrinairism of the Greeks found thus its philosophical formulation and became a welcome conviction for the iron statesmen of republican Rome.

But whatever the particular terms in which the Stoics gave expression to their fundamental thought, this thought itself was everywhere the same, — that life according to Nature and according to reason is a *duty* (καθῆκον) which the wise man has to fulfil, a law to which he has to subject himself in opposition to his sensuous inclinations. And this *feeling of responsibility*, this strict consciousness of the "ought," this recognition of a higher order, gives to their doctrine, as to their life, backbone and marrow.

This demand also, for a life according to duty, we occasionally meet among the Stoics in the one-sided form, that the ethical con-

---

[1] Cf. Diog. Laert. VII. 87.
[2] Thus the formulas ὁμολογουμένως τῇ φύσει ζῆν and ὁμολογουμένως ζῆν have ultimately the same meaning. Stob. *Ecl.* II. 132.

sciousness requires some things on rational grounds, forbids the opposites, and declares all else to be ethically indifferent. What is not commanded and not forbidden, remains morally indifferent (ἀδιάφορον), and from this the Stoics sometimes drew lax consequences, which they perhaps defended more in words than in actual intention. But here, too, the systematic development of the theory created valuable intermediate links. For even if only the Good is unconditionally commanded, yet, in a secondary degree, the desirable must be regarded as ethically advisable; and though baseness proper consists only in willing that which is unconditionally forbidden, the moral man will yet seek to avoid also that which is "to be rejected." Thus, corresponding to the gradation of goods, there was introduced a like gradation of duties, which were distinguished as absolute and "intermediate." So, on the other hand, with regard to the valuation of human actions, a distinction was made on a somewhat different basis between those actions which fulfil the demand of reason[1] externally — these are called "befitting," conformable to duty in the broader sense (καθήκοντα) — and such as fulfil the demand of reason solely from the intention to do the Good. Only in the latter case[2] is there a perfect fulfilment of duty (κατόρθωμα), the opposite of which is the intention that is contrary to duty, as evinced in an action, — sin (ἁμάρτημα). Thus the Stoics, proceeding from the consciousness of duty, entered upon a profound and earnest study, extending sometimes to considerations of casuistry, of the ethical values of human will and action, and we may regard as their most valuable contribution the universally applied thought, that man in all his conduct, outer and inner, is responsible to a higher command.

6. The great difference in apprehension of the ethical life which exists between the Epicureans and the Stoics, in spite of a number of deep and far-reaching common qualities, becomes most clearly manifest in their respective theories of *society* and of the *state*. In this, to be sure, they are both at one almost to verbal agreement in the doctrine that the wise man, in the self-sufficiency of his virtue, needs the state[3] as little as he needs any other society; yes, that in certain circumstances, he should even avoid these in the interest, either of his own enjoyment or of the fulfilment of duty. In this sense, even the Stoics, especially the later Stoics, dissuaded from

---

[1] ὅσα ὁ λόγος αἱρεῖ ποιεῖν; Diog. Laert. VII. 108.
[2] For the contrast here alluded to by the Stoics Kant has made customary the expressions legality and morality; the Latin distinguishes according to Cicero's precedent, *rectum* and *honestum*.
[3] Epic. in Plut. *De Aud. Poet.* 14, 37 (Us. *Fr.* 548).

entrance into the family life and political activity; and for the
Epicureans, the responsibility which marriage and public activity
bring with them was sufficient to justify a very sceptical attitude
toward both, and especially to make the latter appear advisable for
the wise man, only in the case where it is unavoidable, or of quite
certain advantage.   In general, the Epicureans hold to the maxim of
their master, to live in quiet,[1] λάθε βιώσας, in which the inner crumbling of ancient society found its typical expression.

But a greater distinction between the two conceptions of life
shows itself in the fact that, to the Stoics, human society appeared
as a command of reason, which must give way only occasionally to
the wise man's task of personal perfection, while *Epicurus* expressly
denied all natural society among men,[2] and therefore reduced
every form of social conjunction to considerations of utility.   So
the theory of friendship, which in his school was so zealously
pledged, even to the point of sentimentality, did not find the ideal
support which it had received in Aristotle's splendid exposition;[3]
it finds ultimately only the motives of the wise man's enjoyment of
culture as heightened in society.[4]

In particular, however, Epicureanism carried through systematically the ideas already developed in Sophistic teaching concerning
the origin of the political community from the well-weighed interest
of the individuals who formed it. The state is not a natural structure,
but has been brought about by men as the result of reflection, and
for the sake of the advantages which are expected and received from
it.   It grows out of a compact (συνθήκη) which men enter into with
each other in order that they may not injure one another,[5] and the
formation of the state is hence one of the mighty processes through
which the human race has brought itself up from the savage state to
that of civilisation, by virtue of its growing intelligence.[6]   Laws,
therefore, have arisen in every particular case from a convention as
to the common advantage (σύμβολον τοῦ συμφέροντος).   There is
nothing in itself right or wrong; and since in the formation of a
compact the greater intelligence asserts itself to its own advantage

---

[1] Plutarch wrote against this the extant treatise (1128 ff.), εἰ καλῶς λέγεται
τὸ λάθε βιώσας.
[2] Arrian, *Epict. Diss.* I. 23, 1 (Us. *Fr.* 525); ib. II. 20, 6 (523).
[3] Cf. § 13, 12. The extensive literature on friendship is in this respect
a characteristic sign of the time which found its chief interest in the individual
personality and its relations. Cicero's dialogue *Lælius* (*De Amicitia*) reproduces essentially the Peripatetic conception.
[4] Diog. Laert. X. 120 (Us. *Fr.* 540).
[5] Cf. among the κύριαι δόξαι of Epicurus the terse sentences in Diog. Laert. X.
150 f.
[6] Cf. the description in Lucretius, *De Rer. Nat.* V. 922 ff., especially 1103 ff.

as a matter of course, it is for the most part the advantages of the wise that disclose themselves as motives in the enaction of laws.[1] And as is the case for their origin and content, so also for their validity and acknowledgment, the amount of pain which they are adapted to hinder and pleasure which they are adapted to produce, is the only standard. All the main outlines of the *utilitarian theory of society* are logically developed by Epicurus from the atomistic assumption that individuals first exist by and for themselves, and enter voluntarily and with design into the relations of society, only for the sake of the goods which as individuals they could not obtain or could not protect.

7. The *Stoics*, on the contrary, regarded man as already, by virtue of the consubstantiality of his soul with the World-reason, a being constituted by Nature for society,[2] and by reason of this very fact as under obligation by the command of reason to lead a social life, — an obligation which admits of exception only in special cases. As the most immediate relation we have here also friendship, the ethical connection of virtuous individuals who are united in the common employment of proving in action the moral law.[3] But from these purely personal relations the Stoic doctrine at once passes over to the most general, to all rational beings taken as an entirety. As parts of the same one World-reason, gods and men together form one great rational living structure, a πολιτικὸν σύστημα, in which every individual is a necessary member (μέλος), and from this results for the human race the ideal task of forming a *realm of reason* that shall embrace all its members.

The ideal state of the Stoics as it had been already delineated by Zeno, partly in a polemic parallel to that of Plato, knows, accordingly, no bounds of nationality or of the historic state; it is a rational society of all men, — an ideal universal empire. Plutarch, indeed, recognised[4] that in this thought philosophy constructed as rational that which was historically prepared by Alexander the Great, and completed, as we know, by the Romans. But it must not remain unnoticed that the Stoics thought of this empire only secondarily as a political power; primarily it was a spiritual unity of knowledge and will.

It is comprehensible that with such a high-flying idealism the

---

[1] Stob. *Flor.* 43, 139 (Us. *Fr.* 530).

[2] τῶν φύσει πολιτικῶν ζῴων: Stob. *Ecl.* II. 226 ff.

[3] It was, to be sure, extraordinarily difficult for the Stoics to bring the need, which they were obliged to recognise as a fact lying at the basis of the social impulse, into accord with the independence of the wise man, so baldly emphasised by them.

[4] Plut. *De Alex. M. Fort.* I. 6.

Stoics retained only a very weak interest for actual political life in the proper sense. Although the wise man was permitted and indeed charged to take part in the life of some particular state, in order to fulfil his duty to all even in this base world, yet both the particular forms of the state and the individual historical states were held to be ultimately indifferent to him. As to the former, the Stoa could not become enthusiastic for any of the characteristic kinds of government, but, following the Aristotelian suggestion, held rather to a mixed system, something such as Polybius[1] presented as desirable on the ground of his philosophico-historical consideration of the necessary transitions of one-sided forms into each other. To the splitting up of mankind in different states, the Stoics opposed the idea of *cosmopolitanism*, — world-citizenship, — which followed directly from their idea of an ethical community of all men. It corresponded to the great historical movements of the age, that the difference in worth between Hellenes and Barbarians, which had been still maintained even by Aristotle,[2] was set aside by the Stoics as overcome,[3] and though, in accordance with their ethical principle, they were too indifferent to the outer relations of position to enter upon active agitation for social reforms, they demanded, nevertheless, that *justice and the universal love of man*, which resulted as the highest duties from the idea of the realm of reason, should be applied also in full measure, even to the lowest members of human society — the slaves.

In spite of the fact, therefore, that it turned aside from the Greek thought of the national state, to the Stoic ethics belongs the glory that in it the ripest and highest which the ethical life of antiquity produced, and by means of which it transcended itself and pointed to the future, attained its best formulation. The intrinsic worth of moral personality, the overcoming of the world in man's overcoming of himself, the subordination of the individual to a divine law of the world, his disposition in an ideal union of spirits by means of which he is raised far above the bounds of his earthly life, and yet, in connection with this, the energetic feeling of duty that teaches him to fill vigorously his place in the actual world, — all these are the characteristics of a view of life which, though from a scientific point of view it may appear rather as put together than as produced from one principle, presents, nevertheless, one of the most powerful and pregnant creations in the history of the conceptions of human life.

---

[1] In the extant part of the sixth book.

[2] Arist. *Pol.* I. 2, 1252 b 5.

[3] Seneca, *Ep.* 95, 52 ; cf. Strabo, I. 4, 9. The personal composition also of the Stoic school was from its beginning decidedly international.

8. In a concentrated form all these doctrines appear in the conception of the law of life, determined by Nature and reason for all men equally, τὸ φύσει δίκαιον, and this conception, through *Cicero,*[1] became the formative principle of *Roman jurisprudence.*

For, in his eclectic attachment to all the great men of Attic philosophy, Cicero not only held fast objectively with all his energy to the thought of a moral world-order which determines with universal validity the relation of rational beings to each other, but he thought also with regard to the subjective aspect of the question — in correspondence with his epistemological theory (§ 17, 4) — that this command of reason was innate in all men equally, and that it had grown into inseparable connection with their instinct of self-preservation.   Out of this *lex naturæ,* the universally valid natural law which is exalted above all human caprice, and above all change of historical life, develop both the commands of morality in general, and in particular those of human society, — the *jus naturale.*   But while Cicero proceeds to project from this standpoint the ideal form of political life, the Stoic universal state takes on under his hands [2] the outlines of the Roman Empire.   Cosmopolitanism, which had arisen among the Greeks as a distant ideal, in the downfall of their own political importance, becomes with the Romans the proud self-consciousness of their historical mission.

But even in this theoretical development of what the state should be, Cicero interweaves the investigation of what it is.   Not sprung from the consideration or the voluntary choice of individuals, it is rather a product of history, and therefore the ever-valid principles of the law of Nature are mingled in the structures of its life with the historical institutions of positive law.   These latter develop partly as the domestic law of individual states, *jus civile,* partly as the law which the confederates of different states recognise in their relation to one another, *jus gentium.*   Both kinds of positive law coincide to a large extent in their ethical content with the law of Nature, but they supplement this by the multitude of historical elements which in them come into force.   The conceptions thus formed are important not only as constructing the skeleton for a new special science soon to branch off from philosophy; they have also the significance that in them the worth of the *historical* for the first time reaches full philosophical appreciation: and at this point Cicero

---

[1] Two of his treatises, only partly preserved, come into consideration here, *De Republica* and *De Legibus.*   Cf. M. Voigt, *Die Lehre vom jus naturale,* etc. (Leips. 1856), and K. Hildenbrand, *Geschichte und System der Rechts- und Staatsphilosophie,* I. 523 ff.

[2] Cic. *De Rep.* II. 1 ff.

knew how to transform the political greatness of his people into a scientific creation.

§ 15. Mechanism and Teleology.

The practice of the schools in the post-Aristotelian period separated philosophical investigations into three main divisions, — ethics, physics, and logic (the latter called canonic among the Epicureans). The chief interest was everywhere given to ethics, and theoretically the two others were allowed importance only so far as correct action presupposes a knowledge of things, and this in turn a clearness with regard to the right methods of knowledge. Hence the main tendencies of physical and logical theories are undoubtedly determined in this period by the ethical point of view, and the practical need is easily contented by taking up and re-shaping the older teachings; but yet in scientific work the great objects of interest, especially metaphysical and physical problems, assert their fascinating power, and so notwithstanding we see these other branches of philosophy often developing in a way that is not in full conformity with the nature of the ethical trunk from which they spring. Particularly in the case of physics, the rich development of the special sciences must ultimately keep general principles always alive and in a state of flux.

In this respect we notice first that the *Peripatetic* School, during the first generations, made a noteworthy change in the principles for explaining Nature which it had received from its master.

1. The beginning of this is found already with *Theophrastus*, who doubtless defended all the main doctrines of Aristotelianism, especially against the Stoics, but yet in part went his own ways. The extant fragment of his metaphysics discusses, among the aporiæ, principally such difficulties as were contained in the Aristotelian conceptions of the relation of the world to the deity. The Stagirite had conceived of Nature (φύσις) as a being in itself alive (ζῷον), and yet had conceived of its entire motion as a (teleological) effect of the divine Reason; God, as pure Form, was separated from the world, transcendent; and yet, as animating, first-moving power, he was immanent in it. This chief metaphysical problem of the following period was seen by Theophrastus, though his own attitude toward it remained fixed by the bounds of Aristotle's doctrine. On the other hand, he shows a more definite tendency in the closely connected question regarding the relation of reason to the lower psychical activities. The νοῦς was regarded, on the one hand (considered as Form of the animal soul), as immanent, inborn; on the other hand, in its purity, as different in essence, and as having come

into the individual soul from without. Here now Theophrastus decided absolutely against transcendence; he subsumed the νοῦς also as a self-developing activity, under the concept of a cosmic process,[1] of motion (κίνησις), and set it beside the animal soul as something different, not in kind, but in degree only.

Strato proceeded still more energetically in the same direction. He removed completely the limits between reason and the lower activities of ideation. Both, he taught, form an inseparable unity; there is no thought without perceptions, and just as little is there sense-perception without the co-operation of thought; both together belong to the unitary consciousness, which he, with the Stoics, calls τὸ ἡγεμονικόν (cf. § 14, 3). But Strato applied the same thought, which he carried out psychologically, to the analogous metaphysical relation also. The ἡγεμονικόν of the φύσις, also, the Reason of Nature, cannot be regarded as something separated from her. Whether now this may be expressed in the form that Strato did not think the hypothesis of the deity necessary for the explanation of Nature and its phenomena, or in the form that he postulated Nature itself as God, but denied it not only external resemblance to man, but even consciousness,[2] — in any case, Stratonism, regarded from the standpoint of Aristotle's teaching, forms a one-sidedly *naturalistic* or pantheistic modification. He denies spiritual monotheism, the conception of the transcendence of God, and by teaching that a pure Form is as unthinkable as mere matter, he pushes the Platonic element in the Aristotelian metaphysics, which had remained just in the thought of the separation (χωρισμός) of reason from matter, so far into the background that the element derived from Democritus becomes again entirely free. Strato sees in what takes place in the world, only an immanent necessity of Nature, and no longer the working of a spiritual, extramundane cause.

Yet this naturalism remains still in dependence upon Aristotle, in so far as it seeks the natural causes of the cosmic processes, not in the atoms and their quantitative determinations, but expressly in the original qualities (ποιότητες) and powers (δυνάμεις) of things. If among these it emphasised especially warmth and cold, this was quite in the spirit of the *dynamic* conceptions held by the older Hylozoism, and to this, also, Strato seems most nearly related in his undecided, intermediate position between mechanical and teleological explanation of the world. Just for this reason, however, this side-development ran its course with Strato himself without further result, for it was already outrun at the beginning by the Stoic and

---

[1] Simpl. *Phys.* 225 a.   [2] Cic. *Acad.* II. 38, 121 ; *De Nat. Deor.* I. 13, 35.

the Epicurean physics. These both defended also the standpoint of the immanent explanation of Nature, but the former was as outspokenly teleological as the latter was mechanical.

2. The peculiarly involved position of the *Stoics*, in the department of metaphysical and physical questions, resulted from the union of different elements. In the foreground stands the ethical need of deducing from a most general metaphysical principle the content of individual morality which could no longer find its roots in state and nationality as in the period of Grecian greatness, and therefore of so shaping the conception of this principle as to make this deduction possible. But, in opposition to this, stood, as an inheritance from Cynicism, the decided disinclination to regard this principle as a transcendent, supersensuous, and incorporeal principle, out of the world of experience. All the more decisive was the force with which the thoughts suggested in the Peripatetic philosophy of Nature came forward, in which the attempt was made to understand the world as a living being, in purposive motion of itself. For all these motives, the *logos doctrine of Heraclitus* seemed to present itself as in like measure a solution of the problem, and this became, therefore, the central point of the Stoic metaphysics.[1]

The fundamental view of the Stoics is, then, that the entire universe forms a single, unitary, living, connected whole, and that all particular things are the determinate forms assumed by a divine primitive power which is in a state of eternal activity. Their doctrine is in its fundamental principles *pantheism*, and (in opposition to Aristotle) conscious pantheism. The immediate consequence of it, however, is the energetic effort to overcome the Platonic-Aristotelian dualism,[2] and remove the opposition between sensuous and supersensuous, between natural necessity and reason acting according to ends, between Matter and Form. The Stoa attempts this through simple identification of those conceptions whose opposing characters, to be sure, cannot by this means be put out of the world.

Hence it declares the divine World-being to be the primitive power in which are contained in like measure the conditioning laws and the purposeful determination of all things and of all cosmic processes, — the World-ground and the World-mind. As actively productive and formative power, the deity is the λόγος σπερματικός,

---

[1] Cf. H. Siebeck, *Die Umbildung der peripatetischen Naturphilosophie in die der Stoiker* (*Unters. z. Philosophie der Griechen*, 2 Aufl., pp. 181 ff.).

[2] If we were obliged to conceive of the relation of Aristotle to Plato in a similar manner (§ 13, 1–4), just in this point the Stoic philosophy of Nature shows a farther development in the same direction which the Peripatetic takes in Strato.

the *vital principle*, which unfolds itself in the multitude of phenom-ena as their peculiar, particular λόγοι σπερματικοί or *formative forces.* In this organic function, God is, however, also the purposefully creating and guiding Reason, and thus with regard to all particular processes the all-ruling *Providence* (πρόνοια). The determination of the particular by the universe (which constitutes the dominant fundamental conviction of the Stoics) is a completely purposeful and rational *order*,[1] and forms as such the highest *norm* (νόμος), according to which all individual beings should direct themselves in the development of their activity.[2]

But this all-determining "law" is for the Stoics, as it was for Heraclitus, likewise the all-compelling power which, as inviolable *necessity* (ἀνάγκη), and so, as inevitable *destiny* (εἱμαρμένη, *fatum*), brings forth every particular phenomenon in the unalterable succes-sion of causes and effects. Nothing takes place in the world with-out a preceding cause (αἰτία προηγουμένη), and just by virtue of this complete causal determination of every particular does the universe possess its character of a purposeful, connected whole.[3]   Hence Chrysippus combated in the most emphatic manner the conception of chance, and taught that apparent causelessness in a particular event could mean only a kind of causation hidden from human insight.[4] In this assumption of a *natural necessity, admitting of no exceptions* even for the most particular and the least important occurrence, — a conviction which naturally found expression also in the form that the divine providence extends even to the smallest events of l'fe,[5] — the Stoic school agrees even verbally with Democ-ritus, and is the only school in antiquity which carried this most valuable thought of the great Abderite through all branches of theoretical science.

In all other respects, indeed, the Stoics stand in opposition to Democritus and in closer relation to Aristotle. For while in the Atomistic system the natural necessity of all that comes to pass results from the motive impulses of individual things, with the Stoics it flows immediately from the *living activity of the whole*, and

---

[1] As the Platonic Timæus had already taught, § 11, 10.
[2] The normative character in the conception of the *logos* appeared clearly even with Heraclitus (§ 6, 2, p. 63, note 5).
[3] Plut. *De Fato*, 11, 574.   [4] Ib. 7, 572.
[5] Plutarch makes Chrysippus say (*Comm. Not.* 34, 5, 1076) that not even the meanest thing can sustain any other relation than that which accords with the decree of Zeus. Cf. Cic. *De Nat. Deor.* II. 65, 164. Only the circumstance that the Stoa limited the *immediate* action of the divine providence to the pur-poseful determination of the whole, and derived from this that of the particular, explains such modes of expression as the well-known *Magna dii curant, parva negligunt*. Cf. § 16. 2.

as over against the reduction of all qualities to quantitative differences, they held fast to the reality of properties as the peculiar
forces of individual things, and to qualitative alteration (ἀλλοίωσις,
in opposition to motion in space). They directed their polemic
particularly against the purely mechanical explanation of natural
processes by pressure and impact; but in carrying out their *teleology,*
they sank from the great conception of Aristotle, who had everywhere emphasised the immanent purposiveness of the formations in
which the Forms were realised, to the consideration of the benefits
which flow from the phenomena of Nature to meet the needs of
beings endowed with reason, "of gods and men."[1] In particular,
they exaggerated, even to ridiculous Philistinism, the demonstration
of the manner in which heaven and earth and all that in them is,
are arranged with such magnificent *adaptation for man.*[2]

3. In all these theoretical views, and just in these, the *Epicureans*
are diametrically opposed to the Stoics. With the Epicureans, employment with metaphysical and physical problems had in general
only the negative purpose[3] of setting aside the religious ideas
through which the quiet self-enjoyment of the wise man might be
disturbed. Hence it was the chief concern of Epicurus to exclude
from the explanation of Nature every element that would allow a
government of the world, guided by universal ends, to appear as
even possible; hence, on the other hand, the Epicurean view of the
world was absolutely lacking in a positive principle. This explains
the fact that Epicurus, at least, had only a sceptical shrug of the
shoulders for all questions of natural science from which no practical
advantage was to be gained; and though many of his later disciples
seem to have been less limited, and to have thought more scientifically, the ruts of the school's opinion were worn too deep to
allow the attainment of essentially broader aims. The more the
teleological conception of Nature formed, in the course of time, the
common ground on which Academic, Peripatetic, and Stoic doctrines
met in syncretistic blending, the more Epicureanism insisted upon
its isolated standpoint of negation; theoretically, it was essentially
anti-teleological, and in this respect brought forth nothing positive.

It was successful only in combating the anthropological excres-
cences to which the teleological view of the world led, especially

---

[1] Cic. *De Fin.* III. 20, 67 ; *De Nat. Deor.* II. 53 ff.

[2] If one might trust Xenophon's *Memorabilia,* the Stoics had in this no less
a man than Socrates as their predecessor; yet it seems that even in this account,
which is tinctured with Cynicism if not worked over from the Stoic point of
view (Krohn), the general faith of Socrates in a purposeful guiding of the world
by divine providence has descended into the petty. Cf. § 8, 8.

[3] Diog. Laert. X. 143 ; Us. p. 74.

with the Stoics,[1] — a task which was undoubtedly not so very difficult, — but to create from principles a counter-theory it was not prepared. Epicurus, indeed, availed himself for this purpose of the
external data of the materialistic metaphysics, as he was able to
receive them from Democritus; but he was far from attaining the
latter's scientific height. He could follow the great Atomist only
so far as to believe that he himself also, for explaining the world,
needed nothing more than empty space and the corporeal particles
moving within it, countless in number, infinitely varied in form and
size, and indivisible; and to their motion, impact, and pressure he
traced all cosmic processes, and all things and systems of things
(worlds) which arise and again perish, thereby seeking to deduce
all qualitative differences from these purely quantitative relations.[2]
He accepted, accordingly, the purely *mechanical* conception of natural processes, but denied expressly their unconditioned and exceptionless necessity. The doctrine of Democritus, therefore, passed
over to the Epicureans only in so far as it was Atomism and mechanism; with regard to the much deeper and more valuable principle
of the universal reign of law in Nature, his legacy, as we have seen
above, passed to the Stoics.

Meanwhile, just this peculiar relation is most intimately connected with the Epicurean ethics and with the decisive influence
which that exercised upon their physics; indeed, one may say that
the individualising tendency taken by the ethical reflection of the
post-Aristotelian age found its most adequate metaphysics just in
the doctrine of Epicurus. To a morals, which had for its essential
content the independence of the individual and his withdrawal
upon himself, a view of the world must have been welcome which
regarded the prime constituents of reality as completely independent, both of each other and of a single force, and regarded their
activity as determined solely by themselves.[3] Now the doctrine of
Democritus which taught the inevitable, natural necessity of all
that comes to pass, contains unmistakably a (Heraclitic) element
which removes this autonomy of individual things, and just to their
adoption of this element did the Stoics owe the fact (cf. § 14, 5)
that their ethics outgrew the one-sided Cynic presuppositions with
which they started. It is all the more comprehensible that Epicurus let just this element fall away; and his conception of the

---

[1] Cf. especially Lucret. *De Rer. Nat.* I. 1021; V. 156; Diog. Laert. X. 97.
[2] Sext. Emp. *Adv. Math.* X. 42.
[3] Thus Epicurus grounded his deviation from Democritus's explanation of the
world by an appeal to human freedom of the will. Cf. § 16, and also the citations in Zeller IV.[3] 408, 1 [Eng. tr. *Stoics,* etc., p. 446].

world as contrasted with that of the Stoa is characterised precisely by this, that while the latter regarded every individual as determined by the whole, he rather regarded the whole as a product of originally existing and likewise originally functioning individual things.   His doctrine is in every respect consistent *Atomism*.

Thus the system of Democritus had the misfortune to be propagated for traditions of antiquity, and so also for those of the Middle Ages, in a system which indeed retained his Atomistic view, looking in the direction of the exclusive reality of quantitative relations and of the mechanical conception of the cosmic processes, but set aside his thought of Nature as a connected whole, regulated by law.

4. Following this latter direction, Epicurus gave a new form to the doctrine of the origin of the world maintained by Atomism.[1] In contrast with what had been already seen, perhaps by the Pythagoreans, but, at all events, by Democritus, Plato, and Aristotle, that in space in itself there is no other direction than that from the centre toward the periphery, and the reverse, he appeals to the declaration of the senses,[2] — agreeably to his doctrine of knowledge, — according to which there is an absolute up and down, and maintains that the atoms were all originally in motion from above downward by virtue of their weight.   But, in order to derive the origination of atom groups from this universal rain of atoms, he assumed that some of them had voluntarily deviated from the direct line of fall.   From this deviation were explained the impacts, the grouping of atoms, and, ultimately, the whirling motions which lead to the formation of worlds, and which the old Atomism had derived from the meeting of atoms which were moving about in an unordered manner.[3]

It is noteworthy, however, that after he had in this way spoiled the inner coherence of the doctrine of Democritus, Epicurus renounced the voluntary choice of the atoms as a means for the further explanation of the individual processes of Nature, and from the point when the whirling motion of the atom-complexes seemed to him to be explained, allowed only the principle of mechanical

---

[1] Ps.-Plut. *Plac.* I. 3 ; *Dox.* D. 285 ; Cic. *De Fin.* I. 6, 17 ; Guyau, *Morale d'Epic.* 74.

[2] Diog. Laert. X. 60.

[3] Cf. § 4, 9.   It seems that later Epicureans who held fast to the sensuous basis of this idea and yet would exclude the voluntary action of the atoms and carry out more thoroughly the Democritic thought of Nature's conformity to law, hit upon the plan of explaining the grouping (ἀθροισμός) of the atoms on the hypothesis that the more massive fell faster in empty space than the "lighter"; at least, Lucretius combats such theories (*De Rer. Nat.* II. 225 ff.).

necessity to stand.[1] He used, therefore, the voluntary self-determination of the atoms only as a principle to explain the *beginning* of a whirling motion which afterwards went on purely mechanically. He used it, therefore, just as Anaxagoras used his force-matter, νοῦς (cf. p. 52). For upon this metaphysical substructure Epicurus erected a physical theory which acknowledged only the mechanics of atoms as explanation for all phenomena of Nature without any exception, and carried this out, for organisms especially, by employing for the explanation of their purposive formation the Empedoclean thought of the survival of the fit.

Lastly, the Democritic principle of natural necessity asserts itself in the system of Epicurus in his assumption that in the continuous arising and perishing of the worlds which become formed by the assemblages of atoms, every possible combination, and thus every form of world-construction, must ultimately repeat itself. This was proved in a manner which would now be put upon the basis of the theory of probabilities, and the result of this repetition was held to be, that considering the infinitude of time, nothing can happen which has not already existed in the same way.[2] In this doctrine, again, Epicurus agrees with the Stoics, who taught a plurality of worlds, not co-existent, but following one another in time, and yet found themselves forced to maintain that these must be always completely alike, even to the last detail of particular formation and particular events. As the world proceeds forth from the divine primitive fire, so it is each time taken back again into the same after a predetermined period : and then when after the world-conflagration the primitive power begins the construction of a new world, this φύσις (Nature), which remains eternally the same, unfolds itself again and again in the same manner, in correspondence with its own rationality and necessity. This return of all things (παλιγγενεσία or ἀποκατάστασις) appears, accordingly, as a necessary consequence of the two alternative conceptions of the Stoics, λόγος and εἱμαρμένη.

5. The theoretical ideas of these two main schools of later antiquity are accordingly at one only in being completely *material-*

---

[1] Hence in a certain sense it might be said, from the standpoint of present criticism, that the difference between Democritus and Epicurus was only a relative one. The former regards as an unexplained primitive fact the direction which each atom has from the beginning, the latter regards as an unexplained primitive fact a voluntary deviation, taking place at some point of time, from a direction of fall which is uniform for all. The essential difference, however, is that with Democritus this primitive fact is something timeless, while with Epicurus it is a *single* voluntary act *occurring in time*, an act which is expressly compared with the causeless self-determination of the human will (cf. § 16).

[2] Plut. in Euseb. *Dox.* D. 581, 19 ; Us. *Fr.* 266.

istic, and it was just in opposition to Plato and Aristotle that they expressly emphasised this position of theirs. Both maintain that the real (τὰ ὄντα), because it manifests itself in action and passion (ποιεῖν καὶ πάσχειν), can be only corporeal; the Epicureans declared only empty space to be incorporeal. On the contrary, they combated the (Platonic) view that the properties of bodies are something incorporeal *per se* (καθ᾿ ἑαυτό),[1] and the Stoics even went so far as to declare that even the qualities, forces, and relations of things, which present themselves in changing modes in connection with things and yet as actual or real, are "bodies,"[2] and with a mode of thought which reminds us of the coming and going of the homoiomeriæ with Anaxagoras,[3] they regarded the presence and change of properties in things as a kind of inter-mixture of these bodies with others, a view from which resulted the theory of the universal mingling and reciprocal interpenetration of all bodies (κρᾶσις δι᾽ ὅλων).

In carrying out the materialistic theory the Epicureans produced scarcely anything new; on the contrary, the *Stoic doctrine of Nature* shows a number of new views, which are interesting not only in themselves, but also as having marked out the essential lines for the idea of the world held during the following centuries.

First of all, in the Stoic system the two antitheses, which were to be removed or identified in the conception of Nature as one, again part company. The divine primitive essence divides into the active and the passive, into force and matter. As force, the deity is fire or warm, vital breath, *pneuma ;* as matter, it changes itself out of moist vapour (air) partly into water, partly into earth. Thus fire is the soul, and the "moist" is the body, of the World-god; and yet the two form a single being, identical within itself. While the Stoics thus attach themselves, in their doctrine of the transmuta-tion and re-transmutation of substances, to Heraclitus, and in their characterisation of the four elements principally to Aristotle, and follow Aristotle also in the main in their exposition of the world-structure and of the purposive system of its movements, the most important thing in their physics is doubtless the doctrine of the pneuma.

God as creative reason (λόγος σπερματικός) is this warm vital breath, the formative fire-mind which penetrates all things and is

---

[1] Diog. Laert. X. 67.

[2] Plut. *C. Not.* 50, 1085.

[3] A similar materialising of the Platonic doctrine of Ideas (Plat. *Phædo*, 102), which reminds us of Anaxagoras, was apparently worked out by Eudoxos, who belonged to the Academy (p. 103). Arist. *Met.* I. 9, 991 a 17, and also Alex. Aphr. *Schol.* in Arist. 573 a 12.

dominant in them as their active principle; he is the universe regarded as an animate being, spontaneously in motion within itself, and purposefully and regularly developed. All this is comprehended by the Stoics in the conception of the πνεῦμα,[1] an extraordinarily condensed conception, full of relations, — an idea in which suggestions from Heraclitus (λόγος), Anaxagoras (νοῦς), Diogenes of Apollonia (ἀήρ), Democritus (fire-atoms), and not least the Peripatetic natural philosophy and physiology, became intricately combined.[2]

6. The most effective element in this combination proved to be the *analogy between macrocosm and microcosm*, universe and man, which the Stoics adopted from Aristotle. The individual soul, also, the vital force of the body, which holds together and rules the flesh, is fiery breath, pneuma; but all the individual forces which are active in the members and control their purposive functions, are also such vital minds or spirits (*spiritus animales*). In the human and the animal organism the activity of the pneuma appears connected with the blood and its circulation; nevertheless, the pneuma itself — just because it is also a body, said Chrysippus [3] — is separable in detail from the lower elements which it animates, and this separation takes place in death.

At the same time, however, the individual soul, as it is only a part of the universal World-soul, is completely determined in its nature and its activity by this World-soul; it is consubstantial with the divine Pneuma and dependent upon it. Just for this reason the World-reason, the λόγος, is for the soul the highest law (cf. above, § 14, 3). The soul's independence is therefore only one that is limited by time, and in any case it is its ultimate destiny to be taken back into the divine All-mind at the universal conflagration of the world. With regard to the continuance of this independence, *i.e.* as to the extent of individual immortality, various views were current in the school; some recognised the duration of all souls until the time of the universal conflagration, others reserved this for the wise only.

As now the one Pneuma of the universe (whose seat was located by the Stoics sometimes in heaven, sometimes in the sun, sometimes in the midst of the world) pours itself forth into all things as animating force, so the ruling part of the individual soul (τὸ ἡγεμονικόν or λογισμός) in which dwell ideas, judgments, and impulses, and

---

[1] Stob. *Ecl.* I. 374. *Dox.* D. 463, 16: εἶναι τὸ ὂν πνεῦμα κινοῦν ἑαυτὸ πρὸς ἑαυτὸ καὶ ἐξ αὑτοῦ, ἢ πνεῦμα ἑαυτὸ κινοῦν πρόσω καὶ ὀπίσω κτλ.

[2] Cf. H. Siebeck *Zeitsch. f. Völkerpsychologie*, 1881, pp. 364 ff.

[3] Nemesius, *De Nat. Hom.* p. 34.

as whose seat the heart was assumed, was regarded as extending its particular ramifications throughout the whole body, like the "arms of a polyp." Of such particular "pneumata" the Stoa assumed seven,—the five senses, the faculty of speech, and the reproductive power. As the unity of the divine Primitive Being dwells in the universe, so the individual personality lives in the body.

It is characteristic that the Epicureans could entirely adopt this external apparatus of psychological views. For them, too, the soul — which according to Democritus consists of the finest atoms — is a fiery, atmospheric breath (they apply likewise the term "pneuma"); but they see in this breath something that is introduced into the body from without, something held fast by the body and mechanically connected with it, which in death is forthwith scattered. They also distinguish between the rational and the irrational part of the soul, without, however, being able to attribute to the former the metaphysical dignity which it acquired in the Stoic theory. Here, too, their doctrine is, on the whole, insufficient and dependent.

7. In accordance with the pantheistic presupposition of the system, the metaphysics and physics of the *Stoics* form also a *theology*, a system of *natural religion* based on scientific demonstration, and this found also poetic presentations in the school, such as the hymn of Cleanthes. *Epicureanism*, on the contrary, is in its whole nature *anti-religious*. It takes throughout the standpoint of "Enlightenment," that religion has been overcome by science, and that it is the task and triumph of wisdom to put aside the phantoms of superstition which have grown out of fear and ignorance. The poet of this school depicts in grotesque outlines the evils which religion brought on man, and sings the glory of their conquest by scientific knowledge.[1] It is all the more amusing that the Epicurean theory itself fell to depicting a mythology of its own which it regarded as harmless. It believed that a certain degree of truth must attach to the universal faith in gods,[2] but it found that this correct idea was disfigured by false assumptions. These it sought in the myths which feigned a participation of the gods in human life, and an interference on their part in the course of things; even the Stoics' belief in Providence appeared to them in this respect as but a refined illusion. Epicurus, therefore, — following Democritus in his doctrine of the *eidola*, or images (§ 10, 4), — saw in the gods giant forms resembling men, who lead a blessed life of contemplation and spiritual intercourse in the intermediate spaces between the

---

[1] Lucret. *De Rer. Nat.* I. 62 ff.   [2] Diog. Laert. X. 123 f.; Us. p. 59 f.

worlds (*intermundia*), undisturbed by the change of events, and unconcerned as to the destiny of lower beings; and thus this doctrine, also, is fundamentally only the attempt of Epicureanism to put in mythological form its ideal of æsthetic self-enjoyment.

8. It was in an entirely different way that the ideas of the popular religion were fitted into the *Stoic* metaphysics. Whereas, up to this time in the development of Greek thought philosophical theology had separated itself farther and farther from the indigenous mythology, we meet here, for the first time, the systematic attempt to bring *natural and positive religion* into harmony. Accordingly, when the Stoics, also, yielded to the need of recognising the warrant of ideas universally present throughout the human race (cf. § 17, 4), their pneuma doctrine offered them not only a welcome instrument, but suggestions that were determinative. For consideration of the universe must teach them that the divine World-power has evidently taken on mightier forms and those of more vigorous life than individual human souls; and so, beside the one deity without beginning and end, which for the most part they designated as Zeus, a great number of "*gods that had come into existence,*" made their appearance. To these the Stoics, as Plato and Aristotle had already done, reckoned first of all the stars, which they too honoured as higher intelligences and especially pure formations of the primitive fire, and further, the personifications of other natural forces in which the power of Providence, benevolent to man, reveals itself. From this point of view we can understand how an extensive interpretation of myths was the order of the day in the Stoic school, seeking to incorporate the popular figures in its metaphysical system by all kinds of allegories. In addition to this there was an equally welcome use of the Euemeristic theory, which not only explained and justified the deification of prominent men, but taught also to consider the demons sacred, as the guardian spirits of individual men.

Thus the Stoic world became peopled with a whole host of higher and lower gods, but they all appeared as ultimately but emanations of the one highest World-power, — as the subordinate powers or forces which, themselves determined by the universal Pneuma, were conceived of as the ruling spirits of the world's life. They formed, therefore, for the faith of the Stoics, the mediating organs, which represent, each in its realm, the vital force and Providence of the World-reason, and to them the piety of the Stoics turned in the forms of worship of positive religion. The *polytheism* of the popular faith was thus philosophically re-established, and taken up as an integrant constituent into metaphysical pantheism.

In connection with this scientific reconstruction of positive religion stands the theoretical justification of *divination* in the Stoic system where it awakened great interest, except in the case of a few men like Panætius, who thought more coolly. The interconnection and providentially governed unity of the world's processes was held to show itself — as one form of manifestation — in the possibility that different things and processes which stand in no direct causal relation to one another, may yet point to one another by delicate relations, and therefore be able to serve as signs for one another. The human soul is capable of understanding these by virtue of its relationship with the all-ruling Pneuma, but for the full interpretation of such ecstatic revelations the art and science of divination, resting upon experience, must be added. On this basis Stoicism regarded itself as strong enough to elaborate philosophically all the divination of the ancient world. This was especially true of its younger representatives, and in particular, as it seems, of Posidonius.

§ 16. The Freedom of the Will and the Perfection of the World.

The sharp definition of the contrasted mechanical and teleological views of the world, and especially the difference in the conceptional forms in which the thought, common to a certain extent, of Nature's universal conformity to law had been developed, led, in connection with the ethical postulates and presuppositions which controlled the thought of the time, to two new problems, which from the beginning had various complications. These were the problems of the freedom of the human will and of the goodness and perfection of the world. Both problems grew out of contradictions which made their appearance between moral needs and just those metaphysical theories which had been formed to satisfy those needs.

1. The proper home for the formation of these new problems was the *Stoic* system, and they may be understood as the necessary consequence of a deep and ultimately irreconcilable antagonism between the fundamental principles of the system. These principles are *metaphysical monism* and *ethical dualism*. The fundamental moral doctrine of the Stoics, according to which man should overcome the world in his own impulses by virtue, presupposes an anthropological duality, an opposition in human nature in accordance with which reason stands over against a *sensuous nature contrary to reason*. Without this antithesis the whole Stoic ethics is ready to fall. The metaphysical doctrine, however, by which the command of reason in man is to be explained, postulates such an unrestricted and all-

controlling reality of the World-reason that the reality of what is contrary to reason, either in man or in the course of the world, cannot be united therewith. From this source grew the two questions which since then have never ceased to employ man's critical investigation, although all essential points of view that can come into consideration in the case were more or less clearly illumined at that time.

2. The conceptions which form the presuppositions for the *problem of freedom* lie ready at hand in the ethical reflections on the voluntary nature of wrongdoing, which were begun by Socrates and brought to a preliminary conclusion by Aristotle in a brilliant investigation.[1] The motives of these thoughts are ethical throughout, and the domain in which they move is exclusively psychological. The question at issue is hence essentially that of freedom of choice, and while the reality of this is doubtless affirmed upon the basis of immediate feeling, and with reference to man's consciousness of his responsibility, difficulty arises only in consequence of the intellectualistic conception of Socrates, who brought the will into complete dependence upon insight. This difficulty develops primarily in the double meaning of " freedom," or, as it is here still called, " voluntariness " (ἑκούσιον), an ambiguity which has since been repeated again and again in the most variously shifted forms. According to Socrates, all ethically wrong action proceeds from a wrong view — a view clouded by desires. He who thus acts does not "know," therefore, what he is doing, and in this sense he acts involuntarily.[2] That is, only the wise man is free; the wicked is not free.[3] From this *ethical* conception of freedom, however, the *psychological* conception of freedom — *i.e.* the conception of freedom of choice as the ability to decide between different motives — must be carefully separated. Whether Socrates did this is a question;[4] at all events, it was done by Plato. The latter expressly affirmed man's freedom of choice,[5] appealing to his responsibility, — a psychological decision on essentially ethical grounds, — and, at the same time, he held fast to the Socratic doctrine that the wicked man acts involuntarily, *i.e.* is ethically not free. He even connects the two directly when he develops the thought [6] that man may sink into the

---

[1] *Eth. Nic.* III. 1–8.
[2] Xen. *Mem.* III. 9, 4 ; *Cyrop.* III. 1, 38.
[3] Cf. Arist. *Eth. Nic.* III. 7, 113 b 14.
[4] According to a remark in the Peripatetic *Magna Moralia* (I. 9, 1187 a 7) Socrates, indeed, had expressly said, "it is not in our power" to be good or bad. According to this, therefore, he had denied psychological freedom.
[5] Plat. *Rep.* X. 617 ff.
[6] Plat. *Phœd.* 81 B.

condition of ethical non-freedom by his own fault, and, therefore, with psychological freedom.

With *Aristotle*, who separated himself farther from the Socratic intellectualism, the psychological conception of freedom comes out more clearly and independently.   He proceeds from the position that ethical qualification in general is applicable only in the case of "voluntary" actions, and discusses in the first place the prejudices which this voluntariness sustains, partly from external force ($\beta i a$) and psychical compulsion, and partly from ignorance of the matter. That action only is completely voluntary which has its origin in the personality itself, and of which the relations are fully known.[1]   The whole investigation [2] is maintained from the standpoint of responsibility, and the discovered conception of voluntariness is designed to lead to the conception of accountability.   It contains within itself the characteristics of external freedom of action, and of a conception of the situation unclouded by any deception.   But, on this account, it must be still further restricted, for among his voluntary acts a man can be held accountable for those only that proceed from a choice ($\pi \rho o a i \rho \epsilon \sigma \iota s$).[3]   *Freedom of choice*, therefore, which proceeds by reflecting upon ends as well as upon means, is the condition of ethical accountability.

Aristotle avoided a farther entrance upon the psychology of motivation and upon the determining causes of this choice; he contents himself with establishing the position that the personality itself is the sufficient reason for the actions [4] which are ascribed to it; and to this maintenance of the freedom of choice his school, and especially Theophrastus, who composed a treatise of his own on freedom, held fast.

3. On this same basis we find also the *Stoics*, in so far as purely ethical considerations are concerned.   Precisely that lively feeling of responsibility which characterises their morals demanded of them the recognition of this free choice on the part of the individual, and they sought therefore to maintain this in every way.

Their position became critical, however, by reason of the fact that their metaphysics, with its doctrine of fate and providence, drove them beyond this attitude.   For since this theory of fate made man, like all other creatures, determined in all his external and internal formation and in all that he does and suffers, by the

---

[1] *Eth. Nic.* III. 3, 1111 a 73 : οὗ ἡ ἀρχὴ ἐν αὐτῷ εἰδότι τὰ καθ᾽ ἕκαστα ἐν οἷς ἡ :ρᾶξις.

[2] As the reference at the beginning to the right of punishment clearly shows (*Eth. Nic.* 1109 b 34).

[3] Ib. 4, 1112 a 1.

[4] Ib. 5, 1112 b 31 : ἔοικε δὴ . . . ἄνθρωπος εἶναι ἀρχὴ τῶν πράξεων.

all-animating World-power, personality ceased to be the true ground (ἀρχή) of his actions, and these appeared to be, like all else that occurs, but the predetermined and unavoidably necessary operations of the God-Nature.   In fact, the Stoa did not shrink from this extreme consequence of *determinism;* on the contrary, Chrysippus heaped up proof on proof for this doctrine.   He based it upon the principle of sufficient reason (cf. above, § 15, 2); he showed that only by presupposing this could the correctness of judgments concerning the future be maintained, since a criterion for their truth or falsity is given only if the matter is already determined;[1] he also gave to this argument the changed form, that since only the necessary can be known, and not that which is still undecided, the foreknowledge of the gods makes necessary the assumption of determinism; he even did not scorn to adduce the fulfilment of predictions as a welcome argument.

In this doctrine, which, from the standpoint of the Stoic doctrine of the logos, was completely consistent, the opponents of the system saw of course a decided denial of freedom of the will, and of the criticisms which the system experienced this was perhaps the most frequent and at the same time the most incisive.   Among the numerous attacks the best known is the so-called *ignava ratio,* or "lazy reason" (ἀργὸς λόγος), which from the claim of the unavoidable necessity of future events draws the fatalistic conclusion that one should await them inactively, — an attack which Chrysippus did not know how to avoid except by the aid of very forced distinctions.[2]   The Stoics, on the contrary, concerned themselves to show that in spite of this determinism, and rather exactly by virtue of it, man remains the cause of his actions in the sense that he is to be made responsible for them.   On the basis of a distinction[3] between main and accessory causes (which, moreover, reminds us throughout of the Platonic αἴτιον and ξυναίτιον) Chrysippus showed that every decision of the will does indeed necessarily follow from the co-operation of man with his environment, but that just here the outer circumstances are only the accessory causes, while the assent proceeding from the personality is the main cause, and to this accountability applies.   While, however, this voluntarily acting ἡγεμονικόν, or ruling faculty of man, is determined from the universal Pneuma, this Pneuma takes on in every separate being a self-subsistent

---

[1] Cic. *De Fato,* 10, 20.   So far as concerns disjunctive propositions Epicurus also for this reason gave up the truth of disjunction; Cic. *De Nat. Deor.* I. 25, 70.

[2] Cic. *De Fato,* 12, 28 ff.

[3] Cic. *De Fato,* 16, 36 ff.

nature, different from that of others, and this is to be regarded as a proper ἀρχή.[1] In particular, the Stoics make prominent the point that responsibility, as a judgment pronounced on the ethical quality of actions and characters, is quite independent of the question whether the persons or deeds might, in the course of events, have been other than they were, or not.[2]

4. The problem of the freedom of the will, which had been already complicated ethically and psychologically, experienced in this way still further a metaphysical and (in the Stoic sense) theological complication, and the consequence was that the *indeterminists* who were opponents of the Stoa gave a new turn to the conception of freedom which they regarded as threatened by the Stoic doctrine, and brought it into sharp definition.   The assumption of the exceptionless causal nexus to which even the functions of the will were to be subordinated, seemed to exclude the capacity of free decision ; but this freedom of choice had, since Aristotle, been regarded in all schools as the indispensable presupposition of ethical accountability. On this account the opponents thought — and this gave the controversy its especial violence — that they were defending an ethical good when they combated the Stoic doctrine of fate, and with that the Democritic principle of natural necessity.   And if Chrysippus had appealed to the principle of sufficient reason to establish this, *Carneades*, to whom the freedom of the will was an incontestable fact, did not fear to draw in question the universal and invariable validity of this principle.[3]

Epicurus went still farther. He found the Stoic determinism so irreconcilable with the wise man's self-determination which formed the essential feature of his ethical ideal, that he would rather still assume the illusory ideas of religion than believe in such a slavery of the soul.[4] Therefore he, too, denied the universal validity of the causal law and subsumed freedom together with chance under the conception of *uncaused occurrence*. Thus in opposition to Stoic determinism, the *metaphysical conception of freedom* arose, by means of which Epicurus put the uncaused function of the will in man upon a parallel with the causeless deviation of the atoms from their line of fall (cf. § 15, 4).   The freedom of *indeterminism* means, accordingly, a choice between different possibilities that is determined by no causes, and Epicurus thought thereby to rescue moral responsibility.

This metaphysical conception of *freedom as causelessness* is not at

---

all isolated in the scientific thought of antiquity. Only the Stoa held fast inviolably to the principle of causality. Even Aristotle had not followed into details the application of his general principles (cf. p. 143); he had contented himself with the ἐπὶ τὸ πολύ, " for the most part," and had based his renunciation of the attempt fully to comprehend the particular upon the assumption of the contingent in Nature, *i.e.* of the lawless and causeless. In this respect the Stoics alone are to be regarded as forerunners of the modern study of Nature.

5. Stoicism encountered difficulties which were no less great, in carrying out its teleology. The pantheistic system which regarded the whole world as the living product of a divine Reason acting according to ends, and found in this its sole ground of explanation, must of course maintain also the purposiveness, goodness, and *perfection* of this universe; and conversely the Stoics were accustomed to prove the existence of the gods and of Providence by pointing to the purposiveness, beauty, and perfection of the world; that is, by the so-called *physico-theological* method.[1]

The attacks which this line of thought experienced in antiquity were directed not so much against the correctness of the reasoning (though Carneades applied his criticism at this point also) as against the premises; and conversely, the easy exhibition of the many defects and maladaptations, of the evils and the ethical harm in the world was employed as a counter-reason against the assumption of a rational, purposeful World-cause and of a Providence. This was done first and with full energy, naturally, by Epicurus, who asked whether God would remove the evil in the world but could not, or could remove it but would not, or whether perhaps neither of these was true,[2] — and who also pointed to the instances of injustice in which the course of life so often makes the good miserable and the wicked happy.[3]

These objections, intensified and carried out with especial care, were brought into the field by *Carneades.*[4] But to the reference to the evil and injustice of the course of events he added the objection to which the Stoics were most sensitive:[5] " Whence then in this world which has been created by Reason comes that which is void of reason and contrary to reason, whence in this world animated by the divine Spirit come sin and folly, the greatest of all

[1] Cic. *De Nat. Deor.* II. 5, 13 ff.
[2] Lactant. *De Ira Dei,* 13, 19 ; Us. *Fr.* 374.
[3] Id. *Inst. Div.* III. 17, 8 ; Us. *Fr.* 370.
[4] Cic. *Acad.* II. 38, 120 ; *De Nat. Deor.* III. 32, 80 ff.
[5] Cic. *De Nat. Deor.* III. 25–31.

evils? " And if the Stoics, as perhaps occurred in spite of their determinism,[1] wished to make free will responsible for these things, the further question arose, why the almighty World-reason should have given man a freedom which was thus to be abused, and why it should permit this abuse.

6. In the presence of such questions the Stoics with their monistic metaphysics were in a much worse case than Plato and Aristotle, who had been able to trace the maladaptations and evil back to the resistance of the "Not-being," or of matter respectively. In spite of this the Stoics came forward boldly to master these difficulties, and brought to light, not without acute thought, most of those arguments in which at later periods *theodicy* has moved again and again.

The teleological doctrine of the perfection of the universe can be protected against such attacks either by denying the dys-teleological facts, or by justifying them as the indispensable means or attendant result in the purposefully connected whole. Both methods were pursued by the Stoa.

Their psychological and ethical theories permitted the claim that what is called a physical evil is not such in itself, but becomes such by man's assent, that hence, if diseases and the like are brought about by the necessity of the natural course of events, it is only man's fault that makes an evil out of them; just as it is frequently only the wrong use which the foolish man makes of things that makes these injurious,[2] while in themselves they are either indifferent or even beneficial. So the objection based on the injustice of the course of the world is rebutted by the claim that in truth for the good man and the wise man physical evils are no evils at all, and that for the bad man, on the other hand, only a sensuous illusory satisfaction is possible, which does not make him truly happy, but rather only aggravates and strengthens the moral disease which has laid hold of him.[3]

On the other hand, physical evils may also be defended on the ground that they are the inevitable consequences of arrangements of Nature which are in themselves adapted to their ends and do not fail of their purpose, — as Chrysippus, for example, attempted to show in the case of diseases.[4] In particular, however, they have the moral significance of serving partly as reformatory punishments of Providence;[5] partly, also, as a useful stimulus for the exercise of our moral powers.[6]

[1] Cleanth. *Hymn.* v. 17.
[2] Seneca, *Qu. Nat.* V. 18, 4.
[3] Seneca, *Ep.* 87, 11 ff.
[4] Gell. *N. A.* VII. 1, 7 ff.
[5] Plut. *Stoic. Rep.* 35, 1.
[6] Marc. Aurel. VIII. 35.

While external evils were thus justified principally by pointing out their ethical purposiveness, it appeared for the Stoics an all the more urgent problem, though one which proved also the more difficult, to make moral evil or sin comprehensible. Here the negative way of escape was quite impossible, for the reality of baseness in the case of the great majority of men was the favourite subject of declamation in the Stoic discourses on morals. Here, then, was the centre of the whole theodicy, namely, to show how in this world which is the product of divine Reason, that which is contrary to reason in the impulses, dispositions, and actions of rationally endowed beings is possible. Here, therefore, the Stoics resorted to universal considerations. They showed how the perfection of the whole not only does not include that of all the individual parts, but even excludes it,[1] and in this way substantiated their claim that God must necessarily allow even the imperfection and baseness of man. In particular, they emphasised the point that it is only through opposition to evil that good as such is brought about; for were there no sin and folly, there would be no virtue and wisdom.[2] And while vice is thus deduced as the necessary foil for the good, the Stoics give as a final consideration,[3] that the eternal Providence ultimately turns even the evil to good, and has in it but an apparently refractory means for the fulfilment of its own highest ends.[4]

§ 17. The Criteria of Truth.

The philosophical achievements of the post-Aristotelian time were least important in the department of logic. Such a powerful creation as the *Analytics* of the Stagirite, which brought the principles of Greek science in so masterly a fashion to the consciousness of all in a conclusive form, must naturally rule logical thought for a long time, and, in fact, did this until the close of the Middle Ages, and even beyond. The foundations of this system were so firmly laid that at first nothing there was shaken, and there remained for the activity of the schools but to build up individual parts, — an activity in connection with which, even at that time, much of the artificial adornment characteristic of a degenerate age displayed itself.

1. The *Peripatetics* had already attempted to develop the Aristotelian *Analytics* systematically in this direction by a more detailed treatment, by partially new proofs, by farther subdivision, and by more

---

[1] Plut. *Stoic. Rep.* 44, 6.   [3] Ib. 35, 3
[2] Ib. 36, 1.   [4] Cleanth. *Hymn.* vv. 18 f.

methodical formulation. In particular, *Eudemus* and *Theophrastus* undertook investigations concerning the hypothetical and disjunctive judgments, and the extension of the theory of the syllogism occasioned by the appearance of these judgments and premises. The Stoics continued these efforts; they set these new forms of judgment (ἀξίωμα) as composite over against the simple [1] categorical forms, developed into all their details the resulting forms of the syllogism, emphasised also especially the quality [2] of judgments, and deduced the laws of thought in altered forms. In general, however, they spun out the logical rules into a dry schematism and genuine scholastic formalism which thereby became farther and farther removed from the significant fundamental thoughts of the Aristotelian *Analytics*, and became a dead mass of formulæ. The unfruitful subtlety of this process took special delight in the solution of sophistical catches, in which the real meaning was inextricably involved in the contradiction of forms.

It was in these elaborations by the schools that the science of *logic* created by Aristotle first took on the purely *formal* character that it retained up to the time of KANT. The more pedantic the form taken in the development of the particular features, the more the consciousness of the living thought, to which Aristotle had aspired, was replaced by a schoolmaster-like network of rules, — essentially designed to catch thoughts and examine their formal legitimacy, but incapable of doing justice to the creative power of scientific activity. While, even with Aristotle, regard for proof and refutation had occupied the foreground, here it occupies the whole field. Antiquity did not attain a theory of investigation; for the weak beginnings which we find toward this end in the investigations of a younger Epicurean,[3] Philodemus,[4] concerning conclusions from induction and analogy, are relatively isolated, and have no result worthy of mention.

2. In the *doctrine of the Categories*, of the elaboration of which the Stoics made much account, more that was real was to be expected. Here it was indeed quite correct, and yet not very fruitful, to call attention to the fact that the supreme category, of which the rest

---

[1] Sext. Emp. *Adv. Math.* VIII. 93.

[2] Diog. Laert. VII. 65.

[3] Epicurus himself, and his school also, as a whole, did not trouble themselves as to the principles of formal logic. One might regard this as an evidence of taste and intelligence, but it was in truth only indifference toward all that did not promise directly practical advantages.

[4] On his treatise περὶ σημείων καὶ σημειώσεων, discovered in Herculaneum, cf. Th. Gompertz, *Herculanensische Studien*, Heft 1 (Leips. 1865); Fr. Bahusch (Lyck, 1879); R. Philippson (Berlin, 1881).

represent only special determinations, is that of Being (τὸ ὄν)[1] or
Something (τὶ); and the co-ordination of the categories which, at
least as regards the method of their enumeration, was Aristotle's
plan, was replaced by an expressly systematic succession, according
to which each category was to be more exactly determined by the
following one. "What is," or Being, as abiding substrate of all
possible relations, is substance (ὑποκείμενον) ; this is the supporter
(*Träger*) of fixed qualities (ποιόν), and only in this aspect is it
involved in changing states (τὸ πῶς ἔχον), and, in consequence of
these latter, in relations to other substances (τὸ πρός τί πως ἔχον).

Out of the doctrine of the categories grows thus an *ontology*, that
is, a metaphysical theory as to the most general formal relations of
reality, and this theory in the system of the Stoics, agreeably to
their general tendency (cf. § 15, 5), takes on a thoroughly *materialistic* character. As substance, the existent is matter which is in
itself destitute of properties (ὕλη), and the qualities and forces
which are inherent in matter as a whole, as well as in a particular
part (ποιότητες — δυνάμεις), are likewise kinds of matter (atmospheric
currents) which are commingled with it (κρᾶσις δι' ὅλων). In this
connection both substance and attributes are regarded, as well from
the point of view of the general conception as from that of the individual thing, and in the latter aspect it is emphasised that every
individual thing is essentially and definitely distinguished from all
others.[2]

Besides these categories of Being, we find making their appearance among the Stoics those conceptional forms by which the relation of thought to Being is expressed, and in these the *separation of
the subjective from the objective*, for which a preparation had been
growing more and more complete in the development of Greek
thought, now attains definite expression. For while the Stoics
regarded all objects to which thought relates as corporeal, while
they regarded the activity of thought itself, and no less its expression in language[3] as corporeal functions, they were still obliged to
confess that the *content of consciousness* as such (τὸ λεκτόν) is of in-

---

[1] That the Peripatetics also busied themselves with this category is proved
by the definition preserved by Strato: τὸ ὄν ἐστι τὸ τῆς διαμονῆς αἴτιον (Proclus
in Tim. 242 E).

[2] In contrasting the first two with the last two categories, the language relation of noun and verb appears here also (in Stoic terminology πτῶσις and κατη-
γόρημα).

[3] The Stoics laid great weight upon the discriminative comparison of thought
and of speech, of the inner activity of reason (λόγος ἐνδιάθετος), and of its expression through the voice (λόγος προφορικός). Hence, too, the assumption (cf.
§ 15, 6) of the faculty of speech as a proper part of the soul ; hence their thorough treatment of rhetoric and grammar side by side with logic.

corporeal nature. But since the distinction was thus sharply drawn between Being and content of consciousness, the *fundamental epistemological problem* came forward, how the relations by which the ideational content refers to Being and agrees with it, are to be thought.

3. This question was, moreover, also brought home by the vigorous development which *Scepticism* had meanwhile undergone, and by the relatively strong position which it occupied as compared with the dogmatic systems.

Whether by Pyrrho or Timon it matters not, it was at all events at about the same time at which the great school-systems became dogmatically developed and fortified, that all those arguments were systematised into a complete whole, by which the Sophistic period had shaken the naïve trust in man's capacity for knowledge. Although the ethical end of making man independent of fate by withholding judgment was ultimately decisive (cf. § 14, 2), this Scepticism still forms a carefully carried out theoretical doctrine. It doubts the possibility of knowledge in both its forms, the form of perception as truly as that of judging thought, and after it has destructively analysed each of these two factors singly, it adds expressly that just on this account their union can have no certain result.[1]

As regards perception, the Sceptics availed themselves of the Protagorean relativism, and in the so-called *ten Tropes*[2] in which Ænesidemus[3] sets forth the sceptical theory with very defective arrangement, this tendency still occupies the broadest space. Perceptions change not only with the different species of animate beings (1), not only with different men (2), according to their customs (9) and their whole development (10), but even in the case of the same individual at different times (3), in dependence upon bodily conditions (4), and upon the different relations in which the individual finds himself with regard to his object spatially (5). They alter, also, because of the difference in the states of the object (7), and have, therefore, no claim to the value of an immediate report of things, because their origination is conditioned by intermediate states in media such as the air, the co-operating elements furnished by which we are not able to deduct (6). Man is, there-

---

[1] From two deceivers combined it is only right to expect no truth. Diog. Laert. IX. 114.

[2] Sext. Emp. *Pyrrh. Hyp.* I. 38 ff.

[3] It was said by the ancient writers that Ænesidemus was attached, not only to Scepticism, but also to the metaphysics of Heraclitus. The question whether this was actually so, or whether such a relation was only ascribed to him by mistake, has solely antiquarian significance. For had the former been the case, it would have been but another manifestation of a real relationship in thought, to which Plato had already directed attention. *Theæt.* 152 E ff.; cf. p. 92, note 2.

fore, in all ways, not in a condition to know things purely (8), and in the face of the multiplicity of impressions so full of contradictions he has no means of distinguishing a true from a false impression. One is *no more* (οὐ μᾶλλον) valid than another.

Equally relative with man's perceptions are also his opinions (δόξαι). In this aspect the influences of the Eleatic dialectic assert themselves in Pyrrhonism. It is shown that to every opinion the opposite can be opposed with equally good reasons, and this *equilibrium of reasons* (ἰσοσθένεια τῶν λόγων) does not permit us, therefore, to distinguish true and false: in the case of such a contradiction (ἀντιλογία) the one holds *no more* than the other. All opinions accordingly stand — according to the phrase of the Sophists, adopted by the Sceptics — only by convention and custom (νόμῳ τε καὶ ἔθει), not by their essential right and title (φύσει).

More energetically still did the later Scepticism attack the possibility of scientific knowledge, by disclosing the *difficulties of the syllogistic procedure,* and of the methods which Aristotle had built up upon this.[1] In this *Carneades* seems to have led the way, showing that every proof, since it presupposes other proofs for the validity of its premises, makes necessary a *regressus in infinitum* · – an argument that was completely in place for the Sceptic who did not, as did Aristotle, recognise anything as immediately certain (ἄμεσον; cf. § 12, 4). The same argument was carried further by *Agrippa,* who formulated Scepticism in five Tropes[2] much more clearly and comprehensively than Ænesidemus. He called attention again to the relativity of perceptions (3) and of opinions (1); he showed how every proof pushes on into infinity (2 : ὁ εἰς ἄπειρον ἐκβάλλων), and how unjustifiable it is in the process of proof to proceed from premises that are only hypothetically to be assumed (4), and finally, how often it occurs, even in science, that that must be postulated as ground of the premises which is only to be proved by means of the syllogism in question (5 : ὁ διάλληλος). In the latter aspect attention was also called to the fact that in the syllogistic deduction of a particular proposition from a general one, the general would yet from the outset be justified only on condition that the particular were valid.[3]

Since the essential nature of things is thus inaccessible to human

---

[1] Sext. Emp. *Adv. Math.* VIII. 316 ff.
[2] Sext. Emp. *Pyrrh. Hyp.* I. 164 ff.: (1) The conflict of opinions. (2) The endless regress in proving. (3) The relativity of all perceptions. (4) The impossibility of other than hypothetical premises. (5) The circle in the syllogism.
[3] Sext. Emp. *Pyrrh. Hyp.* II. 194 ff. Renewed in J. S. Mill, *Logic,* II. 3, 2; corrected in Chr. Sigwart, *Logik,* I. § 55, 3.

knowledge,[1] the Sceptics demanded that man should suspend judgment so far as possible (ἐποχή). We can say nothing concerning things (ἀφασία); we can only assert that this and that appears so or so, and in so doing we report only our own momentary states (as the Cyrenaics had already taught, § 8, 3). Even the sceptical maintenance of the impossibility of knowledge (in order to avoid the contradiction that here something of a negative character, at least, seems to be maintained and proved)[2] should be conceived of rather as a profession of belief than as knowledge, — more as a withholding of opinion than as a positive assertion.

Cf. V. Brochard, *Les Sceptiques Grecs* (Paris, 1877).

4. The attack of Scepticism was most sharply concentrated in the principle[3] that, in the presence of the deceptions to which man is exposed in all his ideas of whatever origin, there is no univocal, sure sign of knowledge, no *criterion of truth*. If, therefore, the dogmatic schools held fast to the reality of knowledge, even from the Socratic motive that virtue is impossible without knowledge,[4] they found the task assigned them by this sceptical position of announcing such a criterion and of defending it against the sceptical objections. This was done also by the *Epicureans* and *Stoics*, although their materialistic metaphysics and the *sensualistic* psychology connected with it prepared for them serious, and, ultimately, insurmountable difficulties.

In fact, it was the psycho-genetic doctrine of both these schools that the content of all ideas and knowledge arises solely from *sensuous perception*. The origin of sense-perception the Epicureans explained by the image theory of Democritus (§ 10, 3). This theory gave even to the illusions of the senses, to dreams, etc., the character of perceptions corresponding to reality; and even the constructions of the combining fancy or imagination could be explained on this theory by unions which had already taken place objectively between the images. But the Stoics also regarded perception as a bodily process, as an *impression* of outer things upon the soul (τύπωσις), the possibility of which seemed to them to be self-evident, in view of the universal commingling of all bodies. This

---

[1] The simplest formulation of Scepticism, finally, was that which brought Agrippa's five Tropes together into two; there is nothing immediately certain, and just on this account nothing mediately certain; accordingly nothing whatever that is certain. Sext. Emp. *Pyrrh. Hyp.* I. 178 f.

[2] Cic. *Acad.* II. 9, 28 and 34, 109; Sext. Emp. *Adv. Math.* VIII. 463 ff.

[3] Sext. Emp. *Adv. Math.* VII. 159.

[4] Diog. Laert. X. 146 f. K. Δ; Us. p. 76 f., on the other hand, Plut. *Stoic. Rep.* 47, 12.

erassly sensuous conception they expressed by the since frequently repeated comparison, that the soul is originally like a blank tablet, on which the outer world imprints its signs in the course of time.[1] More refined, but more indefinite, and yet absolutely mechanical still in its tone is the designation of Chrysippus, who called perception an alteration of qualities (ἑτεροίωσις) in the soul; for, at all events, the idea or mental presentation (φαντασία) remains for him, too, a corporeal effect or product of that which is presented (φανταστόν).

Both schools explained the presence of conceptions and of general ideas (προλήψεις, and among the Stoics also κοιναὶ ἔννοιαι) solely by the persistence of these impressions, or of parts of them, and by their combination. They combated, therefore, as the Cynics especially had already done, the Platonic-Aristotelian doctrine of Ideas and Forms,[2] especially the assumption of an independent activity or power of forming conceptions, and traced even the most general and abstract conceptions back to this mechanism of elementary perceptions (to which they scarcely gave any further analysis). To these general ideas of experience (ἐμπειρία), which arise naturally and involuntarily (φυσικῶς), the Stoics indeed opposed the conceptions of science produced by the aid of a methodical consciousness; but even the content of these scientific conceptions was held to be exclusively derived from sensations. In this connection, both schools laid especial weight upon the co-operation of language in the origination of conceptions.

But now, in so far as the total content of impressions, and likewise also the nature of thought, are the same among all men, it necessarily follows that under these circumstances the same general ideas will be formed, in both the theoretical and the practical domain, by means of the psychological mechanism. This consequence was drawn especially by the Stoics, whose attention was by their whole metaphysics directed vigorously to the common nature of the psychical functions, which were all held to arise from the divine Pneuma. They taught, therefore, that the surest truth is to be sought in those ideas which develop uniformly among all men with natural necessity, and they liked to take as their starting-point, even for scientific reasonings, these κοιναὶ ἔννοαι, or *communes notiones.* They have a

---

[1] Plut. *Plac.* IV. 11; *Dox.* D. 400; Plut. *Comm. Not.* 47; cf. besides Plat. *Theæt.* 191 C.

[2] Hence the Stoics regard Platonic "Ideas" (class-concepts) as merely structures of the human mind (ἐννοήματα ἡμέτερα; cf. Plut. *Plac.* I. 10, *Dox.* D. 309), and thus gave the first suggestion for the later subjective meaning of the term "idea." Cf. § 19.

predilection for appealing to the *consensus gentium* — the consent of all men, — an argument whose validity it was easy for the Sceptics to shake by pointing to the negative instances of experience.[1]

It was, therefore, not in the spirit of the Stoics that in the later Eclectic literature these common ideas were called *innate* (*innatæ*), and that *Cicero* especially saw in them not only that which Nature teaches equally to all, but also that which Nature or the deity has originally implanted in every one at the same time with his reason. Cicero maintains this, not only for the fundamental conceptions of morality and right, but also for the belief in the deity and in the immortality of the soul: the knowledge of God especially is held to be only man's recollection of his true origin.[2] This doctrine formed the best bridge between the Platonic and the Stoic theories of knowledge, and under the Stoic name of κοιναὶ ἔννοαι the *rationalistic doctrine of knowledge* was propagated on into the beginnings of modern philosophy. Just by this means it retained the *accessory psychologistic meaning* that rational knowledge consists in *innate ideas*.

5. While now the Stoics as well as the Epicureans originally traced back all the contents of ideas to sense-impressions psychogenetically, it was only the Epicureans who drew from this the consistent inference that the sign for the recognition of truth is solely the feeling of the necessity with which a perception forces itself upon consciousness, the irresistible *clearness or vividness* (ἐνάργεια) conjoined with the taking up of reality in the function of the senses. Every perception is as such true and irrefutable; it exists, so to speak, as a self-certain atom of the world of consciousness, free from doubt, independent, and unmovable by any reasons whatever.[3] And if different and mutually contradictory perceptions of the same objects seem to exist, the error lies only in the opinion which refers them, and not in the perceptions which by the very fact of their difference prove that different outer causes correspond to them; relativity is accordingly nothing in point against the correctness of all perceptions.[4]

Meanwhile, opinions (δόξαι) constantly and necessarily go beyond this immediate presence of sense-impressions: for the knowledge requisite for acting needs also knowledge of that which is not immediately perceptible: it needs to know, on the one hand, grounds

---

[1] Cic. *De Nat. Deor.* I. 23, 62 f.

[2] Id. *De Leg.* I. 8, 24: . . . *ut is agnoscat deum, qui unde ortus sit quasi recordetur ac noscat.*

[3] The parallelism of this epistemological Atomism with the physical and ethical Atomism of the Epicureans is obvious.

[4] Sext. Emp. *Adv. Math.* VII. 203 ff.

of phenomena (ἄδηλον), and on the other hand the expectation as to the future that may be inferred from them (προσμένον). But for all these farther functions of the psychical mechanism there is, according to the Epicureans, no other guaranty than perception again. For if conceptions (προλήψεις) are only sense-impressions retained in the memory, they have their own certainty in the clearness or vividness of these impressions, a certainty susceptible neither of proof nor of attack;[1] and hypotheses (ὑπολήψεις), both with regard to the imperceptible grounds of things and also with regard to future events, find their criterion solely in perception, in so far as they are verified by it, or at least not refuted; the former holds for the prediction of the future, the latter for explanatory theories.[2] There is therefore among the Epicureans nothing said of an independent faculty of conviction or belief; whether our expectation of any event is correct we can know only when the event occurs. Thus they renounce on principle any attempt at an actual theory of investigation.

6. It is evident from this that the Epicureans might regard their own Atomistic metaphysics as a hypothesis not refuted by facts, but that they were not permitted to regard it as a hypothesis that was proved. It was a hypothesis, indeed, of which the essential end, as they employed it, was to displace other hypotheses which seemed to them ethically objectionable. Their dogmatism is accordingly only problematical, and their doctrine of knowledge, in so far as it has to do with rational knowledge, is very strongly permeated with scepticism. In so far as they recognise only that which passes with sense-perception as a "fact," but regard such facts as completely certain, their standpoint is to be designated as that of *Positivism.*

This positivism was developed in antiquity still more consistently, and in a form freed from the ethical and metaphysical tendencies of Epicurus, by the theories of the later schools of empirical physicians. These schools went with the Sceptics as regards knowledge of all that is imperceptible by the senses and as regards all rational theories; on the other hand, in their recognition of the sensuous evidence of perceptions, they went with the Epicureans. Observation (τήρησις) is here portrayed as the basis of the physician's art, and observation retained in memory is regarded as the sole essence of his theory: ætiological explanations especially are rejected on principle.

Connected with this is the circumstance that the later Sceptics treated the conception of *causality* in searching investigations and

---

[1] As the final criterion even for the intellectually good is, with Epicurus, sensuous pleasure, so the criterion of the truth of conceptions is only sensuous vividness (*Evidenz*).

[2] Sext. Emp. VII. 211.

discovered its difficulties. Ænesidemus had already propounded a series of such aporiæ,[1] and in Sextus Empiricus we find them developed more broadly and comprehensively.[2] With him not only such defects of ætiological theories are designated as, that they reduce the known to the unknown whicn is just as inexplicable, that they maintain one possibility among many without a sufficient reason, that they do not examine experience carefully enough with a view to possible negative instances, and finally that they after all explain that which is inaccessible to perception by some sort of a scheme known from perception, which is especially simple and therefore apparently intelligible in itself; besides these, he searches out, also, all the general difficulties which prevent us from gaining a clear (picturate) idea of the causal relation. The process of the action of one thing upon another, the passing over of motion from one thing to another, can be made intelligible neither on the assumption that that which acts (as force) is immaterial, nor on the opposite assumption; nor does contact (ἀφή) which is assumed as a *conditio sine qua non* of the causal process (as had been already done by Aristotle) make it any more explicable. So, too, the time relation of cause and effect is extremely difficult to determine. The most important thought in these discussions, however, is the pointing out of the *relativity of the causal relation:* nothing is in itself a cause or effect; each of the two is such only with reference to the other; αἴτιον and πάσχον are correlative terms which must not be absolutely postulated or asserted. The (Stoic) conception of an essentially efficient cause, the conception of a creative deity, is then thereby excluded.

7. The *Sceptics of the Academy* sought in another direction a substitute for the certainty of rational knowledge which they also had given up. Since in practical life suspense cannot be carried out as a principle of conduct and action is indispensable, and since for action determining ideas are requisite, Arcesilaus brought out the view that ideas, even though one refuse them his complete assent, are yet able to move the will,[3] and that in practical life one must content himself with a certain kind of confidence or trust (πίστις), according to which some ideas may in a greater degree than others be regarded as probable (εὔλογον), adapted to the purpose of life, and reasonable.[4]

---

[1] Sext. Emp. *Pyrrh. Hyp.* I. 180 ff.

[2] *Adv. Math.* IX. 195 ff.; cf. K. Göring, *Der Begriff der Ursache in der griechischen Philosophie* (Leips. 1874).

[3] Plut. *Adv. Col.* 26, 3.

[4] Sext. Emp. *Adv. Math.* VII. 158.

The *theory of Probabilism* was carried out farther by *Carneades*[1] in an attempt to define more exactly, according to logical relations, the particular degrees of this "belief." The least degree of *probability* (πιθανότης) is that which (as an indistinct and imperfect form of sensuous clearness or vividness — ἐνάργεια) belongs to the single idea that stands in no farther connections. A higher degree of probability belongs to that idea which can be united (ἀπερίσπαστος), without any contradictions, with other ideas in connection with which it belongs. Lastly, the highest stage of belief is reached where a whole system of such connected ideas is examined as to its complete harmony and verification in experience (περιωδευμένη). Empirical confidence rises, therefore, from the sensuously isolated to the logical systems of scientific research. But though in the latter form it may be completely sufficient for practical life (as Carneades assumed), it is yet not able to lead to a completely certain conviction.

8. In contrast with this, the *Stoics* made the most strenuous efforts to gain an epistemological substructure for their metaphysics, to which they attributed so high a value from considerations of ethical interest, and in spite of psycho-genetic sensualism, to rescue the *rational* character of science.[2] On the principle that like is known by like, their doctrine of the World-reason demanded a knowledge of the external Logos by the internal logos of man, — by his reason;[3] and the ethical antagonism or dualism between virtue and the sensuous impulses required a parallel distinction between knowledge and sensuous ideas. Although, therefore, the whole material of knowledge was held to grow out of sensuous presentations, the Stoics pointed out, on the other hand, that in perception as such, no knowledge whatever is contained; that it is not to be characterised as either true or false. Truth and falsity can be predicated only when *judgments* (ἀξιώματα) have been formed in which something is asserted or denied as to the relation of ideas.[4]

Judgment, nevertheless, is conceived of by the Stoics — and in this they take a new and important position, which, in antiquity, only the Sceptics approach in some degree — by no means merely as the theoretical process of ideation and combination of ideas. They recognised, as the essential characteristic in judgment, the peculiar act of *assent* (συγκατάθεσις), of approval, and of being convinced, with which the mind makes the content of the idea its own, grasps

---

[1] Ib. 166 ff.
[2] Cf. M. Heinze, *Zur Erkenntnisslehre der Stoiker* (Leips. 1880).
[3] Sext. Emp. *Adv. Math.* VII 93.
[4] Sext. Emp. *Adv. Math.* VIII. 13.

it, and in a certain way takes possession of it (καταλαμβάνειν). This act of apprehension the Stoics regard as an independent function of consciousness (ἡγεμονικόν), in the same way as they regard the assent to the impulses, which makes its appearance in passion. The arising of ideas, like that of the excitations of feeling, is a process which is of natural necessity and completely independent of human will (ἀκούσιον) ; but the assent by which we make the one class, judgments, and the other, passions, is a decision (κρίσις) of consciousness, free (ἑκούσιον) from the outer world.[1]

But now in the case of the wise man, by virtue of the identity of the universal with the individual logos, this assent appears only in the case of those ideas which are true : the soul, therefore, in apprehending the content of these ideas, apprehends reality. Such an idea the Stoics called φαντασία καταληπτική,[2] and they were of the conviction that such an idea must call forth the reasonable man's assent with immediate evidence or clearness. Hence assent itself (συγκατάθεσις) is conceived of as an activity of the thinking soul, but individual perceptions appear as the objects of assent as truly as do the intellectual activities of conception, judgment, and reasoning, based upon the individual perceptions.

If thus the Stoics understood by the φαντασία καταληπτική that idea by which the mind lays hold of reality, and which, therefore, so illumines the mind that this, in its assent, makes reality its own, this was indeed the correct expression for the *requirement* which they set up for the true idea,[3] but the definition was not at all adapted to the end for which it was framed: that is, for a sign by which to recognise truth. For as the Sceptics[4] very justly objected, the subjective mark, assent, might be shown as a psychological fact in the case of a multitude of evidently false ideas.

Thus the anthropological discord in the Stoic doctrine manifests

---

[1] Ib. VIII. 39, 7.

[2] In the interpretation of this term there is a wide divergence. According to the sources, it seems now as if the idea were intended which the mind lays hold of, now that which apprehends the real fact, now that by which the mind apprehends reality, and now again that which on its part so lays hold of the mind that the mind must assent to it. It has hence been supposed that the Stoics purposely constructed the expression in this ambiguous form, inasmuch as all these relations would harmonise in it, and perhaps E. Zeller (IV.³ 83) [Eng. tr., *Stoics*, etc., p. 89] intended to repeat this ambiguity by his translation, "conceptional idea or perception" (*begriffliche Vorstellung*), which, however, has an accessory logical sense that the Stoics certainly did not intend.

[3] It is worth while to point out the fact that in their designations for the relation of the knowing mind to the external reality, the Stoics employ, for the most part, expressions from the field of the sense of touch (impression, apprehending, or grasping, etc.), while formerly optical analogies had been preferred. Cf. § 11, 2.

[4] Sext. Emp. *Adv. Math.* VII. 402 ff.

itself even in this central conception of their theory of knowledge.
As it could not be explained in accordance with their metaphysics
how the individual soul arising from the World-reason should fall
under the mastery of sensuous impulses, so it is equally impossible
to understand how theoretical assent should, under certain circumstances, be given even to false ideas.   Both difficulties, however,
have ultimately a common ground.   The Stoics agreed with Heraclitus in identifying in their metaphysics the *normative and the
actual ordering of things,* although these conceptions had meanwhile
become much more clearly separated.   Reason was for them that
which should be, as well as that which is ; it was at the same time
νόμος and φύσις.   And this antithesis, the two sides of which came
into strenuous opposition in their doctrine of freedom and their
theodicy, was the problem of the future.

CHAPTER II.

THE RELIGIOUS PERIOD.

J. Simon, *Histoire de l'École d'Alexandrie.* Paris, 1843 ff.

E. Matter, *Essai sur l'École d'Alexandrie.* Paris, 1840 ff.

E. Vacherot, *Histoire Critique de l'École d'Alexandrie.* Paris, 1846 ff.

[J. Drummond, *Philo Judæus, or the Jewish Alexandrian Philosophy in its Development and Completion.* 2 vols., Lond. 1888.]

Barthélemy St. Hilaire, *Sur le Concours ouvert par l'Académie, etc., sur l'École d'Alexandrie.* Paris, 1845.

K. Vogt, *Neuplatonismus und Christenthum.* Berlin, 1836.

Georgii, *Ueber die Gegensätze in der Auffassung der alexandrinischen Religions- philosophie (Zeitschr. f. hist. Theol. 1839).*

E. Deutinger, *Geist der christlichen Ueberlieferung.* Regensburg, 1850–51.

A. Ritschl, *Die Entstehung der altkatholischen Kirche.* 2d ed., Bonn, 1857.

Chr. Baur, *Das Christenthum der drei ersten Jahrhunderte.* Tübingen, 1860.

J. Alzog, *Grundriss aer Patrologie.* 3d ed., Freiburg i. B. 1876.

[A. V. G. Allen, *The Continuity of Christian Thought.* Boston, 1884.]

Alb. Stöckl, *Geschichte der Philosophie der patristischen Zeit.* Würzburg, 1859.

J. Huber, *Die Philosophie der Kirchenväter.* Munich, 1859.

Fr. Overbeck, *Ueber die Anfänge der patristischen Litteratur (Hist. Zeitschr. 1882).*

A. Harnack, *Lehrbuch der Dogmengeschichte.* 3 vols. Freiburg i. B. 1886–90.

[J. Donaldson, *Critical History of Christian Literature and Doctrine.*]

THE gradual transition of the Hellenistic-Roman philosophy from the ethical to the *religious standpoint* had its inner causes in this philosophy itself, and its external occasion in the imperious de- mands made by the felt need of the time. For the farther the contact between the systems extended, the more it became evident how little able philosophy was to fulfil the task which it had set itself: namely, that of educating man by a sure insight to a state of virtue and happiness, to inner independence of the world. While the sceptical mode of thought, which was extending more and more, already taught that virtue consists rather in the renunciation of the attempt to know, than in knowledge itself, the view forced its way more and more, even among the Stoics, that their ideal of the wise man, so sharply and rigidly drawn, was not entirely realised in any human being, and thus it was felt in every direction that man in his own strength can become neither knowing, nor virtuous and happy.

If, then, a disposition to welcome a higher help for ethical ends was necessarily evoked in philosophy itself, it was also true that the theoretical doctrines of the time contained a great number of religious elements. The Epicureans, to be sure, purposely excluded such, but the Stoics, on the contrary, granted them an entrance that was all the freer. With the Stoics, not only did metaphysics lead to seeking the principle of morals in a divine command, but in their *pneuma* doctrine, the possibility presented itself of giving to the creations of myth a philosophical meaning, which might be shared also by all forms of worship. Finally, the spiritual monotheism in Aristotle's teaching, and that ideal tendency with which Plato sought the abiding essence of things in a higher world of the supersensuous, were not forgotten.

Just this *dualism*, which opposed the earthly world of the perishable to a supersensuous world of the divine, ultimately proved to be the right expression for that inner discord which ran through the entire life of the aging Greek and Roman world. The old craving for sensuous pleasure might still celebrate its orgies in full power and to the intoxication of the senses; but in the midst of it all, out of surfeit and loathing grew a new craving for a purer, higher joy: and in the presence of the tremendous contrasts which the social condition of the Roman Empire brought with it, the look of all the millions that saw themselves excluded from the good things of this earth turned longingly toward a better world. Thus in all ways a deep, passionate need for true salvation of the soul ($\sigma\omega\tau\eta\rho\acute{\iota}a$) came to be increasingly felt, a hunger for something beyond the earthly, a religious urgency without an equal.

This *religious movement* proved its vigour first of all in the eager reception which foreign forms of worship found in the Græco-Roman world, in the mingling and fusing of Oriental and Occidental religions. But with the adjustment which their oppositions found here and there, their strife for the mastery over men's spirits became still more energetic, and thus the soil of the ancient world of civilisation, after bearing the fruits of art and science, became the battleground of religions. Man's essential interest became thereby transferred for long centuries from the earthly to the heavenly sphere; he began to seek his salvation beyond the world of sense.

But the forms in which this *contest of the religions* was waged prove in spite of all what a spiritual and intellectual power Greek science had grown to be. For so strongly was the ancient world "sicklied o'er with the pale cast of thought," so deeply had it become permeated by the feeling of a need for knowledge, that each of the religions desired to satisfy not only the feelings but also the intellect, and was therefore anxious to transform its life into a doctrine. This is true even of *Christianity*, and indeed precisely true of it. The true, victorious power of the religion of Jesus lay, to be sure, in the fact that it entered this decrepit, *blasé* world with the youthful force of a pure, high, religious feeling, and a conviction that was courageous to the death; but it was able to conquer the ancient civilised world only by taking it up into itself and working it over; and as in its external conflict with the old world it shaped its own constitution [1] and thereby ultimately became so strong as to be able to take possession of the Roman state, so also in its defence against the ancient philosophy it made the world of that philosophy's ideas its own, in order thereby to build up its own dogmatic system.

Thus the needs of science and of life met. The former sought the solution of the problems at which it had been labouring in vain, in religion, and the latter desired a scientific formulation and basis for its religious longing or conviction. Hence from this time on, for many centuries, the history of philosophy is grown together with that of dogmatic theology,[2] and the period of *religious metaphysics* begins. The thought of antiquity described a peculiar curve, separating itself farther and farther from religion from which it proceeded, reaching its extreme separation in Epicureanism, and then again steadily drawing near to religion, to return at last entirely within it.

Under these conditions it is possible to understand how that *Weltanschauung* which separated the supersensuous and the sensuous, — looking upon them, from the point of view of value, as divine perfection and earthly baseness, respectively, — constituted the common ground of the whole religious-philosophical movement. This view had already, indeed, been introduced by the Pythagoreans (cf. § 5, 7), and had been maintained even by Aristotle, but it had, without doubt, found its most forcible formulation in the *Platonic metaphysics*. It was, therefore, this latter system which formed the controlling centre for the religious closing development of ancient thought. A religious development of Platonism is the fundamental character of this period.

---

[1] Cf. K. J. Neumann, *Der römische Staat und die allgemeine Kirche bis auf Diocletian* (Vol. I. Leips. 1890).

[2] It will be understood as a matter of course that the following exposition has left at one side all specifically dogmatic elements, except where they are quite inseparably interwoven with philosophical principles.

The geographical centre of the movement, however, is found in that city which, by its history, as well as by its population, represented most distinctly the mingling of peoples and of religions, — *Alexandria.* Here, where in the active work of the museum all treasures of Grecian culture were garnered, all religions and forms of worship crowded together in the great throngs of the commercial metropolis to seek a scientific clarification of the feelings that surged and stormed within them.

The first line of the *Alexandrian philosophy* is the so-called *Neo-Pythagoreanism*, a mode of thought which, proceeding from the religious practice of the Pythagorean mysteries, makes only an external use of the number-mysticism of the old Pythagoreans after whom it calls itself and its writings, while it finds the theoretical setting for its world-renouncing, religious-ascetic ethics in a transformation of the Platonic metaphysics, which became of the profoundest value for the conception of the spiritual nature in the following period. *Apollonius of Tyana*, the founder of a religion, is to be regarded as typical representative of this school.

Not without influence from this school, the *Stoa*, also, in the time of the Empire, brought out more energetically the religious elements in its theory of the world, so that not only did the anthropological dualism of the system become sharpened, but a more theistic mode of thought gradually became substituted for the original pantheism of the school. In men like *Seneca*, *Epictetus*, and *Marcus Aurelius*, the Stoic doctrine became completely a philosophy of deliverance or redemption.

Even *Cynicism* revived again about this time in a religious garb, as a rude, popular preaching of renunciation, and *Demonax* passes for its best-known representative.

Scarcely to be separated from the Neo-Pythagoreans are the *Eclectic Platonists* of the first centuries of our era, such as *Plutarch* of Chæronea and *Apuleius* of Madaura. Later appear *Numenius* of Apamea and *Nicomachus* of Gerasa, who, besides, already stand under Jewish and Christian influences as witnesses of a complete fusion of the two tendencies.

But while, in all these forms, the Hellenic element ever maintains the ascendency over the Oriental, the latter makes its appearance in very much stronger force in the *Jewish philosophy of religion.* As the sect of the Essenes [1] probably proceeded from a contact of Neo-Pythagoreanism with the Hebrew religious life, so the various attempts of learned Jews to draw nearer to Greek science in the

---

[1] Cf. E. Zeller V.[3] 277 ff.

presentation of their dogmas, led ultimately to the doctrine of *Philo of Alexandria*, whose original elaboration of these fermenting bodies of thought influenced their further formation and movement in the most important points.

The *philosophy of Christianity*, which for these first centuries is usually designated by the name *Patristics*, unfolded in an analogous manner upon a larger scale. This philosophical secularisation of the gospel begins with the *Apologists*, who sought to present its religious belief as the only true philosophy, with the purpose of protecting Christianity in the eyes of the cultured world from contempt and persecution, and therefore began to adapt this content of religious faith to the conceptional forms of Greek science: the most important of them are *Justin* and *Minucius Felix*.

But the need of changing faith (πίστις) into knowledge or wisdom (γνῶσις) asserted itself vigorously in the Christian communities, even without this polemical tendency. The first attempts, however, which the *Gnostics* made to create an adequate view of the world for the new religion, proceeded from the excited phantasies of a Syrian mingling of religions, and, in spite of the employment of Hellenistic philosophemes, led to such grotesque constructions, that the Church as it grew stronger and more definitive was obliged to reject them. *Saturninus, Basileides,* and *Valentinus* are to be named as the best known of this class.

In reaction against such over-hasty attempts of religious fantasticalness, a violent aversion toward all philosophical interpretation and adjustment of Christian faith set in, for a time, in Christian literature in the writings of men like *Tatian, Tertullian,* and *Arnobius.* An express *anti-rationalism* thus came forward which nevertheless found it necessary on its part also to return to the related doctrines of Greek philosophy. Without this one-sidedness and with a closer approximation to the older Hellenising Apologists, Gnosticism was combated by *Irenæus* and his disciple *Hippolytus.*

It was not until the beginning of the third century, and after all these preceding attempts, that a positive Christian theology, a system of dogmatics in a complete conceptional form, was established. This came about in the *School for Catechists at Alexandria*, through the leaders of the school, *Clement* and *Origen.* The latter especially is to be regarded as philosophically the most important representative of Christianity in this period.

By his side, however, there went out from the Alexandrian philosophic school the man who undertook to bring the religion-forming tendency of philosophy to an issue solely upon the Hellenistic basis, — *Plotinus,* the greatest thinker of this period. His attempt to

systematise all the main doctrines of Greek and Hellenistic philosophy under the religious principle is designated as *Neo-Platonism.*
His doctrine is the most definitive and thoroughly constructed system of science that antiquity produced.   His disciple *Porphyry,*
however, showed himself already inclined to make a religion out of
this religious teaching, and *Jamblichus,* who is termed the leader of
Syrian Neo-Platonism, transformed it into a *dogmatic theology of polytheism,* with which the learned and political opponents of Christianity,
such as the Emperor Julian, hoped to revive the forms of worship
of the heathen religions, then in a state of dissolution.   After this
attempt had miscarried, the Athenian school of Neo-Platonism, as
the heads of which *Plutarch* of Athens, *Proclus,* and *Damascius*
appear, returned finally to a methodical, scholastic development of
the system of Plotinus.

Thus the Hellenistic efforts to attain to a new religion by means
of science remained without result in this form : the scholars discovered no church.   On the other hand, the need felt by positive
religion to complete and strengthen itself in a scientific doctrine did
attain its goal : the Church created its dogma.   And the great course
of history in this movement was, that the defeated Hellenism in its
powerful death-struggle still created the conceptions by means of
which the new religion shaped itself into a dogma.

While the Pythagorean mysteries had maintained their existence through all
antiquity, scientific **Pythagoreanism** vanished as a proper school after its
incorporation into the Academy (cf. p. 31).   It is not until during the first
century B.C. that specifically Pythagorean doctrines become noticeable again :
they appear in the Pythagorean writings, of which Diogenes Laertius (VIII.
24 ff.), following Alexander Polyhistor, gives an account that leads us to infer
an essentially Stoic influence.   They are renewed expressly by Cicero's learned
friend, **P. Nigidius Figulus** (died 45 B.C.), and find approval also with other
men in Rome.   Cf. M. Herz, *De P. Nig. Fig. Studiis atque Operibus* (Berlin, 1845).

But **Neo-Pythagoreanism** proper was first presented in literary form by
the great number of writings which became public in Alexandria at about the
beginning of our era, under the names of Pythagoras, or Philolaus, or Archytas,
or other older Pythagoreans, the fragments of which give rise to so great difficulties in forming a conception of genuine Pythagoreanism.   Cf. the lit. p. 31.

Of the personalities of the new school, on the contrary, very little is known.
The only distinct figure is **Apollonius** of Tyana, of whose life and nature the
rhetorician Philostratus (ed. by C. L. Kayser, Leips. 1870) gave a romantic
representation at the beginning of the third century, in order to portray in it
the ideal of the Pythagorean life.   Of the works of Apollonius himself, who
lived in the first century A.D., fragments of a biography of Pythagoras and of
a treatise on Sacrifice are extant.   Cf. Chr. Baur, *Apollonius und Christus* in
Drei Abhandl. zur Gesch. d. alt. Philos. (Leips. 1876).   [Tredwell, *Life of
Apollonius of Tyana,* contains a good bibliography, N.Y. 1886.]   His contemporary, **Moderatus** of Gades, might perhaps also be mentioned.

Neo-Pythagorean and Stoic doctrines appear mingled in the Eclectic **Sotion**
of Alexandria, who was affiliated with the Sextians (cf. p. 163).   His disciple,
L. Annæus Seneca of Cordova (4–65 A.D.), was the leader of the **Stoics** in
the time of the Empire.   He was instructor of Nero, was well known because of
his tragic fate, and also as tragic poet unfolded the rigid conceptions of life held

by his school. Of his writings a considerable number of mainly ethical treatises are preserved besides his *Epistolœ* (ed. by Haase, 3 vols., Leips. 1852–3)
[Eng. tr. (or rather paraphrase) by T. Lodge, Lond. 1614, Selections from th.s
and from L'Estrange's *Seneca's Morals by Way of Abstract*, Lond. 1888, Came-
lot series]. Cf. Chr. Baur, *S. und Paulus* in the *Drei Abhandl.;* see above.

Besides him we mentio.1 L. Annæus **Cornutus** (Phurnutus), a chief representative of the Stoic interpretation of myths (Περὶ τῆς τῶν θεῶν φύσεως, ed.
by Osann, Göttingen, 1844), the satiric poet **Persius**, the moralist C. **Musonius**
Rufus, and especially **Epictetus**, who lived at the time of Domitian, and whose
doctrines were published by **Arrian** in two works, Διατριβαί and Ἐγχειρίδιον (ed.
together with the commentary of Simplicius by J. Schweighauser, Leips. 1799 f.)
[tr. by G. Long, Bohn's library; also by T. W. Higginson, Boston, 1865]. Cf.
A. Bonhöffer *E. und die Stoa* (Stuttgart, 1890).

With the noble **Marcus Aurelius Antoninus** the Stoa mounted the Roman
imperial throne (161–180). His reflections τὰ εἰς αὐτόν (ed. by J. Stich, Leips.
1882) are the characteristic monument of this eclectic-religious Stoicism.
[Eng. tr. by G. Long. *The Thoughts of the Emperor, M. Aurelius Antoninus*,
Lond. Bohn's lib.; W. Pater, *Marius the Epicurean*, Lond. and N.Y. 1888; M.
Arnold in *Essays.*]

In the ancient Grecian period, an original figure, that of the monkish wandering preacher Teles, had gone out from the **Cynic** school (cf. v. Wilamovitz-
Möllendorf, *Philol. Unters*, IV. 292 ff.). In the time of the Empire this quaint
creature was frequently copied and exaggerated even to the most ridiculous
extent. Demetrius, Oinomaos of Gadara, Demonax (cf. Fritsche, Leips. 1866),
and Peregrinus Proteus, known through Lucian, belong to these figures. Cf.
J. Bernays, *Lukian und die Kyniker* (Berlin, 1879).

Of the representatives of **religious Platonism** who kept at a distance from
the number theory, may be mentioned the eclectic commentators **Eudorus** and
Arius Didymus, Thrasyllus, the editor of the works of Plato and Democritus,
and especially **Plutarch** of Chæronea (about 100 A.D.), from whom, in addition
to his famous biographies, a great number of other writings are preserved,
especially philosophical treatises of dogmatic and polemical content (*Moralia*,
ed. Dübner; Paris, Didot, Vols. III. and IV. 1855) (cf. R. Volkmann, *Leben,
Schriften und Philosophie des P.*, Berlin, 1872). [Plutarch's *Morals*, trans. ed.
by Goodwin, 5 vols., Boston, 1870; also tr. by Shilleto and by C. W. King, both
in Bohn's lib., Lond. 1888 and 1882 resp.] We mention further **Maximus** of
Tyre of the time of the Antonines; his contemporary, **Apuleius** of Madaura,
who belongs in this series not only on account of his philosophical writings (ed.
by A. Goldbacher, Vienna, 1876), but also on account of his allegorico-satirical
romance, "The Golden Ass" (cf. Hildebrand in the introduction to his collected works, Leips. 1842) [*The Works of Apuleius*, Bohn's lib.]; the opponent of Christianity, **Celsus**, whose treatise ἀληθὴς λόγος (about 180) is known
only from the counter-treatise of Origen, κατὰ Κέλσου (cf. Th. Keim, *C. "wahres
Wort*," Zürich, 1873); and lastly the physician Claudius **Galen**, who died about
200, and might, to be sure, with his broad eclecticism be likewise classed as a Peripatetic and also as a Stoic (cf. K. Sprengel, *Beiträge zur Gesch. d. Medicin*, I.
117 ff.). From the same circle of ideas arose also the writings circulated under
the name of **Hermes** Trismegistus, which belong to the third century (French
tr. by L. Ménard, Paris, 1866; partially published by G. Parthey, Berlin, 1854).

Among the Platonists of the second century **Nicomachus** of Gerasa in Ara-
bia, of whose writings arithmetical text-books and (through Photius) an extract
from a work Ἀριθμητικὰ θεολογούμενα are extant, and **Numenius** of Apamea,
concerning whom we owe our instruction mainly to Eusebius, are strongly Neo-
Pythagorean. Cf. F. Thedinga (Bonn, 1875).

The entrance of Greek philosophy into **Jewish** theology may be traced back
to the middle of the second century B.C., where it can be recognised in the
Biblical explanation of **Aristobulus**; it appears then in a particularly marked
manner, and in a form that is already much nearer the Alexandrian sphere of
thought, in the pseudo-Solomonic *Book of Wisdom*. Yet these are but weak
forerunners of the important creation of **Philo** of Alexandria, of whose life
little more is known than that in the year 39, when already in advanced age, he
was a member of an embassy from his native community to the Emperor Calig

ula. His numerous writings, among which there is also much that is not genuine, were edited by Th. Mangey (Lond. 1742), Leips. stereotype ed., 8 vols., 1851–53; [Eng. tr. by C. D. Yonge, 4 vols., Lond., Bohn's lib.].

F. Dähne, *Die jüdisch-alexandrinische Religionsphilosophie* (Halle, 1834). A.Gfrörer, *Philon und die alexandrinische Theosophie* (Stuttgart, 1835); M. Wolff, *Die philonische Philosophie* (Gothenburg, 1858); Ewald, *Gesch. des Volkes Israel*, VI. 231 ff.

Among the **Christian Apologists** whose writings are collected in the *Corpus Apologetarum Christianorum secundi sœculi*, ed. by Otto (Jena, 1842 ff.), the most prominent is Flavius **Justin Martyr** of Sichem, who lived in the middle of the second century. Two defensive writings and a dialogue with Trypho the Jew are preserved [Eng. tr. in Ante-Nicene Ch. lib., ed. by Roberts and Donaldson, Edinburg, T. & T. Clark, 1867 —]. K. Semisch (2 vols., Breslau, 1840–42), and B. Aubé (Paris, 1861) treat of him. Further Apologists from the Hellenic circle of culture are **Aristides** (whose discourses, discovered in the Armenian language, were printed with a Latin translation, Venice, 1878), **Athenagoras** of Athens (πρεσβεία περὶ Χριστιανῶν addressed to Marcus Aurelius about 176), **Theophilus** of Antioch (a treatise addressed to Autolycus about 180), **Melito** of Sardis, Apollinaris of Hierapolis, and others. — Latin literature presents especially **Minucius Felix**, whose dialogue *Octavius* was written about 200 (ed. in the *Corpus scriptorum ecclesiasticorum latinorum*, by C. Halm, Vienna, 1867). The rhetorician, Firmianus **Lactantius** (about 300), is to be placed in the same series. His main treatise is the *Institutiones Divinæ* [tr. of the above authors in Ante-Nicene lib., see above].

Of the **Gnostics** our information comes essentially through their opponents, Irenæus (140–200; his treatise Ἔλεγχος καὶ ἀνατροπὴ τῆς ψευδωνύμου γνώσεως, ed. by A. Stieren, Leips. 1853), Hippolytus (Κατὰ πασῶν αἱρέσεων ἔλεγχος, ed. by Duncker and Schneidewin, Göttingen, 1859), Tertullian (*Adversus Valentinianos*), etc. [Eng. tr. of the above writings in Ante-Nicene lib., above]. Of Gnostic treatises only one, and that by an unknown author, is extant, Πίστις σοφία (ed. by Petermann, Berlin, 1851). Of the main representatives of this doctrine there were active in the first half of the second century **Saturninus** of Antioch, **Basilides**, a Syrian, and **Carpocrates** in Alexandria; toward the middle of the century **Valentinus**, the most important of them (died about 160); and toward the end of the century **Bardesanes** of Mesopotamia. — *Expositions of the Gnostic Systems* by A. W. Neander (Berlin, 1818) [Eng. tr. by Torrey, Boston, 1865], E. Matter (Paris, 1843), Chr. Baur (Tübingen, 1835), A. Hilgenfeld (Jena, 1884), same author, *Bardesanes, der letzte Gnostiker* (Leips. 1864). — A. Harnack, *Zur Quellenkritik der Geschichte des Gnosticismus* (Leips. 1873); [H. L. Mansel, *Gnostic Heresies*, Lond. 1876].

The most radical opponent of Greek science was **Tatian**, an Assyrian, whose treatise Πρὸς Ἕλληνας arose about 170, but who later became himself an adherent of the Valentinian Gnosticism. The passionate Apologist Qu. Septimius Florens **Tertullian** (165–220, for a time Presbyter in Carthage) ended likewise in opposition to the Catholic Church, in the sect of the Montanists. His works have been edited by Fr. Oehler (3 vols., Leips. 1853 f.), recently by A. Reifferscheid and Wissowa (Vol. I. Vienna, 1890, in *Corp. script. eccl. lat.*) [Eng. tr. in Ante-Nicene lib.]. Cf. A. W. Neander, *Antignosticus, Geist des Tertullian*, etc. (2d ed. Berlin, 1849) [Eng. tr. Bohn's lib., 1851]; A. Hauck, *T.'s Leben und Schriften*, Erlangen, 1877). — In the same series, but from a later·time, is the African rhetorician **Arnobius**, whose seven books, *Adversus Gentes*, were composed about 300 (ed. by A. Reifferscheid in *Corp. script. eccl. lat.*, Vienna, 1875).

Of the writings of **Clement** of Alexandria (died about 217) three treatises are preserved, Λόγος προτρεπτικὸς πρὸς Ἕλληνας — Παιδαγωγός — Στρωματεῖς (ed. by J. Potter, Oxford, 1715) [tr. in Ante-Nicene lib.]. From his school (cf. on the Alex. Catechetical school, Guericke, Halle, 1824 f., and Hasselbach, Stettin, 1826) went forth the founder of Christian theology, **Origen**, surnamed the Adamantine. Born 185 A.D. in Alexandria, equipped with the full education of the time, he came forward early as a teacher, fell into conflicts on account of his doctrines with the Synod, was by it removed from his office, and later lived in Cæsarea and Tyre, dying in the latter place 254. Of his writings, aside from the above-mentioned treatise against Celsus, his work Περὶ ἀρχῶν is of chief importance; it is extant almost only in the Latin version of Rufinus (ed. by

Redepenning, Leips. 1836) [tr. in Ante-Nicene lib.]. Cf. J. Reinkens, *De Clemente Presbytero Al.* (Breslau, 1851); Redepenning, O., *Darstellung seines Lebens und seiner Lehre* (Bonn, 1841–46) [cf. Bigg, *The Christian Platonists of Alexandria*, Oxford, 1887; A. Harnack, Art. *Origen* in *Enc. Brit.*].

A collection of the sources for all the Church writers of this period has been issued by J. P. Migne, *Patrologiœ Cursus Completus* (Paris, 1840 ff.).

A certain **Ammonius Saccus** appears in old traditions as the founder of **Neo-Platonism**, but nothing is known to justify this tradition. To his pupils belonged Plotinus, Origen, the rhetorician **Longinus** (213–273), to whom the book Περὶ ὕψους was ascribed, and another **Origen.**

The true founder of the school was **Plotinus** (204–269). Born in Lycopolis in Egypt, and educated in Alexandria, he became a member of an expedition against the Persians in order to promote his religious studies, made a highly successful appearance as teacher in Rome about 244, and died on a country estate in Campania. His works, written late in life, were published by his disciple Porphyry, arranged in six enneads. Ed. by H. Müller (Leips. 1878–80), with a German translation [Eng. tr. in part by Th. Taylor, Lond. 1787, 1794, 1817, French tr. by Bouillet, Paris, 1857–60]. Cf. H. Kirchner, *Die Philos. des Pl.* (Halle, 1854).— A. Richter, *Neuplatonische Studien* (Halle, 1864 ff.).— H. v. Kleist, *Neuplat. Studien* (Heidelberg, 1883).— [A. Harnack, Art. *Neo-Platonism* in *Enc. Brit.*]

To the **Alexandrian** Neo-Platonism are reckoned further Gentilianus **Amelius** of Ameria, and the Tyrian **Porphyry** (about 230–300). Among the extant writings, aside from the biographies of Plotinus and Pythagoras, are to be mentioned Ἀφορμαὶ πρὸς τὰ νοητά, an aphoristic abridgment of the system of Plotinus (printed in Creuzer's ed. of the works of Plotinus, Paris, 1855), the treatise *On Abstemiousness* (περὶ ἀποχῆς τῶν ἐμψίχων, important on account of its use of the περὶ εὐσεβείας of Theophrastus; cf. J. Bernays, Berlin, 1866), and of the commentaries the Εἰσαγωγὴ εἰς τὰς κατηγορίας (ed. by Busse, Berlin, 1877 · and also in the Berlin ed. of Aristotle, Vol. IV.).

Syrian Neo-Platonism was founded by **Jamblichus** of Chalcis in Cœle-Syria (died about 330), a hearer of Porphyry. His writings were principally commentaries upon Hellenistic and Oriental theology. The following are partially preserved: Περὶ τοῦ Πυθαγορικοῦ βίου (ed. by Westermann, Paris, 1850), Λόγος προτρεπτικὸς εἰς φιλοσοφίαν (ed. by Kiessling, Leips. 1813), Περὶ τῆς κοινῆς μαθηματικῆς ἐπιστήμης (ed. by Villoison, Venice, 1781) [Eng. tr. *Life of Pyth.* by Taylor, Lond. 1818, *Egyptian Mysteries*, by same, Chiswick, 1821].

Of the disciples of the school, **Dexippus** commented on the Aristotelian Categories (ed. by L. Spengel, Munich, 1859), **Sallustius** wrote a compendium of metaphysics (ed. by Orelli, Zürich, 1821), and **Themistius** (about 317–387) made himself known as a paraphrast and commentator upon Aristotelian works. From the same circle comes the treatise *De Mysteriis Ægyptiorum* (ed. by G. Parthey, Berlin, 1857; cf. Harless, Munich, 1858).

This movement had a transient political success by the accession of the Emperor **Julian**, who hoped by its help to renew the old religion and displace Christianity. His writings against the Christians have been edited with a German translation by K. J. Neumann (Leips. 1880). Cf. A. W. Neander, *Ueber den Kaiser J. und sein Zeitalter* (Berlin, 1812).— D. Fr. Strauss, *J. der Abtrünnige, der Romantiker auf dem Throne der Cäsaren* (Mannheim, 1847).— A. Mücke, *J. nach den Quellen* (Gotha, 1866-68).

The founder of **Athenian Neo-Platonism** was **Plutarch** of Athens (died after 430), with his pupils **Syrianus** and **Hierocles.** All these, as well as the following, composed commentaries upon Platonic and Aristotelian or Pythagorean writings, which are in part preserved. More important was **Proclus** (411–485), among whose works the most important is Περὶ τῆς κατὰ Πλάτωνα ϑεολογίας (ed. of his works by V. Cousin, Paris, 1820–25) [Eng. tr. by Th. Taylor]. Cf. H. Kirchner, *De Procl. Metaphysica* (Berlin, 1846). K. Steinhart's Art. in Ersch und Grüber's *Enc.*

The last head of the Platonic Academy was **Damascius**, of whose writings the beginning of a treatise περὶ τῶν πρώτων ἀρχῶν, and the conclusion of a commentary upon the *Parmenides* are extant (ed. by J. Kopp, Frankfort a. M. 1826; cf. E. Heitz in *Strass. Abhdl. für Philos.*, 1884), and also a biography of his teacher Isidorus. Among the commentators of this time **Simplicius is** prominent (on the *Physics*, ed. pr. Venice, 1526, the first four books, Diels, Berlin, 1882; on the *De Cœlo*, Karsten, Utrecht, 1865; on the *De Anima*, Hayduck, Berlin, 1882).

The two latter wandered with their immediate associates for a time toward Persia, when in the year 529 the Emperor Justinian closed the Academy, confiscated its property, and by forbidding lectures on heathen philosophy gave the external confirmation to its close.

§ 18. Authority and Revelation.

The imperturbable self-certainty and self-mastery which the post-Aristotelian philosophy had sought and in part claimed for the wise man, had been so deeply shaken with the progress of time that it had given place to a *feeling of the need of help,* both in the ethical and in the theoretical spheres. The philosophising individual no longer had confidence that he could attain to right insight or to his soul's salvation by his own strength, and sought his help accordingly, partly amid the great monuments of the past, partly in a divine *revelation.* Both tendencies, however, are ultimately upon the same basis, for the confidence which was placed in the men and writings of a previous time rested only upon the fact that they were regarded as especially favoured vessels of higher revelation. *Authority,* therefore, acquired its value as the mediate, historically accredited revelation, while the divine illumination of the individual as immediate revelation came to its assistance. Differently as the relation between these two forms was conceived of, it is yet the common mark of all Alexandrian philosophy that it regards *divine revelation as the highest source of knowledge.* Already in this innovation in the theory of knowledge, we find expressed the heightened value which this period put upon *personality,* and on personality as evincing itself in the feelings. The longing of this time desired that the truth might be found by experience, as an inner communion of man with the Supreme Being.

1. The *appeal to authority* often makes its appearance in Greek and Hellenistic philosophy in the sense of a confirmation and strengthening of an author's own views, but not as a decisive and conclusive argument. The *jurare in verba magistri* might be usual enough among the subordinate members of the schools,[1] but the heads of schools, and in general the men who engaged in independent research, maintained an attitude toward the teachings of the former time that was much more one of criticism than of unconditional subjection;[2] and though in the schools, chiefly the Academic

[1] Though even the well-known αὐτὸς ἔφα [*ipse dixit*] of the Pythagoreans is attested only through later writers (Cicero).

[2] Even the admiration of Socrates, in which all the following schools were at one, did not in itself lead to his being regarded as the valid authority for definite philosophical doctrines.

and Peripatetic, the inclination to preserve and maintain the teaching of the founder as an unassailable treasure was fostered by the custom of commenting upon his works, yet in all the conflict as to the criteria of truth the principle had never been brought forward that something must be believed because this or that great man had said it.

How strongly the need for authority had come to be felt in the later time, we may recognise even from the countless interpolations which were the order of the day in the whole Alexandrian literature. Their authors, who, perhaps, for the most part acted in good faith, since they themselves regarded their thoughts as only developments and continuations of the old doctrines, evidently believed that they could get a hearing for their works in no better way than by assigning to them the name of one of the heroes of wisdom, of an Aristotle, a Plato, or a Pythagoras. This phenomenon appeared most extensively among the Neo-Pythagoreans, whose chief concern it was to invest their new doctrine with the halo of ancient wisdom. But the more the convictions that were to be established in this manner bore a religious character, the more lively became the need to conceive of these authorities themselves as the bearers of a religious revelation, and therefore all the traits that might stamp them as such were sought for within them or even read into them. Not contented, however, with this, the later Greeks believed that they could give a higher sanction to their philosophy, as well as to their entire civilisation, by deriving it from the Oriental religions: thus Numenius[1] did not hesitate to maintain that Pythagoras and Plato had presented only the old wisdom of the Brahmans, Magi, Egyptians, and Jews. As a result of this, the extent of literary authorities increased extraordinarily; the later Neo-Platonists, a Jamblichus and Proclus, commented not only on Greek philosophers, but also upon the entire Hellenic and barbarian theology,[2] and credulously adopted myths and miraculous tales from these sources.

In quite a similar manner Oriental literature testified also to its esteem for Hellenism. Among the predecessors of Philo, Aristobulus especially appealed to verses which were interpolated in Orpheus and Linus, in Homer and Hesiod; and with Philo himself, the great Jewish theologian, the great men of Greek philosophy appear side by side with the Old Testament, as bearers of wisdom.

The felt need of authority naturally asserts itself most strongly in the unconditional faith in religious records. Here the Old Testa-

---

[1] In Eus. *Præp. Ev.* IX. 7   [2] Marinus, *Procl. Vit.* 22.

ment was from the beginning the firm foundation for the science and philosophy of Judaism and also for that of (orthodox) Christianity. But in the Christian Church the need of establishing a collection of writings in which the system of faith should be defined with certainty, first developed with Marcion, and then was gradually satisfied in the completion and conclusion of the New Testament: with Irenæus and Tertullian both Testaments already appear with the full value and validity of churchly authority.

2. If now in this way even scientific thought, which in consequence of sceptical disintegration no longer gave itself credit for the power of truth, subjected itself voluntarily to the authorities of antiquity and to religious institution, it was yet in nowise bound thereby to the extent that we might suppose. This relation rather took the form, along all lines, of extracting from the authoritative sources, and also of reading into them, the scientific doctrines which arose from the new religious movements.[1]

Where in so doing they did not resort expressly to those interpolations which are found more or less in the entire literature of the period as well as in Neo-Pythagoreanism, they employed as their instrument the method of *allegorical interpretation.*

This meets us first in Jewish theology. It had its prototype indeed in the allegorical interpretation of myths, which made its appearance early in Grecian literature, was employed by the Sophists, and extensively prosecuted by the Stoics. It was applied to religious documents by Aristobulus, but it was *Philo*[2] who carried it through methodically, proceeding from the conviction that a distinction must be made in Scripture between the literal and the spiritual meaning, between its body and its soul. In order to teach his commands to the great mass of men, who in their sensuous nature are unable to apprehend the divine purely, God gave to revelation the anthropomorphic form, behind which only the spiritually mature man penetrates to the true sense. This sense is to be sought in the philosophical conceptions which lie hidden in the historical husks. Accordingly, since Philo the task of theology has been directed toward interpreting *religious documents into a system of scientific doctrines;* and if he uses Greek philosophy for this purpose, and finds in it the higher meaning of the Scripture, he

---

[1] Even a man like Plutarch of Chæronea, who follows the writings of Plato as he would the revelations of a religious document, does not scruple to introduce into the teaching of his master Aristotelian and Stoic doctrines as well as his own religious view.

[2] Cf. Siegfried, *Philon v. Alexandria als Ausleger des alten Testaments* (Jena, 1875).

explains this relation on the ground that the thinkers of Greece
have drawn from Mosaic documents.[1]

Following his example, the Gnostics then attempted to transform
Oriental myths into Greek conceptions by allegorical interpretation,
and thought thus to develop a secret doctrine of the Apostolic
tradition, — the Apologists maintained the harmony of Christian
doctrine with the dogmas of Greek philosophy, — even men like
Irenæus and Tertullian worked upon the New Testament, — and
finally *Origen* knew how to bring the philosophy of Christianity
into accord with its documents.   The great Alexandrian theologian,
like the Gnostics who first attempted to create a Christian theology,
distinguished between the carnal (somatic), psychical, and spiritual
(pneumatic) conceptions of the religious records, — corresponding
to the metaphysico-anthropological ideas of the time (cf. § 19 f.).
For him the literal historical tradition yields only a "Christianity
according to the flesh " (χριστιανισμὸς σωματικός), and it is the task of
theology to lead out of this, through the moral significance at which
the "psychical " readers stop, to the ideal content of the Scripture,
which must then illumine the reader as self-evident truth.   Only he
who grasps this last belongs to the pneumatic or spiritual readers,
to whom the *eternal gospel* thus disclosed reveals itself.

This extraction of philosophical meaning from religious tradition
is found in fullest extent among the Neo-Platonists.   Jamblichus
practises it, in accordance with the Stoic model, on all forms of
Oriental and Occidental mythology, and Proclus, too, declares expressly that myths veil the truth from sensuous men who are not
worthy of it.[2]

3. But in all such doctrines, the interest of science (in the Christian teachings, γνῶσις) ultimately predominates over that of faith;
they are accommodations of philosophy to the need of religious
authority, felt at this time.   The essential *identity of authority and
of rational knowledge* obtains, therefore, as the fundamental presupposition; it obtains in such a degree, that just where it seems threatened, all artifices of allegorical interpretation are attempted in order
to rescue it.   This confidence, nevertheless, with which science proceeded to develop its own content as that of the religious documents,
rested ultimately upon the conviction that both historical authority
and scientific doctrine are but different *revelations* of the same divine
Power.

We have seen that the belief in authority in this period grew out
of the felt need of salvation and help.   Another psychological root of

---

[1] Phil. *Vit. Mos.* 657 a. (137 m.).   [2] Procl. *In Remp.* 369.

this belief was the enhanced importance of *personality.* This shows itself in the lively expression of admiration for the great men of the past, as we find it in Philo and in all lines of Platonism, and not less in the unconditional trust of the disciples in their masters, which, especially in later Neo-Platonism, degenerated to exaggerated veneration of the heads of schools.[1] This same motive appears in grandest form as a power in the world's history, in the stupendous, overpowering impression of the personality of Jesus. Faith in him was the uniting bond which held together victoriously the various and manifold tendencies of early Christianity.

But this psychological motive justified itself to theory by the consideration that the admired personality was regarded, in teaching and life, as a revelation of the divine World-reason. The metaphysical and epistemological bases for this were given in Platonism and especially in Stoicism. Attachment to the Platonic doctrine that knowledge is recollection, with the turn already expressed in Cicero that right knowledge is implanted by God in the soul, is innate within it, the carrying out of the Stoic logos doctrine, and of the idea contained in it that the rational part of the soul is a consubstantial emanation from the divine World-reason, — all this led to regarding every form of right knowledge as a kind of divine revelation in man.[2] All knowledge is, as Numenius said,[3] the kindling of the small light from the great light which illumines the world.

It was from this point of view that *Justin,* especially, conceived of the relationship maintained by him between the old philosophy and Christianity, and at the same time conceived the superiority of the latter. God has indeed revealed himself internally through the rational nature [4] (σπέρμα λόγου ἔμφυτον) of man who is created in his image, as he has revealed himself externally through the perfection of his creation; but the development of this *universal,* more potential than actual revelation, is retarded by evil demons and man's sensuous impulses. God has, therefore, for man's help, employed the *special* revelation, which has appeared not only in Moses and the prophets, but also in the men of Greek science.[5] Justin calls the revelation which is extended to the entire human race, the

---

[1] From the point of view of the history of civilisation we may notice the parallel in the boundless deification of the Roman Emperors.

[2] So also by the Stoics of the time of the Empire, philosophy, which among them likewise aimed to be a cure for sick souls (Epictetus, *Dissert.* III. 23, 30), is set forth as a sermon of the deity himself, through the mouth of the wise man (ib. I. 36).

[3] In Euseb. *Præp. Ev.* XI. 18, 8.

[4] *Apol.* II. 8; cf. Min. Fel. *Oct.* 16, 5.

[5] On the other hand, to be sure, Justin as well as Philo derives the Greek philosophy from the Jewish religion, as a borrowing.

λόγος σπερματικός. But that which has appeared in former time, so dispersed and often obscured, is not the full truth : the entire, pure logos has been revealed in Christ, Son of God, and second God.

In this teaching there prevails, on the one hand, with the Apologists, the effort to set forth *Christianity as the true and highest philosophy,* and to show that it unites in itself all teachings [1] of abiding worth that can be discovered in the earlier philosophy. Christ is called the teacher (διδάσκαλος), and this teacher is Reason itself. While Christianity was by this means brought as near as possible to rational philosophy, and philosophy's principle of knowledge made essentially equivalent to that of religion, this had yet at the same time the consequence, that the conception of the religious content itself became strongly rationalistic with Justin and similar Apologists, such as *Minucius Felix:* the specifically religious elements appear more repressed, and Christianity takes on the character of a moralising deism, in which it acquires the greatest similarity to religious Stoicism.[2]

On the other hand, in this relation the self-consciousness of Christianity speaks out, for with its *perfect* revelation it regarded all other kinds of revelation, universal as well as particular, as superfluous; and at this point the Apologetic doctrine became of itself polemic, as is shown especially in *Athenagoras.* Revelation here, too, is still regarded as the truly reasonable, but just on this account the reasonable is not to be demonstrated, but only believed. Philosophers have not found the full truth, because they have not been willing or able to learn God from God himself.

4. Thus, although in the Apologetic doctrine the rational is regarded as supernaturally revealed, there is gradually preparing *an opposition between revelation and knowledge by the reason.* The more the Gnostics, in developing their theological metaphysics, separated themselves from the simple content of Christian faith, the more *Irenæus* [3] warned against the speculations of worldly wisdom, and the more violently *Tatian,* with Oriental contempt of the Greeks, rejected every delusion of the Hellenic philosophy which was always at variance with itself, and of whose teachers each would exalt only his own opinions to the rank of law, while the Christians uniformly subjected themselves to the divine revelation.

This opposition becomes still sharper with *Tertullian* and *Arnobius.* The former, as Tatian had already done in part, adopted the

---

[1] Apol. II. 13, ὅτα παρὰ πᾶσι καλῶς εἴρηται ἡμῶν Χριστιανῶν ἐστιν.

[2] Cf. Min. Fel. *Oct.* 31 ff., where the Christian fellowship of love appears precisely as the Stoic world-state of philosophers.

[3] *Ref.* II. 25 ff.

Stoic materialism in its metaphysical aspect, but drew from it only the logical consequence of a purely sensualistic theory of knowledge. This was carried out in an interesting way by Arnobius, when, to combat the Platonic and Platonising theory of knowledge, he showed that a man left in complete isolation from his birth on would remain mentally empty, and not gain higher knowledge.[1] Since the human soul is by nature limited solely to the impressions of the senses, it is therefore of its own power absolutely incapable of acquiring knowledge of the deity, or of any vocation or destiny of its own that transcends this life. Just for this reason it needs revelation, and finds its salvation only in faith in this. So *sensualism* here shows itself for the first time *as basis for orthodoxy.* The lower the natural knowing faculty of man, and the more it is limited to the senses, the more necessary does revelation appear.

Accordingly, with *Tertullian*, the content of revelation is not only *above reason*, but also in a certain sense *contrary to reason*, in so far as by reason man's natural knowing activity is to be understood. The gospel is not only incomprehensible, but is also in necessary contradiction with worldly discernment: *credibile est quia ineptum est; certum est, quia impossibile est — credo quia absurdum.* Hence Christianity, according to his view, has nothing to do with philosophy, Jerusalem nothing to do with Athens.[2] Philosophy as natural knowledge is unbelief; there is therefore no Christian philosophy.

5. But rationalistic theory also found occasions enough for such a *defining of boundaries between revelation and natural knowledge.* For by their identification the criterion of truth threatened to become lost. The quantity of that which presented itself as revelation, in this time of such agitation in religion, made it indispensable to decide on the right revelation, and the criterion for this could not be sought in turn in the individual's rational knowledge, because the principle of revelation would be thereby injured. This difficulty made itself very noticeable, especially in the Hellenistic line of thought. Plutarch, for example, who regards all knowledge as revelation, follows the Stoic division of theology into three kinds, — viz. of the poets, of the law-givers, and of philosophers, — and would concede to science or philosophy the supreme decision as to religious truth,[3] declaring himself vigorously against superstition[4]

---

[1] Arn. *Adv. Gent.* II. 20 ff.
[2] Tertull. *De Carne Chr.* 5; *De Præscr.* 7. In the latter passage he directs his polemic also expressly against those who present a Stoic or Platonic Christianity. He is the extreme opponent of the Hellenising of dogma; he knows no compromise, and with his hot-blooded nature demands unconditional surrender to revelation. In a still more popular manner Arnobius sets forth the helplessness of natural knowledge (*Adv. Gent.* II. 74 ff.).
[3] *De Isid.* 68. [4] *De Superst.* 14.

(δεισιδαιμονία); but he shows himself to be ultimately as naïve and
credulous as his time, since he takes up into his writings all kinds
of tales of prophecies and miracles; and the incredible absence of
criticism with which the later Neo-Platonists, a Jamblichus and
Proclus proceeded in this respect, shows itself as the consistent
result of the renunciation of the thinker's own discernment, — a
renunciation which the need of revelation brought with it from the
beginning.

Here the development of the Church, which was then in process
of organisation, set in with its principle of *tradition* and *historically
accredited authority*. It regards the religious documents of the Old
and New Testaments as entirely, and also as alone, *inspired*. It
assumes that the authors, in recording this highest truth, were
always in a state of pure receptivity in their relation to the divine
spirit,[1] and finds the verification of this divine origin, not in the
agreement of this truth with the knowledge derived from human
reason, but essentially in the *fulfilment of the prophecies* which are
therein contained, and in the purposeful *connection of their succession
in time*.

The *proof from prophecy*, which became so extraordinarily important for the further development of theology, arose accordingly from
the need of finding a criterion for distinguishing true and false
revelation. Since man is denied knowledge of the future through
natural processes of cognition, the fulfilled predictions of the prophets serve as marks of the *inspiration*, by means of which they have
propounded their doctrines.

To this argument a second is now added. According to the doctrine of the Church, which on this point was supported chiefly by
Irenæus,[2] Old and New Testaments stand in the following connection: the same one God has revealed himself in the course of time
to man in a constantly higher and purer manner, corresponding to
the degree of man's receptive capacity: to the entire race he
reveals himself in the rational nature, which, to be sure, may be mis-
used; to the people of Israel, in the strict law of Moses; to entire
humanity again, in the law of love and freedom which Jesus announced.[3] In this connected *succession of prophets* there is thus
developed the *divine plan of education*, according to which the revelations of the Old Testament are to be regarded as preparations for

---

[1] Just. *Apol.* I. 31.

[2] *Ref.* III. 12; IV. 11 ff.

[3] The Alexandrian theology added, as fourth phase of revelation, the " eternal gospel." which is to be sought in the pneumatic interpretation of the New
Testament. Cf. the carrying out of these thoughts in Lessing's *Education of
the Human Race.*

the New, which in turn confirms them. Here, too, in patristic literature, the fulfilment of prophecies is regarded as the connecting link between the different phases of revelation.

These are the forms of thought in which the divine revelation became fixed for the Christian Church as *historical authority*. But the fundamental psychological power which was active in this process remained, nevertheless, devotion in faith to the person of Jesus, who, as the sum total of divine revelation, formed the centre of Christian life.

6. The development of the doctrine of revelation in the *Hellenistic philosophy* took an entirely different direction. Here the scientific movement lacked the living connection with the Church community, and therefore the support of a historical authority; here, therefore, revelation, which was demanded as a supplement for the natural faculties of knowledge, must be sought in an *immediate illumination of the individual by the deity*. On this account revelation is here held to be a *supra-rational apprehension of divine truth*, an apprehension which the *individual man* comes to possess in immediate contact (ἀφή) with the deity itself: and though it must be admitted that there are but few who attain to this, and that even these attain only in rare moments, a definite, historically authenticated, special revelation, authoritative for all, is nevertheless here put aside. This conception of revelation was later called the mystic conception, and to this extent *Neo-Platonism is the source of all later mysticism.*

The origins of this conception again are to be sought with *Philo*. For he had already taught that all man's virtue can arise and continue only through the working of the divine Logos within us, and that the knowledge of God consists only in the renunciation of self, — in giving up individuality, and in becoming merged in the divine Primordial Being.[1] Knowledge of the Supreme Being is unity of life with him, — immediate contact. The mind that wishes to behold God must *itself become God*.[2] In this state the soul's relation is entirely passive and receptive;[3] it has to renounce all self-activity, all its own thought, and all reflection upon itself. Even the νοῦς, the reason, must be silent in order that the blessedness of the perception of God may come upon man. In this state of *ecstasy* (ἔκστασις) the divine spirit, according to Philo, dwells in man. Hence, in this state, he is a prophet of divine wisdom, a foreteller and miracle-worker. As the Stoa had already traced mantic arts

---

[1] Phil. *Leg. All.* 48 e.; 55 d.; 57 b. (53–62 M.).
[2] Ἀποθεωθῆναι is found also in the Hermetic writings; *Poemand.* 10, 5 ff. The θεοῦσθαι (*deificatio*) is later a general term of Mysticism.
[3] Cf. Plut. *De Pyth. Orac.* 21 ff. (404 ff.).

to the consubstantiality of human and divine spirits (πνεύματα), so too the Alexandrians conceive of this "*deification*" of man from the standpoint of his oneness in essence with the ground of the world. All thought, Plotinus teaches, is inferior to this state of ecstasy; for thought is motion, — a desiring to know. Ecstasy, however, is certainty of God, blessed rest in him;[1] man has share in the divine θεωρία, or contemplation (Aristotle) only when he has raised himself entirely to the deity.

Ecstasy is then a state which transcends the self-consciousness of the individual, as its object transcends all particular determinateness (cf. § 20, 2). It is a sinking into the divine essence with an entire loss of self-consciousness: it is a possession of the deity, a unity of life with him, which mocks at all description, all perception, and all that abstract thought can frame.[2]

How is this state to be attained? It is, in all cases, a gift of the deity, a boon of the Infinite, which takes up the finite into itself. But man, with his free will, has to make himself worthy of this deification. He is to put off all his sensuous nature and all will of his own; he is to turn back from the multitude of individual relations to his pure, simple, essential nature (ἅπλωσις) ;[3] the ways to this are, according to Proclus, love, truth, and faith; but it is only in the last, which transcends all reason, that the soul finds its complete unification with God, and the peace of blessed rapture.[4] As the most effective aid in the preparation for this operation of divine grace, prayer[5] and all acts[6] of religious worship are commended. And if these do not always lead to the highest revelations of the deity, they yet secure at least, as Apuleius[7] had before this supposed, the comforting and helpful revelations of lower gods and demons, of saints and guardian spirits. So, also, in later Neo-Platonism, the raptures of prophecy which the Stoics had taught appear as lower and preparatory forms for the supreme ecstasy of deification. For, ultimately, all forms of worship are to the Neo-Platonist but exercises symbolic of that immediate union of the individual with God.

Thus the theory of inspiration diverged, in Christianity and Neo-Platonism, into two wholly different forms. In the former, divine

---

[1] Plot. *Ennead.* VI. 7.
[2] Ib. V. 3.
[3] An expression which is found even with Marcus Aurelius (Πρὸς ἑαυτ. IV. 26), and which Plotinus also employs (*Enn.* VI. 7, 35).
[4] Procl. *Theol. Plat.* I. 24 f.
[5] Jambl. in Procl. *Tim.* 64 C.
[6] *De Myst. Æg.* II. 11 (96).
[7] Apul. *De Socr.* 6 ff.

revelation is fixed as historical authority; in the latter, it is the process in which the individual man, freed from all eternal relation, sinks into the divine original Ground. The former is for the Middle Ages the source of *Scholasticism;* the latter, that of *Mysticism.*

§ 19. Spirit[1] and Matter.

Among the arguments in which the felt need of revelation develops in the Alexandrian philosophy, none is so incisive as that which proceeds from the premise that man, ensnared in the world of sense, can attain to knowledge of the higher spiritual world only by supernatural help: in this is shown the *religious dualism* which forms the fundamental mode of view of the period. Its roots are partly anthropological, partly metaphysical: the Stoic antithesis of reason and what is contrary to reason is united with the Platonic distinction between the supersensuous world, which remains ever the same, and the sensuous world which is always changing.

The *identification of the spiritual and the immaterial,* which was in nowise made complete with Plato although he prepared the way for it, had been limited by Aristotle to the divine self-consciousness. All the spiritual and mental activities of man, on the contrary, were regarded, even by Plato, as belonging to the world of phenomena (γένεσις), and remained thus excluded from the world of incorporeal Being (οὐσία), however much the rational might be opposed to the sensuous in the interest of ethics and of the theory of knowledge ; and while, in the antagonistic motives which crossed in the Aristotelian doctrine of the νοῦς, the attempt had been made to regard Reason as an immaterial principle, entering the animal soul from without, the development of the Peripatetic School (cf. § 15, 1) at once set this thought aside again. It was, however, in the doctrines of Epicurus and the Stoa that the conscious materialising of the psychical nature and activities attained its strongest expression.

On the other hand, the ethical dualism, which marked off as strongly as possible, man's *inner nature,* withdrawn into itself, as over against the sensuous outer world, became more and more sharply accentuated, and the more it took on religious form, the more it pressed, also, toward a theory of the world that made this opposition its metaphysical principle.

---

[1] [The German " *Geist*," corresponding to both " mind " and " spirit," as used in this period leans sometimes to one, sometimes to the other meaning. In view of the prevailingly religious character of the ideas of the period I have usually rendered it in this section by " spirit," sometimes by the alternative " mind or spirit."]

1. This relation appears in clearest form, perhaps, in the expres. sions of the *later Stoics*, who emphasise anthropological *dualism* so strongly that it comes into palpable contradiction with the metaphysics of the school. The idea of the oneness of man's nature, which the Stoics had taught hitherto, had indeed been already questioned by Posidonius, when he expressed the Platonising opinion, that the passions could not arise from the ἡγεμονικόν, but must come from other irrational parts of the soul.[1] Now, however, we find in Seneca[2] a bald opposition between *soul and "flesh"*; the body is only a husk, it is a fetter, a prison for the mind. So, too, Epictetus calls reason and body the two constituent elements of man,[3] and though Marcus Aurelius makes a distinction in man's sensuous nature between the coarse material and the psychical breath or pneuma which animates it, it is yet his intention to separate all the more sharply from the latter the soul proper, the rational spirit or intelligence (νοῦς and διάνοια), as an incorporeal being.[4] In correspondence with this, we find in all these men an idea of the deity, that retains only the intellectual marks from the Stoic conception, and looks upon matter as a principle opposed to the deity, hostile to reason.[5]

These changes in the Stoa are due, perhaps, to the rising influence of *Neo-Pythagoreanism*, which at first made the Platonic dualism, with its motives of ethical and religious values, the centre of its system. By the adherents of this doctrine the essential difference of soul and body is emphasised in the strongest manner,[6] and with this are most intimately connected,[7] on the one hand, the doctrine which will have God worshipped only spiritually, as a purely spiritual being,[8] by prayer and virtuous intention, not by outward acts, — and on the other hand, the completely *ascetic morals* which aims to free the soul from its ensnarement in matter, and lead it back to its spiritual prime source by washings and purifications, by avoiding certain foods, especially flesh, by sexual continence, and by mortifying all sensuous impulses. Over against the deity, which is the principle of good, matter (ὕλη) is regarded as the ground of all evil, propensity toward it as the peculiar sin of man.

---

[1] Cf. Galen, *De Hipp. et Plat.* IV. 3 ff.
[2] Senec. *Epist.* 65, 22; 92, 13; *Ad Marc.* 24, 5.
[3] Epict. *Dissert.* I. 3, 3.
[4] Marc. Aur. *Med.* II. 2; XII. 3.
[5] Senec. *Ep.* 65. 24; Epict. *Diss.* II. 8, 2; Marc. Aur. *Med.* XII. 2.
[6] Claud. Mam. *De Stratu Anim.* II. 7.
[7] In so far as here, too, man is regarded as a microcosm. Ps.-Pythag. in Phot. *Cod.* 249, p. 440 a.
[8] Apollonius of Tyana (περὶ θυσιῶν) in Eus. *Præp. Ev.* IV. 13.

We meet this same conception ethically, among the Essenes, and theoretically, everywhere in the teaching of *Philo*. He, too, distinguishes between the soul, which as vital force of the bodily organism has its seat in the blood, and the pneuma, which as emanation of the purely spiritual deity, constitutes the true essential nature of man.[1] He, too, finds that this latter is imprisoned in the body, and retarded in its unfolding by the body's sensuous nature (αἴσθεσις), so that since man's universal sinfulness[2] is rooted in this, salvation from this sinfulness must be sought only in the extirpation of all sensuous desires; for him, too, matter is therefore the corporeal substratum, which has indeed been arranged by the deity so as to form the purposive, good world, but which, at the same time, has remained the ground of evil and of imperfection.

2. The Christian Apologists' idea is related to this and yet different. With them the Aristotelian conception of God as pure intellect or spirit (νοῦς τέλειος) is united with the doctrine that God has created the world out of shapeless matter: yet here matter is not regarded immediately as an independent principle, but the ground of evil is sought rather in the perverted use of freedom on the part of man and of the demons who seduce him. Here the ethical and religious character of the dualism of the time appears in its complete purity: matter itself is regarded as something of an indifferent nature, which becomes good or evil only through its use by spiritual powers. In the same manner Hellenistic Platonists like *Plutarch*, proceeding from the conception of matter as formless Notbeing, sought the principle of evil not in it, but rather in a force or power, standing in opposition to the good deity,[3] — a force which, to a certain degree, contends with the deity about the formation of matter. Plutarch found this thought in the myths of different religions, but he might also have referred to a passage where Plato had spoken of the *evil world-soul* in opposition to the good.[4]

Meanwhile, the tendency to identify the antithesis of good and evil with that of mind (or spirit) and matter asserts itself here too, in the fact that the essence of evil is sought again in a propensity

---

[1] In this connection Philo calls πνεῦμα that which among the Stoics, Aristotelians, and Platonists of the time is called νοῦς; cf. Zeller V.³ 395, 3. Yet there occur with him again other expressions in which, quite in the Stoic fashion, the pneuma appears as air, in the sense of a most refined physical reality. Cf. H. Siebeck, *Gesch. d. Psych.* I. b 302 ff.

[2] It is also characteristic that the sinfulness of all men, a doctrine which is completely at variance with the old Stoic faith in the realisation of the ideal of the wise man, is generally acknowledged by the Stoics of the time of the Empire, and regarded as motive for the necessity of supernatural help. Cf. Seneca, *Benef.* I. 10; VII. 27; Epict. *Dissert.* II. 11, 1.

[3] Plut. *De Isid.* 46 ff.

[4] Plat. *Laws*, 896 E.

toward the sensuous and fleshly, — toward matter; while the good, on the contrary, is sought in love to the purely spiritual deity. This is not only a fundamental feature of the early Christian morals, but it is found also, in the same form, among the Platonists above mentioned. For Plutarch, too, liberation from the body is the necessary preparation for that reception of the working of divine grace which forms the goal of human life, and when Numenius carried out his theory further, by teaching that, as in the universe, so also in man, two souls, one good and one evil, contend with each other,[1] he yet also seeks the seat of the evil soul in the body and its desires.

In these doctrines, also, we find everywhere emphasised, not only the pure spirituality and incorporeality of God, but likewise the incorporeality of the individual spirit or mind. With Plutarch this is shown once more in the form that he would separate the νοῦς, the rational spirit, from the ψυχή, which possesses the sensuous nature and the passions together with the power to move the body. So, too, *Irenæus*[2] distinguishes the psychical breath of life (πνοὴ ζωῆς), which is of a temporal nature and bound to the body, from the ani- mating spirit (πνεῦμα ζωοποιοῦν), which is in its nature eternal.

These views of course appear everywhere in connection with the doctrines of immortality or of the pre-existence and transmigration of souls, of the Fall through which or as a punishment for which man has been placed in matter, and of the purification through which he is to free himself from it again; and just in this, too, the synthe- sis in question is completed more and more effectively, inasmuch as the immutable Eternal which remains ever the same (the Platonic οὐσία) is recognised in spirit; the perishable and changeable in matter.

3. In these connections we find developing gradually a separa- tion of the two characteristics which had been originally united in the conception of the soul, — the physiological and the psycholog- ical, the characteristic of vital force and that of the activity of con- sciousness. As in the scheme that had already been employed by Aristotle, so now, side by side with the "soul" which moves the body, appears the "spirit" as self-subsisting and independent principle, and in this spirit is found no longer merely a general rational activ- ity, but the proper essence of the individual (as also of the divine) *personality.* The triple division of man into body, soul, and spirit is introduced in all lines, in the most various modes of expression,[3]

---

[1] Jambl. in Stob. *Ecl.* I. 894.

[2] Iren. *Adv. Hær.* V. 12, 2.

[3] Of the various terminology (ψυχή, anima, πνεῦμα, spiritus, animus, etc.), in which these doctrines appear, examples have already been given above, and

and it is easily understood that in this case, the boundaries, on the one hand between soul and body, and on the other to a still greater degree between soul and spirit, were very fluctuating; for the soul plays here the part of a mean between the two extremes, matter and spirit.

An immediate consequence of this was that a new and deeper idea could be gained of the *activities of consciousness,* which now as "mental" or "spiritual" were separated from the physiological functions of the soul. For, when once removed in essence from the corporeal world, the spirit could not be thought as dependent upon sensuous influences, either in its activity or in the object of its activity; and while, in all Greek philosophy, cognition had been regarded as the perception and taking up of something given, and the attitude of thought as essentially receptive, now the idea of mind or spirit as an independent, productive principle forces its way through.

4. The beginnings for this lie already in the *Neo-Pythagorean* doctrine, in so far as in it the *spirituality of the immaterial world* was first maintained. The immaterial substances of Platonic metaphysics, the Ideas, appear no longer as self-subsistent essences, but as *elements constituting the content of intellectual or spiritual activity;* and while they still remain for human cognition something given and determining, they become *original thoughts of God.*[1] Thus the bodiless archetypes of the world of experience are taken up into the inward nature of mind; reason is no longer merely something which belongs to the οὐσία or which is only akin to it, it is the entire οὐσία itself; the *immaterial world is recognised as the world of mind or spirit.*[2]

In correspondence with this, the rational spirit or intellect (νοῦς) is defined by *Plotinus*[3] as the unity which has plurality within itself, *i.e.* in metaphysical language, as duality determined by unity but in itself indeterminate (cf. § 20), and in anthropological lan-

---

might very easily be multiplied. This doctrine was developed in an especially interesting way by Origen (*De Princ.* III. 1–5), where the "soul" is treated partly as motive power, partly as faculty of ideation and desire, while the spirit, on the contrary, is presented as the principle of judging, on the one hand between good and evil, on the other hand between true and false; in this alone, teaches Origen, consists man's freedom. The like triple division appears with Plotinus in connection with his whole metaphysical construction. *Enn.* II. 9, 2. Cf. § 20.

[1] Cf. Nicomachus, *Arithm. Intr.* I. 6.

[2] With this change the Platonic doctrine of Ideas passed over to the future, because Plotinus, and with him all Neo-Platonism, accepted it. Yet this did not take place without opposition. Longinus at least protested against it, and Porphyry as his disciple wrote a treatise of his own ὅτι ἔξω τοῦ νοῦ ὑφέστηκε τὰ νοητά. Porph. *Vit. Plot.* 18 ff.

[3] Plot. *Enn.* V. 9, 6; 3, 15; 4, 2.

guage, as the *synthetic* function which produces plurality out of its
higher unity.   From this general point of view the *Neo-Platonists*
carried out the psychology of cognition under the principle of the
activity of consciousness.   For according to this, the higher soul can
no longer be looked upon as passive, but must be regarded as essentially active in all its functions.[1]   All its intelligence (σύνεσις) rests
upon the synthesis (σύνθεσις) of various elements;[2] even where the
cognition refers to what is given by the senses, it is only the body
which is passive, while the soul in becoming conscious (συναίσθεσις
and παρακολούθησις) is active;[3] and the same is true of the sensuous
feelings and passions.   Thus in the field of sensation a distinction
is made between the state of excitation and the conscious perception
of this; the former is a passive or receptive state of the body (or
also of the lower soul); the latter even already in conscious perception (ἀντίληψις) is an act of the higher soul, which Plotinus
describes as a kind of bending back of thought — reflection.[4]

While *consciousness* was thus conceived as the active noting of the
mind's own states, functions, and contents, — a theory, which, according to Philoponus, was carried out especially by the Neo-Platonic Plutarch also, — there resulted from this with Plotinus the
conception of *self-consciousness* (παρακολουθεῖν ἑαυτῷ).[5]   His conception
of this was that the intellect, as thought active and in motion
(νόησις), has for its object itself as a resting, objective thought
(νοητόν): intellect as knowledge, and intellect as Being, are in this
case identical.

But the conception of self-consciousness takes on also an ethico-
religious colouring in accordance with the thought of the time.   The
σύνεσις is at the same time συνείδησις — *conscience, i.e.* man's knowledge, not only of his own states and acts, but also of their ethical
worth, and of the commandment by the fulfilment of which the
estimate of this worth is governed; and for this reason the doctrine
of self-consciousness is developed in the doctrine of the Church
Fathers, not only as man's knowledge of his sins, but also as *repentance* (μετάνοια) in actively combating them.

5. The conception of *mind* or *spirit as self-active, creative principle*
did not stop with its significance for psychology, ethics, and theory

---

[1] Porph. *Sentent.* 10, 19 *et al.*

[2] Plot. *Enn.* IV. 3, 26.

[3] Ib. IV. 4, 18 f.   The term συναίσθεσις — whose meaning reminds us besides
of the κοινὸν αἰσθητήριον in Aristotle, and thus ultimately of Plato, *Theæt.* 184 f.
— is found in similar use already in Alexander Aphrodisias, *Quæst.* III. 7,
p. 177, and so, too, Galen employs the expression διάγνωσις to designate the
becoming conscious of the change in the bodily organ as contrasted with that
change itself.

[4] Plot. *Enn.* I. 4, 10.   [5] Ib. III. 9.

of knowledge, but as the ancient world passed out, this conception rose to be the *dominant thought of religious metaphysics.* For by making the attempt to derive matter also from this creative spirit, this conception offered the possibility of finally overcoming that dualism which formed the presupposition of the whole movement of the religious thought of the time.

Hence it became the last and highest pioblem of ancient philosophy to understand *the world as a product of spirit,* to comprehend even the corporeal world with all of its phenomena as essentially intellectual or spiritual in its origin and content. The *spiritualisation of the universe* is the final result of ancient philosophy.

Christianity and Neo-Platonism, Origen and Plotinus, alike worked at this problem. The dualism of spirit and matter remains, indeed, persisting in full force for both so far as they have to do with the conception of the phenomenal world, and especially when they treat ethical questions. The sensuous is still regarded as that which is evil and alien to God, from which the soul must free itself in order to return to unity with pure spirit. But even this dark spot is to be illumined from the eternal light, matter is to be recognised as a creation of spirit. The last standpoint of ancient philosophy is thus *spiritual monism.*

But in the solution of this common problem the philosophy of Christianity and that of Neo-Platonism diverge widely; for this development of the divine spirit into the world of phenomena, even down to its material forms, must evidently be determined by the ideas which obtained of the nature of God and of his relation to the world, and just in this Hellenism found itself working under presuppositions that were completely different from those of the doctrine of the new religion.

§ 20. God and the World.

The peculiar suspense between metaphysical monism and ethico-religious dualism, which defines the character of the entire Alexandrian philosophy, forces together all the thoughts of the time, and condenses them into the most difficult of problems, that of the relation of God and the World.

1. This problem had already been suggested from the purely theoretical side, by the opposition between the Aristotelian and the Stoic philosophy. The former maintained the transcendence of God, *i.e.* his complete separation from the world, as strongly as the latter maintained the immanence of God, *i.e.* the doctrine that God is completely merged in the world. The problem, and the fundamental tendency adopted in its solution, may, therefore, be

recognised already in the eclectic mingling[1] of Peripatetic and Stoic cosmology, as type of which the pseudo-Aristotelian treatise, *Concerning the World* is regarded.[2] With the Aristotelian doctrine that the *essence of God* must be set far above Nature (as the sum-total of all particular things which are moved), and especially above the mutation of earthly existence, is connected here the Stoic endeavour to follow the working of the divine power through the entire universe, even into every detail. While, accordingly, the world was regarded among the Stoics as God himself, while Aristotle saw in it a living being, purposefully moved, whose outermost spheres were set in revolution only by longing for the eternally unmoved, pure Form, — a revolution communicating itself with ever-lessening perfection to the lower spheres, — here the macrocosm appears as the system of individual things existing in relations of mutual sympathy, in which the power of the supra-mundane God is dominant under the most varied forms as the principle of life. The mediation between theism and pantheism is gained, partly by the distinction between the essence and the power of God, partly by the graded scale of the divine workings, which descends from the heaven of the fixed stars to the earth. The pneuma doctrine is united with the Aristotelian conception of God, by conceiving of the forces of Nature's life as the workings of pure Spirit.[3]

This turn, however, but increased the difficulty already inherent in the Aristotelian doctrine of the action of the deity upon the world. For this action was regarded as consisting in the motion of matter, and it was hard to reconcile this materialisation of the divine action with the pure spirituality which was to constitute the essence of the deity. Even Aristotle had not become clear as to the relation of the unmoved mover to that which was moved (cf. § 13.).[4]

2. The problem became more severe as the religious dualism became more pronounced, a dualism which, not satisfied with contrasting God as spirit with matter, the supersensuous sphere with the sensuous, rather followed the tendency to raise the divine being

---

[1] Stratonism as a transformation of the Aristotelian doctrine in the direction of pantheistic immanence, a transformation allied to the doctrine of the Stoa, has been treated above, § 15, 1.

[2] This book (printed among the writings of Aristotle, 391 ff.) may perhaps have arisen in the first century A.D. Apuleius worked it over into Latin.

[3] Cf. principally Ch. 6, 397 b 9.

[4] These difficulties in Aristotle's case became condensed in the concept of the ἁφή. For since the "contact" of the mover with the moved was regarded as the condition of motion, it was necessary to speak also of a "contact" between God and the heaven of the fixed stars. This, however, was liable to objection on account of the purely spiritual essence of the deity, and the ἁφή in this case received a restricted and intellectually transformed meaning ("immediate relation"). Cf. Arist. *De Gen. et Corr.* I. 6, 323 a 20.

above all that can be experienced and above every definite content, and thus to make the *God who is above the world also a God above mind or spirit.* This is found already with the *Neo-Pythagoreans,* among whom a wavering between various stadia of dualism lurks behind their mode of expression in the symbolism of numbers. When the "One" and the "indefinite duality" are maintained to be principles, the latter indeed always means matter as the impure, as the ground of the imperfect and the evil; the One, however, is treated now as pure Form, as spirit, now also as the "cause of causes" which lies above all reason, — as the primordial being which has caused to proceed forth from itself the opposition of the derivative One and duality, of spirit and matter. In this case the second One, the first-born One ($\pi\rho\omega\tau\acute{o}\gamma o\nu o\nu\ \check{\epsilon}\nu$) appears as the perfect image of the highest One.[1]

Inasmuch as mind or spirit was thus made a product of the deity, though the first and most perfect product, this effort led to raising the conception of the deity even to *complete absence of all qualities.* This had been already shown in *Philo,* who emphasised so sharply the contrast between God and everything finite that he designated God expressly as devoid of qualities ($\check{\alpha}\pi o\iota o s$[2]) : for since God is exalted above all, it can be said of him only that he has none of the finite predicates known to human intelligence; no name names him. This type of thought, later called "negative theology," we find also among those Christian *Apologists* that were influenced in their conceptions by Philo, especially with Justin,[3] and likewise in part among the *Gnostics.*

The same meets us also in *Neo-Platonism* in a still more intensified form, if possible. As in the Hermetic writings[4] God had been considered as infinite and incomprehensible, as nameless, exalted above all Being, as the ground of Being and Reason, neither of which exists until created by him, so for Plotinus, the deity is the absolutely transcendent primordial being, exalted as a perfect unity above mind, which, as the principle that contains plurality already in its unity (§ 19, 4), must have proceeded forth from God (and not have been eternal). This One, $\tau\grave{o}\ \check{\epsilon}\nu$, precedes all thought and Being; it is infinite, formless, and "beyond" ($\acute{\epsilon}\pi\acute{\epsilon}\kappa\epsilon\iota\nu a$) the intellectual as well as the sensuous world, and therefore without consciousness and without activity.[5]

---

[1] Nicomachus, *Theol. Arithm.* p. 44.
[2] Phil. *Leg. Alleg.* 47 a ; *Qu. D. S. Immut.* 301 a.
[3] Just. *Apol.* I. 61 ff. [4] *Poemand.* 4 f.
[5] It is easy to understand how a state of ecstasy devoid of will and consciousness and raised above reason, appeared requisite for man's relation to this suprarational God-Being, exalted above all action, will, and thought. Cf. above, § 18, 6.

Finally, while Plotinus still designates this inexpressible First (τὸ πρῶτον) as the One, which is the cause of all thought and of all Being, and as the Good, as the absolute end of all that comes to pass, even this did not satisfy the later members of the school. Jamblichus set above the ἕν of Plotinus a still higher, completely ineffable One (πάντη ἄρρητος ἀρχή[1]), and Proclus followed him in this.

3. In opposition to such dialectical subtilisations, the *development of Christian thought in the Church* preserved its impressive energy by holding fast to the *conception of God as spiritual personality.* It did this, not as the result of philosophical reflection and reasoning, but by virtue of its immediate attachment to the living belief of the Church community, and just in this consisted its psychological strength, its power in the world's history. This faith is breathed in the New Testament; this is defended by all the supporters of patristic theology, and just by this are the limits of the Christian doctrine everywhere defined, as against the Hellenistic solutions of the chief problem in the philosophy of religion.

Hellenism sees in personality, in however purely spiritual a manner it may be conceived, a restriction and a characteristic of the finite, which it would keep at a distance from the Supreme Being, and admit only for the particular gods. Christianity, as a living religion, demands a *personal relation of man to the ground of the world conceived of as supreme personality*, and it expresses this demand in the thought of the *divine sonship* of man.

If, therefore, the conception of personality as intrinsic spirituality (*geistiger Innerlichkeit*) expresses the essentially new result, to yield which, theoretical and ethical motives intertwined in Greek and Hellenistic thought, then it was Christianity which entered upon this inheritance of ancient thought, while *Neo-Platonism* turned back to the old idea that saw in personality only a transitory product of *a life which as a whole is impersonal.* It is the essential feature of the Christian conception of the world that it regards the person and the relations of persons to one another as the essence of reality.

4. In spite of this important difference, all lines of the Alexandrian philosophy were confronted by the same problem, that of placing the deity, thus taken from the sensible world, in those relations which religious need demanded. For the more deeply the opposition between God and the world was felt, the more ardent became the longing to overcome it — to overcome it by a *knowledge* that should understand the world also through God, and by a *life* that should return out of the world to God.

---

[1] Damasc. *De Princ.* 43.

Hence the dualism of God and the world, as well as that of spirit and matter, is but the starting-point — taken in the feelings — and the presupposition of the Alexandrian philosophy: its goal is everywhere, theoretically as well as practically, to vanquish this dualism. Just in this consists the peculiarity of this period, that it is anxious to close, in knowledge and will, the cleft which it finds in its feelings.

This period, to be sure, produced also theories of the world in which *dualism* asserted itself so predominantly as to become fixed as their immovable basis. Here belong primarily Platonists like Plutarch, who not only treated matter as an original principle side by side with the deity, because the deity could in nowise be the ground of the evil, but also assumed beside God, the "evil world-soul" as a third principle in the formation of this indifferent matter into a world. A part of the *Gnostic* systems present themselves here, however, for especial consideration.

This first fantastic attempt at a Christian theology was ruled throughout by the thoughts of sin and redemption, and the fundamental character of Gnosticism consists in this, that from the point of view of these ruling thoughts the conceptions of Greek philosophy were put in relation with the myths of Oriental religions. Thus with *Valentinus*, side by side with the deity ($\pi\rho o\pi \acute{a}\tau\omega\rho$) poured out into the Pleroma or fulness ($\tau\grave{o}$ $\pi\lambda\acute{\eta}\rho\omega\mu a$) of spiritual forms, appears the Void ($\tau\grave{o}$ $\kappa\acute{\epsilon}\nu\omega\mu a$), likewise original and from eternity; beside Form appears matter, beside the good appears the evil, and though from the self-unfolding of the deity (cf. 6, below) an entire spiritual world has been formed in the "fulness" above mentioned, the corporeal world is yet regarded as the work of a fallen Æon (cf. § 21) who builds his inner nature into matter. So, too, *Saturninus* set matter, as the domain of Satan, over against God's realm of light, and regarded the earthly world as a contested boundary province for whose possession the good and evil spirits strive by their action upon man; and in a similar manner the mythology of *Bardesanes* was arranged, which placed beside the "Father of Life" a female deity as the receptive power in the formation of the world.

But dualism reached its culmination in a mixed religion which arose in the third century under the influence of the Gnostic systems combined with a return to the old Persian mythology, — *Manichœism.*[1] The two realms of good and evil, of light and darkness,

---

[1] The founder, Mani (probably 240–280 A.D.), regarded his doctrine as the consummation of Christianity and as a revelation of the Paraclete. He fell a victim to the persecution of the Persian priests, but his religion soon became

of peace and strife, stand here opposed as eternally as their princes, God and Satan. Here, too, the formation of the world is conceived of as a mixture of good and evil elements, — brought about by a violation of the boundaries; in man the conflict of a good soul belonging to the realm of light, and of an evil soul arising from darkness, is assumed, and a redemption is expected that shall completely separate both realms again.

Thus at the close of the period it is shown in the clearest manner that the dualism of the time rested essentially upon ethico-religious motives. By adopting as their point of view for theoretical explanation the judgment of worth, in accordance with which men, things, and relations are characterised as good or bad, these thinkers came to trace the origin of the thus divided universe back to two different causes. In the proper sense of the judgment, only one of these causes, that of the good, should be regarded as positive and have the name of deity, but in a theoretical aspect the other also fully maintains its claim to metaphysical originality and eternity ($o\mathring{v}\sigma\acute{\iota}a$). But even from this relation it may be seen that as soon as the metaphysical relation was completely adapted to the ethical, this must in itself lead to a removal of the dualism.

5. In fact, dualism, from motives that were most peculiarly its own, produced a series of ideas through which it prepared its own overcoming. For the sharper the antithesis between the spiritual God and the material world, and the greater the distance between man and the object of his religious longing, the more the need asserted itself of bringing about again, by *intermediate links*, a union of what was thus separated. The theoretical significance of this was to render comprehensible and free from objections the action of the deity upon matter alien to him and unworthy of him; practically these links had the significance of serving as *mediators* between man and God, having the power to lead man out of his sensuous vileness to the Supreme Being. Both interests were alike suggestive of the methods by which the Stoics had known how to utilise, in their religion of Nature, the popular faith in the lower deities.

This mediation theory was first attempted on a large and thorough plan by *Philo*, who gave it its definite direction by bringing it into close relations, on the one hand, with the Neo-Pythagorean doctrine of Ideas, on the other hand with the doctrine of angels in his

---

greatly extended, and maintained itself in vigour far on into the Middle Ages. We are best instructed with regard to it through Augustine, who was himself for a time an adherent of it. Cf. F. C. Baur, *Das manichäische Religionssystem* (Tübingen, 1836); O. Flügel, *Mani und seine Lehre* (Leips. 1862).

religion. The mediating powers, in considering which Philo had in mind more the theoretical significance and the explanation of the influence of God upon the world, he designates according to the changing point of view of his investigation, now as Ideas, now as acting forces, or again as the angels of God; but with this is always connected the thought that these intermediate members have part in God as in the world, that they belong to God and yet are different from him. So the Ideas are regarded, on the one hand, in Neo-Pythagorean fashion as thoughts of God and content of his wisdom, but again, after the old Platonic thought, as an intelligible world of archetypes, created by God: and if these archetypes are held to be at the same time the active forces which shape the unordered matter according to their purposeful meaning, the forces appear in this case sometimes as powers so independent that by assigning them the formation and preservation of the world, all immediate relation between God and the world is avoided, and sometimes again as something attached to the divine essence and representing it. Finally, as angels they are indeed real mythical forms, and are designated as the servants, the ambassadors, the messengers, of God, but on the other hand they represent the different sides and qualities of the divine essence, which, it is true, is as a whole unknowable and inexpressible in its depth, but which reveals itself just in them. This double nature, conditioned by the fundamental thought of the system itself, brings with it the consequence that these ideal forces have the significance of the contents of general conceptions, and yet are at the same time furnished with all the marks of personality ; and just this peculiar amalgamation of scientific and mythical modes of thought, this indefinite twilight in which the entire doctrine remains, is the essential and important therein.

The same is true of the last inference, with which Philo concluded this line of thought. The fulness of Ideas, forces, and angels was itself in turn an entire world, in which plurality and motion ruled : between it and the one unmoved, changeless deity there was need of still a higher intermediate link. As the Idea is related to the individual phenomena, so the highest of the Ideas (τὸ γενικώτατον), the "Idea of the Ideas," must be related to the Ideas themselves, — as force is related to its activities in the world of sense, so the rational World-force in general must be related to the forces : the world of angels must find its unitary conclusion in an archangel. This sum-total of the divine activity in the world, Philo designates by the Stoic conception of the *Logos*. This also appears with him, on this account, in wavering, changing light. The Logos is, on the one hand, the divine wisdom, resting within

itself (σοφία — λόγος ἐνδιάθετος ; cf. p. 200, note 1), and the producing
rational power of the Supreme Being; it is, on the other hand,
Reason as coming forth from the deity (λόγος προφορικός, "uttered
Reason "), the self-subsistent image, the first-born son, who is not,
as is God, without origin, nor yet has he arisen, as have we men;
he is the *second God*.[1] Through him God formed the world, and he
is in turn also the high priest, who, through his intercession, creates
and preserves relations between man and the deity. He is knowable, while God himself, as exalted above all determination, remains
unknowable : he is God in so far as God forms the life-principle
of the world.

Thus the transcendence and immanence of God divide as separate
potencies, to remain united, nevertheless ; the Logos, as the God
within the world, is the "dwelling-place" of the God without the
world. The more difficult the form which this relation assumes
for abstract thought, the richer the imagery in which it is set forth
by Philo.[2]

6. With this Logos doctrine the first step was taken toward
filling the cleft between God and the sensible world by a definite
graded succession of forms, descending, with gradual transitions,
from unity to plurality, from unchangeableness to changeableness,
from the immaterial to the material, from the spiritual to the sensuous, from the perfect to the imperfect, from the good to the bad ;
and when this series, thus arranged by rank, was conceived of at
the same time as a system of causes and effects which again were
themselves causes, there resulted from this a new exposition of the
cosmogonic process, in which the world of sense was derived from
the divine essence by means of all these intermediate members.
At the same time, the other thought was not far distant, that the
stages of this process should be regarded also in their reverse order,
as the stages by which man, ensnared in the world of sense, becomes
reunited with God. And so, both theoretically and practically, the
path is broken on which dualism is to be overcome.

A problem was thus taken up again which Plato in his latest
Pythagoreanising period had had in mind, and the oldest Academicians as well, when they sought, with the aid of the number theory,

---

[1] Philo in Eus. *Præp. Ev.* VII. 13, 1. With a somewhat stronger emphasis
upon personality, these same conceptions are found in Justin, *Apol.* I. 32 ; *Dial.
c. Tryph.* 56 f.

[2] Connected with all these doctrines is the fact, that with Philo the spiritual
in the world of experience occupies a doubtful position between the immaterial
and the material : the νοῦς of man, the faculty of thought and will, is a part of
the divine Logos (even the demons are designated after the Stoic analogy as
λόγοι), and yet it is again characterised as finest pneuma.

to comprehend how Ideas and things proceeded forth from the
divine unity.   But it had been shown at that time that this scheme
of the development of plurality out of the One, as regards its
relation to the predicates of worth, admitted two opposite interpretations: viz. the Platonic mode of view, defended by Xenocrates,
that the One is the good and the perfect, and that that which is
derived from this is the imperfect and, ultimately, the bad, and the
opposing theory, held by Speusippus, that the good is only the final
product, not the starting-point of the development, and that this
starting-point is to be sought, on the contrary, in the indefinite, the
incomplete.[1]   It is customary to distinguish the above-described
doctrines as the *system of emanation* and the *system of evolution.*
The former term arises from the fact that in this system, which was
decidedly prevalent in the religious philosophy of Alexandrianism,
the separate formations of the world-producing Logos were often
designated by the Stoic term, as "emanations" (ἀπόρροιαι) of the
divine essence.

Yet the Alexandrian philosophy is not lacking in attempts at
evolutionary systems.   In particular, these were especially available for *Gnosticism;* for, in consequence of the degree to which it
had strained the dualism of spirit and matter, this system was
necessarily inclined to seek the monistic way of escape rather in an
indifferent, original ground, which divided itself into the opposites.
Hence where the Gnostics sought to transcend dualism, — and this
was the case with the most important of them, — they projected
not only a cosmogonic but a *theogonic process,* by which the deity
unfolded himself from the darkness of his primeval essence,
through opposition, to complete revelation.   Thus, with *Basileides,*
the nameless, original ground is called the not (yet) existing God
(ὁ οὐκ ὢν θεός).   This being, we hear, produced the world-seed
(πανσπερμία), in which the spiritual forces (υἱότητες) lay unordered
side by side with the material forces (ἀμορφία).   The forming and
ordering of this chaos of forces is completed by their longing for
the deity.   In connection with this process the various "sonships,"
the spiritual world (ὑπερκοσμία), separate themselves from the material world (κόσμος), and in the course of the process of generation all the spheres of the thus developed deity ultimately become
separate; each attains its allotted place, the unrest of striving
ceases, and the peace of glorification rests over the All.

Motives from both systems, that of evolution and that of emanation, appear peculiarly mingled in the doctrine of *Valentinus.*   For

---

[1] Cf. Arist, *Met.* XIV. 4, 1091 b 16; XII. 7, 1072 b 31.

here the spiritual world (πλήρωμα) or system of the "*Æons*," the eternal essences, is developed first as an unfolding of the dark and mysterious primitive Depth (βῦθος) to self-revelation, and in the second place as a descending production of more imperfect forms. The mythical schema in this is the Oriental pairing of male and female deities. In the highest pair or "syzygy" there appears side by side with the original Ground "Silence" (σιγή), which is also called "Thought" (ἔννοια). From this union of the Original Being with the capacity of becoming conscious there proceeds as the first-born the Spirit (here called νοῦς) which in the second syzygy has as its object "Truth," *i.e.* the intelligible world, the realm of Ideas. Thus, having itself come to full revelation, the deity in the third syzygy takes the form of "Reason" (λόγος) and "Life," (ζωή), and in the fourth syzygy becomes the principle of external revelation as "Ideal Man" (ἄνθρωπος) and "Community" (ἐκκλησία, church). While the descending process has thus already begun, it is continued still farther by the fact that from the third and fourth syzygies still other Æons proceed, which, together with the sacred Eight, form the entire Pleroma, but which stand farther and farther removed from the original Ground. It is the last of these Æons, "Wisdom" (σοφία), that, by sinful longing after the original Ground, gives occasion for the separation of this Longing and of its being cast into the material Void, the κένωμα, there to lead to the formation of the earthly world.

If we look at the philosophical thoughts which lie back of these highly ambiguous myth-constructions, it is easy to understand that the school of the Valentinians diverged into various theories. For in no other system of that time are dualistic and monistic mofives of both kinds, from the system of evolution as well as from that of emanation, so intricately mingled.

7. Clarified conceptionally, and freed from mythical apparatus, the like motives appear in the doctrine of *Plotinus,* yet in such a manner that in the system as completed the principle of *emanation* almost entirely crowds out the other two.

The synthesis of transcendence and immanence is sought by Plotinus also in the direction of preserving the essence of God as the absolutely one and unchangeable, while plurality and changeability belong only to his workings.[1] Of the "First," which is exalted above all finite determinations and oppositions, nothing whatever can be predicated in the strict sense (cf. above, 2). It is

---

[1] In so far we find here, coined into theological form, the problem of the Eleatics and Heraclitus, with which Greek metaphysics began, — a problem which also determined the nature of Platonism.

only in an improper sense, in its relation to the world, that it can be designated as the infinite One, as the Good, and as the highest Power or Force (πρώτη δύναμις), and the workings of this Power which constitute the universe are to be regarded, not as ramifications and parts into which the substance of the First divides, and so not as " emanations " in the proper sense, but rather as overflowing by-products which in nowise change the substance itself, even though they proceed from the necessity of its essence.

To express this relation in figurative form Plotinus employs the analogy of *light*, — an analogy which, in turn, has also an influence in determining his conception. Light, without suffering at all in its own essence or itself entering into motion, shines into the darkness and produces about itself an atmosphere of brightness that decreases in intensity more and more from the point which is its source, and finally of itself loses itself in darkness. So likewise the workings of the One and Good, as they become more and more separate from their source, proceeding through the individual spheres, become more and more imperfect and at last change suddenly into the dark, evil opposite — matter.

The first sphere of this divine activity is, according to Plotinus, *mind* or *rational spirit* (νοῦς). in which the sublime unity differentiates itself into the duality of thought and Being, *i.e.* into that of consciousness and its objects. In mind the essence of the deity is preserved as the unity of the thought-function (νόησις) ; for this thought which is identical with Being is not regarded as an activity that begins or ceases, changing as it were with its objects, but as the eternal, pure perception, ever the same, of its own content, which is of like essence with itself. But this content, the world of Ideas, the eternal Being (οὐσία in the Platonic sense) as contrasted with phenomena, is, as intelligible world (κόσμος νοητός), at the same time the principle of plurality. For the Ideas are not merely thoughts and archetypes, but are at the same time the moving forces (νοὶ δυνάμεις) of lower reality. Because, therefore, unity and variety are united in this intelligible world as the principles of persistence and of occurrence and change, and are yet again separated, the fundamental conceptions (categories) of this world are these five,[1] viz. Being or Existing (τὸ ὄν), Rest (στάσις), Motion or Change (κίνησις), Identity (ταὐτότης), and Difference (ἑτερότης). Mind, then, as a function which has determinate contents, and carries plurality within itself, is the form through which the deity causes all empiri-

---

[1] Well known from the dialogue, the *Sophist,* of the *Corpus Platonicum.* Cf. 254 B. ff.

cal reality to proceed forth from itself: God as productive principle, as ground of the world, is mind or rational spirit.

But spirit needs to shine out in a similar manner in order to produce the world from itself; its most immediate product is the *soul*, and this in turn evinces its activity by shaping matter into corporeality. The peculiar position of the "soul" therefore consists in this, that it, perceiving or beholding, receives the content of spirit, the world of Ideas, and after this archetype (εἰκών) forms the world of sense. Contrasted with the creative spirit, it is the receptive, contrasted with matter, the active principle. And this duality of the relations toward the higher and the lower is here so strongly emphasised that just as "spirit" divided into thought and Being, so the soul, for Plotinus, is out and out doubled: as sunk into the blissful contemplation of the Ideas it is the higher soul, the soul proper, the ψυχή in the narrower sense of the word; as formative power, it is the lower soul, the φύσις (equivalent to the λόγος σπερματικός of the Stoics).

All these determinations apply on the one hand to the universal soul (world-soul — Plato), and on the other to the individual souls which have proceeded from it as the particular forms which it has taken on, especially therefore to human souls. The φύσις, the formative power of Nature, is distinguished from the pure, ideal world-soul: from the latter emanate the gods, from the former the demons. Beneath man's knowing soul, which turns back to the spirit, its home, stands the vital force which forms the body. Thus the separation in the characteristics of the concept of the soul — a separation which developed materially from dualism (cf. § 19, 3) — is here demanded formally by the connected whole of the metaphysical system.

In this connection, this working of the soul upon matter is of course conceived of as purposive, that is, as appropriate or adapted for ends, because it ultimately goes back to spirit and reason (λόγος); but since it is a work of the lower soul, it is regarded as undesigned, unconscious direction, which proceeds according to natural necessity. As the outer portions of the rays of light penetrate into the darkness, so it belongs to the nature of the soul to illumine matter with its glory which arises from spirit and from the One.

This *matter*, however, — and this is one of the most essential points in the metaphysics of Plotinus, — must not be looked upon as a corporeal mass subsisting in itself beside the One; it is, rather, itself without body, immaterial.[1] Bodies are indeed formed out of

---

[1] ἀσώματος: *Ennead.* III. 6. 7.

it, but it is itself no body; and since it is thus neither spiritual nor corporeal in its nature, it cannot be determined by any qualities (ἄποιος). But for Plotinus, this epistemological indeterminateness has, at the same time, the force of metaphysical indeterminateness. Matter is for him absolute negativity, pure privation (στέρησις), complete absence of Being, absolute *Non-being:* it is related to the One as darkness to light, as the empty to the full. This ὕλη of the Neo-Platonists is not the Aristotelian or the Stoic, but is once more the Platonic; it is *empty, dark space.*[1] So far in ancient thought does the working of the Eleatic identification of empty space with Non-being, and of the farther extension of this doctrine by Democritus and Plato, extend: in Neo-Platonism, also, space serves as the presupposition for the multiplication which the Ideas find in the phenomenal world of sense. For this reason, with Plotinus, also, the lower soul, or φύσις, whose office it is to shine out upon matter, is the principle of divisibility,[2] while the higher soul possesses the indivisibility which is akin to the rational spirit.

In this pure negativity lies a ground for the possibility of determining by a predicate of worth this matter thus devoid of qualities; it is *the evil.* As absolute want (πενία παντελής), as the negation of the One and of Being, it is also the negation of the Good, ἀπουσία ἀγαθοῦ. But by introducing the conception of evil in this manner, it receives a special form: evil is not itself something positively existent; it is want, or deficiency; it is lack of the Good, *Non-being.* This conception thus formed gave Plotinus a welcome argument for *theodicy;* if the evil *is* not, it need not be justified, and so it follows from the sheer conceptions as so determined that all that is, is good.

For Plotinus, therefore, the world of the senses is not in itself evil any more than it is in itself good; but because in it light passes over into darkness, because it thus presents a mixture of Being and Non-being (the Platonic conception of γένεσις here comes into force anew), it is *good* so far as it has part in God or the Good; i.e. *so far as it is;* and on the other hand, it is *evil* in so far as it has part in matter or the Evil; i.e. *in so far as it is not* [has no real, positive existence]. Evil proper, the true evil (πρῶτον κακόν), is matter, negation; the corporeal world can be called evil only because it is formed out of matter: it is secondary evil (δεύτερον κακόν); and the predicate "evil" belongs to souls only if they give

---

[1] *Ennead.* III. 6, 18. Universal empty space forms the possibility (ὑποκείμενον) for the existence of bodies, while, on the other hand, the particular spatial determinateness is conditioned by the nature of the bodies, II. 4, 12.

[2] Ib. III. 9, 1.

themselves over to matter. To be sure, this entrance into matter belongs to the essential characteristics of the soul itself; the soul forms just that sphere in which the shining forth of the deity passes over into matter, and this participation in evil is, therefore, for the soul, a natural necessity which is to be conceived of as a continuation of its own proceeding forth from the rational spirit.[1]

By this distinction of the world of sense from matter, Plotinus was able to do justice, also, to the positive element in phenomena.[2] For since the original power works through spirit and soul upon matter, all that in the world of sense really exists or *is*, is evidently itself soul and spirit. In this is rooted the spiritualisation of the corporeal world, the idealising of the universe, which forms the characteristic element in the conception of Nature held by Plotinus. The material is but the outer husk, behind which, as the truly active reality, are souls and spirits. A body or corporeal substance is the copy or shadow of the Idea which in it has shaped itself to matter; its true essence is this spiritual or intellectual element which appears as a phenomenon in the image seen by sense.

It is in such shining of the ideal essence through its sensuous phenomenon that *beauty* consists. By virtue of this streaming of the spiritual light into matter the entire world of the senses is beautiful, and likewise the individual thing, formed after its archetype. Here in the treatise of Plotinus on beauty (*Ennead.* I. 6) this conception meets us for the first time among the fundamental conceptions of a theory of the world; it is the first attempt at a metaphysical æsthetics. Hitherto the beautiful had always appeared only in homonomy with the good and the perfect, and the mild attempts to separate the conception and make it independent, which were contained in Plato's *Symposium*, were now taken up again for the first time by Plotinus; for even the theory of art, to which æsthetic science had restricted itself as it appeared most clearly in the fragment of the Aristotelian *Poetic*, considered the beautiful essentially according to its ethical effects (cf. § 13, 14). Ancient life must run its entire course, and that turning toward the inner life, that internalising, as it were, which this life experienced in the religious period, must be completed, to bring about the scientific

---

[1] Therefore, though Plotinus in his ethics emphasised strongly freedom in the sense of responsibility, the great tendency of his metaphysical thought is shown just in this, that he did not make this freedom of "power to the contrary" his explaining principle, but sought to understand the transition of the world into evil as a metaphysical necessity.

[2] Very characteristic in this respect is the treatise (*Ennead.* II. 9) which he wrote against the barbarian contempt of Nature shown by the Gnostics.

consciousness of this finest and highest content of the Grecian world; and the conception in which this takes place is on this account characteristic for the development from which it comes forth; the beauty which the Greeks had created and enjoyed is now recognised as the victorious power of spirit in externalising its sensuous phenomena. This conception also is a triumph of the spirit, which in unfolding its activities has at last apprehended its own essential nature, and has conceived it as a world-principle.

As regards the phenomenal world, Plotinus takes a point of view which must be designated as the *interpretation* of *Nature in terms of psychical life,* and so it turns out that with reference to this antithesis ancient thought described its course from one extreme to the other. The oldest science knew the soul only as one of Nature's products side by side with many others, — for Neo-Platonism the whole of Nature is regarded as real only in so far as it is soul.

But by employing this idealistic principle for explaining individual things and processes in the world of sense, all sobriety and clearness in natural research is at an end. In place of regular, causal connections appears the mysterious, dreamily unconscious weaving of the world-soul, the rule of gods and demons, the spiritual sympathy of all things expressing itself in strange relations among them. All forms of divination, astrology, faith in miracles, naturally stream into this mode of regarding Nature, and man seems to be surrounded by nothing but higher and mysterious forces: this world created by spirit, full of souls, embraces him like a *magic* circle.

The whole process in which the world proceeds forth from the deity appears, accordingly, as a timeless, eternal necessity, and though Plotinus speaks also of a periodical return of the same particular formations, the world-process itself is yet for him without beginning or end. As it belongs to the nature of light to shine forever into the darkness, so God does not exist without the streaming forth with which he creates the world out of matter.

In this *universal life of spirit* the individual personality vanishes, as a subordinate, particular phenomenon. Released from the all-soul as one of countless forms in which that unfolds, it is cast into the sensuous body out of the purer pre-existent state, on account of its guilty inclination toward what is void and vain, and it is its task to estrange itself from the body and from material essence in general, and to "purify" itself again from the body. Only when it has succeeded in this can it hope to traverse backward the stages by which it has proceeded forth from the deity, and so to return to the deity. The first positive step to this exaltation is civic and

political virtue, by which man asserts himself as a rationally formative force in the phenomenal world; but since this virtue evinces
itself only in reference to objects of the senses, the dianoëtic virtue
of knowledge stands far above it (cf. Aristotle), — the virtue by
which the soul sinks into its own spiritual intrinsic life.   As a help
stimulating to this virtue, Plotinus praises the contemplation of
the beautiful, which finds a presentiment of the Idea in the thing
of sense, and, in overcoming the inclination toward matter, rises
from the sensuously beautiful to the spiritually beautiful.   And
even this dianoëtic virtue, this æsthetic θεωρία and self-beholding of
the spirit, is only the preliminary stage for that ecstatic rapture
with which the individual, losing all consciousness, enters into
unity with the ground of the world (§ 18, 6).   The salvation and
the blessedness of the individual is his sinking into the All-One.

The later Neo-Platonists, — Porphyry first, and, still more, Jamblichus and
Proclus, — in the case of this exaltation emphasise, far more than Plotinus,
the help which the individual finds for it in positive religion and its acts of
worship.   For these men largely increased the number of different stages
through which the world proceeds forth from the ''One,'' and identified them
with the forms of the deities in the different ethnic religions by all kinds of
more or less arbitrary allegories.   It was therefore natural, in connection with
the return of the soul to God, since it must traverse the same stages up to
the state of ecstatic deification, to claim the support of these lower gods: and
thus as the metaphysics of the Neo-Platonists degenerated into mythology,
their ethics degenerated into *theurgic* arts.

8. On the whole, therefore, the derivation of the world from God
as set forth by Plotinus, in spite of all its idealising and spiritualising of Nature, follows the *physical* schema of natural processes.
This streaming forth of things from the original Power is an eternal necessity, founded in the essence of this Power; creation is a
purposive working, but unconscious and without design.

But at the same time, a *logical* motive comes into play here, which
has its origin in the old Platonic character of Ideas as class-concepts.   For just as the Idea is related to individual things of sense,
so in turn the deity is related to Ideas, as the universal to the particular.   God is the absolute universal, and according to a law of formal
logic, in accordance with which concepts become poorer in contents
or intension in proportion as their extension increases so that the
content 0 must correspond to the extension ∞, the absolutely universal is also the concept of the ''First,'' void of all content.   But
if from this First proceed first the intelligible, then the psychical,
and finally the sensuous world, this metaphysical relation corresponds to the logical process of *determination* or *partition*.   This
point of view, according to which the more general is throughout
regarded as the higher, metaphysically more primitive reality, while

the particular is held to be, in its metaphysical reality also, a deriv-ative product from the more general, — a view which resulted from hypostatising the syllogistic methods of Aristotle (cf. § 12, 3), — was expressed among the older Neo-Platonists principally by *Porphyry*, in his exegesis of Aristotle's categories.

Meanwhile *Proclus* undertook to carry out methodically this logical schema of emanation, and out of regard for this principle subordinated a number of simple and likewise unknowable "henads" beneath the highest, completely characterless ἕν. In so doing he found himself under the necessity of demanding a proper *dialectical principle* for this logical procession of the particular from the uni-versal. Such a schematism the systematiser of Hellenism found in the logico-metaphysical relation which Plotinus had laid at the basis of the development of the world from the deity. The procession of the Many forth from the One involves, in the first place, that the particular remains like the universal, and thus that the effect abides or persists within the cause; in the second place, that this product is a new self-subsisting entity in contrast with that which has pro-duced it, and that it proceeds forth from the same; and finally, that by virtue of just this antithetic relation the individual strives to return again to its ground. *Persistence, procession*, and *return* (μονή, πρόοδος, ἐπιστροφή), or identity, difference and union of that which has been distinguished, are accordingly the three *momenta* of the dialectical process; and into this formula of emanistic development, by virtue of which every concept should be thought of as in itself — out of itself — returning into itself, Proclus pressed his entire combined metaphysical and mythological construction, — a construc-tion in which he assigned to the systems of deities of the different religions their place in the mystical and magical universe, arranging them in the series divided again and again by threes, according to his law of the determination of concepts.[1]

9. In contrast with this, the peculiarity of *Christian philosophy* consists essentially in this, that in its apprehension of the relation of God to the world, it sought to employ throughout the ethical point of view of free, creative action. Since from the standpoint of its religious conviction it held fast to the conception of the *person-ality of the Original Being,* it conceived of the procedure of the world forth from God, not as a physical or logical necessity of the

---

[1] Personally, Proclus is characterised by the mingling of a superabundant credulous piety with a logical formalism carried even to pedantry, a combina-tion which is highly interesting psychologically. Just for this reason he is, perhaps, the most pronounced type of this period which is concerned in putting its ardent religiosity into a scientific system.

unfolding of his essence, but as an *act of will*, and in consequence of this the creation of the world was regarded not as an eternal process but as a *fact in time that had occurred once for all*. The conception, however, in which these motives of thought became concentrated, was that of the *freedom of the will*.

This conception had had at first the meaning (with Aristotle) of conceding to the finite personality acting ethically the capacity of a decision between different *given* possibilities, independently of external influence and compulsion. The conception had then taken on, with Epicurus, the metaphysical meaning of a causeless activity of individual beings. Applied to the absolute, and regarded as a quality of God, it is developed in the Christian philosophy into the thought of "creation out of nothing," into the doctrine of an un-caused *production of the world from the will of God*. Every attempt at an explanation of the world is thereby put aside; the world is because God has willed it, and it is such as it is because God has willed it so to be. At no point is the contrast between Neo-Platonism and orthodox Christianity sharper than at this.

Meanwhile, this same principle of the freedom of the will is employed to overcome the very difficulties which resulted from it. For the unlimited creative activity of the omnipotent God forces the problem of "theodicy" forward still more urgently than in the other theories of the universe, — the problem how the reality of evil in the world can be united with God's perfect goodness. The *optimism involved in the doctrine of creation*, and the *pessimism involved in the felt need of redemption*, the theoretical and the practical, the metaphysical and the ethical *momenta* of religious faith strike hard against each other. But faith, supported by the feeling of responsibility, finds its way of escape out of these difficulties in the assumption that God provided the spirits and human souls which he created, with a freedom analogous to his own, and that through their guilt evil came into the good world.[1]

This guilt, the thinkers of the Church find not to consist properly in the inclination toward matter or the sensuous; for matter as created by God cannot in itself be evil.[2] The sin of free spirits consists rather in their rebellion against the will of God, in their

---

[1] This is expressed abstractly by Clement of Alexandria (*Strom.* IV. 13, 605) in the form, that evil is only an action, not a substance (οὐσία), and that it there-fore cannot be regarded as the work of God.

[2] Just for this reason the metaphysical dualism of the Gnostics must be in its principle heterodox, and that, too, no matter whether it bore the stamp rather of Oriental mythology or of Hellenistic abstract thought — even though in the ethical consequences which it drew it coincided in great part with the doctrine of the Church.

longing after an unlimited power of self-determination, and only secondarily in the fact that they have turned their love toward God's creations, toward the world instead of toward God himself. Here too, therefore, there prevails in the content of the conception of evil the negative element of departure and falling away from God;[1] but the whole earnestness of the religious consciousness asserts itself in this, that this falling away is conceived of not merely as absence of the good, but as a positive, perverted act of will.

In accordance with this the dualism of God and the world, and that of spirit and matter, become indeed deeply involved in the Christian theory of the world. God and the eternal life of the spirit, the world and the transitory life of the flesh, — these are here, too, sharply enough contrasted. In contradiction with the divine pneuma the world of sense is filled with "hylic" spirits,[2] evil demons, who ensnare man in their pursuits which are animated by hostility to God, stifle in him the voice of universal natural revelation, and thereby make special revelation necessary; and without departure from them and from the sensuous nature there is for the early Christian ethics, also, no rescue of the soul possible.

But still this dualism is not regarded as being in its intrinsic nature either necessary or original. It is not the opposition between God and matter, but that between God and fallen spirits; it is the *purely inner antagonism of the infinite and the finite will.* In this direction Christian philosophy completed through *Origen* the metaphysical *spiritualising* and internalising or idealising of the world of the senses. In it the corporeal world appears as completely permeated and maintained by spiritual functions, — yes, even as much reduced to spiritual functions, as is the case with Plotinus; but here the essential element in these functions is relations of *will.* As the passing over of God into the world is not physical necessity, but ethical freedom, so the material world is not a last streaming forth of spirit and soul, but a creation of God for the punishment and for the overcoming of sin.

To be sure, Origen, in developing these thoughts, took up a motive which was allied to Neo-Platonism, a motive which brought him into conflict with the current mode of thought in the Church. For strongly as he held fast to the conception of the divine personality and to that of creation as a free act of divine goodness, the scientific thought which desires to see action grounded in essence was yet too strong in him to allow him to regard this creation as a causeless

---

[1] In this sense even Origen could call the evil τὸ οὐκ ὄν (in *Joh.* II. 7, 65).
[2] Tatian, *Orat. ad Græc.* 4.

act taking place once for all in time. The eternal, unchangeable
essence of God demands rather the thought that he is creator from
eternity even to all eternity, that he never can be without creating,
that he creates timelessly.[1]

But this creation of the *eternal* will is, therefore, only one that
relates to eternal Being, to the spiritual world (οὐσία). In this
eternal manner, so Origen teaches, God begets the eternal Son, the
Logos, as the sum-total of his world-thoughts (ἰδέα ἰδεῶν), and
through him the *realm of free spirits*, which, limited within itself,
surrounds the deity as an ever-living garment. Those of the spirits
that continue in the knowledge and love of the Creator remain in
unchanged blessedness with him; but those that become weary and
negligent, and turn from him in pride and vainglory, are, for punishment, cast into matter created for this purpose. So arises the
world of sense, which is, therefore, nothing self-subsistent, but
a symbolic eternalisation of spiritual functions. For what may be
regarded as Real in it is not the individual bodies, but rather the
spiritual Ideas which are present, connected and changing within
them.[2]

So, with Origen, Platonism becomes united with the theory of
the creative will. The eternal world of spirits is the eternal product of the changeless divine will. The principle of the temporal
and the sensuous (γένεσις) is the changing will of the spirits.
Corporeality arises on account of their sin, and will vanish again
with their improvement and purification. Thus will, and the *rela-*

---

[1] Orig. *De Princ.* I. 2, 10 ; III. 4, 3.

[2] This idealising of the world of sense was treated in great detail, quite according to the Platonic model, by the most important of the Oriental Church
fathers, *Gregory of Nyssa* (331–394). His main treatise is the λόγος κατηχη-
τικός. Edition of his works by Morellus (Paris, 1675) [Eng. tr. in Vol. V., 2d
series, Lib. Nicene and Post-Nicene Fathers, ed. Schaff and Wace, Oxford,
Lond., and N.Y. 1890]. Cf. J. Rupp, *G. des Bischofs von N. Leben und
Meinungen*, Leips. 1834. — This transformation of Nature into psychical terms
found an extremely poetic exposition among the Gnostics, particularly with the
most ingenious among them, *Valentinus*. The origin of the world of sense
is portrayed as follows in his theogonic-cosmogonic poetic invention : When
the lowest of the Æons, Wisdom (σοφία), in over-hasty longing, would fain
have plunged into the original Ground and had been brought back again to her
place by the Spirit of Measure (ὅρος), the Supreme God separated from her her
passionate longing (πάθος) as a lower Wisdom (κάτω σοφία), called Achamoth,
and banished it into the "void " (cf. § 20, 4). This lower σοφία, nevertheless,
impregnated by ὅρος for her redemption, bore the Demiurge and the world of
sense. On this account that ardent longing of σοφία expresses itself in all
forms and shapes of this world ; it is her feelings that constitute the essence of
phenomena ; her pressure and complaint thrills through all the life of Nature.
From her tears have come fountains, streams, and seas ; from her benumbing
before the divine word, the rocks and mountains ; from her hope of redemption,
light and ether, which in reconciliation stretch above the earth. This poetic
invention is farther carried out with the lamentations and penitential songs of
σοφία in the Gnostic treatise. Πίστις σοφία.

tion of personalities to one another, in particular that of the finite to the infinite personality, are recognised as the ultimate and deepest meaning of all reality.

§ 21. The Problem of Universal History.

With this triumph of religious ethics over cosmological metaphysics, thus sealed by Christianity, is connected the emergence of a farther problem, to solve which a number of important attempts were made — the problem of the *philosophy of history*.

1. Here something which is in its principle *new* comes forward, as over against the Greek view of the world. For Greek science had from the beginning directed its questions with reference to the φύσις, the abiding essence (cf. p. 73), and this mode of stating the question, which proceeded from the need of apprehending Nature, had influenced the progress of forming conceptions so strongly that the chronological course of events had always been treated as something of secondary importance, having no metaphysical interest of its own. In this connection Greek science regarded not only the individual man, but also the whole human race, with all its fortunes, deeds, and experiences, as ultimately but an episode, a special formation of the world-process which repeats itself forever according to like laws.

This is expressed with plain grandeur in the cosmological beginnings of Greek thought; and even after the anthropological tendency had obtained the mastery in philosophy the thought remained in force as theoretical background for every projected plan of the art of living, that human life, as it has sprung forth from the unchanging process of Nature, must flow again into the same (Stoa). Plato had indeed asked for an ultimate end of earthly life, and Aristotle had investigated the regular succession of the forms assumed by political life; but the inquiry for a meaning in *human history taken as a whole*, for a connected plan of historical development, had never once been put forward, and still less had it occurred to any of the old thinkers to see in this the intrinsic, essential nature of the world.

The most characteristic procedure in just this respect is that of Neo-Platonism. Its metaphysics, also, follows the religious motive as its guide; but it gives this motive a genuine Hellenic turn when it regards the procession of the imperfect forth from the perfect as an eternal process of a necessary nature, in which the human individual also finds his place and sees it as his destiny to seek salvation *alone by himself* by return to the infinite.

2. *Christianity*, however, found from the beginning the essence of the whole world-movement in the *experiences of personalities:* for it external nature was but a theatre for the development of the relation of person to person, and especially of the relation of the finite spirit to the deity. And to this were added, as a further determining power, the principle of love, the consciousness of the solidarity of the human race, the deep conviction of the universal sinfulness, and the faith in a common redemption. All this led to regarding the history of the fall and of redemption as the true metaphysical import of the world's reality, and so instead of an eternal process of Nature, the drama of *universal history* as an onward flow of events that were activities of free will, became the content of Christian metaphysics.

There is perhaps no better proof of the power of the impression which the personality of *Jesus of Nazareth* had left, than the fact that all doctrines of Christianity, however widely they may otherwise diverge philosophically or mythically, are yet at one in seeking in him and his appearance the *centre of the world's history.* By him the conflict between good and evil, between light and darkness, is decided.

But this consciousness of victory with which Christianity believed in its Saviour had still another side: to the evil which had been overcome by him belonged also the other religions, as by no means its least important element. For the Christian mode of thought of those days was far from denying the reality of the heathen gods; it regarded them rather as evil demons, fallen spirits who had seduced man and persuaded him to worship them, in order to prevent his returning to the true God.[1]

By this thought the *conflict of religions*, which took place in the Alexandrian period, acquires in the eyes of Christian thinkers a metaphysical significance: the powers whose struggling forms the world's history are the gods of the various religions, and the history of this conflict is the inner significance of all reality. And since every individual man with his ethical life-work is implicated in this great complex process, the importance of individuality becomes raised far above the life of sense, into the sphere of metaphysical reality.

3. With almost all Christian thinkers, accordingly, the world's history appears as a course of inner events which draw after them the origin and fortunes of the world of sense, — a course which takes place *once for all*. It is essentially only Origen who holds fast

---

[1] So even Origen ; cf. *Cont. Cels.* III. 28.

to the fundamental character of Greek science (cf. p. 27, ch. 1). so far as to teach the eternity of the world-process. Between the two motives, the Christian and the Greek, he found a way of escape by making a succession of temporal worlds proceed forth from the eternal spiritual world, which he regarded as the immediate creation of God, and by holding that these temporal worlds take their origin with the declension and fall of a number of free spirits, and are to find their end with the redemption and restitution of the same (ἀποκατάστασις).[1]

The fundamental tendency of Christian thought, on the contrary, was to portray the historical drama of fall and redemption as a connected series of events taking place once for all, which begins with a free decision of lower spirits to sin, and has its turning. point in the redemptive revelation, the resolve of divine freedom. In contrast with the naturalistic conceptions of Greek thought, *history is conceived of as the realm of free acts of personalities, taking place but once,* and the character of these acts, agreeably to the entire consciousness of the time, is of essentially religious significance.

4. It is highly interesting now to see how in the mythico-metaphysical inventions of the *Gnostics,* the peculiar relation of Christianity to *Judaism* is brought to expression in cosmogonic garb. In the Gnostic circles the so-called Gentile Christian tendency is predominant, the tendency which desires to define the new religion as sharply as possible, as over against Judaism, and this tendency just through the Hellenistic philosophy grows to the most open hostility against Judaism.

The mythological form for this is, that the God of the Old Testament, who gave the Mosaic law, is regarded as the fashioner of the world of sense, — for the most part under the Platonic name of the *Demiurge,* — and is assigned that place in the hierarchy of cosmic forms or Æons, as well as in the history of the universe, which belongs to him in accordance with this function.

At the beginning this relation is not yet that of pronounced opposition. A certain *Cerinthus* (about 115 A.D.) had already distinguished the God of the Jews as Demiurge, from the Supreme God who was not defiled by any contact with matter, and had taught that in contrast with the "law" given by the God of the Jews, Jesus had brought the revelation of the Supreme God.[2] So, too,

---

[1] Orig. *De Princ.* III. 1, 3. These worlds, on account of the freedom from which they proceed, are not at all like one another, but are of the most manifold variety; Ib. II. 3, 3 f.

[2] A distinction which Numenius also adopted, evidently under Gnostic influences. Cf. Euseb. *Præp. Ev.* XI. 18.

with *Saturninus*, the God of the Jews appears as the head of the seven planetary spirits, who, as lowest emanation of the spiritual realm, in their desire to rule tore away a portion of matter to form from it the world of sense, and set man as guardian over it.   But a conflict arises, since Satan, to conquer back this part of his kingdom, sends against man his demons and the lower "hylic" race of men. In this conflict the prophets of the Demiurge prove powerless until the Supreme God sends the Æon *νοῦς* as Saviour, in order that he may free pneumatic men and likewise the Demiurge and his spirits from the power of Satan.   This same redemption of the Jewish God also is taught by *Basilides*, who introduces him under the name of the "great Archon" as an efflux of the divine world-seed, as head of the world of sense, and represents him as made to tremble by the Supreme God's message of salvation in Jesus, and as brought to repentance for his undue exaltation.

In a similar manner, the God of the Old Testament, with *Carpocrates*, belongs to the fallen angels, who, commissioned to form the world, completed it according to their own caprice, and founded separate realms in which they got themselves reverenced by subordinate spirits and by men.   But while these particular religions are, like their Gods, in a state of mutual conflict, the Supreme Deity reveals in Jesus the one true universal religion which has Jesus as its object, even as he had already before made revelation in the great educators of humanity, a Pythagoras and a Plato.

In more decided polemic against Judaism *Cerdo* the Syrian further distinguished the God of the Old Testament from that of the New.   The God announced by Moses and the prophets, as the purposeful World-fashioner and as the God of justice is accessible even to natural knowledge — the Stoic conception; the God revealed through Jesus is the unknowable, the good God — the Philonic conception.   The same determinations more sharply defined are employed by *Marcion*[1] (about 150), who conceives of the Christian life in a strongly ascetic manner, and regards it as a warfare against the Demiurge and for the Supreme God revealed through Jesus,[2] and Marcion's disciple *Apelles* even treated the

---

[1] Cf. Volkmar, *Philosophoumena und Marcion* (*Theol. Jahrb.* Tübingen, 1854).   Same author, *Das Evangelium Marcion's* (Leips. 1852).

[2] An extremely piquant mythological modification of this thought is found in the sect of the *Ophites*, who gave to the Hebraic narrative of the fall the interpretation, that the serpent which taught man to eat of the tree of knowledge in Paradise made a beginning of bringing the revelation of the true God to man who had fallen under the dominion of the Demiurge, and that after man had on this account experienced the wrath of the Demiurge, the revelation had appeared victorious in Jesus.   For this knowledge which the serpent desired to teach is the true salvation of man.

Jewish God as Lucifer, who brought carnal sin into the world of sense which had been formed by the good "Demiurge," the highest angel, so that, at the petition of the Demiurge, the Supreme God sent the Redeemer against him.

5. In contrast with this view we find the doctrine firmly held, not only by the *Recognitions*,[1] ascribed to Clement of Rome (which arose about 150 A.D.), but in the entire orthodox development of Christian doctrine, that the Supreme God and the creator of the world, the God of the New and the God of the Old Testaments, are the same. But a *well-planned educative development of the divine revelation* is assumed, and in this the history of salvation, *i.e.* the inner history of the world, is sought. Proceeding in accordance with the suggestions of the Pauline epistles,[2] Justin, and especially Irenæus, took this standpoint. The theory of revelation did not become complete until it found this elaboration in the philosophy of history (cf. § 18).

For the anticipations of Christian revelation, that emerge on the one hand in Jewish prophecy, on the other in Hellenic philosophy, are regarded from this point of view as *pedagogic preparations* for Christianity. And since the redemption of sinful man constitutes, according to the Christian view, the sole significance and value of the world's history, and so of all that is real aside from God, the well-ordered *succession of God's acts of revelation* appears as the essential thing in the entire course of the world's events.

In the main, corresponding to the doctrine of revelation, three stages of this divine, saving activity are distinguished.[3] As divided theoretically there are, first, the universal-human revelation, given objectively by the purposiveness of Nature, subjectively through the rational endowment of the mind; second, the special revelation imparted to the Hebrew people through the Mosaic law and the promises of the prophets; and third, the complete revelation through Jesus. Divided according to time, the periods extended from Adam to Moses, from Moses to Christ, from Christ to the end of the world.[4] This triple division was the more natural for ancient Christianity, the stronger its faith that the closing period of the world's redemp-

---

[1] Edited by Gersdorf (Leips. 1838). Cf. A. Hilgenfeld, *Die clementinischen Recognitionen und Homilien* (Jena, 1848); G. Uhlhorn, *Die Homilien und Recognitionen des Cl. R.* (Göttingen, 1854).

[2] Which treat the "law" as the "schoolmaster" unto Christ ($\pi\alpha\iota\delta\alpha\gamma\omega\gamma\delta\varsigma$ $\epsilon\iota\varsigma$ $X\rho\iota\sigma\tau\delta\nu$); Gal. iii. 24.

[3] This had been done in part already by the Gnostics, by Basilides at least, according to Hippolytus.

[4] The later (heretical) development of eschatology added to these three periods yet a fourth, by the appearance of the "Paraclete." Cf., *e.g.*, Tertullian, *De Virg. Vel.* 1, p. 884 O.

tion, which had begun with the appearance of the Saviour, would be ended in a very short time. The *eschatological* hopes are an essential constituent of the early Christian metaphysics ; for the philosophy of history which made Jesus the turning-point of the world's history had, as by no means its slighest support, the expectation that the Crucified would return again to judge the world, and to complete the victory of light over darkness. However varied these ideas become with time and with the disappointment of the first hopes, however strongly the tendencies of dualism and monism assert themselves here also, by conceiving of the last Judgment either as a definite separation of good and evil, or as a complete overcoming of the latter by the former (ἀποκατάστασις πάντων with Origen), and however much a more material and a more spiritual view of blessedness and unhappiness, of heaven and hell, interplay here also, — in every case the last Judgment forms the conclusion of the work of redemption, and so the consummation of the divine plan of salvation.

6. The points of view from which the world's history is regarded by Christian thinkers are thus indeed exclusively religious ; but the more general principle of a *historical teleology* gains recognition within them. While Greek philosophy had reflected upon the purposiveness of Nature with a depth and an energy which religious thought could not surpass, the completely new thought rises here that the course of events in human life also has a purposeful meaning as a whole. The teleology of history becomes raised above that of Nature, and the former appears as the higher in worth, in whose service the latter is employed.[1]

Such a conception was possible only for a time that from a ripe result looked back upon the vivid memory of a great development in the world's history. The universal civilisation of the Roman Empire found dawning in the self-consciousness of its own inner life the presentiment of a purpose in that working together of national destinies through which it had itself come into existence, and the idea of this mighty process was yielded especially by the continued tradition of *Greek literature* embracing a thousand years. The religious theory of the world, which had developed from this ancient civilisation, gave to that thought the form that the meaning of the historical movement was to be sought in the preparations of God for the salvation of man ; and since the peoples of the ancient civilisation themselves felt that the time of their efficient working was complete, it is comprehensible that they believed they saw the

---

[1] Cf. Irenæus, *Ref.* IV. 38, 4, p. 702 f. *St.*

end of history immediately before them, where the sun of their day was sinking.

But hand in hand with this idea of a systematically planned unity in human history goes the thought of a *unity of the human race,* exalted above space and time. The consciousness of common civilisation, breaking through national boundaries, becomes complete in the belief in a common revelation and redemption of all men. Inasmuch as the salvation of the whole race is made the import of the divine plan for the world, it appears that among the provisions of this plan, the most important is that fellowship (ἐκκλησία) to which all members of the race are called, by sharing in faith the same work of redemption. The conception of the *Church,* shaped out from the life of the Christian community, stands in this connection with the religious philosophy of history, and accordingly, among its constitutive marks or notes, universality or catholicity is one of the most important.

7. In this way, *man and his destiny* becomes the centre of the universe. This *anthropocentric* character distinguishes the Christian view of the world essentially from the Neo-Platonic. The latter, indeed, assigned a high metaphysical position to the human individual, whose psychico-spiritual nature it even held to be capable of deification; it regarded the purposeful connected whole of Nature also from the (Stoic) point of view of its usefulness for man, — but never would Neo-Platonism have consented to declare man, who for it was a part of the phenomena in which divine efficiency appears, to be the end of the whole.

Just this, however, is the case in the philosophy of the Fathers. According to *Irenæus,* man is the end and aim of creation : it is to him as a knowing being that God would reveal himself, and for his sake the rest, the whole of *Nature,* has been created ; he it is, also, who by abuse of the freedom granted him, made farther revelation and redemption necessary ; it is he, therefore, for whose sake all *history* also exists. Man as the highest unfolding of psychical life is, as Gregory of Nyssa teaches, the crown of creation, its master and king : it is creation's destiny to be contemplated by him, and taken back into its original spirituality. But with Origen, too, men are just those fallen spirits, who, for punishment and improvement, have been clothed with the world of sense : Nature exists only on account of their sin, and it will cease again when the historical process has attained its end through the return of all spirits to the Good.

Thus the *anthropological movement,* which at first forced its way into Greek science only as a shifting of the interest, as a change in the statement of the problem, developed during the Hellenistic-Roman period to be more and more the real principle from which the world was considered, and at last in league with the religious need it took possession of metaphysics. The human race has gained the consciousness of the unity of its historical connection and regards the *history of its salvation* as the measure of all finite things. What arises and passes away in space and time has its true significance only in so far as it is taken up into the relation of man to his God.

Being and Becoming were the problems of ancient philosophy at its beginning : the conceptions with which it closes are God and the human race.

PART III.

THE PHILOSOPHY OF THE MIDDLE AGES.

Rousselot, *Études sur la Philosophie du Moyen Âge*. Paris, 1840–42.
B. Hauréau, *De la Philosophie Scholastique*. Paris, 1850.
B. Hauréau, *Histoire de la Philosophie Scholastique*. Paris, 1872–80.
A. Stöckl, *Geschichte der Philosophie des Mittelalters*. Mainz, 1864–66.

WHEN the migration of the peoples broke in devastation over the Roman Empire, and the latter lacked the political strength to defend itself against the northern barbarians, scientific civilisation, also, was in danger of becoming completely crushed out; for the tribes to whom the sceptre now passed brought still less mind and understanding for the finely elaborated structures of philosophy than for the light forms of Grecian art. And, withal, ancient civilisation was in itself so disintegrated, its vital force was so broken, that it seemed incapable of taking the rude victors into its school.

Thus the conquests of the Greek spirit would have been given over to destruction beyond hope of rescue, if in the midst of the breaking down of the old world, a new spiritual power had not grown strong, to which the sons of the North bowed, and which, with firm hand, knew how to rescue for the future the goods of civilisation, and preserve them during the centuries of subversion. This power was the *Christian Church*. What the State could not do, what art and science could not achieve, religion accomplished. Inaccessible still for the fine workings of æsthetic imagination and abstract thought, the Germans were laid hold of in their deepest feelings by the preaching of the gospel, which worked upon them with all the power of its grand simplicity.

Only from this point of religious excitation, therefore, could the process of the appropriation of ancient science by the peoples of the Europe of to-day begin; only at the hand of the Church could the new world enter the school of the old. The natural consequence, however, of this relation was, that at first only that portion of the intellectual content of ancient civilisation remained alive which had been taken up into the doctrine of the Christian Church, and that the teaching authority rigidly excluded all else, and especially that which was opposed to her. By this means, to be sure, confusion in the youthful mind of these nations, which would not have been able to comprehend and elaborate much and many kinds of material, was wisely guarded against; but thereby whole worlds of the intellectual life sank to the depth from which they could only be drawn forth again long after, by toil and conflict.

The Church had grown to its great task of becoming the educator of the European nations, first of all, because from the invisible beginnings of a religious society it had developed with steadily growing power to a unified organisation, which amid the dissolution of political life presented itself as the only power that was firm and sure of itself. And since this organisation was supported by the thought that the Church was called to become the means of bringing the salvation of redemption to all humanity, the religious education of the barbarians was a task prescribed by its own nature. But the Church was all the more able to take this in hand, since in her inner life she had proceeded with the same certainty amid numerous deviating paths, and had attained the goal of a unified and completed system of doctrine. To this was further added the especially favourable circumstance, that at the threshold of the new epoch she was presented with the sum-total of her convictions, worked out into the form of a thorough scientific system by a mind of the first order, — *Augustine.*

Augustine was the true teacher of the Middle Ages. Not only do the threads of Christian and Neo-Platonic thought, the ideas of Origen and of Plotinus, unite in his philosophy, but he also concentrated the entire thought of his time with creative energy about the need of salvation and the fulfilment of this need by the church community. His doctrine is the *philosophy of the Christian Church.* Herewith was given, in pregnant unity, the system which became the basis of the scientific training of the European peoples, and in this form the Romanic and Germanic peoples entered upon the inheritance of the Greeks.

But for this reason the Middle Ages retraced in the reverse direction the path which the Greeks had gone over in their relations to science. In antiquity science had arisen from the pure æsthetic joy in knowledge itself, and had only gradually entered into the service of practical need, of ethical tasks, and of religious longings. The Middle Ages begins with the conscious subordination of knowledge to the great ends of faith; it sees in science at the beginning only the task of the intellect to make clear to itself and express in abstract thought that which it possesses surely and unassailably in feeling and conviction. But in the midst of this work the joy in knowledge itself wakes anew, at first timorously and uncertainly, then with ever-increasing force and self-certainty; it unfolds itself at first scholastically, in fields which seem to lie far distant from faith's unassailable sphere of ideas, and at the end breaks through victoriously when science begins to define her limits as against faith, philosophy hers as against theology, and to assume a conscious independent position.

The *education of the European peoples*, which the history of the philosophy of the Middle Ages sets forth, has then for its starting-point the Church doctrine, and for its goal the development of the scientific spirit. The intellectual civilisation of antiquity is brought to modern peoples in the religious form which it assumed at its close, and develops in them gradually the maturity for properly scientific work.

Under such conditions it is easy to understand that the history of this education awakens psychological interest and an interest connected with the history of civilisation, rather than presents new and independent fruits of philosophical insight. In the appropriation of the presented material the peculiar personality of the disciple may assert itself here and there; the problems and conceptions of ancient philosophy may, therefore, find many fine transformations when thus taken up into the spirit of the new peoples, and in forging out the new Latin terminology in the Middle Ages acuteness and depth often contend emulously with pedantry and insipidity; but in its fundamental philosophical thoughts, mediæval philosophy remains enclosed within the system of conceptions of the Greek and the Hellenistic-Roman philosophy, — not only as regards its problems, but also as regards their solutions. Highly as we must estimate the worth of its labours for the intellectual education of European peoples, its highest achievements remain in the last instance just brilliant productions of scholars or disciples, not of masters, — productions in which only the eye of the most refined detailed investigation can discover the gently germinating beginnings of a new thought, but which show themselves to be, on the whole, an appropriation of the world of thought of the departing antiquity. Mediæval philosophy is, in its entire spirit, solely the continuation of the Hellenistic-Roman, and the essential distinction between the two is that what in the first centuries of our era had been coming into existence amid struggles was, for the Middle Ages, given and regarded as something in the main complete and definitive.

This period, in which the humanity of to-day was at school, lasted a full thousand years, and as if in systematically planned pedagogic steps its education proceeds toward science by the *successive addition of ancient material of culture.* Out of the antitheses which appear in this material grow the problems of philosophy, and the ancient conceptions taken up and amplified give the form to the scientific theories of the world prevalent in the Middle Ages.

An original discord exists in this tradition between Neo-Platonism and the Church doctrine defended by Augustine, — a discord which indeed was not equally strong at all points, since Augustine in very essential points had remained under the control of Neo-Platonism, and yet a discord which amounted to an opposition with reference to the fundamental character of the relation of philosophy to faith. The system of Augustine is concentrated about the conception of the Church; for it philosophy has as its main task to present the Church doctrine as a scientific system, to establish and develop it: in so far as it prosecutes this task mediæval philosophy is the science of the schools, *Scholasticism.* The Neo-Platonic tendency, on the contrary, takes the direction of guiding the individual, through knowledge, to blessed oneness of life with the deity: in so far as the science of the Middle Ages sets itself this end it is *Mysticism.*

Scholasticism and Mysticism accordingly supplement each other without being reciprocally exclusive. As the intuition of the Mystics may become a part of the Scholastic system, so the proclamation of the Mystics may presuppose the system of the Scholastics as its background. Throughout the Middle Ages, therefore, Mysticism is more in danger than Scholasticism of becoming heterodox; but it would be erroneous to see in this an essential mark for distinguishing between the two. Scholasticism is, no doubt, in the main entirely orthodox; but not only do the theories of the Scholastics diverge widely in the treatment of dogmas which are still in the process of formulation, but many of the Scholastics, even in the scientific investigation of the doctrines which were given, proceeded to completely heterodox theories, the expression of which brought them into more or less severe conflicts without and within. As regards Mysticism, the Neo-Platonic tradition often forms the theoretical background of the secret or open opposition offered to the monopolising of the religious life on the part of the Church;[1]

---

[1] Cf. H. Reuter, *Geschichte der religiösen Aufklärung im Mittelalter,* 2 vols. (Berlin, 1875–77). Cf. also H. v. Eicken, *Geschichte der mittelalterlichen Weltanschauung* (Stuttgart, 1888).

but we meet on the other hand enthusiastic Mystics who feel themselves called to take the true faith into their protection against the excesses of Scholastic science.

It appears thus to be inappropriate to give to the philosophy of the Middle Ages the general name of "Scholasticism." It might rather prove, as the result of a more exact estimate, that in the maintenance of scientific tradition as well as in the slow adaptation and transformation of those philosophical doctrines which were effective for the after time, a part belongs to Mysticism which is at least as great as the part played by Scholasticism, and that on the other hand a sharp separation of the two currents is not practicable in the case of a great number of the most prominent philosophic thinkers of the Middle Ages.

Finally, it must be added that even when we put together Scholasticism and Mysticism, we have in nowise exhausted the characteristics of mediæval philosophy. While the nature of both these tendencies is fixed by their relation to the religious presuppositions of thought, — in the one case the established doctrine of the Church, in the other personal piety, — there runs along side by side with these, especially in the later centuries of the Middle Ages though noticeable still earlier, a secular side-current which brings in an increasing degree the rich results of Greek and Roman experience of the world, to science building itself anew. Here, too, at the outset the effort prevails to introduce organically into the Scholastic system this extensive material and the forms of thought which are dominant in it; but the more this part of the sphere of thought develops into an independent significance, the more the entire lines of the scientific consideration of the world become shifted, and while the reflective interpretation and rationalisation of the religious feeling becomes insulated within itself, philosophical knowledge begins to mark off anew for itself the province of purely theoretical investigation.

From this multiplicity of variously interwoven threads of tradition with which ancient science weaves its fabric on into the Middle Ages, we can understand the wealth of colour in which the philosophy of this thousand years spreads out before historical research. In the frequent exchange of friendly and hostile contact, these elements of a tradition changing in compass and content from century to century play back and forth to form ever new pictures; a surprising fineness in the transitions and shadings becomes developed as these elements are woven together, and thus there is developed also a wealth of life in the work of thought, which manifests itself in a considerable number of interesting personalities, in an astonishing amount of literary production, and in a passionate agitation of scientific controversies.

Such living variety in form has as yet by no means everywhere received full justice at the hands of literary-historical research,[1] but the main lines of this development lie before us clearly and distinctly enough for the history of philosophic principles, which nevertheless finds but a meagre field in this period for the reasons already adduced. We must, indeed, be on our guard against aiming to reduce the complex movement of this process to formulas that are all too simple, and against overlooking the multitude of positive and negative relations that have come and gone in shifting forms between the elements of ancient tradition which found their entrance in the course of centuries by irregular intervals into mediæval thought.

In general, the course of science among the European peoples of the Middle Ages proceeded along the following lines.

The profound doctrine of *Augustine* had its first efficiency, not in the direction of its philosophical significance, but as an authoritative presentation of the doctrine of the Church. Side by side with this a Neo-Platonic Mysticism maintained itself, and scientific schooling was limited to unimportant compendiums, and to fragments of the Aristotelian logic. Nevertheless, a logico-metaphysical problem of great importance developed from the elaboration of the logic, and about this problem arose a highly vigorous movement of thought, which, however, threatened to degenerate into barren formalism in consequence of the lack in knowledge to form the content of thought. In contrast with this the Augustinian psychology began gradually to assert its mighty force; and at the same time the first effects of contact with *Arabian* science disclosed themselves, a science to which the West owed, primarily at least, a certain stimulus toward employment with realities, and further a complete widening

---

[1] The grounds for this lie, certainly in part, in the but gradually vanishing prejudices which long stood in the way of a just appreciation of the Middle Ages; but in no less a degree they lie also in this literature itself. The circumstantial and yet for the most part sterile prolixity of the investigations, the schematic uniformity of the methods, the constant repetition and turning of the arguments, the lavish expenditure of acuteness upon artificial and sometimes absolutely silly questions, the uninteresting witticisms of the schools,—all these are features which perhaps belong inevitably to the process of learning, appropriating, and practising, which mediæval philosophy sets forth, but they bring with them the consequence that in the study of this part of the history of philosophy the mass of the material, and the toil involved in its elaboration, stand in an unfavourable relation to the real results. So it has come about that just those investigators who have gone deeply, with industry and perseverance, into mediæval philosophy have often not refrained from a harsh expression of ill-humour as to the object of their research.

and transformation of its horizon. This development was in the main attached to the acquaintance gained by such by-ways with the entire system of *Aristotle*, and the immediate consequence of this acquaintance was that the structure of Church doctrine was projected in the grandest style and carefully wrought out in all its parts with the help of his fundamental metaphysical conceptions. Meanwhile Aristotelianism had been accepted from the Arabians (and Jews) not only in their Latin translation, but also with their commentaries, and in their interpretation which was under strong *Neo-Platonic* influence; and while by this means the Neo-Platonic elements in previous tradition, even in the Augustinian form, found vigorous confirmation in various directions, the specific elements of the *Augustinian metaphysics* were forced into sharper and more energetic expression, in violent reaction against the Neo-Platonic tendency. Thus while both sides lean upon Aristotelianism, a cleft in scientific thought is produced, which finds its expression in the separation of theology and philosophy. This cleft became widened by a new and not less complicated movement. *Empirical research* in medicine and natural science had also made its way from the East, hand in hand with Aristotelianism; it began now to rise also among the European peoples; it conquered the domain of *psychology* not without assistance from the Augustinian current, and favoured the development of the Aristotelian *logic* in a direction which led far from the churchly Aristotelian metaphysics. And while thus the interwoven threads of tradition were separating on all sides, the fine filaments of new beginnings were already finding their way into this loosening web.

With such various relations of mutual support or retardation, and with such numerous changes of front, the thoughts of ancient philosophy move through the Middle Ages; but the most important and decisive turn was doubtless the *reception of Aristotelianism*, which became complete about the year 1200. This divides the whole field naturally into two sections which in their philosophical import are so related that the interests and the problems, the antitheses and the movements, of the first period are repeated in broader, and at the same time deeper, form in the second. The relation of these two divisions, therefore, cannot be generally designated in this case by differences in the subject matter.

CHAPTER I. FIRST PERIOD.

(Until about 1200.)

W. Kaulich, *Geschichte der scholastichen Philosophie*, I. Theil. Prague, 1863.

The line of thought in which mediæval philosophy essentially moved, and in which it continued the principles of the philosophy of antiquity, was prescribed for it by the doctrine of *Augustine*. He had moved the principle of *internality* (*Innerlichkeit*), which had been preparing in the whole closing development of ancient science, for the first time into the controlling central position of philosophic thought, and the position to which he is entitled in the history of philosophy is that of the beginner of a new line of development. For the bringing together of all lines of the Patristic as well as the Hellenistic philosophy of his time, which he completely accomplished, was possible only as these were consciously united in that new thought which was itself to become the germ of the philosophy of the future. But only of a more distant future: his philosophical originality passed over his contemporaries and the immediately following centuries without effect. Within the circuit of the old civilisation the creative power of thought had become extinguished, and the new peoples could only gradually grow into scientific work.

In the cloister and court schools which formed the seats of this newly beginning civilisation, permission for instruction in *dialectic* by the side of the arts most necessary for the training of the clergy had to be conquered step by step. For this elementary logical instruction they possessed in the first centuries of the Middle Ages only the two least important treatises of the Aristotelian Organon, *De Categoriis* and *De Interpretatione*, in a Latin translation with the introduction of Porphyry, and a number of commentaries of the Neo-Platonic time, in particular those of Boethius. For the material of knowledge (of the Quadrivium) they used the compendiums of departing antiquity, which had been prepared by Marcianus Capella, Cassiodorus, and Isidorus of Sevilla. Of the great original works of ancient philosophy, only the Platonic *Timœus* in the translation of Chalcidius was known.

Under these circumstances, scientific activity in the schools was mainly directed toward learning and practising the schematism of formal logic, and the treatment even of the material parts of knowledge, in particular of religious dogma which was indeed regarded as something essentially complete and in its contents unassailable, took the direction of elaborating and setting forth what was given and handed down by tradition, in the forms and according to the rules of the Aristotelian-Stoic logic. In this process the main emphasis must necessarily fall upon formal arrangement, upon the formation and division of class-concepts, upon correct syllogistic conclusions. Already in the Orient the ancient school logic had been put into the service of a rigidly articulated development of Church doctrine by John Damascenus, and now this took place in the schools of the West also.

Meanwhile this pursuit, which had its basis in the conditions of the tradition, had not only the didactic value of a mental exercise in the appropriation of material, but also the consequence that the beginnings of independent reflection necessarily took the direction of an inquiry as to the *significance of logical relations*, and so we find emerging early in the Western literature, investigations as to the relation of the conception on the one hand to the word, and on the other to the thing.

The problem thus formed became strengthened by a peculiar complication. By the side of the Church doctrine there persisted, half tolerated and half condemned, a mystical transmission of Christianity in Neo-Platonic form. It went back to writings which had arisen in the fifth century, but which were ascribed to Dionysius the Areopagite, and it gained wider extension when these writings were translated in the ninth century by *John Scotus Erigena*, and made the basis of his own doctrine. In this doctrine, however, a main point was that identification of the different grades of abstraction with the stages of metaphysical reality, which had been already propounded in the older Platonism and in Neo-Platonism (cf. § 20, 8).

In consequence of these incitements the question as to the *metaphysical significance of logical genera* became, during the next centuries, the centre of philosophic thought. About this were grouped the other logical and metaphysical problems, and the answer given to this question decided the party position of individual thinkers. Amid the great variety of decisions given in this *controversy over universals*, three tendencies are prominent: *Realism,* which main-

tains the independent existence of genera and species, is the doctrine
of Anselm of Canterbury, of William of Champeaux, and of the
Platonists proper, among whom Bernard of Chartres is prominent;
Nominalism, which sees in universals only designations or terms
which apply commonly, is defended in this period principally by
Roscellinus; finally a mediating theory, which has been called
Conceptualism or *Sermonism,* is attached principally to the name of
Abelard.

These conflicts came to an issue principally in the endless disputations at the Paris University. which for this period and on into
the following period formed the centre of scientific life in Europe;
and these battles, conducted with all the arts of dialectical dexterity,
exercised upon this age a fascinating power like that which the
disputes of the Sophists and Socratic circles had once exercised
upon the Greeks. Here as there the unreflective life of the popular
consciousness was awakened to thought, and here as there wider
circles were seized by a feverish thirst for knowledge, and by a passionate desire to take part in such hitherto unwonted intellectual
games. Far beyond the narrow circles of the clergy, who had previously been the transmitters of scientific tradition, the impulse
toward knowledge, thus awakened, forced its way to the surface.

But this excessive vigour in dialectical development found at the
same time manifold opposition. In fact, it hid within itself a serious danger. This brilliant performance, in which abstract thought
proved its power, lacked all basis of real knowledge. With its distinctions and conclusions it was carrying on to a certain extent a
juggler's game in the open air, which indeed set the formal mental
powers into beneficial motion, but which, in spite of all its turns and
windings, could lead to no material knowledge. Hence, from intelligent men like Gerbert, who had received information from the empirical studies of the Arabians, went out the admonition to abandon
the formalism of the schools and turn to the careful examination
of Nature and to the tasks of practical civilisation.

But while such a call still echoed mainly unheard, dialectic met a
more forcible resistance in the piety of faith and in the power of the
Church. The result was inevitable that the logical working over of
the metaphysics of the Church's faith, and the consequences which
were developed in the strife about universals, — at first without any
reference to their religious bearing, — should come into contradiction
with the dogma of the Church; and the more this was repeated, the
more dialectic appeared not only superfluous for the simply pious
mind, but also dangerous to the interests of the Church. In this
spirit it was attacked, sometimes with extreme violence, by the

orthodox Mystics, among whom the most combative was Bernard of Clairvaux, while the Victorines turned back from the excesses of dialectical arrogance to the study of Augustine, and sought to bring out the rich treasure of inner experience which his writings contained, by transferring the fundamental thoughts of his psychology from the metaphysical to the empirical sphere.

Aurelius Augustinus (354–430), born at Thagaste in Numidia, and educated for a jurist there and also in Madaura in Carthage, passed through in his youth almost all phases of the scientific and religious movement of his time. He sought at first in Manichæism religious relief for his burning doubts, then fell into the Academic Scepticism which he had early absorbed from Cicero, passed over from this gradually to the Neo-Platonic doctrine, and was at last won by Ambrose, Bishop of Milan, for Christianity, whose philosopher he was to become. As priest, and later as bishop at Hippo Regius, he was unwearied in practical and literary activity for the unity of the Christian Church and doctrine; his doctrinal system was developed especially in the Donatist and Pelagian controversies. Among his works (in Migne's collection, 16 vóls., Paris, 1835 ff. [tr. ed. by Dods, 15 vols., Edin. 1871–77 ; also in Schaff's lib., Nicene and Post-Nicene Fathers, Vols. 1–8, Buffalo, 1886-88]) those of chief importance for philosophy are his autobiographical *Confessions,* and further *Contra Academicos, De Beata Vita, De Ordine, De Quantitate Animæ, De Libero Arbitrio, De Trinitate, Soliloquia, De Immortalitate Animæ, De Civitate Dei.* — Cf. C. Bindemann, *Der. hlg. A.* (3 Bde. 1844–1869). — Fr. Böhringer, *Kirchengeschichte in Biographien,* XI. Bd. in 2 Thl. (Stuttgart, 1877–78). — A. Dorner, *A.* (Berlin, 1873). — W. Dilthey, *Einleitung in die Geisteswissenschaften,* 1. (Leips. 1883), pp. 322 ff. — J. Storz, *Die Philos. des hlg. A.* (Freiburg, 1892).

The Εἰσαγωγὴ εἰς τὰς κατηγορίας of Porphyry (ed. by Busse, Berlin, 1887), in its translation by Boethius, gave the external occasion for the controversy over universals. **Boethius** (470–525), aside from this, exercised an influence upon the early Middle Ages by his translations and commentaries upon the two Aristotelian treatises, and upon a number of Cicero's writings. In addition to his books there were still others which circulated under the name of Augustine. Cf. Prantl, *Gesch. d. Log. im Abendl.,* II., and A. Jourdain, *Recherches critiques sur l'âge et l'origine des traductions latines d'Aristotle* (Paris, 2 ed., 1843).

Among the *scientific encyclopedias* of departing antiquity, Marcianus Capella (from Carthage, the middle of the fifth century), in his *Satyricon* (ed. by Eyssenhardt, Leips. 1866), after his whimsical introduction *De Nuptiis Mercurii et Philologiæ,* treats the seven liberal arts, of which, as is well known, in the activity of the schools grammar, rhetoric, and dialectic formed the Trivium, arithmetic, geometry, astronomy, and music, including poetics, the Quadrivium. A valuable commentary on Capella was written later by Scotus Erigena (ed. by B. Hauréau, Paris, 1861). — The *Institutiones Divinarum et Sæcularium Lectionum* and *De Artibus ac Disciplinis Litterarum Liberalium* of the Senator Cassiodorus (480–570, Works, Paris, 1588), and the *Originum sive Etymologiarum, Libri XX.* (in Migne) of Isidorus Hispalensis (died 636) are already completely upon theological ground. **John Damascenus** (about 700) in his Πηγὴ γνώσεως (Works, Venice, 1748) gave the classical example for the employment of the ancient school logic in the service of systematising the Church doctrines.

While the storms of the national migrations were blustering upon the continent, scientific study had fled to the British Isles, in particular to Ireland, and later flourished to a certain extent in the school at York under the Venerable Bede. From here learned education was won back to the continent through Alcuin, upon the inducement of Charles the Great ; beside the episcopal and the cloister schools arose the palatinal school, whose seat was fixed by Charles the Bald at Paris. The most important cloister schools were those of Fulda and Tours. At the former worked Rabanus (Rhaban) Maurus (of Mainz, 776–856 ; *De Universo, Libri XXII.*), and Eric (Heiricus) of Auxerre; from it went out, at the end of the ninth century, Remigius of Auxerre and the probable author of the commentary *Super Porphyrium* (printed in Cousin's *Ouvrages Inédits d'Abélard*, Paris, 1836). In Tours Alcuin was followed by the Abbot Frede-gisus, whose letter, *De Nihilo et Tenebris*, is preserved (in Migne, Vol. 105). Later the cloister at St. Gall (Notker Labeo, died 1022) formed a principal seat of scientific tradition.

Cf. also for the literary relations, the *Histoire Littéraire de la France.*

The writings ascribed to the Areopagite (cf. *Acts of the Apostles*, 17 : 34), among which those of chief importance are περὶ μυστικῆς θεολογίας and περὶ τῆς ἱεραρχίας οὐρανίου (in Migne ; German by Engelhardt, Su. zbach, 1823), show the same mixture of Christian and Neo-Platonic philosophy which appeared fre-quently in the Orient (the result of Origen's influence) and in an especially characteristic form in the Bishop Synesius (about 400 ; cf. R. Volkmann, *S. von Cyrene*, Berlin, 1869). The above-named writings of the Pseudo-Dionysius, which probably arose in the fifth century, are first mentioned, 532, and their genuineness is there contested; nevertheless, this was defended by Maximus Confessor (580–662 ; *De Variis Difficilioribus Locis Patrum Dionysii et Gregorii*, ed. Oehler, Halle, 1857).

In connection with this Mysticism develops the first important scientific personality of the Middle Ages, John **Scotus Erigena** (sometimes Jerugena, from Ireland, about 810–880), of whose life it is certainly known that he was called by Charles the Bald to the court school at Paris, and was for a time active there. He translated the writings of the Areopagite, wrote against Gottschalk the treatise *De Prædestinatione*, and put his own theories into his main work, *De Divisione Naturæ* (German by Noack, Leips. 1870–76). The works form Vol. 122 in Migne's collection. Cf. J. Huber, *J. S. E.* (Munich, 1861).

Anselm of Canterbury (1033–1109) came from Aosta, was active for a long time in the Norman cloister at Bec, and was called to become Archbishop of Canterbury in 1093. Of his works (Migne, Vol. 155) the most important for philosophy besides the treatise *Cur Deus Homo?* are the *Monologium* and the *Proslogium*. The two latter are edited by C. Haas (Tübingen, 1863), together with the refutation of a monk, Gaunilo (in the cloister Marmoutier near Tours), *Liber pro Insipiente*, and the reply of Anselm. Cf. Ch. Rémusat, *A. de C.*, *tableau de la vie monastique et de la lutte du pouvoir spirituel avec le pouvoir temporel au 11ᵐᵉ siècle* (2d ed., Paris, 1868).

William of Champeaux (died 1121 as Bishop of Châlons-sur-Marne) was a teacher who was much heard at the cathedral school in Paris, and established studies there in the Augustinian cloister at St. Victor. We are chiefly informed as to his philosophical views by his opponent Abelard ; his logical treatise is lost. Cf. E. Michaud, *G. de Ch. et les écoles de Paris au 12ᵐᵉ siècle* (Paris, 1868).

The **Platonism** of the earlier Middle Ages attached itself essentially to the *Timæus*, and under the influence of the Neo-Platonic interpretation gave to the doctrine of Ideas a form which did not completely correspond to the original sense. The most important figure in this line is **Bernard of Chartres** (in the first half of the twelfth century). His work *De Mundi Universitate sive Mega-· cosmus et Microcosmus* has been edited by C. S. Barach (Innsbruck, 1876). **William of Conches** (*Magna de Naturis Philosophia; Dragmaticon Philoso-phiæ*) and **Walter** of Montagne are regarded as his disciples. **Adélard** of Bath also wrote in the same spirit (*De Eodem et Diverso; Questiones Naturales*).

Roscellinus of Armorica in Brittany came forward as teacher at various places, especially at Locmenach where Abelard was his hearer, and was obliged to retract his opinions at the Council at Soissons. Of his own writings only a letter to Abelard is extant (printed in the *Abhandl. der bair. Akad.*, 1851) ; the sources for his doctrine are Anselm, Abelard, John of Salisbury.

Abelard (Abeillard), the most impressive and energetic personality among the thinkers of this period, was born 1079 at Pallet, in the county of Nantes, and was a pupil of William of Champeaux and of Roscellinus. His own activity as a teacher was developed at Melun and Corbeil, and most successfully in Paris at the cathedral school, and at the logical school St. Geneviève. The misfortune into which his well-known relationship to Heloise plunged him, and the conflicts into which his teaching brought him with the Church authority, chiefly at the instigation of his unwearied prosecutor, Bernard of Clairvaux

(Synods at Soissons 1121, and Sens 1141), did not allow the restless man to attain complete clearness in his mind, and impelled him to seek resting-places in various cloisters : he died 1142 in St. Marcel, near Châlons-sur-Saône. Cf. his *Historia Calamitatum Mearum,* and his correspondence with Heloise (M. Carrière, *A. u. H.,* 2d ed., Giessen, 1853). His works have been edited by V. Cousin in two volumes (Paris, 1849–59). Among these the most important are his *Dialectic, Introductio in Theologium, Theologia Christiana, Dialogus inter Philosophum, Christianum et Judæum,* the treatise *Sic et Non,* and the ethical treatise *Scito Te Ipsum.* Cf. Ch. d. Rémusat, *Abelard* (2 vols., Paris, 1845).

A number of anonymous treatises (published by V. Cousin) occupy a position allied to that of Abelard. Of this description are a commentary on *De Interpretatione, De Intellectibus,* and *De Generibus et Speciebus* (the latter is possibly from Joscellinus, a Bishop of Soissons who died 1151). Related to Abelard is also the philosophico-theological position of **Gilbert** de la Porrée (Gilbertus Porretanus, died 1154 as Bishop of Poitiers), who taught in Chartres and Paris, and was drawn into the prosecution of Abelard by Bernard of Clairvaux. Besides a commentary on the *De Trinitate* and *De Duabus Naturis in Christo* of Pseudo-Boethius, he wrote the *De sex Principiis,* which was much commented upon later.

The consequences of the "dialectic" that were objectionable for the Church showed themselves at an early date especially with **Berengar** of Tours (999–1088), whose doctrine of the Sacrament was combated by **Lanfranc** (1005–1089, Anselm's predecessor at Bec and Canterbury). The latter is probably the author of the treatise formerly ascribed to Anselm and printed among his works, *Elucidarium sive Dialogus Summam Totius Theologiæ Complectens.* In this compendium the effort first appears to give the whole compass of what had been established by the Church, in the form of a logically arranged text-book, putting aside dialectical innovations. From this proceeded later the works of the **Summists** [so called from their writings which took the form of a "Sum" of theology], among whom the most important is **Peter Lombard** (died 1164 as Bishop of Paris). His *Libri IV. Sententiarum* form Vol. 192 in Migne. Among the earlier we may perhaps mention Robert Pulleyn (Robertus Pullus, died 1150) ; among the later, Peter of Poitiers (died 1205) and Alanus Ryssel ("*ab insulis*" ; died 1203). Cf. on him Baumgartner (Münster, 1896).

Gerbert (died 1003 as Pope Sylvester II.) has the merit of having pointed out energetically the necessity of the study of mathematics and natural science. He became acquainted with the work of the Arabians while in Spain and Italy, and acquired an amount of knowledge that made him an object of amazement and suspicion to his contemporaries. Cf. K. Werner, *G. von Aurillac, die Kirche und Wissenschaft seiner Zeit* (2d ed., Vienna, 1881). Like him his disciple, Fulbert (died 1029 as Bishop of Chartres), called men back from dialectic to simple piety, and in the same spirit **Hildebert** of Lavardin was active (1057–1133, Bishop of Tours).

The same thing was done upon a large scale by the orthodox **Mysticism** of the twelfth century. As its most zealous supporter we are met by **Bernard of Clairvaux** (1091–1153). Among his writings those prominent are *De Contemptu Mundi,* and *De Gradibus Humilitatis* (ed. by Mabillon, last ed., Paris, 1839 f.). Cf. Neander, *Der heilige B. und seine Zeit* (3d ed., 1865) ; Morison, *Life and Times of St. B.* (Lond. 1868) ; [R. S. Storrs, *B. of C.* (N.Y. 1892)].

Mysticism became scientifically fruitful among the **Victorines,** the conductors of the cloister school of St. Victor, in Paris. The most important was **Hugo of St. Victor** (born 1096 as Count of Blankenburg in the Harz, died 1141). Among his works (in Migne, Vols. 175–177) the most important is *De Sacramentis Fidei Christianæ;* for the psychology of Mysticism the most important works are the *Soliloquium de Arrha Animæ, De Arca Noe* and *De Vanitate Mundi,* and besides these the encyclopedic work *Eruditio Didascalica.* — Cf. A. Liebner, *H. v. St. V. und die theologischen Richtungen seiner Zeit* (Leips. 1836).

His pupil, **Richard of St. Victor** (a Scot, died 1173), wrote *De Statu, De Eruditione Hominis Interioris, De Preparatione Animi ad Contemplationem,* and *De Gratia Contemplationis.* His works form Vol. 194 in Migne. Cf. W. A. Kaulich, *Die Lehren des H. und R. von St. V.* (in the *Abhandl. der Böhm. Ges. der Wiss.,* 1863 f.). His successor, Walter of St. Victor. distinguished himself in a less scientific polemic against the heretical dialectic (*In Quattuor Labyrinthos Franciæ*).

At the close of this period appear the beginnings of a Humanist reaction against the one-sidedness of the work of the schools, in **John of Salisbury** (Johannes Saresberiensis, died 1180 as Bishop of Chartres), whose writings *Policraticus* and *Metalogicus* (Migne, Vol. 199) form a valuable source for the scientific life of the time. Cf. C. Schaarschmidt, *J. S. nach Leben und Studien, Schriften und Philosophie* (Leips. 1862).

§ 22. The Metaphysics of Inner Experience.

The philosophy of the great Church teacher Augustine is not presented in any of his works as a complete system; rather, it develops incidentally in all his literary activity in connection with the treatment of various subjects, for the most part theological. But from this work as a whole we receive the peculiar impression that these rich masses of thought are in motion in two different directions, and are held together only by the powerful personality of the man. As theologian Augustine throughout all his investigations keeps the *conception of the Church* in mind, as criterion; as philosopher he makes all his ideas centre about the *principle of the absolute and immediate certainty* (*Selbstgewissheit*) *of consciousness.* By their double relation to these two fixed postulates, all questions come into active flux. Augustine's world of thought is like an elliptic system which is constructed by motion about two centres, and this, its inner duality, is frequently that of contradiction.[1]

It becomes the task of the history of philosophy to separate from this complicated system those ideas by which Augustine far transcended his time and likewise the immediately following centuries, and became one of the *founders of modern thought.* All these ideas, however, have their ultimate ground and inner union in the principle of the *immediate certainty of inner experience* (*selbstgewissen Innerlichkeit*), which Augustine first expressed with complete clearness, and formulated and used as the starting-point of philosophy. Under the influence of the ethical and religious interest, metaphysical interest had become gradually and almost imperceptibly shifted from the sphere of the outer to that of the inner life. Psychical conceptions had taken the place of physical, as the fundamental factors in the conception of the world. It was reserved for Augustine to bring into full and conscious use, this, which had already become an accomplished fact in Origen and Plotinus.[2]

---

[1] It is unmistakable that Augustine himself in the course of his development transferred the emphasis of his personality more and more from the philosophical to the Church centre. This comes forward with especial distinctness in his backward look over his own literary activity, the *Retractationes.*

[2] Aug. *De Ver. Rel.* 39, 72. *Noli foras ire; in te ipsum redi:* IN INTERIORE HOMINE *habitat veritas.*

This tendency toward *inner experience* even constitutes his peculiar literary quality. Augustine is a virtuoso in self-observation and self-analysis; he has a mastery in the portrayal of psychical states, which is as admirable as is his ability to analyse these in reflection and lay bare the deepest elements of feeling and impulse. Just for this reason it is from this source almost exclusively that he draws the views with which his metaphysics seeks to comprehend the universe. So there begins, as over against the Greek philosophy, a new course of development, which indeed, during the Middle Ages, made but little progress beyond what was achieved by Augustine in his first cast, and the full development of which is not to be found until the modern period.

1. This makes its appearance clearly already in Augustine's doctrine of the *starting-point* of philosophical knowledge. In correspondence with the course of his personal development he seeks the way to certainty through doubt, and in this process, sceptical theories themselves must break the path. At first, to be sure, with the indomitable thirst of his ardent nature for happiness, he strikes down doubt by the Socratic postulate that the possession of truth (without the presupposition of which there is also no probability) is requisite for happiness, and therefore is to be regarded as attainable: but with greater emphasis he shows that even the sceptic who denies the external reality of the content of perception, or at least leaves it undecided, can yet not involve in doubt the internal existence of the sensation as such. But instead of contenting himself with the relativistic or positivistic interpretations of this fact, Augustine presses forward just from this basis to victorious certainty. He points out that together with the sensation there is given not only its content, which is liable to doubt in one direction or another, but also the reality of the perceiving subject, and this certainty which consciousness has in itself follows first of all from the very act of doubt. In that I doubt, or since I doubt, he says, I know that I, the doubter, am: and thus, just this doubt contains within itself the valuable truth of the *reality of the conscious being.* Even if I should err in all else, I cannot err in this; for in order to err I must exist.[1]

This fundamental certainty extends equally to all *states of con-*

---

[1] Augustine attributed fundamental importance to this line of argument, which he frequently worked out (*De Beata Vita,* 7; *Solil.* II. 1 ff.; *De Ver. Rel.* 72 f.; *De Trin.* X. 14, etc.). That it, however, was not completely unknown to Greek literature also is proved by the passage (III. 6 f.) of the compilation current under the name of "Metaphysics of Herennios." The source of this passage has not as yet been discovered, but is probably late Stoic. Cf. on this E. Heitz in *Sitz.-Ber. der Berl. Ak. d. W.,* 1889, pp. 1167 ff.

sciousness (*cogitare*), and Augustine sought to show that all the various kinds of these states are already included in the act of doubt. He who doubts knows not only that he lives, but also that he remembers, that he knows, and that he wills: for the grounds of his doubt rest upon his former ideas; in estimating the *momenta* of the doubt are developed thought, knowledge, and judgment; and the motive of his doubt is only this, that he is striving after truth. Without particularly reflecting upon this, or drawing farther conclusions from it, Augustine proves in this example his deep insight into the psychical life, since he does not regard the different kinds of psychical activity as separate spheres, but as the aspects of one and the same act, inseparably united with one another. The soul is for him — and by this he rises far above Aristotle, and also above the Neo-Platonists — the living whole of *personality*, whose life is a unity, and which, by its self-consciousness, is certain of its own reality as the surest truth.

2. But from this first certainty Augustine's doctrine at once leads farther, and it is not only his religious conviction, but also a deep epistemological reflection, that makes him regard the idea of God as immediately involved in the certainty which the individual consciousness has of itself. Here, too, the fundamental fact of doubt is of authoritative importance; in this case, also, it already contains implicitly the full truth. How should we come to question and doubt the perceptions of the external world which force themselves upon us with such elementary power, asks Augustine, if we did not possess, besides these, and from other sources, criteria and standards of truths by which to measure and examine these perceptions? He who doubts must know the truth, for only for its sake does he doubt.[1] In reality, continues the philosopher, man possesses, besides sensation (*sensus*), the higher capacity of *reason* (*intellectus, ratio*), *i.e.* of the immediate perception of incorporeal truths;[2] under the latter Augustine understands, not only the logical laws, but also the norms of the good and the beautiful; in general, all those truths not to be attained by sensation, which are requisite to elaborate and judge what is given, — the principles of judging.[3]

---

[1] *De Ver. Rel.* 39, 72 f.

[2] Aspectus animi, quo *per se ipsum* non per corpus verum intuetur: *De Trin.* XII. 2, 2. Cf. *Contra Acad.* III. 13, 29.

[3] The apprehension of these intelligible truths by human consciousness was at the first designated by Augustine quite Platonically ἀνάμνησις. It was orthodox scruples against the assumption of the pre-existence of the soul that led him to regard the reason as the intuitive faculty for the incorporeal world. Cf. also J. Stortz, *Die Philosophie des hl. Augustinus* (Freiburg i. B. 1882).

Such norms of reason assert themselves as standards of judgment in doubt as in all activities of consciousness; but they transcend, as something higher, the individual consciousness into which they enter in the course of time: they are the same for all who think rationally, and experience no alteration in this their worth. Thus the individual consciousness sees itself attached in its own function to something *universally valid* and far reaching.[1]

But it belongs to the essence of truth that it *is* or exists. Augustine also proceeds from this fundamental conception of the ancient, as of every naïve theory of knowledge. But the Being or existence of those universal truths, since they are absolutely incorporeal in their nature, can be thought only as that of the *Ideas in God* — after the Neo-Platonic mode; they are the changeless Forms and norms of all reality (*principales formæ vel rationes rerum stabiles atque incommutabiles, quæ in divino intellectu continentur*), and the determinations of the content of the divine mind. In him they are all contained in highest union; he is the absolute unity, the all-embracing truth; he is the highest Being, the highest Good, perfect Beauty (*unum, verum, bonum*). All rational knowledge is ultimately knowledge of God. Complete knowledge of God, indeed, even according to Augustine's admission, is denied to human insight in the earthly life. Perhaps only the negative element in our idea of him is completely certain; and, in particular, we have no adequate idea of the way in which the different elements of divine truth which the reason beholds are united in him to form the highest real unity. For his incorporeal and changeless essence (*essentia*) far transcends all forms of relation and association that belong to human thought; even the category of substance applies to him as little as do the rest.[2]

3. Directly consistent as these thoughts are with Neo-Platonism,[3] their Christian character is yet preserved in Augustine's presentation by the fact that the religious idea of the deity as absolute personality is inseparably fused with the philosophical conception of the deity as the sum and essence of all truth. But just for this reason the whole Augustinian metaphysics is built up upon the

---

[1] *De Lib. Arb.* II. 7 ff.

[2] The essential thing in this is the insight, that the categories acquired in knowing Nature are inadequate for the peculiar nature of spiritual synthesis (according to which the divine essence should be thought). The new categories of internality are, however, with Augustine only in the process of coming into existence; cf. the following.

[3] In fact, Augustine seeks throughout to identify the νοῦς of Plotinus with the λόγος of Origen; but by dropping from the Neo-Platonic doctrine the emanistic derivation of the νοῦς and its acquirement of independent existence, he abrogates the physical schema of the world potencies in favour of the psychical.

self-knowledge of the finite personality; that is, upon the fact of inner experience. For so far as a comprehension of the divine essence is at all possible for man, it can be gained only after the analogy of human self-knowledge. This, however, shows the following fundamental composition of the inner life: the permanent existence of spiritual Being is given in the sum-total of its content of consciousness, or reproducible ideas; its movement and living activity consists in the processes of uniting and separating these elements in judgments; and the impelling force in this motion is the will, directed toward the attainment of highest blessedness. Thus the three aspects of psychical reality are *idea* (*Vorstellung*), *judgment,* and *will : memoria, intellectus, voluntas,*[1] and Augustine is expressly on his guard against conceiving of these modes of functioning which are peculiar to personality, as the properties of bodies are conceived. Just as little do they mean different strata or spheres of its existence; they form in their indissoluble unity the substance of the soul itself. In accordance with these relations thus recognised in man's mental life, Augustine then not only seeks to gain an analogical idea of the mystery of the Trinity, but recognises, also, in the *esse, nosse,* and *velle* the fundamental determinations of all reality. Being, knowing, and willing comprise all reality, and in omnipotence, omniscience, and perfect goodness, the deity encompasses the universe.

The outspoken opinion of the inadequacy of the physical (Aristotelian) categories reminds us only seemingly of Neo-Platonism, whose intelligible categories (cf. p. 245), as well as its entire metaphysical schema, are throughout physical. It is Augustine who is first in earnest in the attempt to raise the peculiar forms of relation characteristic of the inner nature, to metaphysical principles. Aside from this, his cosmology runs on in the track laid by Neo-Platonism without peculiarities worthy of mention. The doctrine of the two worlds, with its anthropological correlates, forms here the presupposition. The world of sense is known through perceptions, the intelligible world through the reason, and these two given constituents of knowledge are brought into relation with each other by intellectual thought (*ratiocinatio*). For apprehending Nature, the teleology conditioned by the doctrine of Ideas presents itself. The corporeal world also is created out of nothing by divine power, wisdom, and goodness, and bears in its beauty and perfection the sign of its origin. Evil (including moral evil, yet cf. below) is here, too, nothing properly real ; it is not a thing, but an act ; it has no *causa efficiens,* but only a *causa deficiens ;* its origin is to be sought not in the positive Being (God), but in the lack of Being of finite natures ; for these latter, as having been created, possess only a weakened and therefore a defective reality. Augustine's theodicy stands thus essentially upon the ground of that of Origen and Plotinus.

4. A farther and essential consequence of placing philosophy upon a consciously anthropological basis is, in Augustine's case, the central position which he assigned in his theory of the universe to

---

[1] The same triple division of the psychical activities is found among the Stoics. Cf. p. 187.

the *will*. The leading motive in this is doubtless the man's own experience; himself a nature ardent and strong in will, as he examined and scrutinised his own personality he came upon the will as its inmost core. On this account the will is for him the essential element in all : *omnes nihil aliud quam voluntates sunt.*

In his psychology and theory of knowledge this is shown especially in the fact that he seeks to set forth on all sides the controlling position of the will in the entire process of ideation and knowledge.[1] While with reference to sense perception the Neo-Platonists had distinguished between the state of corporeal stimulation and the becoming conscious of the same, Augustine demonstrates by an exact analysis of the act of seeing, that this becoming conscious is essentially an act of will (*intentio animi*). And as physical attention is accordingly a matter of the will, so too the activity of the inner sense (*sensus interior*) shows a quite analogous dependence upon the will. Whether we bring our own states and actions as such to our consciousness or not, depends as truly upon voluntary reflection as does the intentional consideration of something which belongs to our memory, and as does the activity of the combining fantasy when directed toward a definite goal. Finally, the thinking of the intellect (*ratiocinatio*), with its judging and reasoning, is formed completely under the direction of the purposes of the will; for the will must determine the direction and the end according to which the data of outer or inner experience are to be brought under the general truths of rational insight.

In the case of these *cognitions of rational insight* the relation assumes a somewhat more involved form, for in its relation to this higher divine truth the activity of the human mind cannot be given the same play as in the case of its intellectual relation to the outer world and to its own inner world. This is true even on philosophical grounds, for according to the fundamental metaphysical scheme the active part in the causal connection must belong to the more universal as the higher and more efficient Being (*Sein*). The relation of the human mind to this truth, which is metaphysically its superior, can in the main be only a passive one. The knowledge of the intelligible world is for Augustine also, essentially — illumination, revelation. Here, where the mind stands in the presence of its creator, it lacks not only the creative, but even the receptive initiative. Augustine is far from regarding the intuitive knowledge of the intelligible truths as possibly an independent production of the

---

[1] Cf. principally the eleventh book of the treatise *De Trinitate*, and besides, especially W. Kahl, *Die Lehre vom Primat des Willens bei Augustinus, Duns Scotus und Descartes* (Strassburg, 1886).

mind out of its own nature; indeed, he cannot even ascribe to it the same spontaneity of attention or of directing its consciousness (*intentio*) that he ascribes to the empirical cognitions of outer and inner perception : he must, on the contrary, regard the illumination of the individual consciousness by the divine truth as essentially an act of grace (cf. below), in the case of which the individual consciousness occupies an expectant and purely receptive attitude. These metaphysical considerations, which might also have been possible upon the basis of Neo-Platonism, experience in Augustine's case a powerful reinforcement by the emphasis which he laid in his theology upon the divine grace. Knowledge of the truths of reason is an element in blessedness, and blessedness man owes not to his own will, but to that of God.

Nevertheless Augustine here, too, sought to save a certain co-operation for the will of the individual, at least at first. He not only emphasises that God bestows the revelation of his truths upon him only, who through good endeavour and good morals, *i.e.* through the qualities of his will, shows himself a worthy subject for this revelation; he teaches also that the appropriation of divine truth is effected not so much by insight, as through *faith* or belief. Faith or belief, however, as ideation plus assent, though without the act of conception, presupposes indeed the idea of its object, but contains in the factor of assent, which is determined by no intellectual compulsion, an original volitional act of the affirming judgment. The importance of this fact extends so far, in Augustine's opinion, that not only in divine and eternal things, but also in the human and earthly and temporal things, this conviction produced immediately by the will yields the original elements of thought. The insight which conceives and comprehends grows out of these elements by means of the combining reflective procedure of the understanding. Thus even in the most important things, *i.e.* in questions of salvation, faith in the divine revelation and in its appearance in the tradition of the Church — faith dictated by the good will — must precede the knowledge which appropriates and comprehends it intellectually. Full rational insight is indeed first in dignity, but faith in revelation is the first in time.

5. In all these considerations of Augustine, the central point is the conception of the *freedom of the will*, as a decision, choice, or assent of the will, independent of the functions of the understanding, not conditioned by motives of cognition, but rather determining these motives without grounds in consciousness for its acts, and Augustine faithfully exerted himself to maintain this conception against various objections. In addition to the consciousness of

ethical and religious responsibility, it is principally the cause of the divine justice that he here aims to defend: and, on the other hand, most of his difficulties arise from the attempt to unite uncaused action whose opposite is alike possible and objectively thinkable, with the divine prescience. He helps himself here by appealing to the distinction between eternity (timelessness) and time. In an extremely acute investigation [1] he maintains that time has real significance only for the functions of inner experience as they measure and compare: its significance for outer experience also arises only in consequence of this. The so-called foreknowledge of the deity, which is in itself timeless, has as little causally determining power for future events as memory has for those of the past. In these connections, Aristotle is justly regarded as one of the most zealous and forcible defenders of the freedom of the will.

But in opposition to this view, championed essentially with the weapons of former philosophy, there now appears in Augustine's system another line of thought, increasing in force from work to work, which has its germ in the conception of the *Church* and in the doctrine of its redeeming power. Here the principle of historical universality encounters victoriously the principle of the absolute certainty of the individual mind. The idea of the Christian Church, of which Augustine was the most powerful champion, is rooted in the thought that the whole human race is in need of redemption. This latter idea, however, excludes the completely undetermined freedom of the will in the individual man; for it requires the postulate that every individual is necessarily sinful, and therefore in need of redemption. Under the overpowering pressure of this thought, Augustine set another theory by the side of his theory of freedom of the will which was so widely carried out in his philosophical writings; and this second theory runs counter to the first throughout.

Augustine desires to solve the question as to the origin of evil, which is so important for him personally, and to solve it — in opposition to Manichæism — by the conception of the freedom of the will, in order to maintain in this, human responsibility and divine justice; but in his theological system it seems to him to be sufficient to restrict this freedom of will to Adam, the first man. The idea of the substantial oneness of the human race — an idea which was a co-operating element in the faith in the redemption of all by the one Saviour — permitted likewise the doctrine that in

---

[1] In the eleventh book of the *Confessions.* Cf. C. Fortlage, *A. De Tempore Doctrina* (Heidelberg, 1836).

the one man Adam all humanity had sinned.   By the abuse of this freedom of the will on the part of the first man, the whole human nature has been so corrupted that it cannot do otherwise than sin (*non posse non peccare*).   This loss of freedom applies without exception, to the whole race arising from Adam.   Every man brings with him into the world this corrupted nature which is no longer capable of good in its own strength or freedom, and this *inherited sin* is the punishment for original sin.   Just from this it follows that all men, without exception, are *in need* of redemption and of the Church's means of grace.   One as little as another deserves to receive this grace : therefore, thinks Augustine, no injustice can be seen in the fact that God bestows this grace, to which no one has any claim, not upon all, but only upon some ; and it is never known upon whom.   But, on the other hand, the divine justice demands that, at least in the case of some men, the punishment for Adam's fall should be permanently maintained, that these men, therefore, should remain excluded from the working of grace and from redemption.   Since, finally, in consequence of their corrupted nature, all are alike sinful and incapable of any improvement of themselves, it follows that the choice of the favoured ones takes place not according to their worthiness (for there are none worthy before the working of grace), but according to an unsearchable decree of God.   Upon him whom he will redeem he bestows his revelation with its irresistible power : he whom he does not choose, — he can in nowise be redeemed.   Man in his own strength cannot make even a beginning toward the good : all good comes from God and only from him.

In the *doctrine of predestination,* accordingly (and this is its philosophical element), the absolute causality of God suppresses the free will of the individual.   The latter is refused both metaphysical independence and also all spontaneity of action ;   the individual is determined either by his nature to sin or by grace to the good.   So in Augustine's system two powerful streams of thought come into violent opposition.   It will always remain an astonishing fact that the same man who founded his philosophy upon the absolute and independent certainty of the individual conscious mind, who threw the plummet of the most acute examination into the depths of inner experience and discovered in the will the vital ground of spiritual personality, found himself forced by the interests of a theological controversy to a theory of the doctrine of salvation which regards the acts of the individual will as unalterably determined consequences, either of a general corruption or of the divine grace. *Individualism* and *universalism* in the conception of psychical reality stand here in bald opposition, and their clashing contradiction is scarcely concealed by the ambiguity of the word "freedom," which, in the one line, is defended according to its psychological meaning, in the other, according to its ethico-religious meaning. The opposition, however, of the two motives of thought which here lie side by side so irreconcilable, had influence in the succeeding development of philosophy until long past the Middle Ages.

6. In the light of the doctrine of predestination the grand picture of the historical development of humanity, which Augustine drew in the manner and spirit of the old patristic philosophy, takes on dark colours and peculiarly stiff, inflexible forms. For if not only the course of the history of salvation taken as a whole, but also, as in Augustine's system, the position which every individual is to occupy within it, has been previously fixed by divine decree, one cannot rid one's self of the gloomy impression that all man's volitional life in history, with all its thirst for salvation, sinks to a play of shadows and puppets, whose result is infallibly fixed from the beginning.

The spiritual world throughout the whole course of history falls apart, for Augustine, into two spheres, — the realm of God and the realm of the devil. To the former belong the angels that have not fallen, and the men whom God has chosen for his grace; the other embraces, together with the evil demons, all those men who are not predestined to redemption, but are left by God in the state of sin and guilt: the one is the kingdom of heaven, the other that of the world. The two occupy in the course of history a relation like that of two different races which are mingled only in outer action, while internally they are strictly separate. The community of the elect has no home on earth; it lives in the higher unity of divine grace. The community of the condemned, however, is divided within itself by discord; it fights in earthly kingdoms for the illusory worth of power and rule. Christian thought at this stage of development is so little able to master the reality presented by the world, that Augustine sees in the historical states only the provinces of a community of sinners in hostility to God, condemned to quarrel with one another. For him, in fact, the kingdom of God is still not of this world; and the Church is for him the saving institution of the divine kingdom, which enters the temporal life.

The course of the world's history under these presuppositions is so conceived that we find a division entering between the two realms, which becomes sharper and sharper in the course of history, and ultimately results in the complete and definitive separation of the same. In six periods, which correspond to the creative days of the Mosaic cosmogony and are attached to dates of Israelitic history, Augustine constructs his history of the world. In this process he combines a depreciatory estimate of the Roman world with slight understanding of the essential nature of the Grecian. The decisive point in this development is for him, also, the appearance of the Saviour, by which not only the redemption of those chosen by grace is brought to completion, but also their separation from the children of the world. With this begins the last world-period, whose end will be the Judgment: then after the stress of conflict shall enter the Sabbath, the peace of the Lord — but peace only for the elect; for those not predestined to salvation will then be completely separated from the saints, and entirely given over to the pain of their unhappiness.

However spiritually sublime (though never without attendant physical imagery) the conception of happiness and pain here presented, — and this sublimity is especially noteworthy in the thought of unhappiness as a weakening of Being, due to the lack of divine causality, — the dualism of the Good and the Evil is yet unmistakably, for Augustine, the final issue of the world's history. The man assailed by so many powerful motives of thought has not overcome the *Manichæism* of his youthful belief; he has taken it up into Christian doctrine. Among the Manichæans the antithesis of good and evil is held to be original and indelible: with Augustine this antithesis is regarded as one that has come into being, and yet as one that is ineradicable. The omnipotent, omniscient, supremely benevolent God has created a world which is divided forever into his own realm and that of Satan.

7. Among the complicated problems and ideas of universal historical importance which Augustinianism contains, there is still one to be brought forward. It lies in the conception of *blessedness* itself in which all motives of his thought cross. For, strongly as Augustine recognised in the will the inmost motive energy of human nature, deeply as he penetrated the striving after happiness as the impelling motive of all psychical functions, he yet remained firmly convinced that the satisfaction of all this stress and urging is to be found only in *beholding divine truth.* The highest good is God; but God is the truth, and one enjoys truth by beholding it and resting in its contemplation. All urging of the will is but the path to this peace in which it ceases. The last task of the will is to be silent in the gracious working of divine revelation, — to remain quiet when the vision of truth, produced from above, comes over it.

Here are united in common opposition to individualism of will, the Christian idea of the absolute causality of God, and the contemplative mysticism of the Neo-Platonists. From both sides, the same tendency is at work to bring about the conception of man's sanctification as a working of God in him, as a becoming filled and illumined by the highest truth, as a will-less contemplation of the one, infinite Being. Augustine, indeed, worked out forcibly the practical consequences which the working of grace should have in the earthly life, — purification of the disposition and strictness in the conduct of life, — and just in this is shown the comprehensive breadth of his personal nature and his spiritual vision. He develops the vigorous energy of his own combative nature into an ethical doctrine, which, far removed from the asceticism of Neo-Platonism with its weariness of life, sets man in the midst of the world-battle between Good and Evil as a brave fighter for the heavenly kingdom. But the highest reward which beckons this fighter for God is yet, for Augustine, not the restless activity of the will, but the rest of contemplation. *For the temporal life*, Augustine demands the full and never-resting exertion of the struggling and acting soul; *for eternity* he offers the prospect of the peace of becoming absorbed in divine truth. He indeed designates the state of the blessed as the highest of the virtues, as love [1] (*charitas*), but in the eternal blessedness where the resistance of the world and of the sinful will is no longer to be overcome, where love has no longer any want that must be satisfied, there this love is no longer anything other than a God-intoxicated contemplation.

In this duality, also, of the Augustinian ethics, old and new lie close together. With the tense energy of will which is demanded for the earthly life, and with the transfer of the ethical judgment so as to make it apply to the inner disposition, the modern man appears; but in the conception of the highest goal of life the ancient ideal of intellectual contemplation retains the victory.

Here lies in Augustine's doctrine itself a contradiction with the individualism of the will, here at a decisive point an Aristotelian, Neo-Platonic element maintains itself, and this internal opposition unfolds itself in the formation of the problems of the Middle Ages.

§ 23. The Controversy over Universals.

Johannes Saresberiensis, *Metalogicus*, II. cap. 17 f.
J. H. Löwe, *Der Kampf zwischen Nominalismus und Realismus im Mittelalter, sein Ursprung und sein Verlauf* (Prague, 1876).

The schooling in formal logic which the peoples that entered upon the scientific movement at the beginning of the Middle Ages

---

[1] In his system the three Christian virtues, faith, hope, and love, are placed above the practical and dianoëtic virtues of Greek ethics.

were obliged to undergo, developed in connection with the question as to the logical and metaphysical significance of genera and species (*universalia*). But it would be a grave mistake to suppose that this question had only the didactic value of serving as a subject for mental drill, in connection with which the rules of conceptional thought, division, judgment, and inference, were impressed for centuries upon ever new and increasing throngs of scholars. On the contrary, the tenacity with which the science of the Middle Ages — and it is significant that this occurred independently in the Orient as well as in the Occident — held fast to the elaboration of this problem in endless discussions, is rather in itself a proof that in this question a very real and very difficult problem lies before us.

In fact, when Scholasticism, in its timorous beginnings, made the passage in Porphyry's Introduction [1] to the *Categories* of Aristotle which formulated this problem, the starting-point of its own first attempts at thought, it hit with instinctive sagacity upon precisely the same problem which had formed the centre of interest during the great period of Greek philosophy. After Socrates had assigned to science the task of thinking the world in conceptions, the question how the class-concepts, or generic conceptions, are related to reality, became, for the first time, a chief motive of philosophy. It produced the Platonic doctrine of Ideas and the Aristotelian logic; and if the latter had as its essential content (cf. § 12) the doctrine of the forms in which the particular is dependent upon the universal, it is easy to understand that even from so scanty remains and fragments of this doctrine as were at the service of the earliest Middle Ages, the same problem must arise with all its power for the new race also. And it is likewise easy to understand that the old enigmatic question worked upon the naïve minds of the Middle Ages, untrained in thought, in a manner similar to that in which it worked upon the Greeks. In fact, the delight in logical dispute, as this developed after the eleventh century at the schools of Paris, finds its counterpart as a social phenomenon only in the debates of the philosophers at Athens, and in these latter, too, as numerous anecdotes prove, the question as to the reality of universals, which was connected with the doctrine of Ideas, played a leading part.

Nevertheless the problem was renewed under conditions that were essentially less favourable. When this question emerged for the Greeks, they possessed a wealth of proper scientific experience

---

[1] The formulation of the problem in the translation of Boëthius is as follows: "... *de generibus et speciebus — sive subsistant sive in solis nudis intellectibus posita sint, sive subsistentia corporalia an incorporalia, et utrum separata a sensibilibus an in sensibilibus posita et circa hæc consistentia. . . .*"

and a store of real information and knowledge, which, if not always, yet for the most part and on the whole, prevented them from making their discussion solely a game with the abstractions of formal logic. But mediæval science, especially in its beginnings, lacked just this counterpoise, and on this account was obliged to move so long in a circle with the attempt to construct its metaphysics out of purely logical considerations.

That the Middle Ages, in their turn, engaged and persisted so pertinaciously in this controversy which had previously been waged principally between Plato and the Cynics, and afterward between the Academy, the Lyceum, and the Stoa, was not due solely to the fact that in consequence of the defective character of their traditions the thinkers of the Middle Ages knew as good as nothing of those earlier debates; it had yet a deeper ground. The feeling of the peculiar, intrinsic worth of personality, which had gained so powerful expression in Christianity and especially in the Augustinian doctrine, found the liveliest echo and the strongest sympathy among precisely those tribes which were called to become the new bearers of civilisation; and in the hearts of these same peoples urged also the youthful delight in richly coloured reality, in the living, particular appearance. But with the Church doctrine they received a philosophy which, with the measured calm of Greek thought, conceived the essential nature of things to lie in universal connections, a metaphysics which identified the stages of logical universality with intensities of Being of varying worths. In this way an inconsistency which covertly asserted itself, even in Augustinianism, and became a constant stimulus for philosophical reflection.

1. The question as to the individual's ground of Being or existence, from which mediæval thought never became free, was the more natural for it just at its beginning in proportion as the Neo-Platonic metaphysics still maintained itself under the veil of a Christian mysticism. Nothing could be more adapted to call out the contradiction of a natural individualism than the high degree of consistency with which *Scotus Erigena* carried through the fundamental thoughts of the *Neo-Platonic Realism.* Perhaps no philosopher has expressed more clearly and frankly than he the final consequences of the metaphysics which, from the standpoint of the Socratic-Platonic principle that the truth, and therefore also Being, is to be sought in the universal, identifies the stages of universality with those of the intensity and priority of Being. The universal (the class-concept or logical genus) appears here as the essential and original reality, which *produces from itself and contains within itself*

the particular (the species and ultimately the individual). The universals are, therefore, not only substances (*res;* hence the name "Realism"), but, as contrasted with the corporeal individual things, they are the more primitive, the producing and determining substances; they are the more Real substances, and they are *the more Real in proportion as they are the more universal.* In this conception, therefore, the logical relations of concepts immediately become metaphysical relations; formal arrangement contains real significance. Logical subordination becomes changed into a production and inclusion of the particular by the general; logical partition and determination become transformed into a causal process by means of which the universal takes on form and unfolds itself in the particular.

The pyramid of concepts, thus raised to a metaphysical significance, culminates in the concept of the deity as the most universal. But the last product of abstraction, the absolutely universal, is that which has no determinations (cf. p. 250). Hence this doctrine becomes identical with the old "negative theology," according to which we can predicate of God only what he is not;[1] and yet here, too, this highest Being is designated, quite in accord with the thought of Plotinus, as the "uncreated, but self-creating Nature." For this most universal Being produces out of itself all things; these, therefore, contain nothing else than its manifestations, and are related to it as particular specimens or instances are to the class; they are in it and exist only as its modes of appearance. The result of these presuppositions is thus a *logical pantheism:* all things of the world are "theophanies"; the world is God developed into the particular, proceeding out of himself to take on a definite form (*deus explicitus*). God and the world are one. The same "Nature" (φύσις) is, as creative unity, God, and as created plurality, the world.

The process of unfolding (*egressus*) proceeds in the graded scale of logical universality. Out of God comes at first the intelligible world as "the Nature which is created and itself creates," the realm of universals, of Ideas which (as νοῖ in the sense of Plotinus) form the working forces in the sensuous world of phenomena. The Ideas are built up as a heavenly *hierarchy* according to their various grades of universality, and therefore also of intensity of Being, and in connection with this thought Christian Mysticism constructs a

---

[1] In carrying out this Philonic thought (cf. p. 237) the Church Fathers had already employed a course of thought which proceeds by successive abstraction to the concept of God as the undetermined. Cf., *e.g.*, Clement Alex. *Strom.* V, 11 (282).

doctrine of angels after a Neo-Platonic pattern. But in every case beneath the mythical covering the important thought is really active, that real dependence consists in logical dependence; the logical consequence, by which the particular follows from the general, is spuriously substituted for the causal relation.

Hence, then, even in the world of the senses, it is only the universal that is properly active and efficient: corporeal things, as a whole, form the "Nature which is created and does not itself create."[1] In this world the individual thing is not as such active; it is rather active according to the proportion of universal attributes which attain manifestation in it. The individual thing of sense, accordingly, possesses the least force of Being, the weakest and completely dependent species of reality: the Neo-Platonic Idealism is maintained by Scotus Erigena in full.

To the stages of unfolding corresponds in a reverse order the return of all things into God (*regressus*), the resolution of the world of individual forms into the eternal primitive Being, the deification of the world. So thought, as the final goal of all generation and change, as the extinction of all that is particular, God is designated as "the Nature which neither is created nor creates": it is the ideal of motionless unity, of absolute rest at the end of the world-process. All theophanies are destined to return into the unity of the divine All-Being, — that unity which knows no distinctions. Thus, even in the final destiny of things, the superior reality of the universal, which swallows up all that is particular, preserves itself.

2. As in antiquity (cf. § 11, 5), so here, in consequence of the effort to assure truth and reality to universals, the peculiar thought of a graded scale of *Being* appears. Some things (universals), is the doctrine, *are* more than others (particulars). "Being" is looked upon as, like other qualities, capable of comparison, of increase and diminution; it belongs to some things more than to others. So it became the custom to think that the concept of Being (*esse, existere*) has a relation to that which *is* (*essentia*), and a relation of different degrees of intensity, just as other marks and qualities are related to the objects in which they are formed. As a thing possesses more or less extension, force, permanence, so it has also more or less "Being"; and as it can receive or lose other qualities, so it can receive or lose that of Being. This line of thought, peculiar to Realism, must be kept in mind to understand a great number of the

---

[1] It need only be briefly mentioned that this "division of Nature" obviously recalls the Aristotelian distinction of the unmoved mover, the moved mover, and that which neither moves nor is moved. Cf. § 13, 5.

metaphysical theories of the Middle Ages. It explains, in the first place, the most important doctrine which Realism produced, the *ontological argument for the existence of God* which *Anselm of Canterbury* brought forward.

The more universality, the more Reality. From this it follows that if God is the most universal being, he is also the most Real; if he is the absolutely universal being, he is also the absolutely Real being, *ens realissimum*. He has, therefore, according to the conception of him, not only the comparatively greatest Reality, but also absolute Reality; that is, a Reality than which a greater and higher cannot be thought.

But through the whole development which this line of thought had already taken in antiquity, we find that the worth-predicate of *perfection* was inseparably fused with the conception of Being. The degrees of Being are those of perfection; the more anything *is*, the more perfect it is, and, *vice versa*, the more perfect anything is, the more it *is*.[1] The conception of the highest Being is, therefore, also that of an absolute perfection; that is, of a perfection such that it cannot be thought higher and greater : *ens perfectissimum*.

In accordance with these presuppositions, Anselm is perfectly correct in his conclusion that, from the mere conception of God as most perfect and most real Being, it must be possible to infer his existence. But to do this he attempts various modes of proof. In his *Monologium* he follows the old cosmological argument that because there is Being at all, a highest and absolute Being must be assumed from which all else that exists has its Being, and which itself exists only from itself, according to its own essential nature (*aseïtas*). Whereas every individual existent entity can be also thought as non-existent, and therefore owes the reality of its essence not to itself, but to another (the Absolute), the most perfect Being can be thought only as being or existent, and exists accordingly only by virtue of the necessity of its own nature. God's *essence* (and only God's) involves his *existence*. The nerve of this argument is thus ultimately the Eleatic basal thought, ἔστιν εἶναι, Being is, and cannot be thought otherwise than as being or existing.

Anselm, however, involved this same thought in a peculiar complication, while he intended to simplify it and render it independent in itself. In the *Proslogium* he entered upon the ontological argument, properly so called, which maintains that without any reference to the Being of other things, the mere conception of the most per-

---

[1] A principle which lies at the basis of Augustine's theodicy, in so far as with both the existent is held to be *eo ipso* good, and the evil on the contrary, as not truly existent.

fect Being involves its Reality. Inasmuch as this conception is thought, it possesses psychical reality : the most perfect being *is* as a content in consciousness (*esse in intellectu*). But if it existed only as a content in consciousness, and not also in metaphysical reality (*esse etiam in re*), a still more perfect being could evidently be thought, which should possess not only psychical, but also metaphysical reality ; and thus the former would not be the most perfect being possible. It belongs, accordingly, to the conception of the most perfect being (*quo majus cogitari non potest*) that it possesses not only reality in thought, but also absolute reality.

It is obvious that Anselm in this formulation was not fortunate in his shift, and that what hovered before him attained in this proof but a very awkward expression. For it takes little acuteness to see that Anselm proved only that *if* God is thought (as most perfect being), he must be thought also necessarily as being or existent, and cannot be thought as non-existent. But the ontological argument of the *Proslogium* did not show even in the remotest degree that God, *i.e.* that a most perfect being, must be thought. The necessity for this stood fast for Anselm personally, not only because of the conviction of his faith, but also by the cosmological argumentation of the *Monologium*. When he believed that he could dispense with this presupposition and with the help of the mere conception of God arrive at the proof of his existence, he exemplified in typical manner the fundamental idea of Realism, which ascribed to conceptions without any regard to their genesis and basis in the human mind, the character of truth, *i.e.* of Reality. It was on this ground alone that he could attempt to reason from the psychical to the metaphysical reality of the conception of God.

The polemic of *Gaunilo*, therefore, in a certain respect hit the vulnerable point. He argued that according to the methods of Anselm, in quite the same manner the reality of any idea whatever, *e.g.* that of an island, if the mark of perfection were only included within it, might be proved. For the most perfect island, if it were not really in existence, would evidently be surpassed in perfection by the real island, which should possess the same other marks ; the former would be inferior to the latter in the attribute of Being. But instead of showing in his rejoinder, as might have been expected, that the conception of a perfect island is a completely unnecessary arbitrary fiction, or that this conception contains an inner contradiction, while the conception of the most real being is necessary and not contradictory, Anselm expatiates further upon his argument, that if the most perfect being is in the intellect, it must be also *in re.*

However slight the cogency of this attempted proof remains for him who does not, as Anselm does without acknowledging it, regard the conception of an absolute Being as a necessity of thought, the ontological argument is yet valuable as the characteristic feature of mediæval Realism, of which it forms the most consistent expression. For the thought that the highest being owes its reality only to its own essential nature, and that therefore this reality must be capable of being proved from its conception alone, is the natural conclusion of a doctrine which traces the Being of things of perception back to a participation in conceptions, and again within the conceptions themselves sets up a graded scale of reality, employing the degree of universality as the standard.

3. When now the question arose as to the kind of reality which belongs to universals, and as to their relation to the individual things known to the senses, mediæval Realism found itself involved in difficulties quite similar to those which had faced the Platonic Realism. The thought of a second, higher, immaterial world, which at that former period had to be born, was now indeed received as a complete and almost self-evident doctrine, and the religiously disposed thinking could be only sympathetic in its attitude toward the Neo-Platonic conception of the Ideas as contents of the divine mind. Following the pattern of the Platonic Timæus, whose mythical mode of presentation was favourable to this conception, *Bernard of Chartres* sketched an imaginative cosmogonic work of fantastic grotesqueness, and we find with his brother Theodoric, attempts, suggested by the same source, to construct a symbolism of numbers, which undertook not only, as was done in other instances, to develop the dogma of the Trinity, but also to develop further fundamental metaphysical conceptions out of the elements of unity, likeness, and unlikeness.[1]

In addition to this question concerning the archetypal reality of the Ideas in the mind of God, the question is also, what significance is to be conceded to them in the created world. Extreme Realism, as it had been maintained at the outset by *William of Champeaux*, taught the full substantiality of the class-concept in this world also; the universal is present in all its individuals as the undivided essence, everywhere identical with itself. The class accordingly appears as the unitary substance, and the specific marks of the individuals belonging to it appear as the accidents of this substance. It was Abelard's objection that according to this theory mutually contradictory accidents would have to be ascribed to the same sub-

[1] Cf. the extracts in Hauréau, *Hist. d. l. ph. sc.*, I. 396 ff.

stance, which first forced the defender of Realism to give up this extreme position and restrict himself to the defence of the proposition, that the class exists in the individuals, *individualiter;*[1] *i.e.* that its universal, identical essence clothes itself in each particular example in a particular substantial Form.   This view was in touch with the conception of the Neo-Platonists, which had been maintained by Boëthius and Augustine and also occasionally mentioned in the literature of the intervening period, and its exposition moves readily in the Aristotelian terminology, according to which the universal appears as the more indeterminate possibility which realises itself in individuals by means of their peculiar *Forms.* The conception is then no longer substance in the proper sense, but the common substratum which takes on different forms in individual instances.

Walter of Mortagne sought to remove the difficulty in another way, by designating the individualising of the classes or genera to species, and of the species to individual things, as the entering of the substratum into different states (*status*), and yet regarding these states as *realiter* specialising determinations of the universal.

In both these lines of thought, however, Realism was only with difficulty held back from a final consequence which at the first lay in nowise within the purpose of its orthodox supporters.   The relation of the universal to the particular might be regarded as the self-realising of the substratum into individual Forms, or as its specialisation into individual states, — in either case one came ultimately in the ascending line of abstract conceptions to the idea of the *ens generalissimum,* whose self-realisations, or whose modified states, formed in descending line the genera, species, and individuals, *i.e.* to the doctrine that in all phenomena of the world only the one divine substance is to be seen.   *Pantheism* inhered in the blood of Realism by reason of its Neo-Platonic descent and was always making its appearance here and there; and opponents like Abelard did not fail to cast this consequence in the face of Realism.

Meanwhile realistic pantheism did not come to be expressly maintained in this period; on the other hand, Realism in its theory of universals found an instrument for establishing some of the fundamental dogmas, and therefore rejoiced in the approbation of the Church.   The assumption of a substantial reality of the logical genera not only seemed to make possible a rational exposition of the doctrine of the Trinity, but also, as was shown by Anselm and Odo (Odardus) of Cambrey, proved to be a fit phil-

---

[1] For the reading "indifferenter," cf. Löwe, *op. cit.,* 49 ff., and Cl. Bäumker, *Arch. f. Gesch. d. Ph.,* X. 257.

osophical basis for the doctrines of inherited sin and vicarious satisfaction.

4. On the same grounds, we find at first the reverse lot befalling *Nominalism*, which during this period remained more repressed and stifled. Its beginnings[1] were harmless enough. It grew out of the fragments of Aristotelian logic, in particular out of the treatise *De Categoriis*. In this the individual things of experience were designated as the true "first" substances, and here the logico-grammatical rule was propounded that "substance" could not be predicate in a judgment: *res non predicatur*. Since now the logical significance of universals is essentially that of affording the predicates in the judgment, (and in the syllogism), it seemed to follow — this the commentary *Super Porphyrium* had already taught — that universals could not be substances.

What are they, then ? It could be read in Marcianus Capella that a universal was the comprehension of many particularities by one name (*nomen*), by the same word (*vox*); but a word, Boethius had defined as a "motion of the air produced by the tongue." With this all elements of the thesis of extreme Nominalism were given: universals are nothing but collective names, common designations for different things, sounds (*flatus vocis*), which serve as signs for a multiplicity of substances or their accidents.

In what degree the thus formulated Nominalism, which in this extreme form must have ignored even the real occasions for such collective names, was actually propounded and defended during that period[2] can no longer be determined.[3] But the *metaphysics of individualism* which corresponds to such a theory of knowledge meets us clearly and firmly with the claim that only individual things are to be regarded as substances, as truly real. This was doubtless most sharply expressed by *Roscellinus*, when he presented it in a twofold aspect: as the comprehension of many individuals under the same name is only a human designation, so, too, the distinguishing of parts in individual substances is only an analysis for human thought and communication ;[4] the truly real is the individual thing, and that alone.

---

[1] Cf. C. S. Barach, *Zur Geschichte des Nominalismus vor Roscellin* (Vienna, 1866).

[2] It is certain that this did not as yet occur in the beginnings of Nominalism (with Eric of Auxerre, with the author of the commentary *Super Porphyrium*, etc.), for with these writers we find at the same time the expression of Boëthius that *genus* is *substantialis similitudo ex diversis speciebus in cogitatione collecta*.

[3] John of Salisbury says (*Policr.* VII. 12 ; cf. *Metal.* II. 17) that this opinion vanished again with its author Roscellinus.

[4] The example of the house and its wall, which, according to Abelard (*Ouvr. Inéd.* 471), he employed in this connection, was certainly the most unfortunate that could be thought of. How inferior such considerations are to the beginnings of Greek thought)

The individual, however, is that which is given in the world of sensible reality ; hence for this metaphysics, knowledge consists only in the experience of the senses. That this *sensualism* appeared in the train of Nominalism, that there were men who allowed their thinking to go on entirely in corporeal images, we are assured, not only by Anselm, but also by Abelard : but who these men were and how they carried out their theory we do not learn.

This doctrine became momentous through its application to theological questions by Berengar of Tours and Roscellinus. The one contested, in the doctrine of the Sacrament, the possibility of the transmutation of the substance while the former accidents were retained ; the second reached the consequence that the three persons of the divine Trinity were to be looked upon as three different substances, agreeing only in certain qualities and workings (tritheism).

5. In the literary development of these antitheses Realism passed current as Platonic, Nominalism as Aristotelian. The latter designation was evidently much more distorted than the former, but when we consider the defective nature of the transmitted material, we can understand that the mediating tendencies which thrust themselves in between Realism and Nominalism introduced themselves with the endeavour to harmonise the two great thinkers of antiquity. Of such attempts, two are chiefly worthy of mention : from the party of Realism the so-called Indifferentism, from that of Nominalism the doctrine of Abelard.

As soon as Realism abandoned the doctrine of the separate existence of the concepts (the Platonic χωρισμός) and supported only the "*universalia in re,*" the tendency asserted itself to conceive of the different stages of universality as the real states of one and the same substratum. One and the same absolute reality is, in its different "*status,*" animate being, man, Greek, Socrates. As the substratum of these states the moderate Realists regarded the universal, and ultimately the *ens realissimum ;* it was therefore a significant concession to Nominalism when others made the individual the supporter of these states. The truly existent, these latter thinkers conceded, is the individual thing, but the individual thing supports within itself as essential determinations of its own nature certain qualities and groups of qualities which it has in common with others. This real similarity (*consimilitudo*) is the indifferent ("not different") element in all these individuals, and thus the genus is present in its species, the species in its individual examples, *indifferenter.* Adélard of Bath appears as the chief supporter of this line of thought, yet it must have had a wider extension, perhaps with a somewhat stronger nominalistic accent.[1]

6. But it was Abelard[2] with his all-sided activity who formed the vigorous centre in the controversy over universals. The pupil and at the same time the opponent both of Roscellinus and of William of Champeaux, he fought Nominalism and Realism each by means of the other, and since he takes the weapons of his polemic now from the one side now from the other, it could not fail to result that his position should be interpreted and judged oppositely.[3] And yet the outlines of this position are clear and distinct before us. In his polemic against all kinds of Realism, the thought that the logical consequence of Realism is pantheism returns so frequently and energetically that we must see in it, not merely a convenient weapon for use in the ecclesiastical conditions then prevailing, but rather the expression of an individualistic conviction easy to understand in the case of a personality so energetic, self-conscious, and proudly self-reliant. But this individuality had at the same time its inmost essence in clear, sharp, intellectual activity, in genuine French rationality. Hence its no less powerful opposition against the sensualistic tendencies of Nominalism.

Universals, Abelard teaches, cannot be things, but just as little can they be mere words. The word (*vox*) as a complex of sounds, is indeed something singular; it can acquire universal meaning only mediately, by becoming a predicate (*sermo*). Such an employment of a word for a predicate is possible only through conceptional thought (*conceptus*), which, by comparing the contents of perception, gains that which is by its nature adapted to become a predicate (*quod de pluribus natum est prædicari*).[4] The universal is then the conceptual predicate (*Sermonism*), or the concept itself (*Conceptualism*).[5] But if the universal as such gains its existence first in thought and judgment, and in the predicate which is possible only by this means, and exists only there, it is not therefore entirely without relations to absolute reality. Universals could not be the indispensable forms of all knowledge, as they in fact actually are, if there were not something in the nature of things which we

---

[1] According to the statements in the treatise *De Generibus et Speciebus* and the communications of Abelard in his gloss on Isagoge. It seems, too, that William of Champeaux inclined toward Indifferentism at the last.

[2] Cf. S. M. Deutsch, *Peter Abaelard, ein kritischer Theolog. des zwölften Jahrhunderts* (Leips. 1883).

[3] Thus Ritter makes him a Realist; Hauréau, a Nominalist.

[4] Cf. Arist. *De Interpr.* 7, 17 a 39.

[5] It seems that Abelard at different times emphasised sometimes the one alternative, sometimes the other, and perhaps his school also developed differently in accordance with these two lines of thought.

apprehend and predicate in these universals. This something is the likeness or similarity (*conformitas*) of the essential characteristics of individual substances.[1] Not as numerical or substantial identity, but as a multiplicity with like qualities, does the universal exist in Nature, and it becomes a unitary concept which makes predication possible, only when it has been apprehended and conceived by human thought. Even Abelard, however, explains this likeness of character in a multiplicity of individuals upon the hypothesis that God created the world according to archetypes which he carried in his mind (*noys*). Thus, according to his view, the universals exist firstly, *before the things*, as *conceptus mentis* in God ; secondly, *in the things*, as likeness of the essential characteristics of individuals; thirdly, *after things*, in the human understanding as its concepts and predicates acquired by comparative thought.

Thus, in Abelard the different lines of thought of the time become united. But he had developed the individual elements of this theory incidentally, partly in connection with his polemic, and perhaps, also, at different times with varying emphasis on this or that element: a systematic solution of the whole problem he never gave. As regards the real question at issue he had advanced so far that it was essentially his theory that became the ruling doctrine in the formula accepted by the Arabian philosophers (Avicenna), "*universalia ante multiplicitatem, in multiplicitate et post multiplicitatem;*" to universals belongs equally a significance *ante rem* as regards the divine mind, *in re* as regards Nature, and *post rem* as regards human knowledge. And since Thomas and Duns Scotus in the main agreed in this view, the problem of universals, which, to be sure, has not yet been solved,[2] came to a preliminary rest, to come again into the foreground when Nominalism was revived (cf. § 27).

---

[1] Others, who in the main had the same thought, *e.g. Gilbert* de la Porrée, aided themselves with the Aristotelian distinction between first and second substances, or between substance and subsistence ; yet Gilbert uses the latter terms in a changed meaning as compared with their use by Abelard.

[2] Even if the problem as to the universals be restricted, according to the mode of Scholasticism, to the reality of the class-concepts, the problem has gone through essentially new phases in its further development, and cannot be regarded as finally solved by the position taken by science to-day. Behind this, however, rises the more general and more difficult question, what metaphysical significance belongs to those universal determinations, in a knowledge of which all explanatory science practically consists. Cf. H. Lotze, *Logik* (Leips. 1874), §§ 313–321. [Eng. tr. ed. by B. Bosanquet, Oxford and N.Y. 1888.]

To the investigators of to-day, therefore, who would throw the controversy over universals to the lumber pile of past theories, or treat it as a long-outgrown children's disease, so long as they do not know how to state with complete certainty and clearness in what consists the metaphysical reality and efficiency of that which we call a *law of Nature*, we must still cry, "*mutato nomine de te fabula narrata.*" Cf., also, O. Leibmann, *Zur Analysis der Wirklichkeit* (2d ed., Strassburg, 1880), 313 ff., 471 ff., and *Gedanken und Thatsachen* (1 Heft, Strassburg, 1882), 89 ff.

7. But Abelard has a still greater significance than that due to this central position in the controversy over universals, for he manifested in his own person, and expressed in typical form, the attitude which the *dialectic*, unfolding in connection with that controversy, occupied in the mental and spiritual life of that time. He is, so far as it was possible within the limits of the ideas of his time, the spokesman of free science, the prophet of the newly awakened impulse toward real and independent knowledge. Abelard (and with him Gilbert) is first of all a *rationalist;* thought is for him the norm of truth. Dialectic has the task of distinguishing between true and false. He may, indeed, subject himself to revelation preserved in tradition, but, he says, we believe divine revelation only because it is reasonable. Hence dialectic has, in his case, no longer really the task which Anselm, following Augustine, prescribed it, of making the content of faith comprehensible for the intellect; he demands for it also the *critical* right of deciding in doubtful cases according to its own rules. Thus, in the treatise *"Sic et Non,"* he set the views of the Church Fathers over against each other to their reciprocal disintegration dialectically, in order to find at last what is worthy of belief only in what is capable of proof. So, too, in his *Dialogus*, the cognising reason appears as judge over the various religions, and while Abelard regards Christianity as the ideal consummation of the history of religions, there are expressions in his works [1] in which he reduces the content of Christianity to the original moral law, which was re-established by Jesus in its purity. From this standpoint, too, Abelard was the first to win once more a free, unbiassed view for the interpretation of antiquity. Little as he knew of them, he was an admirer of the Greeks; he sees in their philosophers Christs before Christianity, and regarding men like Socrates and Plato as inspired, he asks (reversing the thought of the Church Fathers, cf. p. 223, note 5) whether religious tradition may not perhaps have been partly created by these philosophers. Christianity is regarded by him as the philosophy of the Greeks made democratic.

Abelard, like almost all the "Enlighteners" of the Middle Ages,[2] was an obedient son of the Church. But if this fact were to put us in error as to the significance of his personality in the line just mentioned, — a significance rather for the history of religion and civilisation than as producing something philosophically new, — it would be sufficient to take into account the attacks which he met.

---

[1] Cf. the evidence for what follows in Reuter, *Gesch. der Aufklärung im M.-A.*, I. 183 ff.

[2] A. Harnack, *Dogmengeschichte*, III. 322.

In fact, his controversy with Bernard of Clairvaux is the conflict of knowledge with faith, of reason with authority, of science with the Church. And if Abelard lacked ultimately the weight and staying power of personality to prevail in such a contest,[1] it will be remembered, on the other hand, that a science such as the twelfth century could offer — even aside from the external power to which the Church at that time had attained — must have been inferior to the mighty inward strength of faith, even if it had not been supported by so great and high a personality. For that bold postulate, so full of the future, that only unprejudiced scientific insight should determine faith, — what means did it then possess for its fulfilment? Its only means were the hollow rules of dialectic; and the content which this science had to exhibit, it owed just to that tradition against which it rebelled with its intellectualistic criticism. This science lacked the material strength to carry out the part to which she felt herself called; but she set herself a problem which, while she herself was not able to solve it, has never again vanished from the memory of European peoples.

We hear, indeed, of the disturbing practices of those who would have everything treated only "scientifically";[2] complaints multiply after the time of Anselm over the growing rationalism of the *Zeitgeist,* over the evil men who will believe only what they can comprehend and prove, over the Sophists who, with impudent dexterity, know how to dispute *pro et contra,* over the "deniers," who from rationalists are said to have become materialists and nihilists; — but not even the names of the men who answer to this description have been preserved, to say nothing of their doctrines. And just this lack in proper material of its own was the reason that the dialectic movement, whose prince was Abelard, in spite of all its zeal and all its acuteness, ran out and became exhausted without direct and immediate results.

§ 24. The Dualism of Body and Soul.

On these grounds it is explicable that in the twelfth and, in part, even in the eleventh century, we find the feeling of the unfruitfulness of dialectic as widely extended as the feverish impulse to attain through it to true knowledge. A tendency that indicates disillusion is manifested in this period by the side of the ardent desire for knowledge. Discontented with the subtilties of dialectic, which, even in men like Anselm, had laid itself under obligation to

---

[1] Cf. Th. Ziegler, *Abaelard's Ethica,* in *Strassburg. Abh. z. Philos.* (Freiburg, 1884), p. 221.
[2] "*Puri philosophi.*"

place the ultimate mysteries of faith upon a rational basis, some plunged from unfruitful theory into practical life, "in das Rauschen der Zeit, ins Rollen der Begebenheit," — into the rush of time, the rolling of events, — others plunged into a revelry in supra-rational Mysticism; others, finally, into diligent work in empirical research. All the opposites, into which an intellectual activity that is predominantly logical can pass over, develop by the side of dialectic, and take their position against it in a more or less firmly concluded league, — Practice, Mysticism, and Empiricism.

There resulted from this at first a peculiarly distorted relation to scientific tradition. Aristotle was known only as the father of formal logic and master of dialectic, and in consequence of this ignorance was regarded as the hero of the purely intellectual mode of considering the world. Plato, on the contrary, was known partly as the creator of the doctrine of Ideas (unwittingly falsified in accordance with Neo-Platonic processes), partly, by virtue of the preservation of the *Timæus*, as the founder of a philosophy of Nature whose fundamental teleological character found the liveliest assent in religious thought. Hence when *Gerbert*, as a counterpoise against the pride of dialectic in which he himself had at first made some not very successful attempts, commended the *study of Nature*, to which he had been stimulated by the example of the Arabians, and which corresponded to his own vigorous practical bent toward active life, he could count on approval for this endeavour only among men who, like him, were working toward an extension of material information, and who, in aid of this, were appropriating the results of ancient researches. Thus the *return to antiquity* makes here its first appearance as the source of material knowledge in opposition to the Aristotelian dialectic, — a first weak Renaissance which, half humanistic, half naturalistic, aims to gain a living content of knowledge.[1] Gerbert's disciple, Fulbert (died 1029), opened the school of Chartres, which, in the following period, became the seat of the Platonism that was intimately associated with the study of Nature. Here worked the brothers Theodoric and Bernard of Chartres; from this school William of Conches received his tendency. In their writings the powerful stimulus of classical antiquity unites with the interest of an active and vigorous

---

[1] The cloister Monte Cassino in Italy formed one of the main seats of this movement. Here (about 1050) the monk Constantinus Africanus worked, who, as is known to have been the case also with the Platonist Adélard of Bath, gathered his learning on his journeys in the Orient, and was especially active in the translation of medical treatises by Hippocrates and Galen. The effects of the activity in this cloister are shown not only in literature, but also in the founding of the famous school of Salerno in the middle of the twelfth century.

knowledge of **Nature.** We see here one of the most peculiar shift-ings that have occurred in the history of literature. Plato and Aristotle have exchanged their rôles : the latter appears as the ideal of an abstract science of conceptions, the former as the starting-point for a concrete knowledge of Nature. The knowledge of ex-ternal reality that meets us in this period of mediæval science is attached to the name of Plato. So far as there is a natural science in this age, it is that of the Platonists, — of a Bernard of Chartres, of a William of Conches, and their associates.[1]

But this disposition toward concrete reality, which makes the *Platonists* of the Middle Ages conspicuous as contrasted with the high-soaring metaphysics of the dialecticians, assumed still another form, which was much more valuable. Incapable as yet of gaining from outer experience better results than those already at its hand in the transmitted Greek science, the empirical impulse of the Middle Ages directed its activity to the investigation of the mental life, and unfolded the full energy of real observation and acute analysis in the domain of inner experience — in *psychology.* This is the field of scientific work in which the Middle Ages attained the most valuable results.[2] In this, the experience of practical life as well as that of the sublimest piety was filled with a substantial con-tent, and as such set itself in opposition to the dialectical play of conceptions.

1. The natural leader in this field was *Augustine,* whose psychologi-cal views exercised a mastery that was the stronger in proportion as his views were interwoven with the current religious conviction, and in proportion, also, to the slight extent to which the Aristotelian psychology was known. But Augustine had maintained in his system the complete dualism which regarded the soul as an imma-terial substance, and man as a union of two substances, body and soul. Just for this reason he could not expect to gain a knowledge of the soul from its relations to the body, and took with full con-sciousness of his procedure the *standpoint of inner experience.*

The new principle of method which had thus arisen from meta-physical presuppositions could unfold itself undisturbed so long as the monistic metaphysical psychology of the Peripatetic school re-

---

[1] This humanistic natural science of the early Middle Ages was not at all discriminating in its adoption of ancient tradition ; so, for example, if we may trust the account of Walter of St. Victor (in the extracts made by Bulæus, *Migne,* Vol. 190, p. 1170), William of Conches regarded an atomistic conceptior of Nature as capable of union with his Platonism. (Migne, Vol. 90, pp. 1132 ff.).

[2] Cf. for this and for what follows (as also for § 27, later) the articles by H. Siebeck in Vols. I.–III. of the *Archiv für Geschichte der Philosophie,* and also in Vols. 93, 94, *Zeitschrift für Philos. u. philos. Krit.* (1888–90).

mained unknown. And this unfolding was furthered emphatically
by those needs which brought the Middle Ages to psychology.
Faith sought knowledge of the soul for the purpose of the soul's
salvation, and this salvation was found just in those transcendent
activities through which the soul, estranged from the body, strives
toward a higher world. It was, therefore, principally the *Mystics*
who sought to spy out the secrets of the inner life, and thus became
psychologists.

Weightier and philosophically more significant than the individual
doctrines propounded in this line, which were often very fantastic
and hazy, is the fact that by means of these and connected theories,
the *dualism of the sensuous and super-sensuous worlds* was maintained
in its full strength, and thus formed a strong counterpoise to the
Neo-Platonic monism. But it was not destined to exercise this
metaphysical influence till later : at first, in the more limited form
of the *anthropological dualism* of body and soul, it became the
starting-point for *psychology as the science of inner experience.*[1]

It is, therefore, a very noteworthy phenomenon that the supporters of this psychology as "natural science of the inner sense,"
as it was later called, are precisely the same men who are faithfully
exerting themselves to gain a knowledge of the outer world from all
available material. Having turned away from dialectic, they seek a
knowledge of what is real in experience, a philosophy of Nature ;
but they divide this into two completely separated fields, *physica
corporis* and *physica animæ.* Among the Platonists the preference
for the study of external Nature is predominant, among the Mystics
that for the study of the internal Nature.[2]

2. But we must regard as the characteristic, the essentially new
and beneficial mark of this empirical psychology, the endeavour,
not only to classify the psychical activities and states, but to apprehend them in the living stream of mental life, and to comprehend
their *development.* These men in their pious feelings, in their
struggles for the enjoyment of divine grace, were conscious of an
inner *experience,* of a history of the soul, and were impelled to write
this history ; and while in so doing they used Platonic, Augustinian,

---

[1] Cf. also K. Werner, *Kosmologie und Naturlehre des scholastischen Mittelalters, mit specieller Beziehung auf Wilhelm von Conches ;* and *Der Entwick-
lungsgang der mittelalterlichen Psychologie von Alcuin bis Albertus Magnus*
(off-prints from the *Sitzungsberichten* (Vol. 75), and *Denkschriften* (Vol. 25)
respectively of the *Vienna Acad.*, 1876).

[2] Nevertheless it must be mentioned that Hugo of St. Victor not only shows
an encyclopædic knowledge in his *Eruditio Didascalica,* but also shows that he
is acquainted, even to the most exact detail, with the teachings of ancient medicine, particularly with the theories of physiological psychology (explanation of
perceptions, temperaments, etc.).

and Neo-Platonic conceptions in motley mixture to designate individual facts, the essential and decisive point is that they undertook to exhibit the development of the inner life.

These Mystics, who were not seeking a metaphysics but already possessed one in their faith, were not much troubled by the question which later became so important, of how this duality of body and soul should be understood. *Hugo of St. Victor* is indeed conscious that though the soul is lowest in the immaterial world, and the human body highest in the material world, the two are yet so opposite in constitution that their union (*unio*) remains an incomprehensible enigma; but he thinks that in this very fact God has shown, and desired to show, that for him nothing is impossible. Instead of racking their brains dialetically upon this point, the Mystics rather assume this dualism as a presupposition, in order to isolate the soul for their scientific consideration, and to observe its inner life.

This life, however, is, for Mysticism, a development of the soul to God, and so this *first form of the psychology of the inner sense is the history of salvation in the individual soul.* The Mystics regarded the soul essentially as *Gemüth* ["heart," the seat of sentiment and feeling, rather than intellect]. They show the development of its vital process out of the *feelings*, and prove their literary virtuosoship in their depicting of the states and movements of feeling. They are also the genuine successors of Augustine in examining, in their analysis of this process, the motive *forces of the will*, in investigating the decisions of the will, by virtue of which faith conditions the course of knowledge, and finally in the fact that they ultimately regard as the highest stage in the soul's development the mystical contemplation of God, which, to be sure, is here held to be the same with love. Such, at least, was the activity of the two Victorines, Hugo and Richard, who were completely sustained by the spirit of science, while in the case of Bernard of Clairvaux, the practical factor of the will is much more strongly emphasised. Bernard is unwearied in denouncing as heathenish that pure impulse after knowledge for its own sake which comports with all the virtues and vices, and yet, even for him, the last of the twelve stages of humility is that ecstasy of deification with which the individual disappears in the eternal essence, "as the drop of water in a cask of wine."

The psychology of knowledge, also, is built up with the Victorines upon Augustinian lines. Three eyes are given to man, — the eye of flesh to know the corporeal world, the eye of reason to know himself in his inner nature, the eye of contemplation to know the spiritual world and the deity. While, then, according to Hugo, *cogitatio, meditatio,* and *contemplatio* are the three stages of intellectual activity, the degree to which he emphasises the co-operation of the imagination (*imaginatio*) in all kinds of knowledge is interesting and characteristic of his personality. Even contemplation is a *visio intellectualis,* a mental beholding which alone grasps the highest truth undistorted, while thought is not capable of this.

Old and new are thus variously mingled in the writings of the Victorines. Fantasies of mystic rapture force their way amid the most acute observations and the most delicate portrayals of the psychical functions. The method of self-observation doubtless falls here, too, into the danger of leading to *Schwärmerei,*[1] or ecstatic enthusiasm; but, on the other hand, it wins much fruit of its own, it breaks up the soil for the research of the future, and, above all, it marks off the field on which modern psychology is to grow.

3. This new science received support and enrichment likewise from quite another direction: a side-result of the controversy over universals — and that, too, not the worst result — came to its aid. When Nominalism and Conceptualism combated the doctrine that universals exist in themselves, and declared the species and genera to be subjective creations in the knowing mind, the duty fell on them of making intelligible the process by which these universal ideas arise in the human mind. They found themselves thus sent directly to the empirical study of the *development of ideas,* and supplemented the sublime poesy of the Mystics with results which were indeed sober and dry, but all the more valuable on that account. For, just because the matter in hand required an exhibition of the origin of purely subjective contents of thought, which were.to be explained as the products of man's development in time, this investigation could become only a contribution to the psychology of inner experience.

The very thesis of extreme Nominalism afforded its opponents occasion to treat the relation of word to thought, and in the case of Abelard led to a searching investigation of the co-operating activity that belongs to language in connection with the development of thought. The question as to the meaning of signs and designations in the movement of ideas was by this means raised anew. A still deeper entrance into the heart of theoretical psychology was made by the investigation which is conducted as to the necessary connection between intellect and perception in the treatise *De Intellectibus.* It is here shown how sensation, as *confused idea* (*confusa conceptio*), enters into the perception (*imaginatio*) which grasps and holds it

---

[1] Cf. Kant, *Anthropologie,* § 4.

together with others, and remains preserved reproducible in this imagination; how, then, the understanding by successively running through this manifold material (discursive activity) elaborates it to concepts and judgments; and how, after all these conditions have been fulfilled, opinion, faith, and knowledge arise, in which ultimately the intellect knows its object in a single collective perception or intuition (intuitive activity).

In a similar way *John of Salisbury* set forth the process of psychical development: but in his case the tendency peculiar to the Augustinian conception of the soul asserts itself most strongly, — the tendency to regard the different forms of activity not as strata lying above one another or beside one another, but as ways of functioning in which the same living unity manifests itself. He sees already in the sensation, and in a higher degree in perception or imagination, an act of judgment; and as union of the newly entering sensations with those which are reproduced, imagination contains at the same time the emotional states (*passiones*) of fear and hope. Thus out of imagination as fundamental psychical state develops a twofold series of states of consciousness; in the theoretical series appear first, opinion, and by comparison of opinions, knowledge and rational conviction (*ratio*), both in connection with prudence (*prudentia*), which is an operation of the will; finally, by virtue of the striving after calm wisdom (*sapientia*), we have the contemplative knowledge of the intellect; — in the practical series are given the feelings of pleasure and pain with all their diversifications in the changing states of life.

Thus with John we have indicated the whole programme of the later associational psychology in which his countrymen were to become leaders. And he may be regarded as their prototype not only in his problems, but also in the mode of their treatment. He keeps at a distance from the speculations of dialectic that were so alien to the active world; he has the practical ends of knowledge in his mind, he desires to find his way in the world in which man is to live, and above all in man's actual inner life, and brings with him into philosophy a fineness and freedom of mind characteristic of the man of the world, such as aside from him we do not find at that time. He owes this in no small degree to the education of the taste and of sound cosmopolitan thought which classical studies afford; and in this, too, his countrymen have followed him, not to their injury. He is the precursor of the English Enlightenment as Abelard is of the French.[1]

---

[1] Reuter, *op. cit.*, II. 80, sets thus Roger Bacon and Abelard over against each other; yet precisely the decisive tendency of empirical psychology is present more strongly in the case of John.

4. We notice finally *Abelard's ethics* as a peculiar side-phenomenon
in this process of making more rigid the contrast of outer and inner,
and of transferring the scientific first principle to the inner nature.[1]
Its very title, *Scito Te Ipsum*, announces it as a science based on
inner experience, and its importance consists just in the fact that
here for the first time ethics is again treated as a proper philosophical discipline, and freed from dogmatic metaphysical efforts.[2]
This is true of this ethics although it, too, proceeds from the
Christian consciousness of sin as its fundamental fact. But here
it strives to go at once to the heart of the matter. Good and evil,
it says, consist not in the outward act, but in the action's inner
cause. Nor yet do they consist in the thoughts (*suggestio*), feelings,
and desires (*delectatio*) which precede the decision of the will, but
solely in this resolve or consent to the deed (*consensus*). For the
inclination (*voluntas*), founded in the whole natural disposition and
in part in the bodily constitution, which may lead toward good or
evil, is not itself in the proper sense good or evil. Fault or error
(*vitium*) — to this Abelard reduces inherited sin — becomes sin
(*peccatum*) only through the *consensus*. But if this is present, the
sin is fully and completely there with it, and the bodily executed
action with its external consequences adds nothing ethically.

The essence of the moral is thus placed by Abelard solely in the
resolve of the will (*animi intentio*). But what now is the norm
according to which this resolve of the will is to be characterised as
good or evil? Here, too, Abelard rejects with contempt all external
and objective determination by a law; he finds the norm of judgment solely within the deciding individual, and it consists in the
agreement or non-agreement with the *conscience* (*conscientia*). That
action is good which is in accord with the agent's own conviction;
that only is bad which contradicts this.

And what is conscience? Where Abelard teaches as a philosopher, as the rationalistic dialectician that he was, there conscience
is for him (in accordance with ancient example, Cicero) the natural
moral law, which, though known in varying degree, is common to
all men, and which, as Abelard was convinced, was wakened
to new clearness in the Christian religion, after it had become obscured through human sin and weakness (cf. above, § 23, 7). But

---

[1] Cf. on this Th. Ziegler in the *Strassburger Abhdl. z. Phil.* (Freiburg,
1884).
[2] It throws a surprising light upon the clearness of Abelard's thought when
he incidentally separates the metaphysical conception of the good (perfection =
reality) carefully from the moral conception of the good, with which alone ethics
has to do. He shows in this that he had penetrated this complication of prob-
:ems, one of the most intricate in history.

for the theologian this *lex naturalis* is identical with the will of God.[1] To follow the conscience means, therefore, to obey God; to act against the conscience is to despise God. But where the import of the natural moral law is in any wise doubtful, the only resort for the individual is to decide according to his conscience, that is, according to his knowledge of the divine command.

The *ethics of intention*[2] which was presented by the head of the dialecticians and Peripatetics proves itself to be an enhancement of the Augustinian principles of internalisation and of the individualism of the will, which forces its way out of the system of the great Church teacher and beyond its bounds, to fruitful operation in the future.

---

[1] In his theological metaphysics Abelard seems occasionally to have gone so far as to reduce the content of the moral law to the arbitrary choice of the divine will (*Commentary on the Epistle to the Romans*, II. 241).

[2] The important contrast here presented in various directions to Church theory and practice cannot be brought out here.

CHAPTER II. SECOND PERIOD.

(AFTER ABOUT 1200.)

Karl Werner, *Der hl. Thomas von Aquino.* 3 vols., Regensburg, 1858 ff.
Karl Werner, *Die Scholastik des späteren Mittelalters.* 3 vols., Vienna, 1881 ff.

THE felt need for real knowledge, which mastered Western science after the first enthusiasm for dialectic was past, was very soon to find a satisfaction of unsuspected extent. Contact with the *Oriental civilisation* which at first maintained itself victoriously against the shock of the *Crusades,* disclosed to the peoples of Europe new worlds of intellectual life. Arabian, and in its train Jewish, science[1] made their entry into Paris. They had preserved the tradition of Greek thought and knowledge more immediately and more completely than had the cloisters of the West. A stronger and richer stream of scientific material poured over Bagdad and Cordova than over Rome and York. But the former brought not much more that was new with it than did the latter. Rather, as regards thoughts which discover or establish principles, the Oriental philosophy of the Middle Ages is still poorer than the European. Only, in the breadth and quantity of tradition, in the compass of learned material and in the extent of information in matters of science, the East was far superior, and these treasures now passed over into the possession of the Christian peoples.

From the point of view of philosophy, however, the matter of chief importance was that Parisian science became acquainted not

---

[1] The author believes that he may and ought to decline to give a full exposition of the Arabian and Jewish philosophy of the Middle Ages — ought to, in so far as he is here in great part excluded from penetrating to the original sources, and would therefore find himself forced to reproduce others' expositions at second hand, — may, however, because that which passed over with fructifying influence into European science from this large literature — and it is only this element that could be treated in this presentation of the development of philosophy as a whole — is found to be, with very small exceptions, the spiritual possession of antiquity, of the Greek or the Hellenistic philosophy. On this account there will be given only a brief survey of the Arabian and Jewish philosophy in the Middle Ages, which will be found at the close of the introductory material of this chapter, pp. 316-318.

only with the entire logic of *Aristotle*, but also with all parts of his philosophy that furnished material knowledge. By this "new logic" fresh blood was infused into the already dying dialectic, and while the task of rationally expounding the view of the world held by faith was attacked anew and with a matured technique of thought, there was presented at the same time an almost immeasurable material for arrangement in the metaphysico-religious system.

Mediæval thought showed itself abundantly ready for the problem thus enhanced, and solved it under the after-working of the impression of that most brilliant period in the development of the papacy which Innocent III. had brought about. The Neo-Platonic-Arabian Aristotelianism, which at the first, with its naturalistic consequences, seemed only to strengthen the rationalistic courage of dialectic to victorious pride, was mastered with admirable swiftness and bent to the service of the system of the Church. This, indeed, was possible only in a form in which the intellectualistic elements of Augustinian thought and those allied to Neo-Platonism gained a decided preponderance in this now completely systematic development of a philosophy conformed to the doctrine of faith. In this way was completed an adjustment and arrangement of world-moving thoughts upon the largest and most imposing scale that history has seen, and that, too, without the creative activity of any properly new philosophical principle as its impulse toward the formation of a system. The intellectual founder of this system was *Albert of Bollstädt*. It owes its organic completion in all directions, its literary codification, and thus its historical designation, to *Thomas Aquinas*, and finds its poetical exposition in Dante's *Divine Comedy*.

But while Hellenistic science and Christian faith seemed to be brought into complete harmony in Thomism, the opposition between them broke forth at once all the more violently. Under the influence of Arabian doctrines, the *pantheism* involved in the logical consequence of Realism from being potential became actual in extended circles, and immediately after Thomas, his fellow-Dominican, Master *Eckhart*, developed scholastic intellectualism to the heterodoxy of an *idealistic Mysticism*.

Hence it is comprehensible that Thomism also encountered the resistance of a Platonic-Augustinian tendency, which indeed gladly adopted the increase in the knowledge of Nature (as had been the case before) and the perfection of the logical apparatus, but put aside the intellectualistic metaphysics and developed all the more energetically the opposite elements of Augustinianism.

This tendency reached its full strength in the acutest and deepest thinker of the Christian Middle Ages, *Duns Scotus*, who brought the germs of the philosophy of the will, contained in Augustine's system, to their first important development, and so from the meta‍physical side gave the impulse for a complete change in the direc‍tion of philosophical thought. With him religious and scientific interests, whose fusion had begun in the Hellenistic philosophy, begin to separate.

The *renewal of Nominalism,* in which the intellectual movement of the last century of the Middle Ages culminated in an extremely interesting combination, led to the same result with still more last‍ing force. Dialectic, which had anew obtained the mastery and was flaunting itself in various disputations, developed in its text‍books on logic the Aristotelian schematism. This was worked out especially on the grammatical side, and there developed to a theory which attached the doctrine of judgment and the syllogism to the view that regarded the concepts (*termini*) as subjective signs for really existing individual things. This *Terminism* became united in *William of Occam* with the naturalistic tendencies of the Arabian-Aristotelian theory of knowledge, and these combined combated Realism, which had been maintained alike in Thomism and Scotism. But Terminism also became united with the Augustinian doctrine of the will into a powerful individualism, with the beginnings of the empirical psychology which studied the history of develop‍ment, to a kind of idealism of the inner experience, and with the natural investigation which was conquering wider and wider territory, to an empiricism that was to be fruitful in the future. Thus under the scholastic covering were sprouting the germs of new thought.

Here and there in this extremely diversified movement men still vainly appear with the confidence that they can create a rational system of religious metaphysics, and finally a man of the signifi‍cance of *Nicolaus Cusanus* sought vainly to force all these elements of a new secular science back under the power of a half scholastic, half mystic intellectualism: it was just from his system that those elements exercised an influence upon the future, that was all the stronger because of his work.

The **reception of Aristotle** falls in the century 1150–1250 (for this topic see principally the work of A. Jourdain, cited p. 273). It began with the more val‍uable parts of the *Organon,* hitherto unknown (*vetus — nova logica*), and pro‍ceeded to the metaphysical, physical, and ethical books, always accompanied by the introduction of the Arabian explanatory writings. The Church slowly admitted the *new logic,* although dialectic was again set in fluctuation thereby; for it soon became convinced that the new method which was introduced with the aid of the doctrine of the syllogism, was advantageous for presenting its own teachings.

This **scholastic method** in the proper sense is as follows: a text used as the basis for discussion is broken up by division and explanation into a number of propositions; questions are attached and the possible answers brought together; finally the arguments to be adduced for establishing or refuting these answers are presented in the form of a chain of syllogistic reasoning, leading ultimately to a decision upon the subject.

This scheme was first employed by **Alexander of Hales** (died 1245) in his *Summa Universæ Theologiæ*, with a mastery which was far superior to the mode of treatment of the earlier Summists in wealth of contents, clearness of development, and definiteness of results, and was scarcely surpassed even later.

An analogous change in method was worked out with regard to the material in the encyclopædias of natural science by **Vincent of Beauvais** (Vincentius Bellovacensis, died about 1265), by his *Speculum Quadruplex*, and Johannes Fidanza, called **Bonaventura** (1221–1274), did the same work for the doctrines of Mysticism, especially those of the Victorines. Among Bonaventura's works the *Reductio Artium ad Theologiam* is especially characteristic. Cf. K. Werner, *Die Psychologie und Erkenntnisslehre des B.* (Vienna, 1876).

The Church proceeded in a much more hesitating manner in regard to Aristotle's *Metaphysics* and *Physics*, because these made their entrance in intimate connection with **Averroism**, and because this latter theory had developed to open *pantheism* the Neo-Platonic Mysticism which had never been entirely forgotten since Scotus Erigena. As the defenders of such a system appear **Amalrich** of Bena near Chartres, and **David of Dinant**, about 1200, concerning whose doctrines we are informed only by later writers, especially Albert and Thomas. With the widely extended sect of the Amalricans, which, after the Lateran council of 1215, was persecuted with fire and sword, the "*Eternal Gospel*" of Joachim Floris was also connected. Cf. on this J. N. Schneider (Dillingen, 1873).

The judgment of condemnation passed upon the Averroistic Pan-psychism (cf. § 27) applied at first to Aristotle also. It is the service of the two *mendicant orders*, the Dominicans and Franciscans, to have broken this connection, and to have brought over the power of the Church to the recognition of the Peripatetic system. By a long conflict, which frequently wavered this way and that, they succeeded in founding two chairs of the Aristotelian philosophy at the University of Paris, and finally in having them taken into the faculty (cf. Kaufmann, *Gesch. d. Univ.*, I. 275 ff.). After this victory in 1254, respect for Aristotle rose fast, until he became the highest philosophical authority. He was praised as the forerunner of Christ in matters of Nature as was John the Baptist in matters of grace, and from this time on Christian science (like Averroës) held him to be in such a sense the incarnation of scientific truth, that in the following literature he is often cited only as "Philosophus."

The doctrine of the **Dominicans**, which has remained until the present time the official doctrine of the Catholic Church, was created by Albert and Thomas.

Albert of Bollstädt (Albertus Magnus) was born 1193 at Lauingen in Swabia, studied in Padua and Bologna, taught in Cologne and Paris, became Bishop of Regensburg, and died in Cologne in 1280. His writings consist for the most part of paraphrases and commentaries upon Aristotle; aside from the *Summa* his Botany is particularly of independent value (*De Vegetabilibus, Libri VII.;* ed. by Meyer and Jessen, Berlin, 1867). Cf. J. Sighart, *Al. Mag. sein Leben und seine Wissenschaft* (Regensburg, 1857); v. Hertling, *Al. Mag. und die Wissenschaft seiner Zeit* (in *Hist.-pol. Blätter*, 1874); J. Bach, *Al. Mag.* (Vienna, 1888).

Thomas of Aquino, born 1225 or 27 in Roccasicca, Lower Italy, was educated at first in the cloister Monte Cassino, famous of old for study in natural science, then in Naples, Cologne, and Paris. After this he taught alternately at these universities and also at Rome and Bologna, and died, 1274, in a cloister near Terracina. Besides minor treatises, his works contain commentaries on Aristotle, on the *Liber de Causis* and the *Sentences* of Peter Lombard, and in addition to these, principally the *Summa Theologiæ* and the treatise *De veritate fidei Catholicæ contra gentiles* (*Summa contra gentiles*). The treatise *De Regimine Principum* belongs to him only in part. From the very copious literature concerning him, the following may be named: Ch. Jourdain, *La Philosophie de St. Th.* (Paris, 1858); Z. Gonzalez, *Studien über die Philos. des. hl. Th. v. A.*, translated from the Spanish by Nolte (Regensburg, 1885); R. Eucken, *Die Philos. d. Th. v. A. und die Cultus der Neuzeit* (Halle, 1886); A. Frohschammer, *Die Philosophie des Th. v. A.* (Leips. 1889).

The philosophical importance of **Dante** Alighieri has been best recognised among his editors by Philalethes in the commentary on his translation of the *Divina Commedia.* Besides his great world-poem, the treatise *De Monarchia* should not be forgotten in a philosophical consideration. Cf. A. F. Ozanam, *D. et la Philosophie Catholique au 13ᵐᵉ Siècle* (Paris, 1845); G. Baur, *Boëthius und Dante* (Leips. 1873).

Interest in other Thomists, whose number is great, is only literary-historical. To the Dominican Order belonged also the father of **German Mysticism,** Master **Eckhart,** a younger contemporary of Thomas. Born in the middle of the thirteenth century, probably in Saxony, at about 1300 he was Professor of Philosophy in Paris, became then Provincial of his Order for Saxony, lived for a time in Cologne and Strassburg, and died during the painful discussions concerning the orthodoxy of his doctrine in 1329. The extant writings (collected by F. Pfeiffer, II. Leips. 1857) are principally sermons, tracts, and aphorisms. Cf. C. Ullman, *Reformatoren vor der Reformation*, Vol. II. (Hamburg, 1842); W. Preger, *Gesch. d. deutschen Mystik im Mittelalter* (Leips. 1875, 1881); also the different editions and articles by S. Denifle. On Eckhart in particular, J. Bach, *M. E. der Vater der deutschen Speculation* (Vienna, 1864); A. Lasson, *M. E. der Mystiker* (Berlin, 1868).

In its farther development German Mysticism branched into the heresies of the Beghards and of the " Friends of God " of Basle; in the case of the former it led to the most radical connection with the Averroistic pantheism. It took the form of popular preaching with John **Tauler** at Strassburg (1300–1361), and of poetic song with Heinrich **Suso** of Constance (1300–1365). Its theoretical doctrines maintained themselves, while the heterodoxy was diminished, in the " German Theology " (first edited by Luther, 1516).

The Augustinian Platonic opposition against the suspected Aristotelianism of the Arabians has as its main supporters : —

William of Auvergne, from Aurillac, teacher and Bishop in Paris, where he died in 1249, author of a work *De Universo.* He is treated by K. Werner, *Die Philosophie des W. v. A.* (Vienna, 1873).

Henry of Ghent (Henricus Gandavensis, Heinrich Gœthals of Muda near Ghent, 1217–1293), the valiant defender of the primacy of the will against Thomism. Besides a theological compendium, he wrote a *Summa Quæstionum Ordinarium,* and principally *Quodlibeta Theologica.* Cf. K. Werner, *H. v. G. als Repräsentant des christlichen Platonismus im 13 Jahrhundert* (Vienna, 1878).

Richard of Middletown (R. de Mediavia, died 1300) and William de la Marre, the author of a violent *Correctorium Fratris Thomæ,* may also be named here. In the following centuries an *Augustinian theology* proper maintained itself by the side of Thomism and Scotism. Ægydius of Colonna is regarded as its leader (Æg. Romanus, 1247–1316). Cf. K. Werner, *Schol. d. spät. M.-A.,* III.

The sharpest opposition to Thomism grew out of the Franciscan order. **Roger Bacon's** was a mind fruitfully stimulating in all directions, but not appearing in a fixed and definite form in any one of them. He was born in 1214, near Ilchester, educated in Oxford and Paris, several times persecuted on account of his occupations and theories, which were directed in the line of natural research, protected only for a time by Pope Clement IV., and died soon after 1292. His doctrines are embodied in the *Opus Majus* (ed. by Bridges, Oxford, 1897), and in the form of extracts in his *Opus Minus* (ed. by Brewer, Lond. 1859). Cf. E. Charles, *R. B., sa vie, ses ouvrages, ses doctrines* (Paris, 1861), and K. Werner, in two articles on his psychology, theory of knowledge, and physics (Vienna, 1879).

The most important thinker of the Christian Middle Ages was **Johannes Duns Scotus.** His home (Ireland or Northumberland) and the year of his birth, which was about 1270, are not certainly known. At first a scholar and teacher in Oxford, he then won high reputation at Paris, where he was active after 1304, and in 1308 moved to Cologne, where he died soon after his arrival — all too early. The edition of his works prepared by his Order (12 vols., Lyons, 1639) contains, besides the genuine writings, much that is not genuine or that has been worked over, and especially transcripts of his disputations and lectures. To the latter belongs the so-called *Opus Parisiense,* which forms a commentary upon the *Sentences* of the Lombard. The *Questiones Quodlibetales* have a similar origin. The *Opus Oxoniense,* the original commentary upon the Lombard, is his own writing. Besides this there are his commentaries upon Aristotelian writings and some smaller treatises. His doctrine is expounded in Werner and Stöckl. No exhaustive monograph, corresponding to his importance, exists. Among his numerous adherents, Francis of Mayro, who died 1325, is the best known. The controversy between Thomists and Scotists was a very active one at the beginning of the fourteenth century, and brought many intermediate theories into the field ; but soon both parties had to make common cause in defence against Terminism.

Among the logical school books of the later Scholasticism, the most influential was that of **Petrus Hispanus,** who died 1277 as Pope John XXI. His *Summulæ Logicales* were a translation of a Byzantine-Greek text-book, the Σύνοψις εἰς τὴν Ἀριστοτέλους λογικὴν ἐπιστήμην by Michæl Psellos (in the eleventh century). Imitating the processes in this latter treatise (γράμματα ἔγραψε γραφίδι τεχνικός), the well-known barbarous mnemonic designations for the modes of the syllogism were introduced in the Latin version (*Barbara, celarent,* etc.). Terminism, developed in the nominalistic direction from this rhetorical and grammatical logic, contrasted itself as *logica moderna* with the *logica antiqua* of the Realists, including both Scotists and Thomists under this latter title.

In the renewal of **Nominalism** we find William Durandus of St. Pourçain, who died 1332 as Bishop of Meaux, and Petrus Aureolus, who died at Paris, 1321, the former coming from Thomism, the latter from Scotism. Much more important is **William of Occam,** the Abelard of the second period. With a broad and keen vision for reality, and with a bold, unresting eagerness for innovation, he unites in himself all the elements with the help of which the new science forced its way out of Scholasticism. Born in a village in the County of Surrey, trained under Duns Scotus, he became Professor at Paris, then took an active part in the conflicts of his time between Church and State by joining with Philip the Fair and Lewis of Bavaria in combating the papacy, (*Disputatio inter clericum et militem super potestate ecclesiastica prælatis atque principibus terrarum commissa,* and the *Defensorium* against Pope John XXII.), and died 1347 at Munich. There is no complete edition of his works, but the most important are : *Summa Totius Logices, Expositio Aurea super Artem Veterem, Quodlibeta Septem, Centilogium Theologicum,* and a commentary on Peter Lombard. Cf. W. A. Schreiber, *Die politischen und religiösen Doctrinen unter Ludwig dem Baier* (Landshut, 1858). C. Prantl, *Der Universalienstreit im dreizehnten und vierzehnten Jahrhundert* (*Sitz.-Ber. der Münchener Akad.,* 1874). Occam, too, still waits his philosophically competent biographer.

Of the supporters of terministic Nominalism in the fourteenth century, Johannes Buridan, Rector of the University at Paris, and co-founder of that at Vienna, and Marsilius of Inghen, one of the first teachers at Heidelberg, are usually named. A union of mystical doctrines with the nominalistic rejection of metaphysics is found in Pierre d'Ailly (Petrus de Alliaco, 1350–1425), and in Johannes Gerson (Charlier, 1363–1429).

The attempt at a purely rational exposition of Church doctrine in the interest of apologetics and propagation was made by **Raymundus Lullus** of Catalonia (1235–1315), who is principally known by his curious discovery of the "Great Art," that is, a mechanical device which by combining the fundamental concepts was intended to present the system of all possible cognitions. An extract from this may be found in J. E. Erdmann, *History of Phil.,* I. § 206 [Eng. tr. ed. by Hough]. His efforts were repeated in the fifteenth century by **Raymund of Sabunde,** a Spanish physician, who taught in Toulouse and gained respect by his *Theologia Naturalis* (*sive Liber Creaturarum*). On him cf. D. Matzke (Breslau, 1846); M. Huttler (Augsburg, 1851).

The philosophy of **Nicolaus Cusanus** (Nicolaus Chrypffs, born in Kues (Cusa) near Trier, 1401, died as Cardinal and Bishop of Brixen, 1464), offers an interesting comprehensive view of the intellectual condition of the departing Middle Ages. The main treatise bears the title *De Docta Ignorantia* (ed. in German together with his other most important writings by F. A. Scharpff, Freiburg i. B. 1862). Cf. R. Falckenberg, *Grundzüge der Philos. des N. v. C.* (Breslau, 1880).

Brief Survey of the Arabian and Jewish Philosophy of the Middle Ages.

This period is certainly more interesting from a literary and historical point of view than from that of philosophy, and as yet no competent presentation of the period as a whole has been made. Nor has complete clearness been attained as yet by investigation, but from the literature concerning it the following are to be emphasised : —

Mohammed al Schahrestani, *History of Religious and Philosophical Sects among the Arabs* (German by Haarbrücker, Halle, 1850 f.); A Schmölders, *Documenta Philosophiæ Arabum* (Bonn, 1836), and *Essai sur les Écoles Philosophiques chez les Ar.* (Paris, 1842); Fr. Dieterici, *Die Philosophie der Ar. im zehnten Jahrhundert* (8 Hefte, Leips. 1865–76). Cf. also Hammer-Purgstall, *Gesch. der arabischen Litteratur.*

S. Munk, *Mélanges de philosophie juive et arabe* (Paris, 1859), and the same author's articles on the individual philosophers in the *Dictionnaire des Sciences Philosophiques.* [W. Wallace, Art. *Arabian Phil.* in *Enc. Brit.*, Ueberweg, Erdmann.]

M. Eisler, *Vorlesungen über die jüdischen Philosophen des Mittelalters* (3 vols., Vienna, 1870–84); M. Joël, *Beiträge zur Geschichte der Philosophie* (Breslau, 1876). Cf. also Fürst's *Bibliotheca Judaica*, and histories of Judaism by Graetz and Geiger.

Close as the relations may be which the philosophy of the two civilised Semitic peoples sustained to their religious interests, **Arabian science** especially owes its peculiar character to the circumstance that its founders and supporters were, for the most part, not members of the clergy, as in the West, but *physicians* (cf. F. Wüstenfeld, *Gesch. der arab. Aerzte und Naturforscher*, Göttingen, 1840). Thus from the beginning the study of ancient medicine and natural science went on hand in hand with that of philosophy. Hippocrates and Galen were as much translated (in part through the medium of the Syrian) and read as were Plato, Aristotle, and the Neo-Platonists. Hence in Arabian metaphysics dialectic is always balanced by natural philosophy. But well as this was adapted to afford scientific thought a broader basis of knowledge of facts, we must not, on the other hand, overestimate the independent achievements of the Arabs in medicine and natural science. Here, too, mediæval science is essentially learned tradition. The knowledge which the Arabs were later able to deliver to the West had its origin, in the main, in the books of the Greeks. Nor did even experimental knowledge experience an essential extension through the Arabs' own work ; only in some fields, as, for example, chemistry and mineralogy and in some parts of medicine, *e.g.* physiology, do they appear more independent. In their method, however, in their principles by which they apprehend the universe, and in their entire system of philosophical conceptions, they stand, so far as our information on the subject reaches, entirely under the combined influence of Aristotelianism and Neo-Platonism ; and the same is true of the Jews. Nor can it be maintained that a national peculiarity becomes disclosed in their appropriation of this material. It is rather the case that this whole scientific culture was artificially grafted upon the Arabian civilisation, it can strike no true roots into it, and after a short period of bloom it withers away without vital force. In the history of science as a whole, its mission is only to give back in part to the development of the Western mind the continuity which the latter had itself temporarily lost.

From the nature of the case, the appropriation of ancient science in this case also was completed gradually and by working backward. Beginning with the Neo-Platonism which was still current in Syrian tradition, and which was received with sympathy on account of its religious colouring, the Arabian thinkers proceeded to ascend to the better sources ; but the consequence remained that they saw Aristotle and Plato through the spectacles of Plotinus and Proclus. During the rule of the Abassidæ an active scientific life prevailed in Bagdad, stimulated especially by the Caliph Almamun at the beginning of the ninth century. The Neo-Platonists, the better commentators, almost the entire didactic writings of Aristotle, and the *Republic, Laws*, and *Timæus* of Plato, were known in translations.

The first distinctly emerging personalities, Alkendi, who died about 870, and Alfarabi, who died 950, are scarcely to be distinguished in their teachings from the Neo-Platonic elucidators of Aristotle. A greater importance belongs to **Avicenna** (Ibn Sina, 980–1037), whose "Canon" became the fundamental book of mediæval medicine in the West, as well as in the East, and who also exercised a powerful influence by his extremely numerous philosophical writings, especially his *Metaphysics* and *Logic*. His doctrine comes nearer again to pure Aristotelianism, and perhaps the nearest among all the Arabians.

But the extension of these philosophical views was regarded with jealous eyes by Mohammedan orthodoxy, and the scientific movement experienced so violent persecutions in the tenth century that it took refuge in the secret league of the "Pure Brothers." Avicenna himself was also persecuted. The above-named league embodied the extremely excellent compass of the knowledge of the time in a number of treatises (on this see above, Dieterici), which nevertheless, in contrast with Avicenna, seem to show a stronger leaning toward Neo-Platonism.

Of the scientific achievements of their opponents we know on the one hand the strange metaphysics of the orthodox Motekallemin, who, as against the Aristotelian and Neo-Platonic view of Nature as a living whole, developed an extreme exaggeration of the sole causality of God, and resorted to a distorted Atomism in the greatest metaphysical embarrassment; on the other hand, in the writings of Algazel (1059–1111, *Destructio Philosophorum*) there appears a sceptical and mystical analysis of philosophy.

These latter tendencies won the victory in the Orient the more readily, as the spiritual exaltation of Mohammedanism quickly declined in that quarter. The continuance of Arabian science is to be sought in Andalusia, where Mohammedan civilisation found its short after-bloom. Here, under freer conditions, philosophy developed to vigorous naturalism, which in turn bore a strongly Neo-Platonic stamp.

A characteristic exposition of the doctrine of knowledge in this philosophy is found in the *Conduct of the Solitary* by Avempace, who died 1138, and similar thoughts culminate with Abubacer (Ibn Tophail, died 1185) in an interesting comparison of natural with positive religion. The latter author's philosophical romance *The Living One, the Son of the Waking One*, which sets forth the intellectual development of a man upon a lonely island, excluded from all historical and social relations, was published in a Latin translation by Pocock as *Philosophus Autodidactus* (Oxford, 1671 and 1700, — not twenty years before the appearance of Defoe's *Robinson Crusoe!*) and in a German translation as *Der Naturmensch* by Eichhorn (Berlin, 1783).

But the most important and independent among Arabian thinkers was **Averroës**, who was born 1126 in Cordova, was for a time judge, and then physician in ordinary to the Caliph, was driven afterward by religious persecution to Morocco, and died in 1198. He treated in paraphrases and longer or shorter commentaries, which were printed in the older editions of Aristotle, almost all the didactic writings of Aristotle, who was esteemed by him as the highest teacher of truth. Of his own works (Venice, 1553; some exist now only in the Hebrew version) the refutation of Algazel, *Destructio Destructionis*, is most important. Two of his treatises on the relation of philosophy and theology have been published in German translation by M. J. Müller (Munich, 1875). Cf. E. Renan, *Averroès et l'Averroisme* (3d ed., Paris, 1869).

With the expulsion of the Arabians from Spain traces of their philosophical activity are lost.

Jewish philosophy of the Middle Ages is, in the main, an accompaniment of the Arabian, and dependent upon it. The only exception to this is the Cabbala, that fantastic secret doctrine whose fundamental outlines, which, to be sure, were later much elaborated, show the same peculiar amalgamation of Oriental mythology with ideas of Hellenistic science as does Christian Gnosticism, and go back to the same period and to the same agitated condition of thought attendant upon the mingling of religions. Cf. A. Franck, *Système de la Kabbale* (Paris, 1842; German by Jellinek, Leips. 1844); H. Joël, *Die Religionsphilosophie des Sohar* (Leips. 1849). On the other hand, the main works of Jewish philosophy were originally written in Arabic, and not translated into Hebrew until a relatively late time.

The book of Saadjah Fajjumi (died 942), *Concerning Religions and Philosophies*, which aims to furnish an apology for Jewish doctrine, is related to the earliest Arabian Aristotelianism, and still more closely to the free-thinking Mohammedan theologians, the so-called Mutazilin. In the Neo-Platonic line we meet Avicebron (Ibn Gebirol, a Spanish Jew of the eleventh century), of whose *Fons Vitæ*, Hebrew and Latin versions are extant. **Moses Maimonides** (1135–1204) is regarded as the most important Jewish philosopher of the Middle Ages. In his culture and doctrine he belongs to the phase of Arabian doctrine which has Averroës as its centre. His main treatise, *Guide to the Perplexed* (*Doctor Perplexorum*), has been published in Arabic and French with a commentary by Munk (3 vols., Paris, 1856–66) [Eng. tr. by Friedlander, Trübner, Lond.]. The attachment to Averroës is still closer in the case of Gersonides (Levi ben Gerson, 1288–1344).

The Jews, by means of their widely extended mercantile relations, were the chief contributors to the extension of Oriental philosophy in the West, by sale and translation ; in the thirteenth and fourteenth centuries especially their schools in Southern France formed the medium for this wide-reaching activity.

To the Arabian and Jewish literature, which was taken up by Christian science about 1200, belongs finally a number of *pseudonymous* and *anonymous* writings, which arose in the latest periods of Neo-Platonism, and in part perhaps were of still later date. Among these the principal are the *Theology of Aristotle* (Arabic and German by Dieterici, Leips. 1882–83), and the *Liber de Causis* (*De essentia puræ bonitatis*), an extract from the στοιχείωσις θεολογική ascribed to Proclus, published in Arabic, Latin. and German by O. Bardenhewer (Freiburg i. B. 1882).

§ 25. The Realm of Nature and the Realm of Grace.

Among all the philosphers of the Middle Ages we find existing, with greater or less clearness, a lively feeling of the twofold tradition which forms the presupposition of their thought. In the earlier period all knowledge and thought had arranged itself, as it were, of its own accord within the system of religious metaphysics; and now there appeared by the side of this a powerful, finely articulated, coherent body of thought which the age, thirsting after real contents in its barren dialectic, was ready to take up eagerly. The manifold relations between these two systems which mutually laid hold upon one another and interpenetrated, determine the scientific character of the last centuries of the Middle Ages, and the general course of the development was, that these antagonistic systems, starting from an attitude of abrupt opposition, strove toward reconciliation and adjustment, only to diverge all the more violently after the goal seemed to have been reached. This course of things appeared as necessarily in the conception of the reciprocal relations of the different sciences, as in the view of the ultimate relations of things. In both lines the attempt at synthesis was followed by a separation that went all the deeper.

The religious thought of the West, whose highest problem had been to understand the working of divine grace, was confronted by Oriental philosophy in which the old Grecian philosophical tendency toward knowledge of Nature had at last attained metaphysical sup*r*emacy: and here, too, again the process of appropriation began with the adoption of the last consequences, to ascend only by degrees back to the premises.

1. Hence the form in which Arabian science was first taken up was that of *Averroism*. In this, however, science had marked off its boundaries in the most definite manner as against positive religion. This had taken place not only in reaction against the attacks to which the philosophical movement in the East had been subjected, but still more in consequence of the great mental revolutions which the age of the *Crusades* experienced through the intimate contact of the three monotheistic religions. The more ardently these religions fought in the sphere of historical reality, the more the sharpness of their contrasting doctrines became blunted from the point of view of theory. Those who passed through this conflict of religions as thinking observers could not resist the impulse to seek the common element behind the differences, and to establish above the fields of battle the idea of a universal religion.[1] In order to attain this, every form of special historical revelation must be stripped off, and the path of universally valid scientific knowledge must be taken. So with the aid of Neo-Platonic memories, a return was made to the thought of a universal religion, founded upon science, and the ultimate content of this common conviction was formed by the moral law. As Abelard in his own way had already reached this result, so Roger Bacon later, under Arabian influences, designated morality as the content of the universal religion.

This scientific natural religion, however, had had stamped upon it more and more by the Arabs the exclusive character of an *esoteric* doctrine. The distinction originating with Philo, and current in the entire patristic thought, between a verbal-historical and a spiritually timeless sense[2] of religious documents (cf. § 18, 2) here became the doctrine that positive religion is an indispensable need for the mass of the people, while the man of science seeks the real truth back of religion, and seeks it only there, — a doctrine in which Averroës and Maimonides were at one, and which completely corresponded to the social relations of Arabian science. For Arabian science always moved within narrow and closed circles, and as a foreign growth

---

[1] The court of the highly cultured Hohenstaufen Frederick II. in Sicily appears as a chief seat of this mode of thought, and in general of the exchange of thought between East and West.

[2] Representing this opinion, the *Eternal Gospel* of Joachim of Floris was circulated among the Averroistic Amalricans. This completed for the entire compass of Christian dogma, the transformation of everything external into the internal, all the historical into the timelessly valid: the "pneumatic gospel" of Origen (cf. § 18, 2) was asserted to have here attained reality, the period of the "spirit" to have begun. Cf. J. N. Schneider (Dillingen, 1874).

never gained true sympathy with the mass of the people: Averroës, nevertheless, expressly honours Aristotle as the founder of this high-est, most universal religion of the human race.

Thus in line with this thought, Abubacer made his *" Man in a State of Nature,"* who had attained in his isolation to the philosoph-ical knowledge of God, come into contact again at last with histori-cal humanity, and in so doing discover that what he had known clearly and in abstract thought, is here believed in its picturate wrappings, and that what holds for him as a self-evident demand of the reason is here extorted from the multitude by means of reward and punishment.

If now it is hereby admitted that *natural* and *revealed religion* have ultimately the same content, it still follows that they necessa-rily differ, at least in their expression of the common truth, — that the conceptions which form the expression of philosophical religion are not understood by believers, whiie the picturate ideas of believ-ers are not regarded as the full truth by philosophers. If, then, by theology, we understand the exposition of the positive doctrine of religion, arranged and defended according to the formal laws of science, *i.e.* Aristotelian logic, — and this was the form which the relation of theology to religion had taken in the West as in the East, — it follows that something may be true theologically which is not true philosophically, and *vice versa.* Thus is explained that *doctrine of the twofold truth,*[1] theological and philosophical, which went through the entire later Middle Ages, although we cannot exactly fix the authorship of this formula.[2] It is the adequate expression of the mental state necessarily brought about by the opposition of the two authorities under which the Middle Ages stood, viz. Hellenistic science and religious tradition; and while at a later time it often served to protect scientific theories from the persecution of the Church, it was for the most part, even in these cases, the honest expression of the inner discord in which just the most important minds of the age found themselves.

2. The science of the Christian peoples accepted this antithesis, and while the doctrine of the twofold truth was expressly pro-claimed by bold aialecticians such as Simon of Tournay, or John of Brescia, and was all the more rigidly condemned by the power of

---

[1] Cf. M. Maywald, *Die Lehre von der zweifachen Wahrheit* (Berlin, 1871).

[2] As little can it be fixed with certainty what the origin of that widely ex tended formula was, which designated the founders of the three great positive religions as the three "deceivers" of mankind. Unhistorical, as is every Enlightenment, the philosophical opposition of that day could explain to itself only by empirical interests the mythical which could not stand before compara-tive criticism.

the Church, the leading minds could not evade the fact that philosophy, as it had been developed under the influence of Aristotle and the Arabians, was, and must remain, in its inner nature, alien to precisely those doctrines of the Christian religion which were specific and distinctive. With a full consciousness of this opposition, *Albert* proceeded to his great task. He understood that the *distinction between natural and revealed religion*, which he found in existence, could no longer be put out of sight, that philosophy and theology could no longer be identified, but he hoped and laboured with all his strength that this distinction might not be allowed to become a contradiction. He abandoned the doctrine that the "mysteries" of theology, the doctrines of the Trinity and of the Incarnation, can be made rational, and, on the other hand, he corrected in favour of the Church doctrine the teaching of the "Philosopher" on such important points as the question concerning the eternity or temporal duration of the world. He sought to show that all which is known in philosophy by the *"natural light"* (*lumine naturali*) holds good also in theology, but that the human soul can know completely only that, the principles of which it carries within itself, and that, therefore, in such questions as those in which philosophical knowledge comes to no finally valid decision and must remain standing before the antinomy of different possibilities, revelation gives the decision, — a view in which Albert follows mainly the results of Maimonides. Faith is meritorious just because it cannot be proved or established by any natural insight. Revelation is above reason, but not contrary to reason.

This standpoint for harmonising natural and revealed theology is essentially that taken by *Thomas*, although he seeks to limit still more, if possible, the extent of that which is to be withdrawn from philosophical insight and given into the possession of faith. According to the fundamental thoughts of his system, moreover, he apprehends this relation as a relation of different stages of development, and sees accordingly, in philosophical knowledge, a possibility given in man's natural endowment, which is brought to full and entire realisation only by the grace active in revelation.

It is therefore important to notice that Scholasticism, just in this its highest point, was far from identifying philosophy and theology, or from making the task of the former, as has often been represented, an unresting comprehension of dogma. This conception belongs to the beginnings of mediæval science, *e.g.* to Anselm, and is found sporadically in the times when Scholasticism was entering upon its dissolution. So, for example, Raymundus Lullus projected his "Great Art"[1] essentially in the opinion that this, by making possible a systematic explanation of all truths, will be adapted to convince all "unbelievers" of the truth of the Christian religion. So, too, later, Raymond of Sabunde aimed to prove with the help of Lull's Art that if God has revealed himself in a double manner, in the Bible (*liber scriptus*) and in Nature (*liber vivus*), the contents of these two revelations, of which the one lies at the basis of theology, the other at the basis of philosophy, must evidently be the same. But in the classical time of Scholasticism the distinction between natural and revealed theology was always kept in mind, and was drawn the more sharply, the more the Church had occasion to guard against the confusion of its doctrine with "natural theology."

3. Hence there were very faithful sons of the Church who broadened again the cleft between philosophy and theology, and ultimately made it so wide that it could not be bridged. At their head stands *Duns Scotus*, who taught that theology should be conceived and treated only as a practical discipline; philosophy, on the contrary, as pure theory. Hence for him and for the continuers of his doctrine, the relation between the two is no longer that of supplementation, but that of separation. Between the two opposing territories of revelation and of rational knowledge, natural theology shrivels into an extreme poverty of domain. The compass of the mysteries of theology that are inaccessible for natural knowledge increases more and more; with Duns Scotus the beginning of the created world in time and the immortality of the human soul belong to this sphere; and Occam even denies the cogency of the usual arguments with which rational theology was wont to prove the existence of God.

This criticism is rooted essentially in the purpose to assure to faith its just right, and in this purpose it is completely honest. In connection with the metaphysical dualism which had again become pronounced (see below, No. 5) the knowledge of the understanding, bound as it was to sense-perception, seemed incapable of searching

---

[1] This wrong-headed, and yet in many respects interesting and therefore frequently attempted, discovery, consisted in a system of concentric rings, each of which bore a group of concepts divided into circular compartments. By shifting these rings, all possible combinations between concepts were to be brought about, problems given, and their solutions stated. Thus there was a Figura A (Dei) which contained the whole theology, a Figura Animæ which contained psychology, etc. Mnemo-technic attempts, and such as aim at the discovery of a universal language, or of a system of symbols for expressing philosophical thoughts, have frequently been attached to this *ars combinatoria*. The introduction of the algebraic method of reckoning by letters is also connected with these efforts.

the mysteries of the supernatural world. Thus men like Gerson based their mystical doctrine precisely upon Nominalism. The difference between philosophy and theology is necessary; the contradiction between knowledge and faith is unavoidable. Revelation has its source in grace, and has the divine realm of grace for its content; rational knowledge is a natural process of reciprocal interaction between the knowing mind and the objects of perception. Therefore, though Nominalism escaped from the scholastic method with difficulty, and was late in reaching its goal, it necessarily ended in regarding Nature as the sole object of science. At all events, philosophy now set itself as *secular science,* over against theology as divine science.

So Duns Scotus and Occam employed language which externally is quite in harmony with the "twofold truth." That definition of the boundaries was intended to assert, that in matters of faith dialectic has nothing to say. But it could not fail to be the result, that in the case of others, this separation would lead to the opposite consequence and back to the original meaning of the claim of a double truth. It became a charter of liberty for the "secular philosophy." Dialectical investigation could be pursued even to the boldest propositions, and yet all offence might be avoided if one only added that the proposition was so *secundum rationem,* but that *secundum fidem* the opposite was of course true. This occurred so frequently that the Thomists and Lullists became zealous against it. In the case of many, to be sure, who availed themselves of this principle, we cannot doubt that this was their honest opinion; but it is just as sure that others, with full consciousness of their procedure, found in this only a convenient pretext, in order to present under the protection of this restriction the doctrines of a philosophy that in its inner spirit was at variance with faith. At all events, this applies to the school of the Averroists which flourished in Padua toward the end of the fifteenth century.

4. Parallel to this changeful process of transformation in the relation between theology and philosophy, and in closest connection with it, goes an analogous development of *metaphysical psychology,* and both have reference in like measure to the fundamental relation between the supersensuous and the sensuous worlds. Here, too, dualism is the starting-point, and afterwards again the end. This dualism had been developed to an especial degree of sharpness by the Victorines at the close of the first period. In this Mysticism the last bonds between body and soul were cut, and reconciliation was made impossible. The spiritual and material worlds fell apart as separate spheres of the universal reality.

Now, however, Aristotelianism fulfilled its historical mission of overcoming the two-worlds theory in Augustine, as formerly in Plato, and in the *Thomist psychology* the conception of *development*, and of the gradual building up of phenomena, was intended to bridge that separation. While Hugo of St. Victor had drawn the dividing line in the created world through the midst of man's nature, by emphasising the complete impossibility of any comparison between the two substances there brought together, the human soul was now to be understood as just that connecting link, through the medium of which the two worlds come into organic interaction in the one course of development of all things.

Thomas attains this result by an extraordinarily acute transformation of the Aristotelian doctrine of Forms and their relation to matter. The material and the immaterial worlds are characterised by the fact that, in the latter, pure Forms (*formæ separatæ;* called also subsistent Forms) are real or actual as active intelligences without any attachment to matter, while in the former, Forms realise themselves only in union with matter (inherent Forms). The human soul, as lowest of the pure intelligences, is a *forma separata* (on which rests its immortality) and, at the same time, as entelechy of the body, it is the highest of those Forms which realise themselves in matter. But these two sides of its nature are bound together in it to an absolute substantial unity, and this unity is the only Form which is at the same time subsistent and inherent.[1] In this way the series of individual beings proceeds from the lowest Forms of material existence, on past plant and animal life, *through the human soul*, with uninterrupted continuity over into the world of pure intelligences — the angels,[2] and finally to the absolute Form — the deity. The cleft between the two worlds is closed in Thomism by this central position of metaphysical psychology.

5. But it seemed to the following period that the cleft was closed only by being plastered over, as it were, and that the union of so heterogeneous attributes as the entelechy of the body and the subsistence of a pure intelligence was more of a load than the conception of individual substance was able to bear. Hence *Duns Scotus*, whose metaphysics likewise moves naturally within the Aristotelian terminology, introduced an (inherent) *forma corporeitatis* between the intelligent soul, which he too designates as the "essential Form" of the body, and the body itself; and thus the

---

[1] In this is concentrated in a conception the *anthropocentric* way of viewing the world, which even Thomism did not overcome.

[2] Thomas constructs his scale of forms in the material world according to Aristotle, in the spiritual world according to Dionysius the Areopagite.

Augustinian and Victorinian separation of the conscious essence from the physiological vital force was again re-established.

Occam not only made this distinction his own, but, forced to insert another gradation, analysed the conscious soul into an intellectual and a sensitive part, and ascribed real importance to this separation. It seems to him that the sensuous activities of consciousness can as little be united with the rational nature whose vocation it is to behold the immaterial world, as can the form and motion of the body. Thus for him the soul is split up into a number of individual faculties, to determine the relation of which occasions great difficulties, especially with regard to their spatial inter-relation.

6. The essential thing in this is that the world of consciousness and that of corporeal bodies become again completely separated; and this is shown especially in Occam's theory of knowledge, which proceeded from these presuppositions to an extremely significant innovation.

In their doctrine of the " *species intelligibiles* " the two "Realists," Thomas and Duns Scotus, had alike followed, though with some variations, the old Greek idea, that in the knowing process, by means of the co-operation of the soul and of the external object, a copy of the latter arises, which is then apprehended and beheld by the soul. Occam strikes out these *species intelligibiles* as a useless doubling[1] of the external reality, which according to this view, in so far as it is an object of knowledge, would be assumed as having still another existence (in psychical reality). But by this act *sensuous knowledge loses for him its character of being a copy* as compared with its object. An idea (*conceptus, intellectio rei*) is as such a state or an act of the soul (*passio — intentio animæ*), and forms in this a *sign* (*signum*) for the corresponding external thing. But this inner structure is something of a different nature from the outer reality of which it is the sign, and therefore it is no copy of it. We can speak of a " resemblance " only in so far as in this case the inner reality (*esse objective = content of consciousness*) and the outer reality (*esse formaliter* or *subjective =* objective reality in the present sense of the word "objective" [2]) necessarily relate to each other, and, so to speak, form corresponding points in the two heterogeneous spheres.

Thus the beginning of a psychological and epistemological *idealism*

---

[1] According to his methodical principle : *entia præter necessitatem non esse multiplicanda.*

[2] The terms "objective" and "subjective" in the Middle Ages have accordingly a meaning exactly the reverse of that which they have in present usage.

develops among the Terminists out of the old duality of mind
and body: the world of consciousness is another world than the
world of things. What is found in the former is not a copy, but
only a sign for something without which corresponds to it. Things
are other than our ideas (*ideæ*) of them.

7. Lastly, Augustine's dualism appeared in its complete bald-
ness in his conception of *history*. The realm of God and that of the
devil, the Church and the political state, here confronted each other
in rigid antithesis. The historical conditions of which this doctrine
was the reflex, had become changed completely since Augustine's
day. But hitherto the Middle Ages had not only lacked historical
conceptions which would have been adapted to correct this doctrine,
but scientific thought had been employed in such a one-sidedly theological and dialectical manner, that ethical and social problems had
remained farther outside the horizon of philosophers than had physical problems. And yet at the same time, history was seeing movements of such grand dimensions that science also must necessarily
take a position with regard to it. If she was able to do this in the
second period in a manner completely worthy of the greatness of
the subject, she owed her strength for this again to the Aristotelian
system, which gave the means into her hand of mastering in thought
the great connected structures of political and historical life, of
arranging in her metaphysics these forms of the series of development, and thus of putting into conceptions the mighty import of
that which she was living through. Indeed, in this line in which
the Arabian commentators had not gone before lies the most brilliant
achievement of mediæval philosophy,[1] and since Albert's interest lay
more on the side of physics, the chief credit here falls to *Thomas*.

Thomas regards the political state, not as did Augustine, as a consequence of the fall, but as a necessary member in the world's life.
In his view, therefore, law or right also flows from the divine nature
and must be so conceived; above all human institutions stands the
lex naturalis, upon which rest morality and the life of society. In
particular, however, as is proved by language, by the need of help
which the individual feels, and by the impulse toward society, man
is by his nature destined for life in a state. The end of the state is,
according to Aristotle's teaching, to realise virtue, and from this end
all the characteristics of the state are to be developed (in philosophical law — *Natural Right* or *Law*). But — and here the new thought
begins — that civic virtue to which the state should educate its
citizens does not exhaust man's destiny. In this he fulfils only his

---

[1] Cf. W. Dilthey, *Einleitung in die Geisteswissenschaften*, I. 418 f.

purpose as an earthly being; his higher destiny is the salvation which *grace* offers him in the community of the Church. But as the higher everywhere realises itself through the lower, and the lower exists for the sake of the higher, the political community is to be the preparation for that higher community of the State of God. Thus the state becomes subordinate to the Church as the means to the end, as the preparatory to the complete. The community of the earthly life is the school for that of the heavenly — PRÆAMBULA GRATIÆ.

By the side of the *teleology of Nature* which Greek philosophy had worked out, patristic thought had set the *teleology of history* (cf. § 21, 6); but the two had remained unconnected. The doctrine of the state set forth by Thomas subordinates the one to the other in a system of thought, and in so doing completes the most deeply and widely reaching union of the ancient and Christian conceptions of the world that has ever been attempted.

With this the capstone is fitted to the metaphysical structure of Thomism. By this transition from the community of Nature into that of grace, man fulfils the task which his position in the universe assigns him, but he fulfils it, not as an individual, but only in the race. The ancient thought of the state lives again in Christianity; but the state is no longer an end in itself, it is the best means for carrying out the divine world-plan. *Gratia naturam non tollit sed perficit.*

8. But even this highest synthesis did not long endure. As in political life, so also in theory, the relation of Church and state took on a form that was very much less harmonious. With *Dante* the relation of subordination is already exchanged for that of co-ordination. The poet shares with the metaphysician the thought that because man's destined end is to be attained only in the race, this makes a perfect unity in political organisation requisite. Both demand the *universal state*, the "*monarchia*" and see in the *Empire* the fulfilment of this postulate. But the great Ghibelline cannot think theocratically, as does the Dominican monk; and where the latter assigns to the *imperium* the place of subordination beneath the *sacerdotium*, the former sets the two over against each other as powers of like authority. God has destined man for earthly and for heavenly happiness *in like measure:* to the former he is conducted by the state, by the natural knowledge of philosophy; to the latter he is guided by the Church, by means of revelation. In this co-ordination the joy in the world, characteristic of the Renaissance, bursts forth as victoriously as does the feeling of strength which belongs to the secular state.

And along this line the development proceeded. When the graded scale of reality constructed by Thomas was severed in the midst of man's nature, the spiritual and political powers fell apart, as did the spiritual and corporeal worlds; and the theory afforded the convenient means of banishing the *sacerdotium* to the supra-mundane inner nature, and putting the *imperium* into sole control within the world of sense. This is precisely the point of view from which *Occam*, in his *Disputatio* with reference to the controversy between the papacy and the temporal power, took his position upon the side of the latter. Nor yet is it any longer possible, in accordance with his presuppositions, to base the theory of the state upon the realistic thought of the human race as a whole, bound together for the realisation of one end. The Nominalist sees as a substantial background in social and historical life, only the individuals who will, and he regards state and society as products of interests (*bonum commune*). In theory, as in life, *individualism* prevails.[1]

§ 26. The Primacy of the Will or of the Intellect.

W. Kahl, *Die Lehre vom Primat des Willens bei Augustinus, Duns Scotus und Descartes.*

In closest connection with all these general questions stands a special psychological problem, which was vigorously discussed throughout this whole period, and in reference to which the points of opposition between the parties of the time may be recognised upon a smaller scale, but all the more sharply focussed. It is the question whether among the powers of the soul the higher dignity belongs to the will or to the intellect (*utra potentia nobilior*). It takes so broad a space in the literature of this period that the attempt might have been made to look upon the psychological antithesis which unfolds in connection with it as the leading motive of the whole period. But the course of the development shows too clearly that the real impelling forces lay in religious metaphysics, and the rigidity of systematic conception which distinguishes the philosophical doctrines of this period explains sufficiently why it is that their position with reference to an individual problem may appear as typical for the different thinkers. It still remains characteristic that this problem is a question taken from the domain of the inner world.

---

[1] This doctrine of Occam's concerning secular power and law is followed out to the extreme consequence of the omnipotence of the state by Occam's friend, *Marsilius of Padua*, whose treatise, *Defensor Pacis* (1346), carries out in rigorous lines the attempt to establish the theory of the state upon the utilitarian and nominalistic basis using the Epicurean theory of compact (above, § 14, 6).

In this question, also, the two main bodies of tradition, Augustinianism and Aristotelianism, were not at one ; but their relation was here in nowise that of an outspoken opposition.   For Augustinianism the question was in general awkwardly stated.   For in this system the oneness of nature in the personality was so strongly emphasised, and the inter-relation of the different sides of its activity was so often made prominent, that a relation of rank in the proper sense was really out of the question.   But on the other hand, especially in his doctrine of knowledge, Augustine had assigned to the will as the impelling power — even in the process of ideation — a position so central that it was not shaken in its importance for empirical facts, even though the Neo-Platonic contemplation of the deity was maintained as the final goal of development.   On the contrary, the intellectualism of the Aristotelian system was quite undoubted, and if it still admitted any increase, it had received it from the Arabian philosophy, especially from Averroism.   Thus antitheses presented themselves which were soon enough to break forth to open controversy.

Thomism in this point, also, followed Aristotle unconditionally, finding at its side in this case the nearly related German Mysticism, and as its opponents the Augustinians, Scotists, and Occamists, so that, as thus grouped, the opposition between the Dominicans and the Franciscans finds general expression.

1.   The question as to the pre-eminence of the will or of the intellect develops at first as a purely psychological controversy, and demands a decision upon the point, whether in the course of the psychical life the dependence of the will's decisions upon ideas, or that of the movements of ideas upon the will, is the greater.   It was therefore adapted to further the beginnings of a treatment of psychology that concerned itself especially with the history of mental development (cf. § 24), and it would have been able to do this in a higher degree than was actually the case if it had not always been transferred to the ground of dialectic or to the metaphysical domain. This latter transfer occurred principally in consequence of the fact that the conception of *freedom*, which always involves ethical and religious questions, was looked upon as the point in controversy. Both parties, indeed, desired to maintain or defend man's "freedom" in the interest of responsibility : but this was possible only as they gave different meanings to the word.

Now, in individual cases, Thomas admits an influence of the will, not only upon motion, but also upon affirmation or denial of ideas. In particular, he recognises absolutely such an influence in belief. But in general he regards the will, quite according to the ancient model, as determined by knowledge of the good. The intellect not only apprehends in general the idea of the good, but also, in each individual case, discerns what is good, and thereby determines the will. The will necessarily strives for that which is known to be good; it is therefore dependent upon the intellect. The latter is the *supremus motor* of the psychical life; "rationality," so said *Eckhart* also, is the head of the soul, and even romantic love (*"Minne"*) clings only to knowledge. Freedom (as ethical ideal) is hence, according to Thomas, that necessity which exists upon the basis of knowledge, and, on the other hand, (psychological) freedom of choice (*facultas electiva*) is nevertheless only possible by reason of the fact that the understanding presents to the will various possibilities as means toward its end, the will then deciding for that which is known to be best, — the view held by Albert also. This *intellectualistic determinism*, in connection with which Thomas himself always insisted that the decision of the will depends only upon purely internal knowing activities, was extended by his contemporary *Gottfried of Fontaine* to the point of making even the sensuous presentation (*phantasma*) the *causa efficiens* of the will's activity.

But the opponents made their attack just in connection with this conception of necessary determination. The rising of ideas, so *Henry of Ghent* had already taught, and after him *Duns Scotus*, and still later *Occam*, is a natural process, and the will becomes unavoidably entangled in this if it is to be completely dependent upon ideas. But with this, said Scotus, contingency (*i.e.* possibility of being otherwise or "power to the contrary") in the will's functions is irreconcilable : for the process of Nature is always determined in one way; where it prevails there is no choice. With contingency, however, responsibility also falls to the ground. Responsibility can therefore be preserved only if it is acknowledged that the intellect exercises no compelling power over the will. To be sure, the co-operation of the ideational faculty is indispensable in the case of every activity of the will : it presents the will its objects and the possibilities of its choice. But it does this only as the servant, and the decision remains with the master. The idea is never more than the occasioning cause (*causa per accidens*) of the individual volition; the doctrine of Thomas confuses practical consideration with pure intellect. If the latter gives the object, the decision is still solely a matter of the will; the will is the *movens per se;* to it belongs absolute self-determination.

Indeterminism, as Scotus and Occam teach it, sees therefore in the will the fundamental power of the soul, and maintains conversely, that as a matter of fact the will on its side determines the development of the intellectual activities. Following the procedure of Henry of Ghent,[1] according to whom the theoretical functions become more active according as they are more immaterial, Scotus attempted to prove the proposition just stated, in a highly interesting manner. The natural process, he says, produces as the first content of consciousness (*cogitatio prima*) a multitude of ideas which are more or less confused (*confusæ — indistinctæ*) and imperfect. Of these only those become distinct (*distincta*) and perfect on which the will, which in this process is determined by nothing further, fixes its attention. Scotus also teaches at the same time that the will strengthens in their *intensity* these ideas which it raises from the confused to the distinct condition, and that the ideas to which the will does not apply itself ultimately cease to exist, on account of their weakness.

In addition to these psychological arguments, we find appearing in the controversy appeals to the authority of Anselm and Aristotle on the one side, and to that of Augustine on the other, and further a series of other arguments. These are in part of a purely dialectical nature. Such is the case when Thomas claims that the *verum* toward which the intellect aims is higher in rank than the *bonum* toward which the will strives, and when Scotus doubts the authority for this gradation; and so again when Thomas expresses the opinion that the intellect apprehends the pure, single conception of the good, while the will is concerned only with the special empirical forms assumed by the good, and when Henry of Ghent and Scotus, exactly reversing this statement, develop the thought that the will is always directed only toward the good as such, while the understanding has to show in what the good consists in a particular case. With such variations the matter was later tossed to and fro a great deal, and Johannes *Buridan* is an example of those who stand undecided between determinism and indeterminism. For the latter view speaks responsibility, for the former the principle that every event is necessarily determined by its conditions.

Other arguments which become interwoven in the controversy trench upon the more general domains of the conceptions of the world and of life.

2. To this class belongs, first of all, the transfer of the question of the relative rank of will and intellect to *God.* The extreme intellectualism of the Arabians had, in Averroës, excluded the faculty of will from the Supreme Being, in accordance with the Aristolelian *motif,* that every act of will implies a want, a state of

---

[1] Whose view in this respect Richard of Middletown also completely adopted.

imperfection and dependence; on the contrary Avicebron, who exercised a strong influence upon Duns Scotus, had defended the religious principle that the world was created by the divine will, and in a similar line of thought *William of Auvergne* had maintained the originality of the will as existing side by side with the intellect in the essence of God and in his creative activity. These antitheses were now continued in the controversy between Thomism and Scotism.

Thomas, indeed, as a matter of course, recognises the reality of the divine will, but he regards it as the necessary consequence of the divine intellect, and as determined in its content by the latter. God creates only what in his wisdom he knows to be good; it is necessarily himself, *i.e.* the ideal content of his intellect, that forms the object of his will; he necessarily wills himself, and in this consists the freedom, determined only by himself, with which he wills individual things. Thus the divine will is bound to the divine wisdom, which is superior to it.

But just in this the opponents of Aquinas see a limitation of omnipotence which does not comport with the conception of the *ens realissimum.* A will seems to them sovereign, only if there is for it no kind of determination or restriction. God created the world, according to Scotus, solely from absolute arbitrary will; he might have created it, if he had so willed, in other forms, relations, and conditions; and beyond this his completely undetermined will, there are no causes. The will of God with its undetermined creative resolves is the original fact of all reality, and no further questions must be asked as to its grounds, — even as the decision made by the will of a finite being with its *liberum arbitrium indifferentiæ,* when placed before given possibilities, creates in every instance a new fact which cannot be understood as necessary.

3. The sharpest formulation of this antithesis comes to light in the fundamental metaphysical principles of *ethics.* On both sides the moral law is naturally regarded as God's command. But Thomas teaches that God commands the good because it is good, and is recognised as good by his wisdom; Scotus maintains that it is good only because God has willed and commanded it, and Occam adds to this that God might have fixed something else, might have fixed even the opposite as the content of the moral law. For Thomas, therefore, goodness is the necessary consequence and manifestation of the divine wisdom, and Eckhart also says that "beneath the garment of goodness" the essential nature of God is veiled; intellectualism teaches the *perseïtas boni,* the *rationalty of the good.* For intellectualism, morals is a philosophical discipline

whose principles are to be known by the "natural light." "Conscience" (*synteresis*[1]) is a knowledge of God *sub ratione boni*. With Scotus and Occam, on the contrary, the good cannot be an object of natural knowledge, for it might have been otherwise than it is; it is determined not by reason, but by groundless will. Nothing, so Pierre d'Ailly teaches with extreme consistency, is in itself, or *per se*, sin; it is only the divine command and prohibition which make anything such, — a doctrine whose range is understood when we reflect that, according to the view of these men, God's command becomes known to man only through the mouth of the Church.

It is also closely connected with this that theology, which for Thomas still remained a "speculative" science, became with his opponents, as has been already indicated above (§ 25, 3), a "practical" discipline. Albert had already made intimations of this sort, Richard of Middletown and Bonaventura had emphasised the fact that theology deals with the emotions; Roger Bacon had taught that while all other sciences are based on reason or experience, theology alone has for its foundation the authority of the divine will: Duns Scotus completed and fixed the separation between theology and philosophy by making it a necessary consequence of his metaphysics of the will.

4. The same contrast becomes disclosed with like distinctness in the doctrines of the final destiny of man, of his state in eternal blessedness. The ancient θεωρία, the contemplation of the divine majesty, free from will and from want, had in Augustine's teaching formed the ideal state of the pardoned and glorified man, and this ideal had been made to waver but little by the doctrines of the earlier Mystics. Now it found new support in the Aristotelian intellectualism, in accordance with which *Albert* thought that man, in so far as he is truly man, is intellect. The participation in the divine being which man attains by knowledge is the highest stage of life which he can reach. On this account Thomas, too, sets the dianoëtic virtues above the practical, on this account the *visio divinæ essentiæ*, the intuitive, eternal vision of God, which is removed beyond all that is temporal, is for him the goal of all human striving. From this vision follows *eo ipso* the love of God, just as every determinate

---

[1] This word (written also *sinderesis, scinderesis*) has, since Albert of Bollstädt, occasioned much etymological cudgelling of brains. Since, however, among the later physicians of antiquity (Sext. Emp.) τήρησις appears as a technical term for "observation," it may be that συντήρησις, which is attested in the fourth century, originally signified "self-observation" in analogy with the Neo-Platonic usage in συναίσθησις or συνείδησις (cf. p. 234), and thus took on the ethico-religious sense of "conscience" (*conscientia*).

state of the will is necessarily attached to the corresponding state of the intellect. Just this tendency of Thomism was given its most beautiful expression by Dante, the poet of the system. Beatrice is the poetic embodiment of this ideal, for all time.

Meanwhile a counter-current manifests its force on this point also. Hugo of St. Victor had characterised the supreme angel choir by love, and the second by wisdom; and while Bonaventura regarded contemplation as the highest stage in the imitation of Christ, he emphasised expressly the fact that this contemplation is identical with "love." Duns Scotus, however, taught with a decided polemical tendency that blessedness is a state of the will, and that, too, of the will directed toward God alone; he sees man's last glorification, not in contemplation, but in love, which is superior to contemplation, and he appeals to the word of the Apostle, "The greatest of these is love."

Hence as Thomas regarded the intellect, and Duns Scotus the will, as the decisive and determining element of man's nature, Thomas could hold fast to Augustine's doctrine of the *gratia irresistibilis*, according to which revelation determines irresistibly the intellect and with it the will of man, while Duns Scotus found himself forced to the "synergistic" view, that the reception of the operation of divine grace is to a certain extent conditioned by the free will of the individual. So the great successor of Augustine, with strict logical consistency, decided against the Augustinian doctrine of predestination.

5. On the other hand, the intellectualism of Thomas develops its extreme consequences in *German Mysticism*, whose founder, Eckhart, is entirely dependent upon the teacher of his Order in the conceptional outlines of his doctrine.[1] Eckhart goes far beyond his master only in the one respect that as a much more original personality he is unwearied in his effort to translate the deep and mighty feeling of his piety into knowledge, and thus urged on by his inner nature he breaks through the statutory restrictions before which Thomas had halted. Convinced that the view of the world given in the religious consciousness must be capable of being made also the content of the highest knowledge, he sublimates his pious faith to a speculative knowledge, and in contrast with the pure spirituality of this he looks upon the Church dogma as only the external, temporal symbol. But while this tendency is one that he shares with many

---

[1] Cf. S. Denifle in the *Archiv für Litterat.- u. Kult.-Gesch. d. M.-A.*, II. 417 ff. So far, therefore, as Eckhart was really to be the "Father of German speculation," this speculation had its source in Thomas Aquinas and his teacher Albert

other systems, it is his peculiarity that he does not wish to have the inmost and truest truth kept as the privilege of an exclusive circle, but desires rather to communicate it to all people. He believes that the right understanding for this deepest essence of religious doctrine is to be found precisely in connection with simple piety,[1] and so he throws down from the pulpit among the people the finest conceptions constructed by science. With a mastery of language that marks the genius he coins Scholasticism into impressive preaching, and creates for his nation the beginnings of its philosophical modes of expression,—beginnings which were of determining influence for the future.

But in his teaching the combined mystical and intellectualistic elements of Thomism become intensified by the Neo-Platonic idealism, which had probably reached him through the medium of Scotus Erigena, to the last logical consequence. *Being and knowledge are one*, and all that takes place in the world is in its deepest essence a knowing process. The procedure of the world forth out of God is a process of knowledge, of self-revelation,—the return of things into God is a process of knowledge, of higher and higher intuition. The ideal existence of all that is real—so at a later time said Nicolaus Cusanus, who made this doctrine of Eckhart's his own—is truer than the corporeal existence which appears in space and time.

The original ground of all things, the deity, must therefore lie beyond Being and knowledge;[2] it is above reason, above Being; it has no determination or quality, it is "Nothing." But this "deity" (of negative theology) reveals itself in the triune God,[3] and the God who is and knows creates out of nothing the creatures whose Ideas he knows within himself; for this knowing is his creating. This process of self-revelation belongs to the essence of the deity; it is hence a timeless necessity, and no act of will in the proper sense of the word is required for God to produce the world. The deity, as productive or generative essence, as "un-natured Nature" [or Nature that has not yet taken on a nature], is real or actual only by knowing and unfolding itself in God and the world as produced

---

[1] German Mysticism is thus connected with the more general phenomenon, that the fast increasing externalisation which seized upon the life of the Church in the thirteenth and fourteenth centuries drove piety everywhere into paths that lay outside the Church.

[2] Evidently the same relation that subsisted in the system of Plotinus between the ἕν and the νοῦς, a relation in which thought and Being were held to coincide.

[3] The distinction between deity and God (*divinitas* and *deus*) was made dialectically by Gilbert de la Porrée in connection with the controversy over universals and its relations to the doctrine of the Trinity.

reality, as natured Nature.[1] God creates all — said Nicolaus Cusanus — that is to say, he is all. And on the other hand, according to Eckhart, all things have essence or substance only in so far as they are themselves God ; whatever else appears in them as phenomena, their determination in space and time, their " here " and " now " (" *Hie* " und " *Nu*," *hic et nunc* with Thomas), is nothing.[2]

The human soul, also, is therefore in its inmost nature of the divine essence, and it is only as a phenomenon in time that it possesses the variety of " powers " or " faculties " with which it is active as a member of the *natura naturata*. That inmost essence Eckhart calls the " Spark," [3] and in this he recognises the living point at which the world-process begins its return.

For to the " Becoming " corresponds the reverse process, the " Anti-becoming " (" *Entwerden* "), the disappearing. And this, too, is the act of knowledge by means of which the things which have been made external to the deity are taken back into the original Ground. By being known by man the world of sense finds again its true spiritual nature. Hence human cognition, with its ascent from sense perception to rational insight,[4] consists in the " elimination " (" *Abscheiden* ") of plurality and multiplicity; the spiritual essence is freed from its enveloping husks. And this is man's highest task in the temporal life, since knowledge is the most valuable of man's powers. He should indeed be also active in this world, and thus bring his rational nature to assert itself and gain control, but above all outer action, above the righteousness of works which belongs to the sphere of sense, stands first the " inner work," cleanness of disposition, purity of heart, and above this in turn stands retirement or " decease " (*Abgeschiedenheit*) and " poverty " of soul, the complete withdrawal of the soul from the outer world into its inmost essence, into the deity. In the act of knowing it reaches that purposelessness of action, that action not constrained by an end, that freedom within itself, in which its beauty consists.

But even this is not perfect so long as the knowing process does not find its consummation. The goal of all life is the knowledge of

---

[1] On the terms *natura naturans* and *natura naturata*, which were probably brought into use by Averroism (cf. § 27, 1), cf. H. Siebeck, *Archiv f. Gesch. d. Phil.*, III. 370 ff.

[2] Accordingly without accepting the dialectical formulas, Eckhart treats the Thomistic doctrine of Ideas quite in the sense of the strict Realism of Scotus Erigena. He speaks slightingly of the Nominalists of his time as " little masters."

[3] Also the " Gemüthe " or Synteresis = *scintilla conscientiæ*.

[4] The single stages of this process are developed by Eckhart according to the Thomistic-Augustinian scheme.

God, but knowing is Being; it is a community of life and of Being with that which is known. If the soul would know God, it must be God, it must cease to be itself. It must renounce not only sin and the world, but itself also. It must strip off all its acquired knowledge, and all present knowing of phenomena; as the deity is "Nothing," so it is apprehended only in this knowledge that is a not-knowing — *docta ignorantia*, it was later called by Nicolaus; and as that "Nothing" is the original ground of all reality, so this not-knowing is the highest, the most blessed contemplation. It is no longer an act of the individual, it is the act of God in man; God begets his own essence within the soul, and in his pure eternal nature the "Spark" has stripped off all its powers through which it works in time, and has effaced their distinction. This is the state of supra-rational knowing when man ends his life in God, — the state, of which Nicolaus of Cusa said, it is the eternal love (*charitas*), which is known by love (*amore*) and loved by knowledge.

§ 27. The Problem of Individuality.

The doctrine of German Mysticism, which had arisen from the deepest personal piety and from a genuine individual need felt in a life whose religion was purely internal, thus runs out into an ideal of exaltation, of self-denial, of renunciation of the world, in the presence of which everything that is particular, every individual reality, appears as sin or imperfection, as had been the case in the ancient Oriental view. In this thought the contradiction that was inherent in the depths of the Augustinian system (cf. p. 287) became fully developed and immediately palpable, and it thus becomes evident that the Neo-Platonic intellectualism, in whatever form it appeared from the time of Augustine to that of Master Eckhart, was *in itself alone* always necessarily inclined to contest the metaphysical self-subsistence of the individual, while the other party maintained this self-subsistence as a postulate of the doctrine of the will. Accordingly, when in connection with the increase of intellectualism the *universalistic* tendency increased also, the counter-current was necessarily evoked all the more powerfully, and the same antithesis in motives of thought which had led to the dialectic of the controversy over universals (cf. p. 289) now took on a more real and metaphysical form in the question as to the ground of existence in individual beings (*principium individuationis*).

1. The stimulus for this was furnished by the far-reaching consequences to which universalism and intellectualism had led among the Arabians. For the Arabians, in interpreting the Aristotelian

system, had proceeded in the direction which had been introduced in antiquity by Strato (cf. p. 179 f.), and which among the later commentators had been maintained chiefly by Alexander of Aphrodisias. This direction was that of naturalism, which would fain remove from the system of the Stagirite even the last traces of a metaphysical separation between the ideal and the sensuous. This effort had become concentrated upon two points : upon the relation of God to the world, and upon that of the reason to the other faculties. In both these lines the peculiar nature of the Arabian Peripatetic doctrine developed, and this took place by complicated transformations of the Aristotelian conceptions of Form and Matter.

In general, we find in this connection in the Andalusian philosophy a tendency to make matter metaphysically self-subsistent. It is conceived of, not as that which is merely abstractly possible, but as that which bears within itself as living germs the Forms peculiar to it, and brings them to realisation in its movement. At the same time *Averroës*, as regards particular cosmic processes, held fast to the Aristotelian principle that every movement of matter by which it realises out of itself a lower Form, must be called forth by a higher Form, and the graded series of Forms finds its termination above in God, as the highest and first mover. The transcendence of God could be united with this view, as the doctrine of *Avicebron* shows, only if matter were regarded as itself created by the divine will. But on the other hand, this same Jewish philosopher, proceeding from the same presuppositions, insisted that with the exception of the deity, no being could be thought of otherwise than as connected with matter, that accordingly even the spiritual Forms need for their reality a matter in which they inhere, and that finally the living community of the universe demands a single matter as basis for the entire realm of Forms. The more, however, in the system of *Averroës*, matter was regarded as eternally in motion within itself, and as actuated by unity of life, the less could the moving Form be separated from it *realiter*, and thus the same divine All-being appeared on the one hand as Form and moving force (*natura naturans*), and on the other hand as matter, as moved world (*natura naturata*).

This doctrine with regard to *matter*, that it is *one in nature, is informed within, and is eternally in motion of itself*, became extended with Averroism as an extremely naturalistic interpretation of the philosophy of Aristotle. It now became reinforced by those consequences of dialectical Realism which compelled the view that God, as the *ens generalissimum*, is the only substance, and that individual things are but the more or less transient Forms in which this single substance becomes realised (cf. § 23). The *Amalricans* thus teach that God is the one single essence (*essentia*) of all things, and that creation is only an assuming of form on the part of this divine essence, a realising, completed in eternal movement, of all possibilities contained in this one single matter. *David* of Dinant[1] establishes this same *pantheism* with the help of Avicebron's conceptions, by teaching that as "hyle" (*i.e.* corporeal matter) is the substance of all bodies, so mind (*ratio — mens*) is the substance of all souls; that, however, since God, as the most universal of all essences, is the substance of all things whatever, God, matter, and mind are, in the last resort, identical, and the world is but their self-realisation in particular forms.

2. But the metaphysical self-subsistence of the *individual mind* was involved in doubt by yet another line of thought. Aristotle had made the νοῦς, as the everywhere identical rational activity, join the animal soul "from without," and had escaped the difficulties of this doctrine because the *problem of personality*, which emerged only with the Stoic conception of the ἡγεμονικόν, did not as yet lie within the horizon of his thought. But the commentators, Greek and Arabian, who developed his system did not shrink before the consequences that resulted from it for the metaphysical value of mental and spiritual individuality.

In the thought of *Alexander of Aphrodisias* we meet, under the name of the "passive intellect" (cf. p. 150), the capacity of the individual psyche to take up into itself, in accordance with its whole animal and empirical disposition, the operation of the active reason, and this *intellectus agens* (agreeably to the naturalistic conception of the whole system) is here identified with the divine mind, which is still thought only as "separate Form" (*intellectus separatus*). But with *Simplicius*, in accordance with the Neo-Platonic metaphysics, this *intellectus agens* which realises itself in man's rational knowledge has already become the lowest of the intelligences who rule the sublunary world.[2] This doctrine finds an original development in the thought of *Averroës*.[3] According to his view, the *intellectus passivus* is to be sought in the individual's *capacity* for knowledge, a capacity which, like the individual himself, arises and perishes as Form of the individual body; it has validity, therefore, only for the individual, and for that which concerns the particular. The *intellectus*

---

[1] Following the *Liber de Causis* and the pseudo-Boethian treatise *De Uno et Unitate;* cf. B. Hauréau in the *Mémoires de l'Acad. des Inscript.*, XXIX. (1877), and also A. Jundt, *Histoire du Panthéisme Populaire au M.-A.* (Paris, 1875).

[2] The so-called "Theology of Aristotle" identifies this νοῦς with the λόγος. For particulars, see E. Renan, *Av. et l'Av.*, II. § 6 ff.

[3] Cf. principally his treatise *De Animæ Beatitudine.*

agens, on the contrary, as a Form existing apart from empirical individuals and independent of them, is the *eternal generic reason of the human race,* which neither arises nor perishes, and which contains the universal truths in a manner valid for all.   It is the substance of the truly intellectual life, and the knowing *activity* of the individual is but a special manifestation of it.   This (actual) knowing activity (as *intellectus acquisitus*) is indeed in its content, in its essence, eternal, since in so far it is just the active reason itself; on the contrary, as empirical function of an individual knowing process, it is as transitory as the individual soul itself. The completest incarnation of the active reason has, according to Averroës, been given in Aristotle.[1]   Man's rational knowing is, then, an impersonal or supra-personal function : it is the individual's temporal participation in the eternal generic reason.   This latter is the unitary essence which realises itself in the most valuable activities of personality.

Intimations of this *pan-psychism* occasionally appear in the train of Neo-Platonic Mysticism at an earlier period in Western literature ; as an outspoken and extended doctrine it appears by the side of Averroism about 1200 ; the two are everywhere named in conjunction at the first when the erroneous doctrines of the Arabian Peripatetic thought are condemned, and it is one main effort of the Dominicans to protect Aristotle himself from being confused with this doctrine.   Albert and Thomas both write a *De Unitate Intellectus* against the Averroists.

3. Pan-psychism encounters with Christian thinkers an opposition in which the determining factor is the feeling of the metaphysical value of *personality,* — the feeling which had been nourished by *Augustine.*   This is the standpoint from which men like William of Auvergne and Henry of Ghent oppose Averroës.   And this is also the real reason why the main systems of Scholasticism — in diametrical contrast with Eckhart's Mysticism — did not allow the Realism which was inherent in the intellectualistic bases of their metaphysics to come to complete development.   *Thomism* was here in the more difficult case, for it maintained indeed, following Avicenna's formula (cf. p. 299), that universals, and therefore also the genus " soul," exist only " individualised," *i.e.* in the individual empirical examples as their universal essence (*quidditas*), but it ascribed to them, nevertheless, metaphysical priority in the divine mind.   It was therefore obliged to explain how it comes

---

[1] And with this the unconditional recognition of the authority of the Stagirite is theoretically justified by Averroës.

about that this one essence as universal matter presents itself in such manifold forms. That is to say, it asked after the PRINCIPIUM INDIVIDUATIONIS, and found it in the consideration that matter in space and time is *quantitatively determined (materia signata)*. In the capacity of matter to assume quantitative differences consists the possibility of individuation, *i.e.* the possibility that the same Form (*e.g.* humanity) is actual in different instances or examples as individual substances. Hence, according to Thomas, pure Forms (*separatæ sive subsistentes*) are individualised only through themselves; that is, there is but one example which corresponds to them. Every angel is a genus and an individual at the same time. The inherent Forms, on the contrary, to which the human soul also belongs in spite of its subsistence (cf. p. 324), are actual in many examples, in accordance with the quantitative differences of space and time which their matter presents.

This view was opposed by the *Franciscans*, whose religious and metaphysical psychology had developed in intimate relation with Augustine's teaching. In their thought, first the individual soul, and then, with a consistent extension in general metaphysics, individual beings in general, are regarded as self-subsisting realities. They rejected the distinction of separate and inherent Forms. Bonaventura, Henry of Ghent, and still more energetically Duns Scotus, maintained, following Avicebron, that even intellectual Forms have their own matter, and Scotus teaches that the "soul" is not individualised and substantialised only after, and by means of, its relation to a definite body, as Thomas had taught, but that it is already in itself individualised and substantialised. On this point *Scotism* shows a discord which had evidently not come to notice in the mind of its author. It emphasises on the one hand, in the strongest manner, the Reality of the universal, by maintaining the unity of matter (*materia primo-prima*) quite in the Arabian sense, and on the other hand it teaches that this universal is only actual by being realised by the series of Forms descending from the universal to the particular, and ultimately by means of the definite individual Form (*hæcceitas*). This individual Form is therefore for Duns Scotus an original fact; no farther question as to its ground is permissible. He designates individuality (both in the sense of individual substance and in that of individual occurrence) as the *contingent (contingens)*; that is, as that which is not to be deduced from a universal ground, but is only to be verified as actual fact. For him, therefore, as for his predecessor Roger Bacon, the inquiry for the principle of individuation has no meaning : the individual is the "last" Form of all reality, by means of which alone universal matter exists, and the question rather is how, in presence of the fact that the individual being with its determined form is the only Reality, one can still speak of a Reality of universal "natures."[1]

From this noteworthy limitation of the doctrine of Scotus it becomes explicable that while some of its adherents, as for example Francis of Mayron, proceeded from it to extreme Realism, it suddenly changed with *Occam* into the *renewal of the nominalistic thesis*, that only the individual is real and that the universal is but a product of comparative thought.

4. The victorious development which Nominalism experienced in the second period of mediæval philosophy rests upon an extremely peculiar combination of very different motives of thought. In the depths of this stream of development is dominant the Augustinian *moment* of feeling, which seeks to see the proper metaphysical value secured to the individual personality ; in the main philosophical current the anti-Platonic tendency of the Aristotelian theory of knowledge, now just becoming known, asserts itself, throwing its influence toward conceding the value of "first substance" to the empirical individual only; and on the surface plays a logico-grammatical schematism, which has its origin in the first operation of the Byzantine tradition of ancient thought.[2] All these influences become concentrated in the impassioned, impressive personality of William of *Occam*.

In their exposition of the doctrine of concepts and its application to the judgment and syllogism, the text-books of "modern" logic, as type of which that of Petrus Hispanus may serve, lay an important emphasis upon the theory of "*supposition*" in a manner which is not without its precedent in antiquity.[3] According to this theory a class-concept or term (*terminus*) may, in language, and, as was then supposed, in logic also, stand for the sum of its species, and a species-concept for the sum of all its individual examples (*homo = omnes homines*), so that in the operations of thought a term is employed as a *sign* for that which it means. Occam develops Nominalism in the forms of this *Terminism*[4] (cf. pp. 325 f). Individual

---

[1] This method for the solution of the problem of universals, peculiar to Duns Scotus, is usually called *Formalism*.

[2] In fact, we may see in the working of the text-book of Michael Psellos the first impetus of that accession of ancient material of culture which the West received by way of Byzantium, and which later in the Renaissance became definitely united with the two other lines of tradition that came, the one by way of Rome and York, the other by way of Bagdad and Cordova.

[3] The reader need only be reminded of the investigations of Philodemus on signs and things signified (p. 162 ; cf. also p. 198).

[4] Cf. K. Prantl in the *Sitz.-Ber. der Münch. Acad.*, 1864, II. a 58 ff.

things, to which Occam, following Scotus, concedes the Reality of original Forms, are represented in thought by us *intuitively*, without the mediation of *species intelligibiles;* but these ideas or mental representations are only the "natural" signs for the things represented. They have only a necessary reference to them, and have real similarity with them as little as any sign is necessarily like the object designated. This relation is that of "first intention." But now as individual ideas stand for (*supponunt*) individual things, so, in thought, speech, and writing, the "undetermined" general ideas of abstract knowledge, or the spoken or written words which in turn express these general ideas, may stand for the individual idea. This "second intention," in which the general idea with the help of the word refers no longer directly to the thing itself, but primarily to the idea of the thing, is no longer natural, but arbitrary or according to one's liking (*ad placitum instituta*).[1] Upon this distinction Occam rests also that of *real* and *rational* science : the former relates immediately or intuitively to things, the latter relates abstractly to the immanent relations between ideas.

It is clear, according to this, that rational science also presupposes "real" science and is bound to the empirical material presented in the form of ideas by this real science, but it is also clear that even "real" knowledge apprehends only an inner world of ideas, which may indeed serve as "signs" of things, but are different from things themselves. The mind — so Albert had incidentally said, and Nicolaus Cusanus at a later time carried out the thought — knows only what it has within itself; its knowledge of the world, terministic Nominalism reasons, refers to the inner states into which its living connection with the real world puts it. As contrasted with the true essence of things, teaches *Nicolaus Cusanus*, who committed himself absolutely to this *idealistic Nominalism*, human thought possesses only *conjectures*, that is, only modes of representation which correspond to its own nature, and the knowledge of this relativity of all positive predicates, the knowledge of this non-knowledge, the *docta ignorantia*, is the only way to go beyond rational science and attain to the inexpressible, signless, immediate community of knowledge with true Being, the deity.

5. In spite of this far-reaching epistemological restriction, the real vital energy of Nominalism was directed toward the development of natural science ; and if its results during the fourteenth and fifteenth centuries remained very limited, the essential reason for this

---

[1] The agreement of this with the contrast between θέσις and φύσις, which had been asserted also in the ancient philosophy of language (Plato's *Cratylus*), is obvious.

was that the scholastic method with its bookish discussion of authorities, which had now attained full perfection, controlled absolutely later as well as earlier the prosecution of science, and that the new ideas forced into this form could not unfold freely, — a phenomenon, moreover, which continues far into the philosophy of the Renaissance. For all that, Duns Scotus and Occam gave the chief impetus to the movement in which philosophy, taking its place beside the metaphysics whose interests had hitherto been essentially religious, made itself again a *secular science of concrete, actual fact*, and placed itself with more and more definite consciousness upon the basis of *empiricism*. When Duns Scotus designated the *hœcceitas* or original individual Form, as contingent, this meant that it was to be known, not by logical deduction, but only by actual verification as fact; and when Occam declared the individual being to be the alone truly Real, he was thereby pointing out to " real science " the way to the immediate apprehension of the actual world. But in this point the two Franciscans are under the influence of *Roger Bacon*, who with all his energy had called the science of his time from authorities to things, from opinions to sources, from dialectic to experience, from books to Nature. At his side in this movement stood *Albert*, who supported the same line of thought among the Dominicans, knew how to value the worth of original observation and experiment, and gave brilliant proof in his botanical studies of the independence of his own research. But strongly as Roger Bacon, following Arabian models, urged quantitative determinations in observation, and mathematical training, the time was not yet ripe for natural research. Attempts like those of Alexander Nekkam (about 1200), or those of Nicolaus d'Autricuria, at a later time (about 1350), passed away without effect.

The fruitful development of empiricism during this period was only in the line of *psychology*. Under the influence of the Arabs, especially of Avicenna and of the physiological optics of Alhacen, investigations concerning the psychical life took on a tendency directed more toward establishing and arranging the facts of experience. This had been begun even by Alexander of Hales, by his pupil, Johann of Rochelle, by Vincent of Beauvais, and especially by Albert; and in the system of Alfred the Englishman (Alfred de Sereshel, in the first half of the thirteenth century) we find a purely physiological psychology with all its radical consequences. These stirrings of a physiological empiricism would, however, have been repressed by the metaphysical psychology of Thomism, if they had not found their support in the Augustinian influence, which held fast to the *experience which personality has of itself*, as its highest principle. In this attitude *Henry of Ghent,* especially, came forward in opposition to Thomism. He formulated sharply the standpoint of inner experience and gave it decisive value, particularly in the investigation of the states of feeling. Just in this point, in the empirical apprehension of the life of feeling, the theory of which became thus emancipated at the same time from that of the will and that of the intellect, he met support in *Roger Bacon,* who, with clear insight and without the admixture of metaphysical points of view, distinctly apprehended the difference in principle between outer and inner experience.

Thus the remarkable result ensued, that purely theoretical science developed in opposition to intellectualistic Thomism, and in connection with the Augustinian doctrine of the self-certainty of personality. This self-knowledge was regarded as the most certain fact of "real science," even as it appeared among the nominalistic Mystics such as Pierre d'Ailly. Hence "real science" in the departing Middle Ages allied itself rather to active human life than to Nature ; and the beginnings of a " secular " science of the inter-relations of human society are found not only in the theories of Occam and Marsilius of Padua (cf. p. 328), not only in the rise of a richer, more living, and more "inward " writing of history, but also in an empirical consideration of the social relations, in which a *Nicolas d'Oresme,*[1] who died 1382, broke the path.

6. The divided frame of mind in which the departing Middle Ages found itself, between the original presuppositions of its thought and these beginnings of a new, experientially vigorous research, finds nowhere a more lively expression than in the philosophy of *Nicolaus Cusanus,* which is capable of so many interpretations. Seized in every fibre of his being by the fresh impulse of the time, he nevertheless could not give up the purpose of arranging his new thoughts in the system of the old conception of the world.

This attempt acquires a heightened interest from the conceptions which furnished the forms in which he undertook to arrange his thoughts. The leading motive is to show that the individual, even in his metaphysical separateness, is identical with the most universal, the divine essence. To this end Nicolaus employs for the first time, in a thoroughly systematic way, the related conceptions of *the infinite* and *the finite.* All antiquity had held the perfect to be that which is limited within itself and had regarded only indefinite possibility as infinite. In the Alexandrian philosophy,

---

Cf. concerning him W. Roscher, *Zeitschr. f. Staatswissenschaft,* 1863, 305 ff.

on the contrary, the highest being was stripped of all finite at tributes. In Plotinus the "One" as the all-forming power is provided with an unlimited intensity of Being on account of the infinity of matter in which it discloses itself; and also in Christian thought the power, as well as the will and the knowledge of God, had been thought more and more as boundless. Here the main additional motive was, that the will even in the individual is felt as a restless, never quiet striving, and that this *infinity of inner experience* was exalted to a metaphysical principle. But Nicolaus was the first to give the method of negative theology its positive expression by treating *infinity as the essential characteristic of God* in antithesis to the world. The identity of God with the world, required as well by the mystical view of the world as by the naturalistic, received, therefore, the formulation that in God the same absolute Being is contained infinitely, which in the world presents itself in finite forms.

In this was given the farther *antithesis of unity and plurality.* The infinite is the living and eternal unity of that which in the finite appears as extended plurality. But this plurality — and Cusanus lays special weight on this point — is also that of opposites. What in the finite world appears divided into different elements, and only by this means possible as one thing by the side of another in space, must become adjusted and harmonised in the infinitude of the divine nature. God is the unity of all opposites, the *coincidentia oppositorum.*[1] He is, therefore, the absolute reality in which all possibilities are *eo ipso* realised (*possest,* can-is), while each of the many finite entities is in itself only possible, and is real or actual only through him.[2]

Among the oppositions which are united in God, those between him and the world, — that is, those of the infinite and the finite, and of unity and plurality, — appear as the most important. In consequence of this union the infinite is at the same time finite; in each of his manifestations in phenomena the unitary *deus implicitus* is at the same time the *deus explicitus* poured forth into plurality (cf. p. 290). God is the greatest (*maximum*) and at the same time also

---

[1] Nicolaus also designates his own doctrine, in contrast with opposing systems, as a *coincidentia oppositorum,* since it aims to do justice to all motives of earlier philosophy. Cf. the passages in Falckenberg, *op. cit.,* pp. 60 ff.

[2] Thomas expressed the same thought as follows: God is the only necessary being, *i.e.* that which exists by virtue of its own nature (a thought which is to be regarded as an embodiment of Anselm's ontological argument, cf; § 23, 2), while in the case of all creatures, essence (or *quidditas* — whatness) is really separate from existence in such a way that the former is in itself merely possible and that the latter is added to it as realisation. The relation of this doctrine to the fundamental Aristotelian conceptions, *actus* and *potentia,* is obvious.

the smallest (*minimum*). But, on the other hand, in consequence of this union it follows also that this smallest and finite is in its own manner participant in the infinite, and presents within itself, as does the whole, a harmonious unity of the many.

Accordingly, the universe is also infinite, not indeed in the same sense in which God is infinite, but in its own way; that is, it is unlimited in space and time (*interminatum,* or privitively infinite). But a certain infinity belongs likewise to each individual thing, in the sense that in the characteristics of its essence it carries within itself also the characteristics of all other individuals. All is in all: *omnia ubique.* In this way every individual contains within itself the universe, though in a limited form peculiar to this individual alone and differing from all others. *In omnibus partibus relucet totum.* Every individual thing is, if rightly and fully known, a *mirror of the universe,* — a thought which had already been expressed incidentally by the Arabian philosopher Alkendi.

Naturally this is particularly true in the case of man, and in his conception of man as a microcosm Nicolaus attaches himself ingeniously to the terministic doctrine. The particular manner in which other things are contained in man is characterised by the ideas which form in him signs for the outer world. Man mirrors the universe by his "conjectures," by the mode of mental representation peculiar to him (cf. above, p. 343).

Thus the finite also is given with and in the infinite, the individual with and in the universal. At the same time the infinite is necessary in itself; the finite, however (following Duns Scotus), is absolutely contingent, *i.e.* mere fact. There is no proportion between the infinite and the finite; even the endless series of the finite remains incommensurable with the truly infinite. The derivation of the world from God is incomprehensible, and from the knowledge of the finite no path leads to the infinite. That which is real as an individual is empirically known, its relations and the oppositions prevailing in it are apprehended and distinguished by the understanding, but the perception or intuition of the infinite unity, which, exalted above all these opposites, includes them all within itself, is possible only by stripping off all such finite knowledge, by the mystical exaltation of the *docta ignorantia.* Thus the elements which Cusanus desired to unite fall apart again, even in the very process of union. The attempt to complete the mediæval philosophy and make it perfect on all sides leads to its inner disintegration.

APPENDIX.

P. 12.   Line 15.   Add: —

On the pragmatic factor, cf. C. Herrmann, *Der pragmatische Zusammenhang in der Geschichte der Philosophie* (Dresden, 1863).

P. 12.   Line 10 from foot of the text.   Add as foot-note, affixed to the word "positive": —

A similar, but quite mistaken attempt has been recently made in this direction by Fr. Brentano, *Die vier Phasen in der Philosophie und ihr gegenwärtiger Stand* (Vienna, 1895).   Here belong also the analogies, always more or less artificial, which have been attempted between the course of development in the ancient and that in the modern philosophy.   Cf. *e.g.* v. Reichlin-Meldegg, *Der Parallelismus der alten und neueren Philosophie* (Leips. and Heidelb. 1865).

P. 16.   Line 6 from foot of text, add: —

In all previous expositions of the history of philosophy, whether upon a larger or smaller scale, a chronological arrangement has been adopted, following the order and succession of the more important philosophies and schools.   These various arrangements have differed only in details, and these not always important.   Among the most recent might be named in addition, that of J. Bergmann, whose treatment shows taste and insight (2 vols., Berlin, 1892).   A treatment marked by originality and fineness of thought, in which the usual scheme has been happily broken through by emphasis upon the great movements and inter-relations of the world's history, is presented by R. Eucken, *Die Lebensanschauungen der grossen Denker* (2d ed., Leips. 1898).

P. 23.   To the foot-note, add: —

Windischmann, earlier (*Die Philosophie im Fortgang der Weltgeschichte*, Bonn, 1827–1834), and recently P. Deussen (*Allgemeine Geschichte der Philosophie*, I. 1, Leips. 1894) have made a beginning toward the work of relating this Oriental thought to the whole history of philosophy.

P. 24.   Line 8.   Affix as foot-note: —

E. Rohde has set forth with great insight and discrimination the rich suggestions for philosophy in the following period, which grew out of the transformations of the religious ideas (*Psyche*, 2d ed., 1897).

P. 27.   To the lit. on the Period, add: —

A. Fairbanks, *The First Philosophers of Greece*, N.Y. 1898.

P. 30.   Line 30.   To the notice of Heraclitus, add: —

He was apparently the first who, from the standpoint of scientific insight, undertook to reform the public life and combat the dangers of anarchy.   Himself an austere and rigorous personality, he preached the law of order, which ought to prevail in human life as in nature.

P. 30. Line 19 from the foot. To the notice of Anaxagoras, add: —

His scientific employments were essentially astronomical in their nature. Neglecting earthly interests, he is said to have declared the heavens to be his fatherland, and the observation of the stars to be his life work. Metrodorus and Archelaus are named as his disciples.

P. 42. Foot-note 1. Relating to the νοῦς of Anaxagoras, add: —

Cf., however, M. Heinze in the *Ber. d. Sächs. Ges. d. Wiss.*, 1890.

P. 46. Last line of text. To the word "curved," affix as foot-note: —

The tradition (Arist., *loc. cit.*) shows this collocation ; whereas, from the cosmology of the Pythagoreans and likewise from that of Plato and Aristotle, we should expect the reverse order.

P. 55. To the notice of Diogenes of Apollonia, add: —

He was the most important of the eclectics of the fifth century. So little is known as to his life that it is even doubtful whether Apollonia was his home. Of his writings, even Simplicius had only the περὶ φύσεως before him (*Phys.*, 32 V. 151, 24 D).

P. 62. Add to foot-note 1: —

because in this phase of Greek thought they run along as yet unrelated lines of thought, side by side with the theories of natural science. Only the Pythagoreans seem as yet to have begun the combination between theology and philosophy, which later became through Plato a controlling influence.

P. 68. Prefix to par. 4, which begins with "But while," the following sentence: —

A preparation for this transition was made by the circumstance that even in the investigation of nature, interest in fundamental principles had grown weaker after the first creative development, and science had begun to scatter her labours over special fields.

P. 71. To the personal notice of Socrates, add: —

He considered this enlightenment of himself and fellow-citizens a divine vocation (Plato's *Apology*), giving this work precedence even over his care of his family (Xanthippe). He gathered about him the noblest youth of Athens, such as Alcibiades, who honoured in him the ideal and the teacher of virtue. He appeared thus as leader of an intellectual aristocracy, and just by this means came into opposition to the dominant democracy. [K. Joël, *Der echte u. d. Xenophontische Sokrates,* Vol. I., Berlin, 1893. Vol. II. in 2 pts., 1901. Kralik, *Sokrates,* 1899.]

P. 96. Line 23. Insert after Plato: —

And of their materialism which he so vigorously opposed.

P. 102. At close of par. 4, insert: —

This personal influence he himself regarded as the most important part of his activity. For scientific investigation was only one side of his rich nature. The demand for ethical teaching and for political and social efficiency had a still stronger life within him. He had an open vision for the evils of his time. He united an adherence to the aristocratic party with an activity in the direction indicated by Socrates, and never quite gave up the hope of reforming the life of his time through his science. To this was added as a third element in his personality that pre-eminent artistic disposition which could clothe his ideals with poetic exposition in the most splendid language.

P. 103. To references on Plato, add : —

P. Lutowslawski, *Origin and Growth of Plato's Logic* (1897).
[R. L. Nettleship, *Philos. Lectures,* ed. by Bradley and Benson, 1897. W. Windelband, *Plato,* Stuttgart, 1900.]

P. 104. After first par., insert : —

In comparison with the high flight of Plato, the personality and life-work of Aristotle appear throughout of cooler and soberer type. But if he lacks the impulse toward an active influence in public life, and also the poetic charm of diction and composition, he has, instead, all the more effective a substitute in the power of thought with which he surveys and masters his field, in the clarity and purity of his scientific temper, in the certainty and power with which he disposes and moulds the results gathered from the intellectual labours of many contributors. Aristotle is an incarnation of the spirit of science such as the world has never seen again, and in this direction his incomparable influence has lain. He will always remain the leading thinker in the realm of investigation which seeks to comprehend reality with keen look, unbiassed by any interest derived from feeling.

P. 104. Line 10. After " knowledge," insert : —

The recently discovered main fragment of his Πολιτεία τῶν 'Αθηναίων is a valuable example of the completeness of this part, also, of his literary work. In the main only his scientific, etc.

P. 104. [Especially valuable in the recent literature upon Aristotle are : H. Meier, *Die Syllogistik des Aristoteles.* Vol. I., 1896, Vol. II. in 2 pts., 1900 ; G. Rodier, *Aristote, Traité de l'Ame, trad. et annotée.* 2 vols., Paris, 1900. Cf. also W. A. Hammond, *A.'s Psychology : The De Anima and Parva Nat., tr. with Int. and Notes,* Lond. and N.Y. 1901 ; H. Siebeck, *A.,* Stuttgart, 1899.]

P. 112. As note to close of first par., attached to words " in the middle " : —

Cf., however, on this, A. Goedeke-Meyer, *Die Naturphilosophie Epikur's in ihrem Verhältniss zu Demokrit,* Strassburg, 1897.

P. 119. Line 17. After "back," insert : —

according to the general laws of association and reproduction (*Phaedo,* 72 ff.).

P. 123. Insert after the first par. under 6, the following par. : —

This completely new attempt on Plato's part was supported by the theological doctrines which he was able to take from the Mysteries of Dionysus. Here the individual soul was regarded as a " daimon " or spirit which had journeyed or been banished from another world into the body, and during its earthly life maintained mysterious emotional relations to its original home. Such theological ideas were brought by the philosopher into his scientific system, not without serious difficulties.

P. 135. Note attached to the word "not" in line 11 (from foot) : —

For Aristotle means nothing else, even where, as is frequently the case in the *Analytics,* he expresses the relation by saying that the question is whether the one concept is affirmed or predicated (κατηγορεῖν) of the other.

P. 142. After the first sentence in the last par., insert: —

" The subordination of the single thing under the general concept is for him too, not an arbitrary act of the intellect in its work of comparison; it is an act of knowledge which takes us into the nature of things and reproduces the actual relations which obtain there."

P. 148. Line 3. After " world," insert: —

Every element has thus its " natural " motion in a certain direction and its " natural " place in the universe. Only by collision with others ($\beta i\alpha$) is it turned aside or crowded out.

P. 162. Before second par., insert: —

" In the history of the *Stoa* we have to distinguish an older period which was predominantly ethical, a middle period which was eclectic, and a later period which was religious."

P. 162. To references on Stoicism, add: —

A. Schmekel, *Die mittlere Stoa* (Berlin, 1892).

P. 162. Line 6 from foot. To references on Lucretius, add: —

R. Heinze's Com. on 3d Book (Leips. 1877).

P. 163. Line 20. Add: —

Cf. E. Pappenheim (Berlin, 1874 f., Leips. 1877 and 1881).

P. 163. To references on Scepticism, add: —

V. Brochard, *Les Sceptiques Grecs* (Paris, 1887). [M. M. Patrick, *Sextus Empiricus and Greek Scepticism* (contains trans. of the " Pyrrhonic Sketches," Camb. and Lond. 1899).]

P. 163. Line 35. After " principle," insert: —

Cicero stands nearest to the position of Probabilism as maintained by the Academy. See below, § 17, 7.

P. 163. To the material before § 14, add: —

A **popular moral eclecticism** was represented by certain preachers of morals who were more or less closely related to the principles of the Cynics. These scourged the social and moral conditions of the Hellenistic and later of the Roman world with harsh and outspoken criticism. Among them were Teles (cf. v. Wilamowitz-Möllendorf, *Philologische Untersuchungen*, IV., 292 ff. ; *Fragments*, ed. by O. Hense, Freiburg, 1899), Bion of Borysthenes (cf. R. Heinze, *de Horatio Bionis Imitatore*, Bonn, 1889) of a later period, Demetrius, Oenomaos, and Demonax. Cf. J. Bernays, *Lukian und die Kyniker* (Berlin, 1879). In this connection Dio Chrysostomos is also to be named. Cf. H. v. Arnim (Berlin, 1898).

P 174. Line 8. Add to this paragraph: —

In many cases, however, notably in the Imperial age of Rome, this maxim appears as the easily intelligible principle of the honourable man who finds himself repelled by the corruption and partisan self-seeking of political life, and can have nothing to do with it.

P. 181. Add to the second par. the following (in part new) : —

Nevertheless, inasmuch as they, like Heraclitus, treated the necessary course of events and providence as equivalent terms, the Stoic formulation of the principle of sufficient reason (*i.e.* that everything which comes to be has a ground or reason) may also be expressed in the form that not even the least thing in the world can be otherwise than in accord with the decree of Zeus.

P. 186. Line 8 from foot of text, after "Heraclitus" insert : —

"and in part to the later philosophy of nature as influenced by him. (Pseudo-Hippoc. περὶ διαίτης ; cf. above p. 67, note 1.)

P. 189. Line 12 from foot, add the following : —

Finally this web of syncretistic theology received the metaphysical strand, to which the Older Academy with Pythagorean tendencies (especially Xenocrates) had begun to attach the hierarchy of mythical forms (cf. § 11, 5). The combination of all these theological tendencies was completed in the middle, eclectic Stoa, especially through Posidonius.

P. 204. Note 4, add : —

Hence Epicurus did not regard it necessary to decide on theoretical grounds between different modes of explaining particular phenomena : the one mode was no more valid (οὐ μᾶλλον) than the other, to use the sceptical phrase.

P. 210. Line 20. Add : —

trans. as Harnack's *History of Doctrine*, by N. Buchanan, Lond. 1894.

P. 210. Add to references : —

Fr. Susemihl, *Geschichte der griechischen Litteratur in der Alexandrinerzeit* (2 vols., Leips. 1891).

P. 216. Line 26. To the lit., add : —

H. v. Arnim, *Dion von Prusa* (Leips. 1896), pp. 4–114.

P. 216. Line 16 from foot. To the notice of Galen, add : —

He was frequently referred to as philosophical authority in the humanistic literature of the Renaissance. His treatise, *De placitis Hippocratis et Platonis*, has been edited by J. Müller (Leips. 1874), the *Protrepticus*, by G. Kaibel (Leips. 1894), the εἰσαγωγὴ διαλεκτική, by C. Kalbfleisch (Leips. 1896). J. Müller has discussed the περὶ ἀποδείξεως.

P. 217. Line 3. Add : —

Of the new Berlin ed. of Philo, by L. Cohn and P. Wendland, Vols. I. and II. have appeared (1896–1897).

P. 217. Line 14. To the lit. on Justin Martyr, add : —

H. Veil (Strassburg, 1893).

P. 217.　Line 20 from foot.　To the notice of Tertullian, add : —

He was a partisan whose hot-headed fanaticism did not shrink from any paradoxical consequence.

P. 217.　Line 3 from foot.　To the notice of Clement, add : —

With iron will and tireless activity he united the peaceful and conciliatory
spirit of scientific culture, with which he sought to exercise an influence in the
passionate ecclesiastical controversies of his time.

P. 218.　Line 15.　To the notice of Plotinus, add : —

A fine, noble nature, in whom the deep inwardising and spiritualising of life,
which was the most valuable result of ancient civilisation, found its best embodiment.

P. 218.　Line 29.　Add : —

Porphyry's Εἰσαγωγὴ εἰς τὰς κατηγορίας was usually known in the Middle Ages
by the title *de quinque vocibus.*

P. 224.　Line 3.　Add a foot-note : —

Similarly in the Epistle to the Hebrews, the relation of Jesus to the angels
is set forth in the manner in which it is presented by Philo.

P. 234.　Line 3 from foot of text, add : —

This transition is also connected with the fact that in the Christian view the activity of consciousness just described was considered
less from the theoretical than from the practical standpoint. The
freedom of the will is here the central conception. The Oriental
Church fathers in part stood nearer the intellectualism of the Hellenistic philosophy, or at least made concessions to it; on the other
hand, among the western teachers of the Church who were in closer
touch with Rome the will was most strongly emphasised in both
psychology and theology. Among the latter the tendency is dominant to regard the spiritual or immaterial principle as passive and
determined by its object in so far as it is knowledge, but as active
and determining in so far as it is will.

P. 238.　After line 6, insert the following paragraph : —

In this connection the *conception of the infinite* underwent a
transformation which gave it a radically different value (cf. Jon.
Cohn, *Geschichte des Unendlichkeitsproblems*, Leips. 1896). The mind
of the Greeks, directed as it was upon measure and definite limitation, had originally looked upon the infinite as the incomplete and
imperfect; it was only with reluctance that when considering the
infinitude of space and time metaphysics had allowed itself to
ascribe to the infinite a second subordinate kind of reality, as was
done by the Pythagoreans, the Atomists, and Plato — aside from
the isolated case of Anaximander, whose influence lay in another
direction. Now, infinitude had become the only predicate which

could be ascribed to the highest reality or to the deity, as over against the finite things of the world. Even the "negative" theology could permit this expression. The name "infinite" must be applied to the divine power which in the Stoic and Neo-Pythagorean philosophy of nature was regarded as the essence pervading and informing the world with its workings; to the One from which Neo-Platonism regarded worthy of the world's forms as flowing forth; to the creative divine will which, according to Christian teaching, had called forth the world from nothing, and thus shown its freedom from all limitation; and finally to this supreme personality himself in contrast with finite persons. Thus through this final development of ancient philosophy the conception of the infinite became the constituent mark of the highest metaphysical reality; it belongs not only to the universe as extended in space, but also to the inmost essence of things, and, above all, to the deity. This latter fusion became so fixed and sure that to-day it appears entirely a matter of course in the sphere of thought, as well as in that of feeling, to conceive of the supreme being as the Infinite, in contrast with all finite things and relations.

P. 256.   Line 11.   To the phrase "drama of universal history" affix the following foot-note: —

This expression has in this connection, as we see, a broader meaning, and one which conforms much more to the meaning of the words, than in its ordinary use.

P. 263.   To the literature of the period, add: —

B. Hauréau, *Notices et Extraits de quelques Manuscripts de la Bibliothèque Nationale.* 6 vols., Paris, 1890–1893; H. Denifle and E. Chatelain, *Chartularium Universitatis Parisiensis.* 2 vols, Paris, 1890–1894; H. Denifle and Fr. Ehrle, *Arch. f. Litt. u. Kirch. Gesch. d. Mittelalters,* 1885 ff.

P. 273.   Line 13.   To the notice of Augustine, add: —

His youth was in part wild and irregular. His father, Patricius, belonged to the old religion; his mother, Monica, to Christianity. To a deeply passionate nature he joined not only dialectical skill and keen intelligence, but also philosophical subtlety and a wide intellectual and spiritual vision, which was narrowed only at the last by ecclesiastical partisanship. He was made bishop 391.

P. 274.   Line 19.

"Eriugena" is given as first form of the name, with "Erigena" and "Jerugena" as variants.

P. 274.   Line 17, from foot, add: —

Recently his authorship has been doubted and the work assigned to a Bernhard Silvestris (also Bernhard of Tours).

P. 274.   Line 14, from foot, add: —

Cf. A. Clerval, *Les Écoles de Chartres au Moyen-âge* (Chartres, 1895).

P. 275. Line 5. To the notice of Abelard, add:—

The dialectical virtuosoship to which he owed his success and his fame deceived both him and his time as to the slightness of his knowledge. On the other hand, the freer and bolder convictions which he had gained in the ethical and religious field by the keenness of his intellect could not overcome the counter-tendency of his age, because they did not find sufficient support in his vain and weak personality. In addition to the ed. in two vols. of his work, Cousin has edited also *Ouvrages inédits* (Paris, 1836). Cf. S. M. Deutsch, *P. A. ein kritischer Theolog. des 12 Jahrhunderts* (Leips. 1883); A. Hausrath, *Peter Abälard* (Leips. 1893).

P. 313. Line 25. To the lit. on the Amalricans, add:—

Cf. the *Treatise against the Amalricans*, ed. by Cl. Bäumker (*Jahrb. f. Philos u. spec. Theol.*, VII., Paderborn, 1893).

P. 313. Line 15 from foot. To the lit. on Albert, add:—

V. Hertling, *A. M. Beiträge zu seiner Würdigung* (Cöln, 1880).

P. 316. To the general lit. add:—

[T. J. de Boer, *Gesch. d. Philos. in Islam* (Stuttgart, 1901).]

P. 317. Add to third par.:—

Cf. T. de Boer, *Die Widersprüche d. Philosophie nach Algazalli und ihr Ausgleich durch Ibn Roschd* (Strassburg, 1894).

P. 320. Line 11, add:—

But the " natural " man finds that even among a highly developed people the pure teaching of the natural religion meets in most cases only misunderstanding and disfavour. He turns back to his isolation with the one friend whom he has gained (cf. Pocock's ed. pp. 192 ff.).

P. 330. Line 3 from foot. To " Scotus," affix the reference:—

Cf. H. Siebeck, *Die Willenslehre bei Duns Scotus u. seinen Nachfolgern, Zeitschr f. Philos.* Vol. 112, pp. 179 ff.

P. 331. Line 9 from foot, add:—

It was a great service on the part of Buridan that, in order to grasp the problem more exactly, he sought to state the question once more in purely psychological terms. He sought to do justice to the arguments on each side, and made it his purpose to develop the conception of *ethical* freedom, in which indifferentism should lose the element of arbitrary caprice, and determinism should lose the character of natural necessity. Nevertheless, he did not succeed in completely clearing up the complication of problems which inhere in the word " freedom."

P. 333. Foot-note on word " synteresis," add:—

Cf., however, recently, H. Siebeck in *Arch. f. Gesch. d. Philos.*, X. 520 ff.

P. 339. Foot-note 1. For " and the pseudo," read:—

" and perhaps the pseudo."

P. 342. Line 24. Affix to "Occam," the reference: —

Cf. H. Siebeck, *Occam's Erkenntnisslehre in ihrer historischer Stellung* *Arch. f. Gesch. d. Philos.*, X. 317 ff.).

INDEX TO VOLUME I

harper ✦ torchbooks

HUMANITIES AND SOCIAL SCIENCES

American Studies: General

LOUIS D. BRANDEIS: Other People's Money, and How the Bankers Use It. ‡ Ed. with an Intro. by Richard M. Abrams   TB/3081

THOMAS C. COCHRAN: The Inner Revolution. Essays on the Social Sciences in History   TB/1140

HENRY STEELE COMMAGER, Ed.: The Struggle for Racial Equality   TB/1300

EDWARD S. CORWIN: American Constitutional History. Essays edited by Alpheus T. Mason and Gerald Garvey △   TB/1136

CARL N. DEGLER, Ed.: Pivotal Interpretations of American History   Vol. I TB/1240; Vol. II TB/1241

A. HUNTER DUPREE: Science in the Federal Government: A History of Policies and Activities to 1940   TB/573

A. S. EISENSTADT, Ed.: The Craft of American History: Recent Essays in American Historical Writing
Vol. I TB/1255; Vol. II TB/1256

CHARLOTTE P. GILMAN: Women and Economics: A Study of the Economic Relation between Men and Women as a Factor in Social Evolution. ‡ Ed. with an Introduction by Carl N. Degler   TB/3073

OSCAR HANDLIN, Ed.: This Was America: As Recorded by European Travelers in the Eighteenth, Nineteenth and Twentieth Centuries. Illus.   TB/1119

MARCUS LEE HANSEN: The Atlantic Migration: 1607-1860. Edited by Arthur M. Schlesinger   TB/1052

MARCUS LEE HANSEN: The Immigrant in American History.   TB/1120

JOHN HIGHAM, Ed.: The Reconstruction of American History △   TB/1068

ROBERT H. JACKSON: The Supreme Court in the American System of Government   TB/1106

JOHN F. KENNEDY: A Nation of Immigrants. △ Illus.   TB/1118

LEONARD W. LEVY, Ed.: American Constitutional Law: Historical Essays   TB/1285

LEONARD W. LEVY, Ed.: Judicial Review and the Supreme Court   TB/1296

LEONARD W. LEVY: The Law of the Commonwealth and Chief Justice Shaw   TB/1309

HENRY F. MAY: Protestant Churches and Industrial America. New Intro. by the Author   TB/1334

RALPH BARTON PERRY: Puritanism and Democracy   TB/1138

ARNOLD ROSE: The Negro in America   TB/3048

MAURICE R. STEIN: The Eclipse of Community. An Interpretation of American Studies   TB/1128

W. LLOYD WARNER and Associates: Democracy in Jonesville: A Study in Quality and Inequality ¶ TB/1129

W. LLOYD WARNER: Social Class in America: The Evaluation of Status   TB/1013

American Studies: Colonial

BERNARD BAILYN, Ed.: Apologia of Robert Keayne: Self-Portrait of a Puritan Merchant   TB/1201

BERNARD BAILYN: The New England Merchants in the Seventeenth Century   TB/1149

JOSEPH CHARLES: The Origins of the American Party System   TB/1049

HENRY STEELE COMMAGER & ELMO GIORDANETTI, Eds.: Was America a Mistake? An Eighteenth Century Controversy   TB/1329

CHARLES GIBSON: Spain in America †   TB/3077

LAWRENCE HENRY GIPSON: The Coming of the Revolution: 1763-1775. † Illus.   TB/3007

LEONARD W. LEVY: Freedom of Speech and Press in Early American History: Legacy of Suppression TB/1109

PERRY MILLER: Errand Into the Wilderness   TB/1139

PERRY MILLER & T. H. JOHNSON, Eds.: The Puritans: A Sourcebook of Their Writings
Vol. I TB/1093; Vol. II TB/1094

EDMUND S. MORGAN, Ed.: The Diary of Michael Wigglesworth, 1653-1657: The Conscience of a Puritan   TB/1228

EDMUND S. MORGAN: The Puritan Family: Religion and Domestic Relations in Seventeenth-Century New England   TB/1227

RICHARD B. MORRIS: Government and Labor in Early America   TB/1244

KENNETH B. MURDOCK: Literature and Theology in Colonial New England   TB/99

WALLACE NOTESTEIN: The English People on the Eve of Colonization: 1603-1630. † Illus.   TB/3006

JOHN P. ROCHE: Origins of American Political Thought: Selected Readings   TB/1301

JOHN SMITH: Captain John Smith's America: Selections from His Writings. Ed. with Intro. by John Lankford   TB/3078

LOUIS B. WRIGHT: The Cultural Life of the American Colonies: 1607-1763. † Illus.   TB/3005

American Studies: From the Revolution to 1860

JOHN R. ALDEN: The American Revolution: 1775-1783. † Illus.   TB/3011

MAX BELOFF, Ed.: The Debate on the American Revolution, 1761-1783: A Sourcebook △   TB/1225

RAY A. BILLINGTON: The Far Western Frontier: 1830-1860. † Illus.   TB/3012

EDMUND BURKE: On the American Revolution: Selected Speeches and Letters. ‡ Edited by Elliott Robert Barkan   TB/3068

WHITNEY R. CROSS: The Burned-Over District: The Social and Intellectual History of Enthusiastic Religion in Western New York, 1800-1850 △   TB/1242

GEORGE DANGERFIELD: The Awakening of American Nationalism: 1815-1828. † Illus.   TB/3061

The New American Nation Series, edited by Henry Steele Commager and Richard B. Morris.
American Perspectives series, edited by Bernard Wishy and William E. Leuchtenburg.
The Rise of Modern Europe series, edited by William L. Langer.
* History of Europe series, edited by J. H. Plumb.
Researches in the Social, Cultural and Behavioral Sciences, edited by Benjamin Nelson.
The Library of Religion and Culture, edited by Benjamin Nelson.
Harper Modern Science Series, edited by James R. Newman.
Not for sale in Canada.
Not for sale in the U. K.

L. S. B. LEAKEY: Adam's Ancestors: *The Evolution of Man and His Culture.* △ *Illus.* TB/1019

EDWARD BURNETT TYLOR: Religion in Primitive Culture. *Part II of "Primitive Culture."* § *Intro. by Paul Radin* TB/34

W. LLOYD WARNER: A Black Civilization: *A Study of an Australian Tribe.* ¶ *Illus.* TB/3056

Art and Art History

WALTER LOWRIE: Art in the Early Church. *Revised Edition. 452 illus.* TB/124

EMILE MÂLE: The Gothic Image: *Religious Art in France of the Thirteenth Century.* § △ *190 illus.* TB/44

MILLARD MEISS: Painting in Florence and Siena after the Black Death: *The Arts, Religion and Society in the Mid-Fourteenth Century. 169 illus.* TB/1148

ERICH NEUMANN: The Archetypal World of Henry Moore. △ *107 illus.* TB/2020

DORA & ERWIN PANOFSKY: Pandora's Box: *The Changing Aspects of a Mythical Symbol. Revised Edition. Illus.* TB/2021

ERWIN PANOFSKY: Studies in Iconology: *Humanistic Themes in the Art of the Renaissance.* △ *180 illustrations* TB/1077

ALEXANDRE PIANKOFF: The Shrines of Tut-Ankh-Amon. *Edited by N. Rambova. 117 illus.* TB/2011

JEAN SEZNEC: The Survival of the Pagan Gods: *The Mythological Tradition and Its Place in Renaissance Humanism and Art. 108 illustrations* TB/2004

OTTO VON SIMSON: The Gothic Cathedral: *Origins of Gothic Architecture and the Medieval Concept of Order.* △ *58 illus.* TB/2018

HEINRICH ZIMMER: Myth and Symbols in Indian Art and Civilization. *70 illustrations* TB/2005

Business, Economics & Economic History

REINHARD BENDIX: Work and Authority in Industry: *Ideologies of Management in the Course of Industrialization* TB/3035

GILBERT BURCK & EDITORS OF FORTUNE: The Computer Age: *And Its Potential for Management* TB/1179

THOMAS C. COCHRAN: The American Business System: *A Historical Perspective, 1900-1955* TB/1080

THOMAS C. COCHRAN: The Inner Revolution: *Essays on the Social Sciences in History* △ TB/1140

THOMAS C. COCHRAN & WILLIAM MILLER: The Age of Enterprise: *A Social History of Industrial America* TB/1054

ROBERT DAHL & CHARLES E. LINDBLOM: Politics, Economics, and Welfare: *Planning and Politico-Economic Systems Resolved into Basic Social Processes* TB/3037

PETER F. DRUCKER: The New Society: *The Anatomy of Industrial Order* △ TB/1082

EDITORS OF FORTUNE: America in the Sixties: *The Economy and the Society* TB/1015

ROBERT L. HEILBRONER: The Great Ascent: *The Struggle for Economic Development in Our Time* TB/3030

ROBERT L. HEILBRONER: The Limits of American Capitalism TB/1305

FRANK H. KNIGHT: The Economic Organization TB/1214

FRANK H. KNIGHT: Risk, Uncertainty and Profit TB/1215

ABBA P. LERNER: Everybody's Business: *Current Assumptions in Economics and Public Policy* TB/3051

ROBERT GREEN MC CLOSKEY: American Conservatism in the Age of Enterprise, 1865-1910 △ TB/1137

PAUL MANTOUX: The Industrial Revolution in the Eighteenth Century: *The Beginnings of the Modern Factory System in England* ○ △ TB/1079

WILLIAM MILLER, Ed.: Men in Business: *Essays on the Historical Role of the Entrepreneur* TB/1081

RICHARD B. MORRIS: Government and Labor in Early America △ TB/1244

HERBERT SIMON: The Shape of Automation: *For Men and Management* TB/1245

PERRIN STRYKER: The Character of the Executive: *Eleven Studies in Managerial Qualities* TB/1041

Education

JACQUES BARZUN: The House of Intellect △ TB/1051

RICHARD M. JONES, Ed.: Contemporary Educational Psychology: *Selected Readings* TB/1292

CLARK KERR: The Uses of the University TB/1264

JOHN U. NEF: Cultural Foundations of Industrial Civilization △ TB/1024

Historiography & Philosophy of History

JACOB BURCKHARDT: On History and Historians. △ *Introduction by H. R. Trevor-Roper* TB/1216

WILHELM DILTHEY: Pattern and Meaning in History: *Thoughts on History and Society.* ○ △ *Edited with an Introduction by H. P. Rickman* TB/1075

J. H. HEXTER: Reappraisals in History: *New Views on History & Society in Early Modern Europe* △ TB/1100

H. STUART HUGHES: History as Art and as Science: *Twin Vistas on the Past* TB/1207

RAYMOND KLIBANSKY & H. J. PATON, Eds.: Philosophy and History: *The Ernst Cassirer Festschrift. Illus.* TB/1115

ARNALDO MOMIGLIANO: Studies in Historiography ○ △ TB/1283

GEORGE H. NADEL, Ed.: Studies in the Philosophy of History: *Selected Essays from History and Theory* TB/1208

JOSE ORTEGA Y GASSET: The Modern Theme. *Introduction by Jose Ferrater Mora* TB/1038

KARL R. POPPER: The Open Society and Its Enemies △
Vol. I: *The Spell of Plato* TB/1101
Vol. II: *The High Tide of Prophecy: Hegel, Marx and the Aftermath* TB/1102

KARL R. POPPER: The Poverty of Historicism ○ △ TB/1126

G. J. RENIER: History: *Its Purpose and Method* △ TB/1209

W. H. WALSH: Philosophy of History: *An Introduction* △ TB/1020

History: General

WOLFGANG FRANKE: China and the West. *Trans by R. A. Wilson* TB/1326

L. CARRINGTON GOODRICH: A Short History of the Chinese People. △ *Illus.* TB/3015

DAN N. JACOBS & HANS H. BAERWALD: Chinese Communism: *Selected Documents* TB/3031

BERNARD LEWIS: The Arabs in History △ TB/1029

BERNARD LEWIS: The Middle East and the West ○ △ TB/1274

History: Ancient

A. ANDREWES: The Greek Tyrants △ TB/1103

ADOLF ERMAN, Ed. The Ancient Egyptians: *A Sourcebook of Their Writings. New material and Introduction by William Kelly Simpson* TB/1233

MICHAEL GRANT: Ancient History ○ △ TB/1190

SAMUEL NOAH KRAMER: Sumerian Mythology TB/1055

NAPHTALI LEWIS & MEYER REINHOLD, Eds.: Roman Civilization. *Sourcebook I: The Republic* TB/1231

NAPHTALI LEWIS & MEYER REINHOLD, Eds.: Roman Civilization. *Sourcebook II: The Empire* TB/1232

History: Medieval

P. BOISSONNADE: Life and Work in Medieval Europe: *The Evolution of the Medieval Economy, the 5th to the 15th Century.* ○ △ *Preface by Lynn White, Jr.* TB/1141

HELEN CAM: England before Elizabeth △ TB/1026

NORMAN COHN: The Pursuit of the Millennium: *Revolutionary Messianism in Medieval and Reformation Europe* △ TB/1037

3

4

Intellectual History & History of Ideas

Law

Literature, Poetry, The Novel & Criticism

Myth, Symbol & Folklore

Philosophy

Political Science & Government

Christianity: The Middle Ages and The Reformation

Christianity: The Protestant Tradition

Christianity: The Roman and Eastern Traditions

12